The Student Teacher
in the Elementary School

The Student Teacher in the Elementary School

by

LESTER D. CROW, Ph.D.

PROFESSOR OF EDUCATION
FORMERLY DIRECTOR OF STUDENT TEACHING
BROOKLYN COLLEGE

and

ALICE CROW, Ph.D.

FORMERLY ASSOCIATE PROFESSOR OF EDUCATION
AND SUPERVISOR OF STUDENT TEACHING
BROOKLYN COLLEGE

DAVID McKAY COMPANY, INC.

NEW YORK

Preface

Parents and other community members are becoming increasingly concerned about the educational fundamentals that are made available to children. No longer are they satisfied only with the mastery of the three R's. In addition, children on the elementary level are expected to gain an understanding of those knowledges, to achieve facility in those skills, and to discover those positive attitudes that can serve as the bases of continued education. To this point in your teacher education, you have been exposed to the theory of education. You have learned about child development, have reviewed the subject matter included in the elementary curriculum, and have had some experience with elementary teaching approaches. Now you are engaging in the practical application of theory.

You are in the position of discovering the problems inherent in teaching children and of gaining skill in handling them. You want to be an effective elementary teacher. Student teaching can be extremely valuable to you in helping you achieve your purpose. *The Student Teacher in the Elementary School* can be used as a guide as you move ahead in your student-teaching activities. The authors treat in detail the various aspects of an elementary teacher's responsibilities in guiding children's learning activities. They also present the role of the student teacher in the setting in which she finds herself.

You are alerted to significant factors inherent in your orientation to student teaching as well as to important personal and professional attributes of good teachers. Since effective teaching depends, in good part, on your understanding of your pupils, the authors discuss children's characteristics and present some approaches to child study that you may find helpful. Attention also is directed toward the kind of relationships you should develop with the various faculty members of your cooperating school, the college faculty, and the school community.

What you have learned in your college classrooms about teaching methodology acquires practical significance when you experience actual teaching-learning situations. Hence many helpful suggestions pertaining to them are included. Consideration is given to such problems as (1) broad areas of planning in light of accepted objectives of elementary education, (2) unit and daily lesson planning, and (3) teaching techniques appropriate to the learning needs of children. In addition, your attention is directed toward the special learning problems of rapid and slow learners. Suggestions also are offered for the utilization of various supplementary teaching aids, as well as for the teacher's responsibility in classroom management and for out-of-class teacher-pupil activities.

Many beginning teachers report that they have difficulty with disciplinary problems. Hence the role of the teacher is carefully explored in relation to the factors involved in an understanding of discipline and the development of self-discipline among children. Another concern to the neophyte teacher is the importance of measurement and evaluation in teaching. To this end, considerable attention is devoted to pupil evaluation and to reporting pupil progress. Finally, the problems of teacher placement and orientation are treated, including numerous practical suggestions and programs.

The authors wish to thank all who have permitted the reprinting of material from their publications. Some of the material of this book has been adapted from *The Student Teacher in the Secondary School* by Crow and Crow and used with the permission of the publisher, David McKay Company, Inc.

LESTER D. CROW
ALICE CROW

Contents

The Student Teacher
in the Elementary School

1

ORIENTATION TO STUDENT TEACHING

Student-teaching experiences, under wise guidance and supervision, are intended to help you adapt constructively to the various activities that constitute teaching responsibilities. Your experiences as a student teacher should result in your gaining an understanding of the many personal and professional aspects of your chosen lifework and motivate you to achieve a high level of teaching competence. These experiences should help you, as a beginning teacher, to face many problems in adjusting to your new profession.

FUNCTIONS OF STUDENT TEACHING

To the present, you probably have viewed teaching from the point of view of a student. You have evaluated the worth of your teachers in light of their effect upon you and your educational progress. Now the situation is about to be reversed. You are being encouraged to evaluate teaching success according to the effect of your teaching procedures upon your pupils—their attitudes toward you, their classroom behavior, and their evidenced degree of success in subject-matter and skill mastery. The main functions or purposes of the student-teaching experience are to assist you (1) to achieve success in teaching-learning situations and (2) to achieve adequate control of teaching-learning conditions.

Some of the functional phases of teaching activities with which you can become acquainted as a student teacher are described here briefly. Later in the chapter, we shall discuss (1) the theoretical background of teacher education to which you probably have been exposed, and (2) the practical application of theory in student teaching.

Understanding Elementary School Objectives

The broad functions of elementary education are to help children achieve command of fundamental knowledge and skills, develop good physical and mental health, practice constructive social relationships, and begin to develop their special aptitudes. In your college classes you have discussed the aims of education on the elementary school level, but the approach was more or less academic. Now you will have an opportunity to observe educational objectives in action.

You can evaluate the ways in which and the extent to which educational purposes are being fulfilled in the school or schools with which you are associated. Your understanding of educational philosophy will be quickened. You will learn to apply those principles of elementary education that will enable you to become an effective teacher.

Need for Knowing Children

How well do you understand elementary school boys and girls? You probably are young enough to believe that you know something about the joys and sorrows, the trials and tribulations, and the ambitions and interests commonly associated with childhood.

Your childhood experiences were rooted in a specific family and personal background. Your attitudes and behavior, your interests and ambitions, and your school and social relationships have been uniquely your own. As an elementary school teacher, you need to understand differences among children and to adapt your attitudes and behavior in light of those displayed by your pupils.

As you work with young learners during your student-teaching activities, you are enabled thereby to deepen your insight into the whys and wherefores of differences among them. What you learn during this training period will have value when later, as a regular teacher, you are responsible for the personal and academic development of the boys and girls whose learning you are attempting to guide.

Need to Appreciate the Total Concept of Teaching

In your own school experiences to the present, you may have envisaged the functions of the teacher to be those of assigning study units and then discovering how well pupils master learning content. You may have conceded that some teachers, but not all, attempt to help children overcome learning difficulties. This, of course, is an immature point of view.

Your student-teaching experiences should alert you to the various facets of the teaching process. You will come to recognize the many broad as well as specific duties that are included in the teaching concept. You will discover that the effective teacher:

1. Guides his pupils in the mastery of subject matter.
2. Helps his pupils improve needed skills.
3. Assists children in the solution of their personal problems.
4. Organizes and conducts efficiently all of the many activities that constitute classroom management.
5. Develops satisfactory relationships with administrators, supervisors, fellow teachers, and parents.
6. Participates in out-of-class experiences.
7. Cooperates with the administration in all matters of school management.
8. Becomes acquainted with and cooperates with the community in which the school is located.
9. Learns to meet and work with parents.
10. Gives evidence of a love of teaching and a professional attitude toward teaching.

The foregoing list of teacher responsibilities covers broad areas of activities. You realize the fact that, during the school day, week, month, or year, a teacher can be called upon to participate in many specific situations that have for their purpose the furthering of pupil welfare. As a student teacher, you are afforded an opportunity to observe regular teachers in action as well as to share some of their many responsibilities. Student teaching is an excellent medium for alerting you to the important role of the teacher in the lives of young, eager learners.

ORGANIZATION AND CONDUCT OF STUDENT TEACHING

Various factors will affect your experiences as a student teacher. These factors include (1) the school to which you are assigned, (2) the classroom teacher (cooperating teacher) with whom you work, (3) the amount of time you spend in the student-teaching activity, (4) your relationships with your college supervisor, and (5) the procedures employed in the school.

School Assignment

Colleges and other teacher-training institutions differ in their arrangements for student teaching. Some colleges maintain campus schools to which teacher trainees are assigned for observation and, if the number of trainees is not too large, for actual practice as well. Consequently, some college students may complete their practice in the campus school while others are assigned to community schools.

Some colleges use neighboring public schools or send their student teachers to schools in communities that are removed from the college campus or are in another town. If it is feasible, a trainee may be assigned to a school in a community in or near which he later may wish to serve as a full-time teacher.

Unless you are acquainted with your assigned school, you would be well advised to discover some things about it before you begin your practice period there. It would be helpful for you to know the following:

1. Location of the building
2. Size and age of the building
3. Number and types of children
4. Kinds and amount of teaching aids
5. Composition of the faculty
6. Attitude of faculty toward student teaching and student teachers
7. Community attitudes toward education

The more you know about the school and its environs the easier it probably will be for you to adapt yourself to participation in its activities. It is satisfying to feel wanted and to feel adequate in whatever you attempt.

Student-Teaching Arrangements

The amount of time that you are expected to devote to student teaching and the manner in which the time is apportioned differ with college communities. You can check minimums required by various states.[1] You may find also that individual colleges set a period of time for student teaching that is in excess of the minimum set by the state.

The student teacher can be assigned to a school for a block of time such as eight or ten weeks, during which he spends all of the school day in the school and engages in class and out-of-class activities. According to this arrangement, the trainee may both observe and teach, give learning help to individual or small groups of pupils who need it, attend faculty meetings, and work with parents. In fact, he is given an opportunity to get the feel of a total teaching situation.

Some colleges, especially those in large urban areas, prefer to utilize a split program—i.e., part of each day (two to three hours), throughout the entire semester, is devoted to student teaching in a laboratory school or a neighboring public school, and the remainder of the college day is spent in regular college classrooms where the trainees continue their academic study.

The following of the dual program mentioned in the foregoing has advantages as well as disadvantages. The trainee plays a dual role; he is both a student teacher and a student. Since his time in the practice school is relatively short, he is associated only with one, at the most two, teachers of any grade. He does, however, have the opportunity to observe and teach in several grades. He is denied full contact with the school as a community agency. Yet, his returning to college for part of a day affords him an opportunity to discuss his practical experiences with his college instructors and fellow trainees. He also can use this experience as background in class discussion to understand better the material he is studying.

[1] See *A Manual on Certification for School Personnel in the United States,* National Commission on Teacher Education and Professional Standards (Washington, D.C.: National Education Association, 1962).

Supervisory Personnel

During your practice-teaching experiences you will be associated with members of both the college and the school personnel. In most education departments of colleges and universities or in teacher-training institutions, one member of the faculty is responsible for assigning student teachers to appropriate schools and classes. This usually is done in consultation with individual trainees and is concerned with matters such as suitable conferences with teacher, period of service, travel conditions, college program, and the like. If possible, the trainee is given some choice in the school assignment.

College supervisor. While you are on the job, you receive a certain amount of supervision and guidance of your activities. You will be assigned to a member of the college faculty who then becomes your college supervisor. Through regular visitations and conferences, this person aids you in your adjustment to your teaching responsibilities.

Cooperating teacher. The man or woman in whose classroom you are working usually is called the cooperating teacher. In your day-by-day association with him you can learn much by observing his attitudes and techniques and by attempting to follow them.

School Procedures

Schools differ in their educational outlook and modes of procedure. This difference is found in schools of the same as well as in widely separated communities: You may be assigned to a school in which traditional methods are employed, or you may find yourself in a school that follows modern educational principles. Since the latter approach probably is characteristic of the college in which you are studying, you may feel at a loss in a more traditional school.

To observe teaching procedures and to practice those that seem to vary widely from the educational principles taught you at college may pose problems of adjustment. The situation is worsened if your college supervisor expects you to follow modern trends in your teaching, but the cooperating teacher insists that you fall in line with his mode of procedure.

Even though the situation is difficult, you need to keep in mind that you are a guest in the practice school. There is no compulsion for the school to accept student teachers. Moreover, your cooperating teacher is responsible for the academic achievement of his pupils. He is guiding their learning progress in light of school standards.

It is your obligation to help keep the wheels running smoothly by following the teacher's lead even though you disapprove of his teaching methods. Perhaps, in so doing, you can strengthen your own attitude toward proper teaching approaches to be utilized.

If any conflict or misunderstanding arises between you and your cooperating teacher, you probably can discuss the situation with your college supervisor, who is likely to understand the difficulty involved and be able to help you bring about a compromise between your educational principles and the practices you observe. You even may find that some so-called traditional approaches to learning are effective.

PREPARATION FOR STUDENT TEACHING

The question often arises as to whether teachers are born or made. The fact must be recognized that some people seem to have a flair for teaching. They are able, with a minimum of training, to assist others to learn. One also finds persons who, in spite of having experienced considerable teacher education, become and remain mediocre teachers.

Importance of Selecting Qualified Candidates

In order to insure for our children the services of superior teachers, it is important that all college departments of teacher education and teacher-training institutions exercise care in selecting teacher trainees from among applicants. They need to select those men and women who seem to have an inherent aptitude for teaching, and then provide them with as extensive and intensive a program of teacher education as is possible.

We shall not dwell here at length upon the various techniques utilized for the selection of candidates. Do you recall on what basis you were chosen? In some training institutions, the selection is made when the student enters the freshman year. In most colleges, however, the final decision comes at the end of the sophomore year. Selection usually is based upon such factors as health and physical fitness, and personal qualities (including voice, academic achievement, and evidenced interest in the profession). We are concerned at this point with the kind of educational preparation needed for entrance into teaching.

Need for Liberal Arts Background

The holding of a bachelor's degree is becoming a generally accepted state requirement for teaching in the elementary school. All states, except one, now require the degree for eligibility to teach. Some states are showing an interest in requiring some graduate courses. Anyone who is preparing to teach needs to possess a broad cultural background as well as a thorough mastery of subject matter.

In most colleges, the freshman and sophomore years are devoted to what sometimes is referred to as "general education," with concentration on a major field such as psychology, sociology, or a similar broad area. Some students, of course, do not decide on teaching until their junior or senior year. Regardless of when the decision to teach is made, a good background of liberal arts education is an asset to success in the teaching profession.

Need for Courses in Education

At one time, all that a man or woman (usually a woman) needed to be eligible for teaching elementary school children was a high school education and a good grounding in the 3 R's. As psychologists and other researchers discovered that children differ in their personal attributes and in their degree of ability to learn, educational leaders began to recognize the value to elementary school teachers of understanding differences among their pupils and of adjusting teaching techniques in light of children's differing abilities and interests. Consequently, in order to meet the growing need for improved teacher preparation, teacher-training schools were established. Later, they developed into four-year teachers colleges and gradually were transformed into colleges with broader curriculum offerings. Also, liberal arts colleges and universities have instituted departments of education.

For elementary school teachers to motivate any boy or girl to benefit from school learning requires that teachers know and can apply the principles basic to effective teaching and learning. Hence teacher-education curriculums include such areas of study as child psychology, sociological backgrounds, educational philosophy, and principles and techniques of teaching.

In addition to courses in the liberal arts, you probably already have completed much of your study of educational theory. Now you are ready to apply the knowledge and skills you have learned in your education courses before and during your student-teaching experiences. In fact, even after you have become a regular teacher you probably will find it helpful to continue advanced or graduate study in these and related areas.

Need for Practical Experience

In the foregoing, we have seemed to stress theory at the expense of practice. This is not the intention, however. In an increasing number of colleges, teacher trainees are being given an opportunity to apply some of the theory that they are learning in the classroom before they begin actual student teaching. A few such experiences that precede student teaching are listed here.

Observation. If the college has a campus school, students, during the junior year or earlier, are assigned in small groups to observe children in action in the laboratory school. If the college is in an urban community, groups of students visit neighboring schools, travel through the building, and sit in on classroom discussions. In either case, what has been observed is discussed later in the appropriate college classroom. In some colleges, the students are provided with a kind of questionnaire to guide their observation.

Community agency participation. Large cities have many welfare agencies, which, during late afternoons and evenings, provide many activities for young people. These usually include athletics, crafts, dancing, and various social activities. Since these community agencies often are understaffed with paid personnel, college upper classmen are welcomed as volunteer workers.

Colleges in urban areas often cooperate closely with these agencies. During the junior year, teacher trainees are given an opportunity in connection with an appropriate course in education, to serve as volunteer workers in an assigned community agency. This is an integral part of the course and must be completed if the student is to receive credit for the course.

A trainee spends two or three hours weekly after the college day in an agency where he works with a group of the children and young people who frequent the agency. He works directly under the supervision of the personnel in the agency. His duties may include any one of the following—helping to supervise athletics activity, teaching arts or crafts, or sponsoring social activities.

The college student, by participating in the various activities and offerings of the agency, gains a more intimate knowledge of young people, including their behavior and attitudes. Through these experiences, he gets the feel of working with children in these relatively unstructured situations. He also gains experience in working with experienced social workers and learns how to cooperate with fellow workers.

Value of Teacher Aides

Some colleges afford their students still another means of becoming acquainted with school procedures while they are mastering educational theory and before they begin student teaching. A student is assigned to a teacher in a neighboring public school as a teacher aide for a specific number of periods each school week.

The trainee's duties consist of helping the cooperating teacher with such matters as caring for routines associated with class management (such as preparing and distributing materials, proctoring tests, correcting papers submitted by the pupils, working with individual pupils or small groups of those who need help in their studies, and the like). Serving as a teacher's aide is valuable to the trainee in that it gives him an opportunity to become acquainted with the school situation. This experience gives him confidence in himself, thus minimizing the normal fear that he might experience when he begins his student teaching.

Other Areas of Valuable Experience

In addition to the experiences in dealing with children that are provided by the college, some trainees engage in similar activities on their own.

Camp experience. An increasing number of young men and women are participating in camp activities. They serve as camp counselors. Living and working with children in a summer camp provide them with excellent opportunities to study youngsters and to gain confidence in themselves as being able to meet and cope with individuals in these situations. These experiences prove to be invaluable to teacher trainees in their efforts to guide the various activities of children in school situations.

Importance of participating in religious activities. Good practical preparation for teaching also can be obtained by your participating in religious school teaching. The informal relationship that exists between teacher and pupils in the religious day or Sunday school class enables you to gain some knowledge of children's interests and ambitions as well as of the problems of growing up. If this experience is available to you, seize it as one to serve others as well as to receive your own personal rewards.

Value of home influences. You also may be fortunate enough to have younger brothers and sisters with whose attitudes and behavior you are well acquainted. The meeting of child problems in the home can serve you well as you encounter similar problems in the classroom. Although you may not have reflected on this before, you might evaluate some of those experiences as you go forward in your student-teaching activities.

Conceptual Scheme for Teacher Education

The schematic representation proposed by Elizabeth Z. Howard [2] illustrates, in summary fashion, the important considerations and relationships that operate in a good teacher education program. It is presented in Figure 1.

TEACHING AS A CAREER

As you begin the student-teaching phase of your teacher education, it might be well for you to evaluate yourself—your potentialities for and attitudes toward teaching as a lifework.

---

[2] Elizabeth Z. Howard, "Needed: A Conceptual Scheme for Teacher Education," *The School Review*, LXXI, No. 1 (Spring, 1963), 15. Copyright 1963 by The University of Chicago.

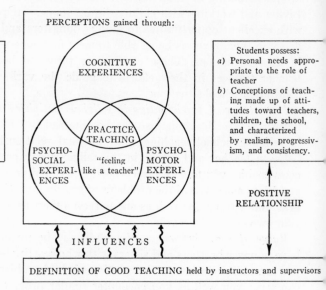

BEGINNING OF PROGRAM ➤ PROFESSIONAL TEACHER TRAINING ➤ END OF PROGRAM

Students possess:
a) Personal needs appropriate to the role of student
b) Conceptions of teaching made up of attitudes toward teachers, children, the school, and characterized by idealism, traditionalism, and inconsistency.

PERCEPTIONS gained through:

COGNITIVE EXPERIENCES

PRACTICE TEACHING

PSYCHO-SOCIAL EXPERIENCES

"feeling like a teacher"

PSYCHO-MOTOR EXPERIENCES

Students possess:
a) Personal needs appropriate to the role of teacher
b) Conceptions of teaching made up of attitudes toward teachers, children, the school, and characterized by realism, progressivism, and consistency.

POSITIVE RELATIONSHIP

INFLUENCES

DEFINITION OF GOOD TEACHING held by instructors and supervisors

FIG. 1.—Conceptual scheme for professional teacher education.

Your Selection of Teaching as a Career

When did you decide to become a teacher? Various studies have been made to discover answers to this question. According to one study,[3] in about 60 per cent of the replies the decision was made between the junior year of high school and the sophomore year of college (inclusive), with 16 per cent at an earlier time and 24 per cent at a later time. A very small percentage of decisions was made by the sixth grade or earlier. A somewhat larger percentage is indicated for "after college." (See Figure 2.)

As you can see by studying Figure 2, women tended to decide earlier than men to go into teaching. One reason for this difference may be that men have a wider range of choice among occupations than do women.

Why did you decide upon teaching as a career? Perhaps you are

[3] See Ward S. Mason, *The Beginning Teacher: Status and Career Orientations* (Washington, D.C.: U.S. Department of Health, Education and Welfare, 1961), pp. 96–98.

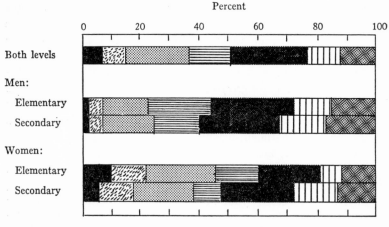

Fig. 2.—Educational level at which beginning teachers had decided to enter teaching, by sex and teaching level: 1956–57.*

not certain. Family members who either are or wanted to become teachers may have influenced your decision. Teaching may have seemed to offer greater security—both financial and emotional— than other fields. You may have been intrigued by working conditions—long vacations and relatively short working days.

Your actual vocational interest may lie in another field. Preparation for that field may have appeared to be too difficult, causing you to switch to teaching, or you may plan to engage in teaching while you are continuing to prepare yourself for another profession. Of course, the best motive for selecting teaching is a deep interest in working with people, especially young people.

Your Fitness for Student Teaching

Whatever the reason for your decision, you now have committed yourself, tentatively at least, to teaching as your lifework. As you evaluate your potentialities during your student-teaching experi-

* Ward S. Mason, *ibid.*, p. 96.

ences, you can discover to some degree whether you have made a wise choice. The possession of certain qualities or characteristics is essential to success in student teaching as well as in full-time teaching.

Some of your teacher qualities are rooted in your basic personality pattern; others are outgrowths of your educational experiences. Regardless of whether your various characteristics are innate or acquired, they can be improved as a result of intelligent and serious application to your student-teaching obligations.

In the following, we list some of the essentials of good teaching. No attempt has been made to arrange the items in rank order, since all of them are significant. As you begin your student-teaching activities, try to assess your strong and weak points and resolve to achieve whatever improvement you believe to be needed. Be honest in your self-evaluation. "Know thyself" is an excellent motto to follow.

Interest in young people. Children are sensitive to adults' attitudes toward them. They seem to be able to recognize whether a teacher likes them and is concerned about their welfare. They respect the teacher who gives evidence of understanding them and their whims and foibles and who, patiently but firmly, attempts to encourage them to maintain high standards of conduct.

What is your attitude toward children? Do you like them? Can you appreciate their problems of growing up? Are you perhaps somewhat afraid of them, believing that any uncooperative behavior displayed by them is aimed at you personally rather than a symptom of an urge for independence of action? The attitude you display in your dealings with young pupils exercises a tremendous effect upon your degree of success as a teacher.

Knowledge of subject matter. How well grounded are you in the content of the subjects you are preparing yourself to teach? Are you enthusiastic about teaching them and eager to share your enthusiasm with your pupils? Do you believe that you will be able to present the learning material so clearly and succinctly that learners will enjoy studying and will benefit from their learning experience?

It usually does not take long for pupils, especially upper elementary school pupils, to evaluate their teacher's mastery of and attitude toward subject matter. They know whether he is attempting to "bluff" his way through the presentation of a teaching unit because he is not sure of his facts. They judge his teaching in light of his ability to answer questions that go beyond the requirements of the assigned unit of study. They are quick to discover whether the teacher enjoys teaching or regards teaching as a chore.

We have stressed the fact that you should know your subject matter thoroughly. You need to be careful, however, that your mastery of the advanced phases of a subject has not caused you to forget the difficulties that can be present in the early stages of its study. Too often one hears pupils complain that a certain teacher knows so much about a subject that in his presentation of it he is not able to get down to their level of little or no acquaintance with it. It is important to present material on pupils' learning level.

Be careful not to become impatient with the apparent inability of learners to grasp the rudimentary principles that are involved. This often is the experience of beginning teachers. You can learn much about presenting subject matter as you observe skilled teachers in action.

Personal qualities needed for successful teaching. First impressions are important in the classroom. On your first day as a student teacher, you probably will come to a conclusion—either right or wrong—about the learners you are meeting. The children too will be "sizing you up." They will respond favorably or unfavorably to your clothing, hairdo, voice, and manner. They tend to be severe critics. You need to behave properly to feel confident that you will meet this first test.

As you continue your student-teaching activities, you will give evidence of other personal characteristics that can affect the attitude toward you of those with whom you will be working. In Chapter 2, we discuss the assessment of teacher effectiveness. Hence, at this point, we shall list a few questions that you can use as a guide toward evaluating some of your personal characteristics as they may be rated by others.

1. Are your clothes appropriate and becoming?
2. Do you keep your clothes well pressed, clean and free from body odors, and your shoes shined and in good repair?
3. Is your hair neatly arranged, free from dandruff, and frequently washed?

4. Are your nails carefully manicured, and is your skin free from blemishes?
5. If you are a woman, do you avoid the excessive use of cosmetics?
6. Do you have an upright posture and a free-swinging walk?
7. Are your teeth in good condition, and is your breath free from unpleasant odors?
8. Is your voice resonant, distinct, clear, and properly modulated?
9. Do you have an adequate vocabulary, pronounce words distinctly, and employ correct English?
10. Do you avoid affected mannerisms, grimaces, loud laughter, and other unpleasant behavior habits?
11. Are you reliable? Can you be counted on to meet your obligations adequately and on time?
12. Have you a good sense of humor?
13. Do you regard yourself as patient, cheerful, and cooperative in your relations with other people?
14. Do you believe that children should be treated impartially but with kindness and consideration?
15. Are you prepared to maintain a democratic attitude in the classroom?

You may find it difficult to answer all of these questions in the affirmative. As you pass through student-teaching experiences, keep them in mind and work toward effecting any improvement in your personal characteristics that seems to be necessary to achieving success in the classroom.

Your Attitude toward Criticism

You know that your student-teaching activities will be supervised by your college supervisor and your cooperating teacher. At times, a member of the administrative staff will observe you in action. What do you think your reaction will be to critical evaluations of you and your work?

When you are trying your best to succeed in an endeavor, it sometimes is disheartening to find that someone else is not completely satisfied with the results obtained. This situation is one that you may experience often during your neophyte days as a teacher. You are not perfect—no one is. No matter how sincere you are in your desire to do a good job, you still have much to learn about the many practical aspects of teaching. Constructive criticism of your activities is essential to your growth as a teacher.

Your attitude toward supervisory criticism will vary in light of your own evaluation of your purposes and behavior. You will accept some criticism without question, recognizing its validity. In some instances, you may believe that an unsatisfactory criticism is too harsh, that the critic did not fully realize what you were trying to accomplish.

A supervisory criticism may give evidence of serious divergence between educational points of view. This situation sometimes occurs when a student teacher attempts to apply educational principles learned in the college classroom. These principles may differ from those applied to the situation by a cooperating teacher. A conference in which the difference of opinion is discussed can help clear the air in a situation of this kind. The two of you may find that when each clearly understands what the other had in mind, you are not so far apart as you had thought.

Regardless of its emotional effect on you at the time, you should welcome constructive criticism and learn from it. It is important that you begin early to assess your strengths and weaknesses. A supervisor who is called upon to evaluate your work probably will find much to commend in what you do. He, thereby, is emphasizing your strengths. Cherish these comments. At the same time, heed well his suggestions for improvement. They are the foundation blocks upon which is built the structure of effective teaching.

When You Begin Your Student Teaching

You probably are beginning your student-teaching experience with ambivalent feelings. You are about to play a new educational role. In the past, you have been concerned with your own academic achievements; now you are about to take some responsibility for the academic achievement of others.

You probably are looking forward eagerly to practical participation in your chosen profession. You may believe (wrongly, of course) that to the present you have been no more than a passive recipient of educational materials and that now you will be actively engaged in proving yourself. Many young men and women tend to regard student teaching as the most, if not the only, professional experience that has value in teacher education. They underplay and misevaluate their previous study in the field.

College students often do not recognize the fact that mastery of theory is essential to effective practice. As you attempt to meet your student-teaching obligations, you will find yourself applying the principles of education that you learned in the college classroom.

In addition, no matter how interested you are in beginning your student teaching, you probably are approaching it with some degree of apprehension. You want to succeed in it, but it is a new experience. You may have doubts concerning your ability to meet adequately all the requirements of this period of training. An apprehensive attitude is not unusual and should not be regarded as undesirable. In fact, a little cautious fear may motivate you toward better achievement.

As you begin your student teaching, a certain amount of humility in your approach to the situation can indicate a degree of sensitivity that will serve you well as you continue your teaching efforts. Moreover, as a student teacher you are not entirely on your own. Experienced college and school personnel are prepared to help you as you encounter rough spots. In addition, a careful reading of this book and an intelligent application of its suggestions can aid you further in your preparation for teaching.

QUESTIONS AND TOPICS FOR DISCUSSION

1. Ask your college supervisor or another college instructor what he considers to be the chief function of student teaching. How does his opinion compare with what is said in this chapter?
2. On what bases have you been assigned to student teaching? Would you have prepared another plan? Why or why not?
3. With how many of the items listed on page 4 were you acquainted when you started your student teaching? How did you acquire the information?
4. If you have decided on the state in which you wish to teach, consult the requirements for teaching in that state. To what extent are you fulfilling those requirements?
5. What is your present attitude toward the teaching procedures utilized in your school? How do you plan to adjust to them?

6. What prestudent teaching experiences with young people have you had? How can these help you now? Be specific.
7. Why did you select teaching as a career? Be honest in your answer.
8. Assess your personal qualities according to the list on pages 15–16. In which of them do you believe you need improvement? What can you do about them?

2

THE EFFECTIVE TEACHER

During your years in school, you have met various kinds of teachers. Some you will remember for many years, either because you liked them very much or because you disliked them intensely. Others you have forgotten or will soon forget since your attitude toward them was neutral; they made little or no impression on you.

YOUR IMPRESSION OF GOOD TEACHING

Try this little project. Jot down the names of those school teachers whom you remember well. How do you explain the fact that these names come to your memory so quickly? Check the names of those teachers who leave pleasant memories. Cross the names of those teachers in whose classes you were not happy. What is at the root of your evaluation of these men and women? What were the differentiating characteristics?

Select one teacher who might serve as a model of the kind of teacher you would like to be. Do you have any reservations about the person you have chosen? You realize, of course, that what you have just done is to evaluate those qualities that make for a good or a poor teacher, according to your personal standards of what constitutes teaching competence.

The personal and professional attitudes and behavior of teachers probably have already been discussed in some of your college education courses. You have formed some conclusions concerning the kind of teacher you would like to be. You also have answered the questions about yourself as a potential teacher that appear in Chapter 1. Now you are having an opportunity to observe teachers in action as you meet them and work with them during your student-teaching experiences. Perhaps what we say in this chapter will enable you better to discriminate between a more or less effective teacher.

PRESENT CONCERN ABOUT TEACHING COMPETENCE

The educational facilities available to young people are matters of extreme importance to all of the citizens of the United States. In our fifty states as well as in our many local communities, more and more financial support is being made available to schools. The federal government is allocating an increasing amount of money to meet evidenced educational needs throughout the country.

Curriculum modifications and special programs are being constructed by school people to provide for the special schooling needs and interests of our large and diverse school population. Moreover, it is being recognized that the achieving of worthwhile educational results depends not only on the content of school offerings but also on the teaching skill by which young people are motivated to learn. Hence teachers, buildings and equipment, and learning materials are important if learners are to be helped to develop their capacities to the fullest.

The Importance of the Teacher

The present century is notable for the interest displayed by educators and the lay public in attempts to find an answer to the question: Who is an effective teacher? Many informal and more formal studies have been conducted to ascertain the attributes of apparently successful leaders of young people's learning. The significance of the teacher in the complex totality of the teaching-learning process cannot be minimized. We quote:

A good teacher and the quality of his teaching have always been of paramount importance to free men and to a free society. As society increases in complexity and as the concept of democracy strikes a responsive note in the culture of peoples throughout the world, the need for good teaching is accentuated. This need can be met only as we draw on our warehouse of research findings to improve teacher competence everywhere.[1]

[1] From "Foreword" in *Who's A Good Teacher?* written by Anita Ruffing, President NEA Department of Classroom Teachers; Theodore C. Sargent, President, National School Boards Association; Benjamin C. Willis, President, American Association of School Administrators, in *Who's A Good Teacher?* eds. W. J. Ellena, M. Stevenson, and H. V. Webb (Washington, D.C.: American Association of School Administrators, Department of Classroom Teachers of the NEA, and National School Boards Association, 1961).

In a recent publication, *Teaching as a Career,* the Teacher Education Staff of the Bureau of Educational Research and Development, Office of Education, gave the following as an answer to the question "What is a good teacher?"

The good teacher enjoys teaching; he has a strong desire to learn and wants to kindle this desire in others. He works effectively with others. He is able to see and accept people as they really are. He respects individuality. In the classroom he regards each of his students as a person; he appreciates the uniqueness and the personal beliefs of each one.

The good teacher has confidence in his ability to do a first-class job although he is never completely satisfied with the results. He has a talent for creativeness and the ability to arouse the interest of his students. He has a ready sense of humor—a real asset when the unexpected occurs, as so often happens in any class.

The good teacher is well prepared in the subjects he teaches and he has mastered effective techniques for getting his subjects across. He knows his students. He is skillful in directing their learning in terms of their abilities, interests, and needs. Like members of other professions, he is alert and keeps abreast of current developments: new methods of teaching, the latest teaching aids, research both in the field of education generally and in his own teaching field.

Good teachers find their work deeply rewarding. They receive great personal satisfaction from working with their students, their colleagues, and the public in advancing the objectives of American education. They understand the problems and difficulties of the job, but they are happy that they selected teaching as a career.[2]

State and local school administrators, boards of education, and other groups of school executives tend to construct lists of the qualities they expect their teachers to possess and responsibilities they expect them to assume. The State Department of Education of Florida expects that:[3]

As a person, the teacher needs:

1. To maintain a steadfast and informed loyalty to the values and processes of the American heritage.

[2] Teacher Education Staff, Bureau of Educational Research and Development, *Teaching as a Career,* Pamphlet No. 122 (Washington, D.C.: U.S. Department of Health, Education and Welfare, Office of Education, 1963), p. 3.

[3] Thomas D. Bailey, *A Guide: Teaching Moral and Spiritual Values in Florida Schools,* Bulletin 14 (Tallahassee, Fla.: State Department of Education, 1962), pp. 17–18. Reprinted by permission.

2. To have developed a set of values to serve as guideposts to a philosophy of life.
3. To incorporate these values in all his human relationships with others, both in and outside school.
4. To evaluate at regular intervals these values, critically and reflectively, as they serve him in his daily life.

Only as values increase the teacher's capacity to make mature personal adjustments to society can he begin to help his students develop their own values.

As a member of the profession, the teacher needs:

1. To have a positive attitude toward the worth, importance, and values of his profession.
2. To have a knowledge of child development and its application to intellectual, emotional, social, spiritual, and physical growth.
3. To create with his pupils a classroom climate free from tension and anxiety by establishing a relationship of mutual respect through affection, acceptance, and security. In such an atmosphere creative thinking, originality, initiative, and independence are most likely to flourish.
4. To develop skills in communication in order to interpret the curriculum to parents and to the community as it affects the life of children.
5. To participate actively in shaping educational policies.
6. To execute loyally those policies which have been approved by the school system.
7. To achieve and sustain a high level of professional competence.

As a member of the community, the teacher needs:

1. To provide educational leadership for the community.
2. To establish a condition of mutual trust, understanding, and sympathy with people within the community.
3. To establish himself as a person whose moral and spiritual values are reflected in his personal way of life.
4. To participate in community activities to an appropriate degree, keeping in mind that his primary responsibility is to the classroom.

GENERAL DUTIES, POLICIES, AND PRACTICES
IN SELECTED SCHOOL SYSTEMS

The Board of Education, Syracuse, New York, provides new teachers with the following teacher responsibilities:

DUTIES OF TEACHERS [4]

Personal Responsibilities—Each teacher shall:

1. keep a valid teaching certificate at all times;
2. familiarize himself, after proper orientation, with his entire schedule of duties and meet fully and promptly every obligation of that schedule;
3. be in his room at least fifteen minutes before the time for the opening of school in the morning and ten minutes after school in the afternoon; that is, at 8:15 in the morning in both elementary and secondary schools; in the afternoon to remain until 3:20 in the elementary schools and until 3:10 in the secondary schools;
4. check by initial at designated point his arrival and departure each school day;
5. cooperate mutually with the principal in all matters generally recognized as relating to the welfare of the school;
6. refrain from sending pupils on errands off school property during school time;
7. refrain from presenting a prize, premium, advertising, or gift to a pupil, except such as are permitted by the Board of Education policy;
8. use reasonable and purposeful tact in discouraging pupils and parents from presenting the teacher with gifts of significant value;
9. refrain from requiring any pupil to purchase any text or work book for use in school except such as are on the list approved by the Board of Education, which list the Board of Education will supply;
10. refrain from tutoring for money or other gain any pupil in his own classes;
11. attend, unless he is duly excused, meetings to which he is called after ample notice by the administrative and supervisory staff.

Plans and Records—Each teacher shall:

1. meet each class promptly with activities planned for the class period;
2. keep accurately all attendance records required;
3. keep required records of the proficiency of the pupils in their studies;
4. report all accidents immediately on proper form;
5. have class lists, up-to-date seating charts, and daily lesson plans for one week in advance available for use of substitute teachers;
6. share equitably the handling of details of records, attendance, and extracurricular activities.

[4] *Welcome to Syracuse: Teachers' Orientation Booklet* (Syracuse, N.Y.: Board of Education, Syracuse, 1963), pp. 12–14. Reprinted by permission.

Physical Appearance of Room—Each teacher shall:

1. be responsible for checking the general appearance and orderliness of his room.

Referrals—Each teacher shall:

1. refer cases of illness to school nurse or designated representative;
2. refer discipline cases to designated authority, when considered necessary by the teacher;
3. refer deviates to proper school service such as school doctor, nurse, counselor, or visiting teacher;
4. report loiterers to the principal;
5. confiscate any items that may be harmful to others, and turn such items over to the principal.

Discipline—Each teacher shall:

1. maintain classroom discipline with the backing of the principal;
2. in the absence of Board of Education regulations, make rules for the conduct in his classroom, and shall enforce them as if they have been adopted by the Board;
3. together with all other members of the staff, help to maintain through conduct and conversation, the respect of students for all staff members.

The Independent School District, San Antonio, Texas, provides each teacher with a plan of relationships with others and individual responsibilities, as follows:

GENERAL POLICIES AND PRACTICES IN ALL SCHOOLS [5]

Classroom Management

The classroom provides excellent opportunities for the teacher to make practical applications of the democratic way of life. A successful teacher will make the most of these opportunities. Although democratic procedures will permit the pupils to share in the development of many phases of classroom

[5] Oscar E. Miller, *Handbook for Teachers* (San Antonio, Texas: San Antonio Independent School District, 1963), pp. 15–19. Reprinted by permission.

activity and management, they should not include ideas of unrestricted freedom. Pupils must definitely learn that the teacher is the guide and leader and *in this capacity is always in charge of the classroom situation.*

Pupil Behavior

Attitudes of friendliness and cooperation between the teacher and pupils will do much to prevent the development of behavior problems. A carefully planned program of activities that involves pupils in work that is interesting, challenging, and within the range of their abilities will tend to promote a wholesome atmosphere and will reduce the likelihood of undesirable conduct.

A strong teacher will be able to deal skillfully in handling behavior problems if and when they arise and, in most cases, will not need assistance from higher authority. Whenever a case becomes serious and acute, however, and the teacher feels the need for assistance, the principal should be consulted. Such a case should not be sent to the principal without advising him or her in advance, giving full details regarding the case.

Fairness in dealing with pupils is a very important policy which, coupled with firmness when necessary, will enable the teacher to cope successfully with most classroom problems. The good teacher will be certain that all pupils fully understand the standards of behavior and will then be consistent in enforcing them. Self-control on the part of the teacher is the foundation on which control of the pupils is built. Classroom control based on kindness, firmness, and understanding is most effective. A natural, well-modulated speaking voice, when used consistently by the teacher, will set a very desirable tone pattern that is conducive to good order in the classroom.

Teacher-Pupil Relationships

A genuine interest in the pupils will aid the teacher in establishing a friendly atmosphere within the classroom. The classroom in which attitudes of courtesy and respect prevail provides a desirable setting for profitable learning experiences. A cooperative teacher-pupil planning approach in developing the learning activities will do much to establish the desirable rapport between teacher and pupil.

A good teacher is friendly but must always be careful to maintain the proper adult professional status. He or she may be one WITH the pupils but not one OF them. It is important, too, that the pupils be brought to the realization that they must maintain the proper respect for the teacher's authority at all times.

Every pupil should understand that he is under the supervision of every faculty member in the building and not just his own class teachers, home room teacher, or adviser.

Teacher-School Relationships

Each teacher is a member of a "team" that works as a unit in maintaining a well-organized and efficiently operating school. In this relationship teachers have responsibilities, other than those related specifically to the classroom, which include duties in connection with recess and the noon hour, before and after school activities, and others which the principal may assign. An alert teacher will become informed about the entire program of the school and will find his or her place in it.

Teacher-Community Relationships

Participation in community affairs, particularly in those which relate directly to the school of which a teacher is a part, is a good public relations activity. Active participation in the work of the Parent-Teacher Association is one way in which proper relationships between parents and teachers may be built and strengthened.

Advance Preparation for Classroom Activities

The successful teacher will give a great deal of thought and consideration to advance planning for the framework around which the classroom activities will be built. Teachers should prepare weekly and daily plans which should be realistic and flexible, and should provide for the entire range of abilities of the pupils within a classroom.

The Teacher's Folder

Every teacher should have a folder, to be kept in his or her desk, that contains the following records and information:
Weekly lesson plans
Copy of the daily program
Seating plan
Register containing all class rolls
Daily report forms
List of textbooks in current use for the grade or subjects taught
Notes for a substitute
Copy of the room inventory
Fire drill procedures
Rainy day schedule

Quality of Classwork

Each pupil should be encouraged to give his best effort to his work. Individual progress graphs and charts provide motivation for improvement. High standards should be set and neatness should be stressed in all work. Written work which does not represent the pupil's best effort should not be accepted.

Records

The keeping of records is an important phase of a teacher's responsibility. Neat, accurate, and complete records, which are kept up-to-date, are essential in a well-organized school system. Addresses and telephone numbers need to be checked frequently.

In addition to keeping records of the individual progress of pupils in classroom activities, each teacher is responsible for maintaining accurate records of attendance. Inasmuch as the attendance records serve as a basis for the allotment of State funds that are distributed through the Texas Education Agency to our school district, it is imperative that these records meet the standards set forth by the Agency, under "General Instructions," in the front of the Teacher's Daily Register. This information is also used as a basis for pupil accounting in secondary schools. Attendance records *must* be kept in ink with no erasures. Age-Grade Residence cards, properly signed by parents, must be secured on all pupils residing within the school district.

TEACHER QUALITIES DESIRED BY VARIOUS GROUPS

The many studies of teacher efficiency that have been conducted during the present century (and earlier) have been affected somewhat by the purposes and points of view of those who undertook the particular study. You, as a beginner in the teaching field, want to know what you should be and do to earn success in the profession. Administrators, pupils, and parents, and other members of the lay public have specific goals in mind as they attempt to discover what constitutes effective teaching. Let us analyze briefly some of these specific purposes.

Qualities administrators want in teachers. Although certain educational principles can be applied generally to all learning situations, each school community is likely to present teaching-learning conditions that differ somewhat from those of other communities. Educational needs may differ from school to school, especially in large urban communities. Hence administrative personnel, such as superintendents, principals, and other men and women associated with school administration and supervision, tend to evaluate teacher services in light of the educational needs of their districts and schools.

Administrators of elementary schools want teachers who are well-grounded in the material they are teaching. They expect their teachers to understand and like children, and have the ability to earn the respect and cooperation of their pupils. Administrators also appreciate teachers who can get along amicably with their colleagues, and who are willing to submit intelligently to constructive supervisory evaluation of their teaching efficiency.

In the modern school, a teacher's responsibilities go beyond the immediate classroom. He is expected to participate in out-of-class school activities, to establish a good relationship with parents, and to be actively interested in community welfare. Administrators approve of the teacher who is able to meet the more or less non-instructional aspects of his total teaching responsibilities.

An important duty of a school administrator or supervisor is to rate or assess the efficiency of his teachers. He can do this by (1) observing a teacher functioning in the classroom, (2) evaluating, by means of standardized or school-constructed tests, the progress of the pupils' learning achievement, and (3) alerting himself to the attitudes displayed toward a teacher by children, their parents, and other persons within and outside the school with whom the teacher is professionally associated.

It is evident that an administrator's evaluation of teacher competence is influenced by his own concept of what a good teacher is like in his particular school or school system. We need further to keep in mind that an administrator or supervisor, like any other human being, can be influenced in his rating of teacher effectiveness by personal bias or prejudice. His evaluation also can be affected by his own earlier experiences as a teacher.

Community attitudes toward teaching and teachers. Many teachers are dedicated members of their profession. They are sincere in their desire to meet the demands of teaching as effectively as is possible for them to do. Their difficulty is that they do not always understand fully what is expected of them. They are sensitive to pupils' attitudes toward them, to administrative criticism of their activities, and to public opinion concerning their status in society. They cannot help resenting such popular evaluations of their worth as "Those who can, do; those who cannot, teach."

Attitudes toward teachers vary with communities. Among some of our communities, the teacher is treated with great respect. In fact, he may be regarded as a superior being who can bring about all the desirable changes in their children that they themselves cannot effect.

In some localities, the teacher has not always been accepted as a worthy member of the community. Rather was he regarded as a kind of public servant who should be willing to subsist on a low living wage and be subservient to the will of community leaders. It is no wonder that many teachers of the past found it difficult to maintain self-respect and evaluate rightly their teaching effectiveness.

Fortunately, with increased public emphasis on the value of continued education for American youth has come a new appreciation of the part played by the teacher in the educational progress of young people. Earlier community restrictions on the social activities of a teacher have gradually been withdrawn, and teacher salaries are increasing. The teacher is coming to be a respected member of most community groups. This general change in attitude toward teachers and teaching has helped the members of the profession to view themselves as solid citizens who have a worthwhile contribution to make to society.

Qualities teachers want to possess. Their newly won status often makes it increasingly difficult for teachers to assess objectively the qualities that are essential to efficiency on the job. In too many communities, school programs are set up by lay and professional "higher ups," and the classroom teacher is expected to follow a curriculum, for example, which, in light of his teaching experience, is inadequate or inappropriate. How well can he function in a situation of this kind? What are the teacher qualities needed by him to perform effectively? The teacher does not know—he is confused. His one hope is that eventually he may be included among members of a planning committee for school programs, as is now the situation in some progressive school systems.

It is satisfying for a teacher to be afforded an opportunity to discover the extent to which he has the ability to work effectively in an educational framework that he has helped to erect. Yet, since the master teacher is likely to have set high standards of accomplishment for himself, more often than not he is unsatisfied with his work; he tries in various ways to motivate young people to want to learn.

The serious-minded teacher thrills to his successes, but becomes depressed if he believes that he has failed in his endeavors. More and more, teachers are evincing a serious interest in research concerning teacher effectiveness and are attempting to rate themselves honestly on the various teacher rating scales that are being made available for their use.

Qualities of teachers preferred by pupils. When pupils are asked to list the characteristics that they would like a teacher to possess, they usually include all or most of the following traits:

Interest in children	Ability to control class
Patience	Sincerity
Adaptability	Enthusiasm and cheerfulness
Knowledge of subject matter	Friendliness
Good organization of subject matter	Consideration of others
Daily preparation	Tactfulness
Attention to the needs of individuals	Cooperation
	Sense of justice
Stimulation of thought	Sense of humor
	Impartiality

You will notice that many of these characteristics have to do with human relationships. The rank order of these characteristics varies with groups. Children rarely approve of the easy-going, overly-permissive teacher or the teacher who "plays favorites." A child has little respect for the teacher who disregards or overlooks displays of youthful whims.

Interest of parents in good teachers. Parents have begun to assume a more realistic point of view toward the men and women who teach their children. They recognize and appreciate the worth of the teacher who displays a sincere interest in young people, who can motivate them to profit from their school experiences, and who cooperates with parents in helping children develop mature attitudes and behavior patterns.

The increasing interest in the nation's schools is accompanied by concern about the kind and number of teachers needed for the guidance of young people's learning. State and local communities demand that their teachers be persons who are interested in and understand their pupils, are well-gounded in subject matter, and find satisfaction in teaching.

Various approaches are utilized to insure the obtaining of competent teachers. The lay public is demanding that elementary school teachers, for example, receive an adequate preteaching education, develop an understanding of child psychology, have a good cultural background, and complete sufficient study in the field of teacher preparation to enable them to motivate learning progress effectively. The majority of teacher trainees are educated in state- and/or community-financed colleges and universities. Many communities also offer an in-service program aimed at alerting teachers to educational changes and advances, and to ways of improving their teaching approaches and techniques.

Increasing birthrates, especially during the past twenty years, have resulted in a serious teacher shortage. Communities not only wish to procure well-trained beginning teachers but they also want to keep them. Hence, within their financial ability to do so, they gradually have been increasing teachers' salaries and in other ways are attempting to make teaching an attractive profession for ambitious and able young men and women.

Local boards of education, as well as educational leaders, recognize the fact that teaching is a complex, demanding vocational field. Consequently, they are cooperating in efforts to lighten the teacher's burdens. These include the provision of good pensions, hygienic teaching conditions, adequate supplies, helpful teaching aids, and other personal and social advantages.

Interest in school by parents. In general, parents tend to be very much interested in the elementary schools that their children attend. For many years, Parents Associations have worked in close cooperation with elementary school people. These groups have been active in assisting principals and teachers in furthering their children's early education. Class mothers have served in various ways to lighten teachers' work. Parents also show concern about teacher attitudes, characteristics, and behavior.

Growing public concern with teachers and teaching is evidenced also in an increasing attempt to discover what constitutes teacher efficiency. Competent teachers are wanted; but who is a competent teacher? Public and private organizations are devoting considerable time, energy, and money to research projects in this field of investigation. Informal studies are giving way to attempts to measure objectively and scientifically those personal and professional attributes that differentiate the effective teacher from the less competent teacher.

The parents of elementary school children usually welcome opportunities to discuss with teachers and other school personnel their children's interests, behavior patterns, and learning progress. At one time, especially in some large urban areas, a parent rarely sought a conference with his or her child's teacher. Moreover, a teacher tended to limit his communication with parents to complaints about their child's uncooperative behavior or unsatisfactory learning progress. At present, in an increasing number of elementary schools, parents and teachers work together to further children's welfare.

DISTINGUISHING ASPECTS OF TEACHER COMPETENCE

As we have indicated earlier in the chapter, many investigations of teachers' personal and professional competencies have been constructed. We now shall consider the items included in some of these studies.

Lists of Teacher Qualities

If you were to analyze the many questionnaires that deal with teacher evaluation, you would find that certain broad areas of personal and professional characteristics appear on many of them. There is agreement among most researchers that the successful teacher has achieved proficiency in (1) guiding the learning process, (2) motivating pupils to learn, (3) improving teaching techniques, (4) encouraging young people to develop desirable attitudes, (5) encouraging young people to develop desirable behavior, and (6) developing those personal and social traits that are conducive to effective teaching.

As you read the foregoing list of six areas of teaching responsibilities, you might comment on them somewhat as follows: "I agree that these items represent important activities and attributes, but they do not indicate how they are to be achieved. How shall I guide or motivate pupils? What are 'desirable' attitudes? Which teaching techniques can or shall I improve? How do I know whether my particular traits are conducive to effective teaching?" These general fields need to be so analyzed that anyone rating a teacher's competence can apply them in practical situations.

It is desirable that all important areas of teacher competence be considered in the evaluation of teachers and teaching effectiveness. A teacher should display an understanding of learning procedures and know how to utilize them in the teaching function. The competent teacher should:

1. Understand the accepted principles of education and how to function within their framework.
2. Understand the areas for service and demonstrate ability to perform those services.
3. Understand the value of planning and of using those plans in his teaching.
4. Understand the principles of healthy living and how to apply those principles to his teaching.
5. Understand child development and how to adapt his teaching accordingly.
6. Understand differences among individuals and how to meet these individual differences in his teaching.
7. Understand the guidance function and how to apply its principles in the education of children.
8. Understand teaching-learning material and how to present this material to his learners.
9. Understand the function of extracurricular activities and what he can do to incorporate them into his teaching.
10. Understand the nature and use of evaluation in the education of children.
11. Understand the interrelating functions of the community and the school in the education of children.
12. Understand the utilization of audio-visual and other aids in the teaching-learning situation.

It will be noted that in the construction of this list an attempt was made to explain the connotation of each general aim by means of its possible applications.

Significant studies of teacher characteristics. A well-known investigator of the literature dealing with teacher characteristics was A. S. Barr, who, before his death, was at the University of Wisconsin. Barr found that, in general, constructors of lists of teacher characteristics tend to use three differing approaches:

1. Personal qualities
2. Behavior of the teacher
3. The teacher's knowledge, special skills, and attitudes [6]

In his discussion of "Characteristics of Successful Teachers," Barr presents the following succinct points of view: [7]

When one attempts to describe the successful teacher in terms of personal qualities one is confronted with an overwhelming wealth of descriptive terms. One of the problems that confronts the worker in this field is to telescope and organize these many qualities to a more manageable shorter list. Several years ago the author proposed some twelve qualities, as follows:

1. *Resourcefulness*
Originality, creativeness, initiative, versatility, imagination, adventurousness, progressiveness.

2. *Intelligence*
Foresight, judgment, intellectual acuity, understanding, mental ability, intellectual capacity, common sense.

3. *Emotional Stability*
Poise, self-control, steadfastness, sobriety, reserve, dignity, non-neuroticism, emotional maturity, adjustment, constancy, loyalty, easy-going realism in facing life, not excitable, stable, integrated character.

4. *Considerateness*
Appreciativeness, kindliness, friendliness, courteousness, sympathy, tact, good-naturedness, helpfulness, patience, politeness, thoughtfulness, tolerance.

5. *Buoyancy*
Optimism, enthusiasm, cheerfulness, gregariousness, fluency, talkativeness, sense of humor, pleasantness, carefreeness, vivaciousness, alertness, animation, idealism, articulativeness, expressiveness, wit.

6. *Objectivity*
Fairness, impartiality, open-mindedness, freedom from prejudice, sense of evidence.

---

[6] See A. S. Barr, "The Measurement and Prediction of Teacher Efficiency: A Summary of Investigations," *Journal of Experimental Education,* XVI (June, 1948), 202–8; and A. S. Barr, "Characteristics of Successful Teachers," *Phi Delta Kappan* (March, 1958), pp. 282–84.

[7] A. S. Barr, "Characteristics of Successful Teachers," *Phi Delta Kappan* (March, 1958), pp. 282–84. Reprinted by permission.

7. *Drive*

Physical vigor, energy, perseverance, ambition, industry, endurance, motivation, purposefulness, speediness, zealousness, quickness.

8. *Dominance*

Self-confidence, forcefulness, decisiveness, courageousness, independence, insensitiveness to social approval, self-sufficiency, determination, thick-skinnedness, self-reliance, self-assertiveness.

9. *Attractiveness*

Dress, physique, freedom from physical defects, personal magnetism, neatness, cleanliness, posture, personal charm, appearance.

10. *Refinement*

Good taste, modesty, morality, conventionality, culture, polish, well-readness.

11. *Cooperativeness*

Friendliness, easy-goingness, geniality, generosity, adaptability, flexibility, responsiveness, trustfulness, warm-heartedness, unselfishness, charitableness.

12. *Reliability*

Accuracy, dependability, honesty, punctuality, responsibility, conscientiousness, painstakingness, trustworthiness, consistency, sincerity. . . .

There are hundreds of illustrative behaviors associated with buoyancy. Only five illustrations have been given here.

If one considers the successful teacher from the point of view of observable behaviors, one might center attention upon items such as:

1. Behaviors associated with identifying pupil needs.
2. Behaviors associated with setting and defining goals.
3. Behaviors associated with creating favorable mind sets and motivation.
4. Behaviors associated with choosing learning experiences.
5. Behaviors associated with providing for individual differences.
6. Behaviors associated with making activities meaningful.
7. Behaviors associated with the analysis and organization of learning experiences.
8. Behaviors associated with the direction of group activities.
9. Behaviors associated with the use of learning aids.
10. Behaviors associated with teacher-pupil relations.
11. Behaviors associated with the evaluation of pupil growth and achievement.

Much has been written on all the above items. It is not enough to list them. They must be defined, preferably in an operational way.

A third approach to the characteristics of the successful teacher is through the knowledges, attitudes, and special skills that teachers need to be considered competent. Among the knowledges there are four that are usually listed as essential to successful teaching:

1. Good cultural background.
2. Substantial knowledge of the subject taught, or of some area of specialization.

3. Substantial knowledge of human development and learning.
4. Substantial knowledge of professional practices and techniques.

Among the generalized skills the following are frequently emphasized:
1. Skill in the use of language, spoken and written.
2. Skill in human relationships.
3. Skill in research and educational problem-solving.
4. Effective work habits.

Among the interest and attitudes frequently emphasized are the following:
1. Interest in pupil.
2. Interest in a subject or area of specialization.
3. Interest in teaching.
4. Interest in the school and the community.
5. Interest in professional cooperation.
6. Interest in professional growth.

Note carefully the various items on Barr's list. Ask someone who knows you well to give you some idea where you stand in reference to the teacher traits mentioned. Note the traits on which you are not considered to be very proficient. Discuss with the rater the reasons for the evaluations given. Do you find it difficult to accept adverse comments? It probably was not easy for your friend to give you an honest appraisal of what he considers to be your strong and weak characteristics for teaching. This experience should be helpful to you when later you are officially rated by your supervisors.

We need not remind you that when supervisors rate you, their judgments are based on your observable modes of behavior. You need constantly to be aware of the kind of impression you are making on those with whom you work. Moreover, it is practically impossible for a rater to be completely objective. Personal interest or bias is likely to affect the evaluation of a teacher by a supervisor.

Differentiation among Teacher Trait Values

Various possible aspects of teaching competence are included in the many lists of teacher characteristics that now are available. It probably is a fact that the possession of these characteristics contributes to teaching effectiveness, yet it also is probable that some qualities and behavior reactions are more valuable as predictors of teacher competence than are others.

More than a quarter of a century ago, a study of teacher qualities was completed that attempted to distinguish between the more significant and the less significant of fifty traits as having predictive value in rating teacher effectiveness.

Each of sixty supervisors, two hundred teachers, and three hundred fifty student teachers rated two excellent and two ineffective teachers they knew on each of the fifty listed items using the following seven-point scale.

Almost totally lacking	Noticeably below average	Slightly inferior to average	In no way unusual	Noticeably superior	Unusually superior	Nothing left to be desired
1	2	3	4	5	6	7

A rater might be so enthusiastic about an excellent teacher that he would rate him 7 in each item (a total of 350 points) or disapprove so heartily of a poor teacher that he would rate him no more than 1 in each item (total 50 points). Since no one tends to be perfect in all characteristics and no one probably is almost totally lacking in them, the raters were limited to a total of 275 points for the excellent teacher and 125 points for the poor teacher. These limitations compelled the rater to place special emphasis on those traits that in his estimation were the most predictive, thereby understressing relatively unimportant items.

The fifty items then were arranged in rank order, according to the *point divergence* between respective arithmetic means. The greatest divergence between judgments of excellent and poor teachers was 3.51 (*Ability to develop pupil's self-control*) and 1.96 (*Health*). These figures can be interpreted to mean that the raters considered the *Ability to develop pupil's self-control* as the most significant difference between the excellent teacher and the ineffective teacher, and *Health* as the least predictive.

According to the findings, the ten most significant and the ten least significant items are given in Table 1.

Correct interpretation of these data is very important. One should not conclude that the last ten qualities are not important. They are, but, by comparison, they are not so significant as the first ten in distinguishing between the competent and the less competent teacher.

TABLE 1

THE TEN MOST IMPORTANT AND THE TEN LEAST IMPORTANT TRAITS TO
DIFFERENTIATE GOOD FROM POOR TEACHERS

Most Significant Traits	Least Significant Traits
1. Ability to develop pupil's self-control	41. Interest in community
2. Personal influence	42. Punctuality, attendance
3. Ability to teach how to study	43. Intellectual capacity
4. Enthusiasm	44. Posture
5. Ability to stimulate thinking	45. Voice
6. Skill in questioning	46. Use of English
7. Ability to discipline	47. Care of light, heat, etc.
8. Ability to motivate students	48. Economy of using material
9. Definite aim	49. Dress
10. Care of individual needs	50. Health

We shall illustrate our point. A teacher should have good health, but most teachers do, regardless of the quality of their teaching. Of course, a teacher should possess superior intelligence. However, a young person having inferior or mediocre mental ability would scarcely be able to achieve successfully in his many years of study before he becomes a teacher. Similarly, good posture, proper dress, correct use of English, and pleasantness of voice are attributes that result from general educational experiences. A teacher's interest in the school community is desirable, but may have comparatively little effect upon his efficiency in the classroom. You will notice also that the ten most significant characteristics are closely associated with individual attitudes and behavior.

This early study and others like it that have been conducted through the years indicate the direction being taken by recent research in this area. The three national associations, mentioned earlier, expressed a similar point of view in *Who's a Good Teacher?* The traits listed in this publication as being closely associated with teacher competence include:

. . . intelligence, knowledge of subject matter, scholarship, educational background, age and experience, professional knowledge, cultural background, socio-economic background, teaching attitude and interest, and voice and speech characteristics.[8]

[8] W. J. Ellena *et al., op. cit.,* p. 22.

The authors then proceed to assess the relationship of each of these traits with observable teacher success. They conclude their discussion of effectiveness as an elusive quality with this statement:

> In most of the studies of unsuccessful teachers, poor maintenance of discipline and lack of cooperation tend to be found as the chief causes of failure. Health, educational background, preparation, age, and knowledge of subject matter, on the other hand, appear to be relatively unimportant factors in terms of teacher failure.[9]

In light of what is now known, eductors might wish to give different weights to different items in evaluating teacher competence. If we turn to the fifty items used to discover the differences between "good" and "poor" teachers and consider how each might be weighted in the evaluation of teachers, we would be able to construct a scale that might be meaningful. We present a teacher rating scale with appropriate weights assigned to each item on the scale. In this type of scale, provision for only three evaluations (Poor—1) (Average—2) (Good—3) is sufficient to arrive at the index for each teacher. This approach, if adopted, would make it possible to compare one teacher with another by use of a single index.

TABLE 2

WEIGHTED RATING SCALE FOR TEACHERS

Student's Name _____	Poor	Average	Good	Weight	Total
Trait for Evaluation	1	2	3		
Ability to develop pupil's self-control				2.5	
Personal influence					
Ability to teach how to study					
Enthusiasm					
Ability to stimulate thinking					
Skill in questioning					
Ability to discipline					
Ability to motivate students					
Definite aim					
Care of individual needs					
Ability to develop good habits				2.0	
Ability to understand the learner					
Attention to responses of pupils					

[9] *Ibid.*, p. 26.

TABLE 2 (*Cont.*)

WEIGHTED RATING SCALE FOR TEACHERS

Student's Name _____	Poor	Average	Good	Weight	Total
Trait for Evaluation	1	2	3		
General growth				2.0	
Adaptability					
Skill in making assignments					
Interest in pupils					
Ability to organize subject matter					
Growth in subject					
Cheerfulness					
Ability to be tactful					
Choice of subject matter					
Practice of self-control					
Ability to be sympathetic				1.5	
Sincerity					
Sense of justice					
Attention to health of pupils					
Daily preparation					
Initiative, self-reliance					
Ability to cooperate					
Professional interest					
Attention to punctuality of pupils					
Sense of humor					
Accuracy					
Industry					
Interest in school					
Grasp of subject matter					
Care of routine					
Attention to neatness of room					
Promptness with reports					
Interest in community				1.0	
Punctuality, attendance					
Intellectual capacity					
Posture					
Voice					
Use of English					
Care of light, heat, ventilation					
Economy of using material					
Dress					
Health					

Total Index

CODE OF ETHICS FOR STUDENT TEACHERS

In order to assist student teachers to understand their professional responsibility, the California Student Teachers Association, in 1963, revised its *Code of Ethics for Students of Education.* We present it in this chapter along with the specific suggestions for implementing its provisions. Likewise, as a means of pinpointing a teacher's responsibility in relation to students, the community, and the profession, and to acquaint you with professional employment practices, the Committee on Professional Ethics of the National Education Association drew up the *Code of Ethics for the Education Profession* that appears in Chapter 17.

As you consult these codes you realize that basic to their construction are various teacher characteristics that have been stressed in the foregoing discussion. Each code sets down in practical terminology those professional qualities that are important in effective teacher relationships. Note, especially, your responsibility to pupils, to the teacher-education institution, to the profession, and to society as outlined in the "applications of the student teachers' code of ethics."

CODE OF ETHICS
STUDENT CALIFORNIA TEACHERS ASSOCIATION [10]

A Code for Students of Education: The objectives of the Student of Education are to gain insight into teaching skills and to develop professional integrity; therefore, it is necessary that he accept these responsibilities:

Responsibility to the Pupil

The first consideration of the Student of Education is the welfare of his pupils and future pupils. He seeks to gain a firm foundation in all subject matter in order to make himself an informed, prepared person. As a Student Teacher he respects the judgment of and assists the Supervising Teacher in guiding the pupil toward mature responsibility in the school, the home, and the community.

[10] Courtesy of Charles E. Hamilton, State Adviser, Student California Teachers Association. Revised Code Approved, 1963.

Responsibility to the Teacher Education Institution

The Student of Education observes the professional and personal standards expected by his college and welcomes the guidance of its representatives. As a Student Teacher he becomes informed on and supports the policies of the school in which he is doing his Directed Teaching and develops satisfactory rapport with the Supervising Teacher and other personnel.

Responsibility to the Profession

The Student of Education strives to develop his professional skills and attitudes and maintains a constructive and cooperative relationship with his associates.

Responsibility to Society

The Student of Education recognizes the concern of society for the education of its youth and is ready to preserve the social heritage and promote the democratic way of life.

APPLICATIONS OF THE STUDENT TEACHERS' CODE OF ETHICS

The following applications of the preceding Code are designed to implement the interpretation of each of the four general responsibilities.

I. Responsibility to Pupils

1. The Student of Education, realizing that he has a responsibility to his future pupils, prepares himself with a sound foundation in the liberal arts, as well as in his technical professional preparation.
2. The Student Teacher respects the confidence of a pupil; information given in confidence should be passed on only to authorized persons or agencies that are attempting to aid the pupil.
3. The Student Teacher is an example to his pupils physically, mentally, intellectually, morally, and ethically.
4. The Student Teacher refrains from indoctrinating his pupils with his religious or political views.
5. The Student Teacher recognizes the need for understanding child growth and development. On the basis of this understanding, he develops:
   a) a learning program oriented to the individual capacities of his pupils, and

    b) a social climate which encourages personal integrity and societal responsibility.

6. The Student Teacher deals sympathetically with each pupil without prejudice or partiality.

II. *Responsibility to the Teacher Education Institution*

1. Having established an affiliation as a student with a college, the Student of Education upholds its academic standards.
2. The Student of Education approaches all of his opportunities for academic and professional preparation with a constructive attitude.
3. The Student of Education appreciates the assistance of the school in which his student teaching is done.
4. Realizing that the supervising teacher is legally responsible for the class, the Student Teacher assumes only the authority which has been delegated to him.
5. The Student of Education respects the rights and the dignity of all members of the profession and conducts himself so that he is worthy of equal respect.

III. *Responsibility to the Profession*

1. The Student of Education shows pride in and considers himself a member of the profession and he acts according to professional ethics.
2. The Student of Education continues to inform himself about academic, professional, and current affairs.
3. The Student of Education is informed on the legal aspects of his profession.
4. The Student of Education includes the professional organization as an instrument for solving the problems related to education.
5. Placement: The Student Teacher
    a) uses only professional methods in obtaining a position.
    b) does not apply or underbid for a position held by a qualified teacher.
    c) will be honest in the statement of his competencies in order that the employing district may best utilize the prospective teacher's abilities.

IV. *Responsibility to Society*

1. The Student of Education maintains an open mind toward the attitudes and activities of the community and takes an increasing interest in community life.
2. The Student of Education assumes the responsibility of informing society of the purposes and activities of the American schools.

As you reflect on the material in this chapter, keep in mind that all of the qualities and attributes listed are important, but that some have a higher degree of significance in distinguishing between the good and the poor teacher than do others. You already possess many of the success-encouraging characteristics; others you are achieving through your teacher-training experiences. Much that follows in this book can aid you in developing, through practice, whatever strengths you need to acquire.

QUESTIONS AND TOPICS FOR DISCUSSION

1. Write a description of the teacher whose attitudes and behavior you would like to emulate when you are a teacher.
2. What are some of the factors inherent in present-day concern about teaching and teachers?
3. What do you think administrators can do to foster among teachers the teaching qualities they desire?
4. What are the general attitudes toward teachers in your home community?
5. Why do teachers find it difficult to meet present high standards of teaching?
6. What were your relationships with your teachers when you were an elementary school pupil? Be specific.
7. Reread the list of teacher qualities. Rearrange them according to your judgment of their importance.
8. What was your parents' attitude toward your elementary school and your experiences in it?
9. What evidences have you of an increased interest in education on the part of your home community or elsewhere?
10. How well do you think you meet Barr's list of teacher characteristics?

3

RELATIONSHIPS WITH YOUR PUPILS

You are hoping that your student-teaching experiences will help prepare you to guide effectively the learning activities of boys and girls. You want to gain confidence in the ability to work cooperatively with the many whom you will be meeting in various school situations. In order to achieve your purpose, it is essential that you know something about them—their abilities, their likes, and dislikes; their attitudes toward themselves and toward other people; their aims and ambitions.

The college courses you have taken to this point probably included a course in child psychology in which you traced the pattern of child development and adjustment. Now you are beginning to work closely with these children about whom you have studied. You find that no two children are exactly alike.

You know as never before that each of your pupils has a unique personality. This fact requires that you (1) recognize the differences that exist among children, (2) know how and to what extent your pupils differ from one another, and (3) learn how to deal effectively with the differing attitudes and behavior patterns that they exhibit.

THE CHILD AND HIS DEVELOPMENT

Childhood is an exciting and challenging period. A child's developing personality pattern reflects the effects on his attitudes and behavior of the potentialities he inherits from his family line as these are influenced by his experiences in the home, school, and community. A young person's interactions with younger, same-age, and older relatives, friends, and neighbors help him develop self-understanding. He gradually comes to recognize himself as an individual, both similar to and different from other individuals in his environment.

Changes in Adult Attitudes toward the Child

Adults have differed in their concepts of the significance of child-hood. Religious and social factors have influenced people's inter-pretation of child nature. Some religious groups, believing that the child was born in sin, envisioned their responsibility as that of "driving the devil out of him," by means of rigid disciplining. Other such groups held that the newborn infant was good and pure; any undesirable characteristic that he later might exhibit resulted from the effects on him of forces in this wicked world to which he might respond. Another point of view, having a social background, was the concept of a child as a miniature adult who, although differing in size from older individuals, was expected to understand adult con-ventions and values and to conform to them.

As a result of continuing child study, adult attitudes toward child-hood gradually have changed. A child now is recognized to be a young person who is developing a physical, mental, emotional, and social pattern peculiar to himself. His inner drives are moulded by the environmental factors to which he is exposed. Parents differ in child-rearing practices. Some still employ rigid practices of behavior control; others are unduly permissive in their attitudes toward the child; still others treat the child as if he were a mature adult and able to control his behavior according to adult standards. As a teacher, you need to be thoroughly acquainted with current theories concerning child nature and to keep informed on the latest findings in the field of child study. In addition, as you attempt to guide the learning of your pupils, you should try to discover how their atti-tudes and behavior are related to their home conditions, especially to parental concepts of child-rearing procedures.

Differences among Children

An individual's most rapid rate of growth and development takes place during the first six years of his life. The active, alert, ele-mentary school entrant is very different from the helpless infant he had been some five years earlier. He has grown physically; his inner organs probably are functioning adequately; his attitudes and be-havior reflect maturational development as well as earlier childhood experiences. He has formed certain behavior habits that may persist through much or all of his life span.

In general, the average six-year-old child gives evidence of the kind of person he can be expected to become in his later years. Yet, an individual child may differ greatly in one or more characteristics from others of his age group. You, as a teacher, need to recognize and meet adequately any such differences.

Differences among elementary school children are many. Some children are tall for their age, others are below average in height; some are healthy, others are delicate; some are mentally superior, others have average intelligence, and still others are slow learners; some are maturing rapidly, others are slow maturers; some are enjoying rich home experiences, others are products of underprivileged homes.

The Child as an Imitator

Many attitudes and behavior patterns of children are the results of their imitation of the attitudes and behavior of other persons with whom they are associated. For example, fundamental speech patterns are learned in the home. Children who are products of homes in which there is constant bickering and quarreling among family members are likely to be emotionally disturbed; they may be extremely aggressive or unduly submissive.

The social activities of the family affect children's attitudes toward people outside the home. The child whose parents relate well with friends and neighbors of all ages is likely to be well poised and at ease with his teacher and schoolmates. The child whose close family relatives find it difficult to make and keep friends often experiences similar difficulties in adjusting to the demands of membership in the social groupings found in the school. Other personal qualities exhibited by children that are rooted in adult example as well as in precept include the development of positive or negative attitudes toward cleanliness, neatness, punctuality, industry, cooperation with other people and consideration for their rights, and conformity to school rules and regulations.

In your relationships with children during your student-teaching experiences you should keep in mind that not only have your pupils acquired many of their existing attitudes and behavior habits through imitation but that they also are still in the formative stage. Elementary school children tend, either consciously or unconsciously, to imitate their teacher's mannerisms and ways of doing things and to reflect in their own attitudes the kinds of attitudes he or she displays.

To illustrate the influence a teacher can exert on developing children we cite the case of Miss B, a middle-aged woman who likes children, is well-grounded in subject content, and apparently likes teaching. In her school relationships, however, she always has been sensitive to the attitudes displayed toward her by her pupils and her coworkers. She also is generous in the expenditure of money, time, and energy in behalf of others' welfare. In fact, it would seem sometimes that her generosity is used as a means of earning for herself the good opinion of pupils and colleagues.

Miss B is beginning to exhibit symptoms of a kind of emotional disorganization that is causing her to lose a proper perspective of teacher-pupil relationships, thereby encouraging among her pupils attitudes of laxity in the fulfillment of school responsibilities and of lack of respect for authority. For example, last year she was teaching a class of bright fourth-graders. She became involved emotionally with these boys and girls to the point of urging them to address her by her first name (to the dismay of many parents).

In her teaching Miss B offered these mentally superior children satisfying intellectual challenge but she did little, if anything, toward motivating them to adhere to necessary rules and regulations. She permitted the pupils to move around the classroom, talk to one another, or engage in personal projects, at will. She accepted, without comment, carelessly prepared papers, and condoned any lack of completion of assigned tasks. Throughout the year, Miss B showered the children with gifts, and constantly emphasized their individual strengths and minimized their weaknesses. By the end of the school year many of these youngsters had developed strong emotionalized attitudes.

The case of Miss B is an extreme example of a teacher's influence on young learners. The teacher who received these children the next year in the fifth grade likes to refer to them as her "prima donnas." She enjoys meeting the intellectual challenge they present, but is finding it difficult to retrain them in good behavior habits.

During your student-teaching experiences you will have an opportunity to observe differences among children and to discover what your cooperating teacher does to meet them. At the same time, you need to evaluate your own personality traits and attempt to develop those qualities that can be worthy models for children to imitate.

THE DEVELOPING NEEDS OF ELEMENTARY SCHOOL CHILDREN

Everyone, regardless of his age, experiences certain basic needs that demand fulfillment. Although a child's growth pattern tends to be continuous but uneven, an elementary school child gives evidence of physical, mental, emotional, and social wants, urges, and drives that persist through childhood and beyond. The child's physical needs include a healthful diet, interesting but not too strenuous physical activity, and sufficient rest and sleep.

The child needs intellectual challenge that is suited to his degree of mental ability to profit from learning experiences. Emotionally, he needs love and affection, freedom from unreasonable fears, and the power to adjust well to disappointments and frustrations, and to achieve control of anger, jealousy, and similar disruptive emotions. In his social relationships, the child needs to experience a feeling of belongingness. He should be secure in the knowledge that parents, teachers, and peer associates accept him as a worthy member of the group and that he can share with them his interests and activities.

The ways in which a child's needs can best be fulfilled depend in good part on the characteristic attitudes and behavior patterns he displays at different periods of his development. It is important, therefore, that you, as a student teacher, understand the changes that are likely to take place in the child's personality from his entrance into the elementary school at about the age of six years to his graduation at the age of twelve from a six-year school, or at fourteen from an eight-year elementary school. Your knowledge concerning the child's developmental progress can aid you to meet more effectively the needs of children that are peculiar to specific age periods.[1]

[1] For a detailed discussion of the developmental process through the early school years consult A. L. Gesell and F. Ilg, *The Child from Five to Ten* (New York: Harper & Row, Pub., Inc., 1946). Also R. I. Watson, *Psychology of the Child* (New York: John Wiley & Sons, Inc., 1959), and L. D. Crow and Alice Crow, *Child Development and Adjustment* (New York: Macmillan Co., 1962).

The Child from Six through Eight Years

Unless the child has had nursery school and/or kindergarten experiences, the elementary school entrant is faced with meeting a situation that represents a transition from the relatively sheltered environment of the home and immediate neighborhood to a larger social group that includes a stranger in the form of the teacher and many children whom he does not know. If parents encourage the child to regard "going to school" as an exciting new adventure and if older children seem to enjoy their school experiences, the child is likely to look forward with pleasant anticipation to his own school activities.

The child who is overprotected in the home may be so fearful of the new and the different that entering the elementary school becomes a dread-arousing experience. Such a child needs sympathetic and understanding treatment by the teacher. You may need to help the eager, outgoing youngster control his effervescent behavior; you should not try to "push" unduly the fearful, retiring child but encourage a gradual adjustment to the new and strange school situation in which he finds himself.

As a teacher in the primary grades your relationship with your pupils is that of a mother substitute. Like the mother you must gear your handling of them in light of those characteristics that are relatively common among children of this age period.

A young elementary school child tends to be egocentric: he is concerned with the satisfaction of his felt needs and drives; he seems to regard himself as the center of his little world; he may act as though the chief function of adults were to cater to his every whim and fancy.

The six-year-old may exhibit contradictory moods. At one time he may be "demanding and explosive"; at another time he may be shy and retiring; he may shift from affectionate behavior to antagonism and *vice versa*. Gradually, however, as the child participates with his teacher and classmates in shared activities, he develops a new awareness of these others as individuals and self-interest gives way, partially at least, to interest in them and concern for their welfare. He becomes sensitive to the attitudes toward him of adults and his peer associates.

The primary school child has a short attention span. Hence you should limit the time spent on any one area of learning to what the child can take without becoming bored or restless. Although even the young pupil needs to learn what it means to participate in serious work, it should be continued only so long as interest in it can be maintained. Work periods should be interspersed with play activity that can release any emotional tensions. Also, you should keep in mind that during this age period the child is likely to be interested only in his immediate environment and in current happenings. He is not yet able to project himself into a world that extends beyond present happenings and circumstances.

The young child is able to recognize cause-and-effect relationships but these need to be associated with concrete situations rather than with abstract concepts. For example, the adage, "Honesty is the best policy," means nothing to the child but he probably understands that for him to take something that belongs to another child is wrong and will result in his being punished for the misdeed.

The child wants to learn about himself and about things and other people in his immediate environment. He asks many questions, sometimes not waiting for an answer to one before he raises another. He seems to be trying constantly to find reasons for that which he observes. He also enjoys developing simple skills.

Child differences that need attention. One difference among pupils that is important for teachers to recognize is an individual child's readiness to participate in one or another learning activity. Although degree of learning readiness differs among children of any age it is particularly significant during the early years of school attendance. At one time it was believed that by the age of six years, for example, all children were equally able to begin to master the 3 R's. Now we realize that all six-year-old children have not developed sufficiently mentally and emotionally to benefit similarly from instruction.

It has been found that some children do not respond in the same way to attempts to guide their learning in areas such as reading and the understanding of number concepts. Hence test constructors have devised reading and arithmetic readiness tests to discover the kind of teaching approach that would be most beneficial for young pupils in light of their degree of learning readiness. Curriculum planning takes into account the general readiness of children to learn as well as the specific learning problems of individual pupils.

School people also are giving attention to the health needs of their pupils. Milk and snacks as well as hot lunches are being provided for children. In some schools in underprivileged neighborhoods food is provided at no cost to the children. Also, in some schools, the custom common to nursery schools and kindergartens of allowing periods of needed rest for the children is continued in the early primary grades.

The Child from Nine through Eleven

The child in the intermediate grades continues to experience the fundamental needs that were characteristic of him earlier, but his ways of satisfying them are different. Physically, the nine-to-eleven-year-old tends to develop gradually a pattern of growth that gives some indication of adult status. He can be expected to be healthy and energetic. His rapid mental maturation makes him a joy to teach. He is intellectually curious and is becoming interested in learning about people and happenings that in time and space are outside his immediate neighborhood experiences. He also is less interested in the fanciful and more in the realistic, scientific, and adventurous.

During this age period the child gradually gains greater control of his emotions. His earlier displayed emotional outbursts and temper tantrums become less frequent or disappear. He also is likely to be more restrained in his show of affection. He can differentiate well between right and wrong, and has high standards of conduct for himself and for others. He does not always live up to his ideals, however. His great energy and increasing curiosity often impel him to take part in mischievous acts.

Individual differences are becoming increasingly evident. Not only does each child differ from other children but also, as he matures, differences occur in his own pattern of behavior. Since girls mature more rapidly than boys, girls tend to become aware of differences between the sexes earlier than do boys and are more interested in boy-girl relationships.

This is a period of the formation of gangs among boys and of "best friend" among girls. For both sexes, group loyalties usually are of short duration. There tends to be a succession of gangs or best friends. Although the child still tends to learn through imitation, the attitudes and behavior of peer-age associates tend to influence him more than does adult example.

The preadolescent is gaining greater personal control of his conduct and is exhibiting some understanding of group interaction. In general, this is a happy and zestful period during which the child is making good progress toward eventual maturity.

The Young Person from Twelve through Fourteen

If you are student teaching in an eight-year elementary school you may have the experience of working with pubescents and young adolescents. The years from twelve through fourteen can represent a difficult period of adjustment. Basic needs, such as the need to belong and to be secure in the affection of associates, for example, tend to persist. The physical changes that are taking place within the developing young person are likely to give rise to new needs that he may not yet be ready to meet. He is beginning to view himself as an adult and craves to achieve freedom from adult control, especially that of parents. Yet when things go wrong, he needs and seeks adult help.

Some young people pass through the early pubescent stage with relative ease. If they have been wisely prepared for the physical changes that they will experience, they can accept them in their stride and gradually acquire new interests and a wholesome degree of self-dependence. Other pubescents can become very much disturbed by the changes that are taking place within them. They come to realize suddenly that they no longer are children, but they are not quite certain what their present role should be.

Former interests and activities of older children are spurned by them as "childish" or "silly." They begin to recognize within themselves a new attitude tward members of the opposite sex. The fact that girls tend to mature earlier than boys may give rise to conflict between the sexes. Younger adolescent boys especially seem to be interested in same-sex group activities, although they are willing to share some of their activities with girls who are "good sports."

Rate of anatomical growth differs among young adolescents. In too many instances, this growth is uneven. Hands and feet may seem to be inordinately large in comparison to the growth pattern of other parts of the body. This condition causes awkwardness of movement. The boy more than the girl constantly stumbles over his feet or drops books, or other things, to the amusement of his classmates. At this age, young people often are cruel in their appraisal of one another's peculiarities. The young adolescent girl who suddenly "shoots up" like a weed, or the short, dumpy young adolescent boy may suffer much embarrassment in the presence of more evenly growing young associates.

During this age period, most young people are enthusiasts. They want to be up and doing. They also want to know about all kinds of people and things, but may not always recognize the value to themselves of some of their school studies. Yet, they tend to like their teachers and respect those teachers who exercise sensible control over their conduct. They want to be popular with same-age associates and they become increasingly sensitive to adverse criticism of their personal appearance, manners, and general behavior by other people, especially their age peers.

Young adolescents are likely not to be so generally good-natured as they were during the preceding age period, although they tend to be more genial away from home than with the family. They also may indulge in periods of moodiness and often engage in "thinking things through," either alone or with close pals. Teaching these young people offers considerable challenge, but the experience can be richly rewarding if you have sufficient patience to live with them and all of their vagaries.

QUALITIES CHILDREN NEED AS ADEQUATE PERSONS [2]

In the resolutions they adopted, participants in the White House Conference showed that they hope education will help children of our Nation develop certain qualities appropriate for satisfying and useful living in a democracy. Members of the followup conference interpreted in the following ways these qualities in terms of characteristics of the individual.

With relation to *self*, each individual should have:

A healthy and realistic self concept; self-esteem, including an understanding of one's own capabilities and limitations.

[2] Elementary School Section, Division of State and Local Schools, *Implications for Elementary Education,* Follow-up on the 1960 White House Conference on Children and Youth (Washington, D.C.: U.S. Department of Health, Education and Welfare, Office of Education, 1961), pp. 7–9.

Aspiration to levels of achievement in keeping with individual development, interests, and aptitudes in order to develop one's own potential to its fullest.

Realistic self-evaluation in terms of one's own potential.

Understanding of one's role in the home and family, society, and the world at large.

Self-reliance.

Serenity in the face of changes, such as those caused by mobility.

Character, discipline, and responsibility.

With respect to *human relationships in a free society,* each individual should have:

Belief that all persons should have an equal opportunity for their fullest development regardless of race, creed, social status, or national origin.

Recognition and understanding of the dignity and worth of all individuals.

Belief in the free association of persons of different age, color, creed, and economic or social situation in open communities.

Experience in democratic processes as a method of problem solving.

With relation to *values* each individual should have:

Faith in the moral and spiritual foundations of our democracy, and in the family as the basic unit of our society.

Recognition of the influence of literature, newspapers, magazines, movies, radio, and television in the development of values.

Respect for the uniqueness and dignity of every human being.

Appreciation of the democratic heritage and a sense of his responsibility to maintain and improve it.

Increasing responsibility for high standards of personal, family, and group integrity and conduct. Desire to serve God and his fellowmen.

With relation to *problem-solving and critical thinking,* each individual should:

Enjoy and appreciate intellectual freedom.

Have intellectual curiosity.

Have the skills to pursue individual inquiry.

Have mastery of the basic and academic skills: reading, writing, and number.

Have preparation for coping with the scientific and social problems of an automated world.

Use originality.

Be experienced in the democratic processes of problem-solving.

Have ability to use knowledge, conviction, and courage in making the free choices which are his right to make.

Face situations critically and constructively.

With relation to *safe and healthful living* each should:

Have good health habits.

Have good knowledge of nutrition.

Understand the ill effects of alcohol and tobacco.

Enjoy the best possible physical and mental health.

Have a decent, safe, and sanitary house, security of person and property; protection of physical and mental health, continuous medical and dental care, including vision, hearing, and lingual problems, early detection and treatment of defects and abnormalities, as well as the prevention and treatment of disease; have recourse to ample health facilities, such as hospitals and clinics.

Have access to schools and play areas free from health and safety hazards; be free from exploiting pressures of adults in competitive sports.

With relation to *the use of leisure time* each individual should:

Have interests, attitudes, and appreciations basic to the worthy use of leisure time.

Enjoy participation in recreational endeavors such as sports; creative activities including writing, art, drama, literature, and music; and social activities.

Enjoy exploring and developing his own interests.

Your Childhood Experiences

In the foregoing pages, we have reviewed some of the differentiating characteristics of your pupils. You recall your own childhood attitudes and interests. During that period you recognized the fact that some of your schoolmates differed from yourself, but you did not think too much about these differences. You may have experienced some difficulties of adjustment, but you probably were able to solve them satisfactorily. Now you are viewing children from a different point of view. It is your responsibility as a teacher to recognize differences among them and to do what you can to help all of your pupils become fine, upstanding young people.

You need to be careful to refrain from judging your pupils' behavior according to standards that you and/or your parents set up for you during your childhood. You represented a specific social and economic status that was accompanied by adherence to certain mores and customs according to which you charted your life course.

Some of your pupils are the products of homes that may differ much from that in which you grew up. You need to avoid snap judgments about these young people. Rather should you attempt to discover and take into account all of the factors that are basic to pupils' displayed modes of conduct. The various techniques and approaches utilized in studying and evaluating childrens' developmental progress are discussed at some length in Chapters 4 and 15. At this point we survey briefly some of the media you can employ to learn about students.

LEARNING ABOUT YOUR PUPILS

To face a class of children with the realization that included in the group are many differing personalities can be a fear-producing experience. You realize that if you are to be effective in your guidance of their learning you need to know as much as you can about their differing abilities, interests, and attitudes. This requires that you become acquainted with each of them and discover all that you can about him.

You are limited, of course, in what you are able to discover about your pupils by the amount of time your total college and practice program permits you to devote to this project, as well as by the availability of material. You probably will not be able to learn everything about every pupil with whom you work, but you can make a good beginning by gathering data about some of them, thereby gaining practice in performing an activity that is an important responsibility of the regular teacher.

Suggestions for Getting Acquainted

At your first meeting with the class, prepare a seating chart or utilize one prepared by your cooperating teacher. By referring to the chart during class discussion, you can begin to associate names with the proper individuals. Watch their reactions to you, the class teacher, and teaching procedures. After several sessions, you probably will discover differences in their attitudes. You may decide early that you need to know more about some of them, if you are to deal with them effectively.

You now are ready to obtain some helpful information about these pupils. You know what they look like; you have memorized their names; and you have observed some of their class behavior. What else can you discover about them? Where can you go to obtain needed information?

Utilize Various Sources of Information

Your cooperating teacher can be helpful by (1) acquainting you with the cumulative record of your pupils, and (2) supplying pertinent information concerning the home background of a pupil, any serious problems he may be experiencing, or his relations with other pupils, for example. You also can learn much about a pupil's attitudes toward you, his studies, the school, and life in general through friendly, informal little conferences with him, if you have the time and opportunity to arrange with him for them outside regular class hours. On occasions, you may need to consult the child's guidance counselor to obtain personal help in dealing with him.

Maintaining a Confidential Attitude

Perhaps, a word of caution is in order. Remember that any information you gather about a pupil, or obtain from him should be treated as confidential material. Too often, enthusiastic student teachers become so much interested in some of the young people whom they meet in the practice school that they are moved to discuss them with their college classmates, and with their family or friends. To do so is highly unethical.

Even though you may believe that a particular pupil has a personal problem with the solution of which you would like to help, seek advice from authorized members of the school personnel. Consult such individuals as your cooperating teacher and the school guidance counselor, or an administrator. Do not gossip about the situation with other people—not even with your most intimate friends. You cannot know who may report your gossip to someone who is acquainted with the pupil. Anyone to whom you speak may report the matter to his family, with undesirable results.

DEALING EFFECTIVELY WITH ELEMENTARY SCHOOL PUPILS

You may recall that in a previous chapter we listed the characteristics that elementary school pupils would like their teacher to possess. Here we shall indicate briefly how you can apply, in practice, some of these qualities admired by children.

Show a Genuine Interest in Children

You can give expression to your interest in your pupils in various little ways. Be quick to commend an especially fine bit of behavior, but do not expand upon it to the extent that other members of the class come to believe that you are "playing favorites." Spread your commendations among the entire group insofar as this is possible. Be ready to lend a sympathetic ear to any reports of pupils concerning interesting things that are happening to them.

Be willing to help your pupils when they bring some of their simple problems to you for your advice. You must keep in mind, however, that your time is limited. You cannot afford to give any one child more attention than you give to others, unless the need is great. Then, as already indicated, you should seek the help of other qualified personnel in solving a problem.

Most pupils are careful not to be too demanding of your time and attention, but they do want to be assured of your interest in them and your desire to be helpful in suitable ways. Interest in your pupils is closely associated with other personal attributes. We shall refer to some of these briefly.

Show Friendliness and Consideration to Children

Many opportunities arise in the classroom for you to display attitudes of friendliness and consideration. As your pupils enter the classroom, they like to be greeted with a friendly smile. Children are extremely sensitive to adult attitudes toward them. No matter how independent they may seem to be or how casual their treatment of you, they want to feel that your attitude toward them is one of friendliness and consideration of their interests. This does not mean, of course, that your face during the recitation period should continue to resemble that of the famous Cheshire cat in *Alice in Wonderland,* but they do appreciate your maintaining a pleasant attitude toward them.

The tone of voice you employ is important. Requests usually are better than commands. "Please" or "Will you?" is likely to be heeded promptly. At times, such directives as "Open your textbook to page—" may be desirable. You can either utter these words so sternly or harshly as to imply that you do not expect them to obey or indicate by your friendly, businesslike approach that you expect them to comply with your request as a matter of course.

You can gain the respect and admiration of your pupils by displaying consideration for their feelings. Do not harangue a child for a misdeed in the presence of his classmates. When a child engages in a bit of mischief or is otherwise uncooperative, you cannot permit him to interfere with the study activities of his classmates or disrupt the class, but, as we suggest in Chapter 13, in which we discuss discipline, let him know that you are aware of his undesirable behavior by a glance in his direction or a word of admonition. Speak further with him about the matter in a private conference. If his class behavior does not improve, report his conduct to the cooperating teacher who then will either settle the issue or consult the guidance counselor or someone else in authority.

Most classes usually include at least one member who is so much interested in the class discussion that he wants to preempt an undue amount of class time. He may blurt out answers, without raising his hand or waiting for you to call on him or on another member. You realize that he does not mean to be officious—he is being carried away by his enthusiasm. To reprimand him publicly might cause him to feel that you do not appreciate his study efforts; his feelings are hurt.

A good way to handle such a situation is to say quietly something like this, "Not now, John. You know the answer, but let us hear what Max has to say about it." Several repetitions of this kind of treatment usually are sufficient to convince him that he needs to employ self-restraint. Especially is this so if, on occasions, you call on him to summarize what other pupils have said or to add a point that they have omitted. In addition, you can explain in private to a too active pupil that everyone in the class has the same rights that he has.

There are many other ways through the following of which you can convince your pupils of your friendly and understanding consideration of their feelings. For example, you have requested a pupil to read to the class a paper that you have assigned on a specific topic or to place on the chalkboard a diagram or outline that he has prepared. He is having some difficulty in finding the material. It is extremely embarrassing for the child to have you, the teacher, sit in silence while he fumbles through his books to find his material. Better results are obtained if you fill the gap by addressing some pertinent comments to the class until he is ready. He will appreciate your helping him out in this way.

Display a Sense of Justice

We often hear children say of a teacher, "He's not fair!" They thereby are giving expression to the difference between children's and adults' attitudes concerning what should be considered to be right and just. Children tend to evaluate adult attitudes toward them in light of their own subjective interpretation of what is due them. Most adults have learned to view their experiences more objectively. They have learned that, although rules and regulations, for example, do not please them personally, such regulators of behavior are aimed at the common good. The child cannot project his thinking beyond his own immediate interests and desires.

The administrators of the school in which you are doing your student teaching have established certain rules of conduct to which the pupils are expected to conform. These may include directives concerning matters such as mode of dress in school, passing through corridors, punctuality in meeting school responsibilities, respect for authority, and similar aspects of behavior. It is your obligation to know these regulations and to make certain that your pupils obey them.

You cannot afford to permit any child to flout prescribed school dicta in your presence. Perhaps, because of your youth and newness in the school, a child may attempt to "get away" with a form of forbidden conduct that he would not attempt in the presence of one of his regular teachers. You must be alert to the possibility of such an attempt to try you out.

Be mentally prepared to let any miscreant pupil know that you are aware of his intentions and warn him that you will not tolerate a repetition of undesirable behavior. You may need to penalize any individual who repeats the offense. If he persists in his misbehavior, you should report him to your cooperating teacher. It usually is better for you, yourself, to handle infraction of rules, however. Too much reporting of misdeeds to a person higher than yourself in authority may earn for you a reputation among the pupils of being an unfair talebearer.

Another area of class procedure concerning which children accuse their teachers of injustice is that of the administration of tests. In order to give you practice in evaluating learning progress, your cooperating teacher may permit you to construct, administer, and mark class tests. Although you consult him in the preparation of testing material, you are more than likely to include questions that will be disapproved by some members of the class.

You may safely assume that one or more pupils will complain that the material on the test had not been covered in class, that the test was so long they could not complete it, or that the questions were too difficult. In addition, some pupils will accuse you of marking their papers unfairly. They may insist that their answers were similar to those of other pupils to which you assigned a higher rating than you did to theirs. This is a common experience of most teachers. It often is difficult for young people to evaluate their own performances. Hence they are likely to blame you for their failure to achieve desired success in a test.

Since the evaluation of learner progress is discussed in later chapters, here we do no more than suggest the following testing procedures. Adherence to them will be helpful to you.

1. Be certain that the content of the test does not include anything that has not been assigned for study. If a thought question is included, it should be based on a background of learned material.

2. After you have constructed the questions, put them aside for a while. Then read them to make sure that their meaning is clear.

3. Before you start to mark any pupil's answers, read all the papers through quickly in order to discover the general trends in the

answers. If the test includes several essay questions, a good plan is to grade one question on all of the papers before you start on another question. In this way, you can keep in mind what you expect to find included in the answer and can assign grades on a relative basis.

4. No matter how carefully you mark papers, you may make mistakes. You can misinterpret an answer that is correct but differs somewhat from the answer you wanted. If a pupil calls this fact to your attention, be willing to admit your error and make correction by reevaluating the answer. Do not let this situation occur too often, however, lest you be bombarded with demands for reconsideration of many other papers. If it happens occasionally and you are gracious in your attitude toward giving a pupil all the credit he deserves for his performance, you soon earn the reputation of being a fair and just teacher.

During your day-by-day contacts with pupils, many incidents occur that cause children to rate you as just or unjust. The best you can do is to display a *sincere attitude* of interest in the welfare of every child in the room. Inadvertently, you may seem to single out one or a few pupils to the exclusion of others. You may commend one pupil for work well done, for example, but disregard others who have performed equally well.

At one time you may call a pupil to account for a wrongdoing but, at another time, fail to notice that another pupil is engaging in the same kind of behavior. You may grant a request to one pupil but deny the same request to another. In justice to all pupils, you need to be consistent in your behavior toward each of them.

Importance of Being Tactful

In dealing with your pupils much tact is needed. You know that children are easily aroused emotionally. Their feelings are hurt if they believe that anyone is belittling them in the opinion of their peers. A child is sensitive to the recognition of any way in which he may seem to be inferior to other members of his group. You therefore need to handle tactfully any situation in the classroom that may cause one child to be criticized adversely by his classmates, especially if the condition is not of his own making. We cite a few examples.

Speech defects, such as stammering or stuttering, are not uncommon among children. A tense, high-strung young person finds it difficult to enunciate clearly when he is called upon to recite. The attitude of the other members of the class toward the defect reflects your own attitude toward it. Do not frown or give evidence of impatience. Encourage him with a smile to try to answer the question, warning the others with a glance to desist from laughing at him.

Young people can be cruel to their peers, but they also can be sympathetic and willing to take their cue from your leadership in situations of speech difficulties. If the defect is serious, the child probably is receiving therapeutic treatment from a special speech teacher. Your cooperating teacher will acquaint you with this fact and tell you how you best can help the pupil. Be sure to follow any such suggestions given you.

You also need to be tactful in your personal relations with children. Sometimes, because they like you, they want to know all they can about you. Hence they are motivated to ask you questions about yourself. How old are you? Do you live at home? What is your address? What does your father do?

Once pupils are given an opening they will continue to ply you with questions. They might continue with such questions as the following. Do you have brothers and sisters? How old are they? Do you dance and/or go to parties? Have you a girl friend (boy friend)? There sometimes seems to be no end to the personal questions they ask you.

You need to realize that usually children are not trying to be pert or "fresh." They just want to know. You need to be tactful in your answers to their questions, however. Some matters are none of their business. Yet, you cannot put them off completely. Answer truthfully whatever you think they have the right to know. Give a general answer to others.

It usually is unwise to give pupils your address unless you would welcome them in your home as visitors. Some regular teachers invite their pupils to their homes for special purposes. It usually is better for a student teacher not to encourage any visiting between himself and his pupils. If you are in a school that is close to your home and a pupil's parents are friends of your family, you cannot avoid meeting this child socially. Be careful, however, to avoid discussing with him either members of the school faculty or his classmates.

IMPORTANCE OF SUBJECT MATTER

Since the advent of Sputnik, subject matter even on the elementary school level has received added attention from educators. Middle- and upper-grade pupils learn much of their subject matter through reading what is written on the printed page. Hence to acquire needed knowledge, children need to achieve the ability to read with under-standing.

Teachers in the early grades need to place considerable emphasis on helping children not only to master this tool of learning but also to enjoy using it. Unfortunately, too many children find it difficult to learn to read. They become slow or retarded readers who have trouble keeping up in the study of subject matter with average or superior readers even on the high school and college levels.

Your Knowledge of Subject Matter

If you hope to earn success as a student teacher you need to know your pupils and how to deal with them. Consequently, adequate preparation requires an understanding and application of certain psychological and sociological principals that are fundamental to achieving positive teacher-pupil relationships. It is equally important that you are well-grounded in subject matter. Your primary goal as a teacher is to guide children's learning progress to the end that they can apply what they have acquired—knowledge, skills, or atti-tudes—in the conduct of their lives. Other aspects of teacher educa-tion are means to an end.

Regardless of their own attitudes toward study materials, children expect their teachers to have a thorough knowledge of subject matter. They want to feel that they can bring any of their questions to a teacher and receive a satisfactory answer. As we have suggested earlier, you may find occasionally that you cannot supply an answer on the spur of the moment. You should know, however, where to find it. Admit this fact to the pupils and, either alone or assisted by them, obtain the correct data.

Do not hedge. Do not give a vague or incomplete answer to a question and expect your pupils to be satisfied. Keep up-to-date, especially in the fields of science and world affairs. Many older

children like to read newspapers and magazines and to follow radio
and television programs that deal with current happenings. Your
pupils can embarrass you by referring to new developments unless
you keep one step ahead of them. Be informed concerning the kind
of information in which they are likely to be interested and about
which they can learn outside the classroom. They often appreciate
your alerting them to such material.

No matter how thorough your mastery of subject matter has been
during your preteaching education, you probably will need to continue your studies during your entire teaching career. New information, improvement of techniques and skills, greater understandings,
and more realistic appreciations challenge you from day to day and
require that you continue to be a student as well as a teacher.
Moreover, as you yourself engage in continued learning, you are
enabled to maintain a student point of view and become increasingly
aware of the learning problems of your pupils.

Your Organization of Subject Matter

Later we shall discuss lesson planning and all that it entails. We
want here to stress the importance of so organizing your presentation of learning materials that your pupils can get a clear understanding of relationships between various phases and units of study.

You need to help your pupils build each unit of knowledge or
skill on a thoroughly recognized and understood base. You must
avoid rambling from one topic to another or leaving a topic hanging
in midair. Your own thinking needs to be clear and well organized
in order to help the pupils follow you step by step in the learning
process of the material under consideration.

Your Daily Preparation

As a student teacher, you probably will receive considerable assistance from your cooperating teacher and your college supervisor
in the matter of preparing the material that you expect to teach
each day. There are certain suggestions that, if you follow now,
will develop habits that can be valuable to you as a beginning
teacher.

Know exactly *what* and *how much* you expect to cover during recitation. This you learn from experience. The beginning teacher is likely to attempt to include either too much or too little material.

The points to be included in the lesson should follow a well-thought-through sequence. You may find that questions arise in class that indicate lack of understanding of the material on the part of some students. If you are well prepared for the lesson, you probably have foreseen such difficulties and will be able to meet them. The important point is that you start the day's work promptly and that you carry it through in an interesting and worthwhile fashion.

YOUR ATTITUDE TOWARD TEACHING IN THE ELEMENTARY SCHOOL

Some people regard teaching on the elementary school level to be an easier and more simple task than guiding the learning activities of secondary school and college students. Such individuals seem to believe that all children can and want to master the fundamentals on which are built later more advanced study materials. In spite of their own elementary school experiences, they still may think that all the elementary school teacher does is to help able and willing youngsters learn how to read and write and gain facility in handling simple arithmetic processes. These people fail to realize that children differ in their ability to learn and that they do not achieve equal success in the mastery of the 3 R's.

Moreover, you, as an elementary school teacher, are responsible for aiding your pupils to acquire other basic skills and the beginnings of knowledge about themselves, other people, and the world about them. Also, one of your chief functions is to inculcate in them positive attitudes toward learning and effective study habits. Hence, contrary to more or less popular belief, an elementary school teacher exerts a powerful influence not only on children's present learning but also on their attitudes toward continued study.

Attitudes are acquired in various settings; they are not taught. If you bring to your teaching a high degree of enthusiasm born of your deep interest in children and subject content, you are likely to engender in your pupils a similar attitude toward their learning activities. At present, you probably are enthusiastic about guiding the learning of young children. That is why you have selected teaching on the elementary school level as your professional activity.

You need to take care, however, that as you continue through the years to teach on this school level you do not allow your work to become so routinized that you lose your present interest in it and enthusiasm for it.

QUESTIONS AND TOPICS FOR DISCUSSION

1. Recall four of your elementary school pals. List ways in which these young people differed from one another.
2. What were your interests as a preadolescent?
3. Why do some educators consider preadolescents difficult to teach?
4. Select three pupils in your class about whom you would like to have more information. Ask permission to consult their cumulative records and study them. To what extent did the data help you understand these children?
5. If you have had a conference with any of your pupils, write a brief report of what transpired at it.
6. Cite examples of your cooperating teacher's consideration of his pupils' feelings.
7. Have you had any difficulties with pupil behavior? If so, how have you handled such situations?
8. If you have been the victim of a tactless teacher, explain how his behavior affected your attitude toward him.

4

GENERAL ASSESSMENT OF PUPILS

Throughout your teacher-training courses you have had your attention called to the need to understand pupils as individuals. As a student teacher, you find yourself face to face with situations in which you must be able not only to distinguish one individual from another but also to understand what the differences are among individuals, how they come about, and what can be done to meet them.

Your attention already has been directed toward individual differences and how they affect your relationships with your pupils. During your observation of your cooperating teacher, you have noticed how some of the differences have been met by him, how he has handled deviant behavior, and what can be done for pupils who suffer serious problems of adjustment.

VALUE OF STUDYING CHILDREN

You will find as you enter the teaching profession that the more you know about learners the better are you able to help them individually. If you wish to be most effective in your stimulation of learners toward a well-rounded education you will want to acquaint yourself with the extent of their mental, emotional, and social development.

An understanding of the psychological factors involved in human development and learning enables you, as time and energy permit, to deal effectively with the class as a whole and with members individually. It is your duty to identify and concern yourself with those individual differences that exert a significant influence on learning, and that necessitate adequate differential treatment in the teaching-learning situation. You will need to have some knowledge relative to the kinds of information available and be able to evaluate the qualitative effect of each on effective learning.

Ability Differences among Children

Every teacher knows that no two of his learners are alike. The ways in which and the extent to which these differences occur may be difficult to discern. You soon discover, however, that the more nearly equated your pupils are in ability to achieve the better teaching-learning climate will there be in your classroom. Before long, school administrators may realize that optimal learning conditions prevail in those classrooms in which the learners are able to cope with study material without too wide a gap among their basic potentialities in that area of learning. In other words, classes will be organized according to levels of ability or extent of achievement.

We have known for a long time that every measurable trait of individuals tends to distribute itself according to a normal curve of distribution. (See Figure 3.) This seems to be true whether the trait is one of height, weight, mental ability, or other measurable human quality. For example, if mental ability is measured, we find a wide range of capacity for those individuals having low ability to those displaying superior ability, with the larger number clustering near the middle or average. (See Figure 3.)

When norms are established for the determination of a reading grade level in the sixth grade, for example, the median score obtained from administration of a reading test to a large number of learners in that particular grade is used as its norm. However, the results of a reading test administered to all of the sixth-grade pupils indicate that the range of responses probably will vary from third- to twelfth-grade norms. A similar wide spread of abilities usually can be found in any heterogeneously grouped class. If your class is organized according to ability or achievement level, you should find a smaller range of differences in reading ability and mental capacity. You also should encounter fewer problems as you attempt to meet the learning needs of all of the pupils in the class.

Behavior Differences among Children

It does not take you long to become aware of the overt behavior characteristics of your pupils and to realize that there are significant differences among them. You need to learn to recognize and identify behavior differences and come to appreciate the extent to which these children are alike and different in their ways of responding to classroom procedures. Moreover, you know a child's personality characteristics do not consist of a single entity but represent a combination of traits that is a resultant of integrating factors serving his immediate needs.

To be alert to your pupils' daily behavior in the classroom is a valuable teaching asset. It not only will make you aware of present behavior but may be an indication of what can be expected in the future. Also, usually anticipated behavior follows a pattern of past practices. To have information regarding a pupil's past as well as present behavior should be helpful to you in your attempts to encourage him to bring about needed improvement in his behavior.

Pupil Attitudes as Revealed in School Setting

In addition to observing a pupil's commonly displayed behavior, it is necessary to try to discover why he behaves as he does. He may exhibit a deep prejudice or a noncooperative attitude. When these traits are discovered, it is worth while to study the child's characteristics intensively in order to discover how any undesirable trait fits into his total personality pattern. As we suggested earlier, you may find it profitable to learn all that you can about such characteristics as his physical structure, health, mental ability, special aptitudes, interests, and emotional and social status.

Effect of Out-of-School Environment

If you wish to achieve a well-rounded understanding of the forces and influences that have an impact on the pupils in your class, you will need to know something about the kind of homes from which they come, the types of recreational activities available in the immediate neighborhood, the level of training of the parents, the economic level represented in the community, and other factors that affect the out-of-school life of your pupils. You need to realize that you do not deal with learners in a vacuum, but rather with young people who are constantly interacting in their school and out-of-school environment.

You will discover that classroom behavior of most learners is

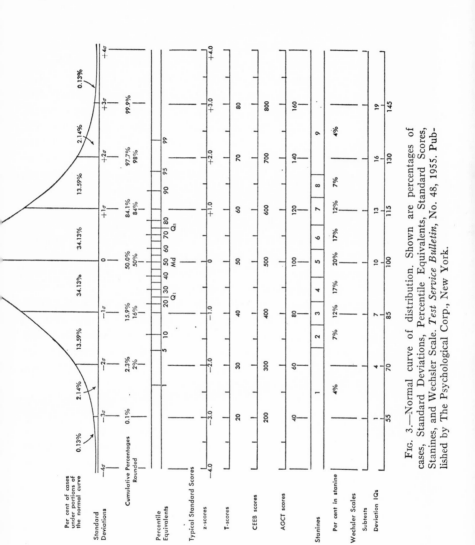

Fig. 3.—Normal curve of distribution. Shown are percentages of cases, Standard Deviations, Percentile Equivalents, Standard Scores, Stanines, and Wechsler Scale. *Test Service Bulletin*, No. 48, 1955. Published by The Psychological Corp., New York.

markedly affected by environmental factors, both within and outside the school. As a teacher, you have some influence over the behavior of children within your class or within the confines of the school; you have little or no control over the outside influences to which they are exposed. Yet, your ability to evaluate the school behavior of your pupils will be enhanced to the extent that you are acquainted with such factors. Your greater understanding of a child's total life pattern has value in helping you work effectively with him.

Sources of Information about Learners

It is not difficult for you to understand the value of studying your pupils in order to provide them with appropriate learning conditions. It is essential that you know where and how significant information about them can be obtained. In Chapter 3, we surveyed briefly ways in which you can learn about various characteristics of children. In this chapter we treat in greater detail some general study approaches and other more specific areas of study in which you might participate and the results of which would have value for you. Among the sources of information available to you are (1) the results of major studies of child development and adjustment, (2) cumulative records of pertinent data, and (3) evaluative techniques, some of which can be used by you in the classroom.

GENERAL APPROACHES TO CHILD STUDY

In your psychology and education courses you have reviewed some of the major studies that have been conducted by researchers in the field of child development and adjustment. These studies, for the most part, are general in that they stress common developmental trends, although individual differences are not neglected. In fact, some studies deal specifically with the problems of individual differences.

In many instances, the results of studies reveal to you the extent to which certain characteristics can be expected to show themselves at specific stages of growth. An understanding of the general trends can help you determine the ways in which and the extent to which specific pupils in your class differ from a more or less to-be-expected pattern. There are various approaches to the study of young people.

They may be studied individually or in groups of differing sizes.

As a teacher in the classroom, you should be well acquainted with the results of valid and reliable research studies so that you can evaluate your pupils, both individually and as a group, according to derived norms or standards of behavior. You should know also the study approach utilized by a researcher for arriving at his conclusions.

A developmental or adjustment study may be based on either (1) the *cross-sectional* approach (horizontal study), or (2) the *longitudinal* approach (vertical study). The cross-sectional approach is a normative study and usually involves large numbers of individuals at one time. For example, same-age or same-grade young people are studied to discover various facts about "normal" or average characteristics of the particular group studied. These data are valuable for teachers dealing with pupils of this age or grade to use as standards of comparison. The longitudinal approach is employed when the purpose of the study is to discover the sequential developmental pattern of an individual or a group of individuals during a more or less extended period of time.

Interpretation of Horizontal Studies

The results of many child studies with which you are acquainted were obtained by means of the utilization of the horizontal or cross-sectional approach. To the extent that you have familiarized yourself with general growth or developmental trends of same-age children you can "spot" the individual or individuals among them who deviate from the expected "average" and therefore are atypical. In a sixth-grade class, for example, you may find that the majority of its members vary little from the height norm for their age, but that a few of them may be extremely short and several others are as tall as or taller than average tenth-graders.

Children who deviate in height require special consideration in the matter of seating arrangements. You also may find that the height deviation affects their attitude toward their classmates and the latter's behavior toward them. The very short boy is denied participation in some of the sports activities of his classmates. The tall boy may be regarded as a leader, even though he possesses little or no leadership abilities. The extremely tall eighth-grade girl may display awkwardness of movement and feel ill at ease among the average-height boys and girls in her class.

As you work with your pupils, you are likely to discover young people in the class who appear to be atypical in one or another aspect of development—physical, physiological, mental, or emotional. It is your responsibility, of course, to attempt, insofar as you are able, to meet the needs of the deviate. At the same time, you must be reasonably certain that the standards according to which you are evaluating your pupils represent conclusions from horizontal studies that are based on samplings inclusive of a sufficient number of the population to make them valid for general application.

In addition, the usability of the results of a cross-sectional study as a standard of comparison depends on the extent to which the research involved has followed strict scientific procedure. Much information now is available on various traits of children that has been obtained through horizontal studies.

Interpretation of Vertical Studies

School people as well as parents are interested in knowing something about the developmental history of young people. They want to know what to expect at the different stages of the total growth and developmental pattern. The results of well-organized and scientifically conducted vertical or longitudinal studies can answer some of their questions.

Several vertical studies have been made to provide us with information concerning developmental and maturational processes and progress over a long time, such as during the first eighteen years of life. You may recall reading about some of these studies. A valid and comprehensive vertical study usually takes many years to complete and involves the utilization of various techniques of evaluation. Significant longitudinal studies have been completed at Harvard University in the Center for Research in Child Health and Development by Shuttleworth, and at the University of California in the Institute of Child Welfare by Jones and Bayley.

When a sufficient number of the same individuals are included in the longitudinal study, the cross-sectional or horizontal approach can be utilized to obtain information about them at the respective stages of their development. This is particularly true of the study of 134 children made by Reed and Stuart on height and weight over a period of eighteen years.[1] It should be noted that a relatively complete research study of child and adolescent development usually employs both the vertical and horizontal approach.

As a student teacher, it is unlikely that you will be asked to participate in a vertical study or a horizontal study. However, you should know about such research activities and apply their findings in your practice teaching and later in your regular teaching assignments. There are many cross-sectional studies to which you can have access.[2] An excellent source of a collection of longitudinal studies can be found in Stone and Onque, *Longitudinal Studies of Child Personality.*[3]

RECORDS OF PERTINENT DATA

When a child begins his formal education by enrollment in the kindergarten or first grade of an elementary school, a record card is started for him on which will be reported, grade by grade, appropriate data concerning him, his activities, and his learning achievement. In some school systems the cumulative record card, as it usually is called, accompanies the young person through high school.

In an appropriate office of the school, you will find for each pupil a cumulative record of various items of interest about him as well as a record of his school progress. The record may be contained in a folder with other pertinent data. As a student teacher, you probably will be permitted access to this confidential material. By consulting a child's record card, you can obtain information about him, such as his age and school grade; his record of attendance; the results of standardized tests that have been administered to him, including some or all of the following—intelligence, special aptitudes and interests, emotional and/or social status, or any other areas of personal adjustment; his general achievement record; his learning progress, grade by grade.

[1] See R. B. Reed and H. C. Stuart, "Patterns of Growth in Height and Weight from Birth to Eighteen Years of Age," in *Supplement to Pediatrics* (Springfield, Ill.: Charles C Thomas, Pub., 1959).

[2] See Paul H. Mussen (ed.), *Handbook of Research Methods in Child Development* (New York: John Wiley & Sons, Inc., 1960).

[3] See A. A. Stone and G. C. Onque, *Longitudinal Studies of Child Personality* (Cambridge, Mass.: Harvard Univ. Press, 1959).

Other significant data that may be recorded on the cumulative record form are the pupil's special activities, and personality ratings assigned to him by his various teachers. Notations concerning the health status of a child may be very valuable. Some pupil folders also include anecdotal reports concerning his behavior and attitudes.

During your student-teaching assignment, you should learn to study these records so that you learn what they contain and how to make use of the information you find there.

CLASSROOM PROCEDURES FOR THE STUDY OF LEARNERS

Fortunately, school people are concerned with evaluating more than merely the school achievement of a learner. Modern emphasis on the development of the "whole" individual implies the need to evaluate all aspects of an individual's personality. We now concern ourselves with the nature and extent of the child's physical, intellectual, emotional, and social characteristics. Human traits developed in the classroom almost defy your ability to measure them objectively. Yet, although subjective elements are involved in evaluating approaches, you should get some training and experience in their use during your student-teaching activities.

Need for the Utilization of Various Procedures

You will need to utilize various study procedures in your efforts to carry on pupil-appraisal activities. Whatever evidence you obtain concerning the degree of progress of individual children in the development of knowledge, skill, and behavior attitudes tends to improve your effectiveness in your working relations with them. Young people like a teacher who is expert in evaluating their behavior and achievement; they lose confidence in one who seems to lack this facility.

The teacher has many avenues available to him that he may utilize in his discovery of the differences and likenesses among his pupils. Among the informal procedures that are helpful in studying pupils are: (1) observing pupil behavior, (2) writing anecdotal reports, (3) having the pupils write autobiographical sketches, (4) using sociograms, (5) assigning individual or group projects, and (6) holding informal conferences.

You will find it helpful to develop skill in the utilization of various evaluative techniques during your student-teaching experiences. The first step toward success in their use is to adopt a positive mental set (attitude) toward their value as a teaching aid. Unless you believe that these techniques can improve your teaching effectiveness, they may be a burden rather than a help.

Observation of Pupil Behavior

The teacher has a continuous opportunity to observe pupil behavior. The alert teacher attempts to keep informed concerning whatever is transpiring in the classroom. Try as he may he does not always know all that is happening, however. He may observe deviant behavior, overhear an unusual comment, or note a questioning expression on the face of a pupil. These observations are important to him in learning about pupil reactions to classroom procedures.

You should be interested in the various patterns of behavior that are displayed in the classroom. However, you need to evaluate these overt expressions objectively, realizing that some may have no more than momentary significance but that others may be symptomatic of behavior that needs to be corrected. Your ability to assess classroom incidents correctly can be helpful to the pupils involved as well as to yourself.

The student teacher and observation. It may seem to you that to expect a teacher to be aware of what every pupil is doing at every minutes of the school day is assigning him an almost impossible task. The teacher is concentrating on his presentation of subject matter and evaluating responses to his questions. At the same time, he needs to know what John (who is sitting in the rear of the room) is doing, that Jane (at the side of the room) is trying to whisper to her schoolmate, that Ethel is writing, or why George is fussing under his desk. Yet, you have known teachers who have been able to carry on learning activities and also keep aware of pupil behavior.

Education departments in colleges and universities in teacher-education institutions realize the fact that student teachers need training in multiple-attention giving. Hence, before you are assigned the responsibility of teaching a class under supervision, you have opportunities to observe teachers and their classes in action. In these experiences, you can observe teaching approaches and watch pupil behavior. This is good practice since, when you are teaching a class (especially as a beginner), you may overlook many activities that you can detect as a visitor whose objective is to note the teacher's and the pupils' behavior.

When you begin your observations of teaching methods, pupil responses, and general classroom behavior, you may not know to what matters you should direct your attention. You need to be helped to develop skill in observation. In order for you to keep alert to pupils' reactions, you can be asked to employ the open-end approach by using a class seating chart to record any observed behavior characteristics of individuals. Another approach is to supply you with a prepared list of more or less typical behavior responses on which you can check your observation of attitudes and behavior. By utilizing both the seating chart and a list of suggested activities, you can spot the particular activities of individual pupils.

Suggested list of pupil activities. Various lists have been devised to guide student teachers in their beginning participation in observation of pupil behavior. You may find the following list of suggestions helpful. The list includes:

1. Manner of entering classroom and taking seat
2. Promptness in coming to attention
3. Specific kinds of behavior displayed in attempts to gain peer attention or teacher approval
4. Extent of participation of individual pupils in class discussion
5. Types of pupil responses
6. Tendencies of pupils to dominate the discussion
7. Tendency to engage in irrelevant activities or to tease classmates
8. Care with which pupils have prepared assigned work
9. Nature and extent of displayed interest in learning
10. Types of questions, if any, asked by pupils
11. Ability of individual pupils to read with understanding
12. Nature of observable physical handicaps.
13. Speech or language problems of pupils
14. Displayed tendency toward leadership
15. Individual reaction to deserved punishment
16. Attempts to monopolize the attention of the teacher

17. Attempts at cheating or other forms of dishonesty
18. Work or study habits displayed by individuals
19. Special cooperative or noncooperative acts
20. General social atmosphere in the classroom

As you learn to observe pupil behavior and make notations, you can become proficient in utilizing ways of discovering much about each learner. Your interest in your pupils tends to increase as you come to know more about them and their displayed attitudes.

Observation of Teaching Procedures

Watching pupils and their responses is only one aspect of your total observational activity. You need also to discover what is being done by the teacher and to note the skill with which he conducts the lesson. You should attempt not only to discover what he does to increase his understanding of his pupils but also to observe the respective steps taken by him in his development of the ideas associated with the learning experience.

A list of suggestions that you can use to guide your observation during your early observational experiences may prove helpful. We suggest that as you observe your cooperating teacher you can be rewarded greatly by noting such aspects of his procedure as:

1. The manner in which the teacher starts a lesson
2. The intrinsic and extrinsic rewards utilized to motivate the pupils' learning activities
3. The use made of visual aids; chalkboards, charts, slides, film-strips, motion pictures, programmed learning, and the like
4. The ways in which the teacher helps the learners draw upon their previous experiences
5. The extent to which pupils are stimulated toward the development of mental readiness for engaging in a specific unit of study
6. The number of pupils who are drawn into the class discussion
7. The means used by the teacher to engender self-discipline
8. The ways in which pupils are encouraged to develop good habits of work
9. The way in which full use is made of available time

10. The influence on pupils of the teacher's attitude and behavior
11. The extent to which the lesson is developed step by step
12. The variations that are made in methods of presentation that are in accord with differences among learners

As you observe a teacher conduct a lesson, you must keep in mind that your function is not to criticize adversely what you observe. In Chapter 8 we note that in spite of college courses in methods of teaching, you can learn much from watching a teacher in action. You may not agree with everything that is done. If time permits, you will find it helpful to discuss with the teacher whom you observed his reasons for employing certain techniques rather than others.

Writing Anecdotal Reports

The recording of information concerning an individual pupil is referred to as an anecdotal report. During your observation of your cooperating teacher and his class, you will have many opportunities to make entries of specific characteristics of individual pupils. You can take notes on types of responses displayed, such as actual behavior during recitation, span of attention, willingness to participate in the discussion, interest in the subject, attempts to converse with a neighbor, tendency to daydream, and the like. You then can report the incident in the form of an anecdotal report.

Before you write an anecdotal report you should evaluate the data and decide what you want to keep on record and what you may wish to discard. Although this phase of evaluation may not seem to be important to you, it may be one of the most important steps in pupil evaluation. It represents what you believe to be significant in pupil responses.

Need for accuracy in reporting. You must learn to be accurate and objective in what you record and make every effort to avoid any personal biases or prejudices. This suggests the recording of everything that you observe happening in connection with a particular pupil in a particular situation. You should not select only certain aspects of the situation. Record the facts as you observed them. However, after you have made your preliminary notes you should evaluate their worth. Decide whether they are important enough to be retained as a permanent record.

In your observation of behavior, try to be accurate and reliable. As you rise above an injection of personal bias in your interpretation of an incident, to that extent will you become objective in dealing with children's behavior. When these records are kept, from year to year, by teachers of various grades there is built a cumulative record that tends to inscribe a profile of the student.

Some teachers seem to believe, mistakenly, that anecdotal records are to be used only to report incidents that reflect undesirable or uncooperative behavior. This is not the only purpose of such reports. Rather are they intended to record unusual incidents concerning a pupil or pupils. They may represent behavior that is superior or inferior to the average. All entries should be made in light of an individual's assets or liabilities in a given situation.

It takes time and considerable thought to write a good anecdotal report. As you practice writing them, develop the habit of reporting a significant incident as soon after it occurs as is possible, thus avoiding a failure to include significant aspects of the situation (which you may forget if you allow too much time to elapse between the incident and your reporting of it). Include the date on which the incident occurred and sign the report. Also, be terse and to the point. Your job is to report and not to evaluate the incident or give your personal opinion concerning it. Here are several examples of anecdotal reports.

On November 16, 1964, one of the boys of Grade 4B forgot his necktie, the wearing of which is required for a boy's attendance at assembly exercises. Bill Grant lent him an extra one that, as Bill says, he keeps in his desk for the time when he forgets his. Bill, however, never has forgotten his necktie; he always is carefully and neatly dressed.

During the week of October 19, 1964, Charles Avery's parents noticed that he seemed to have no homework. When they questioned him, he said that he had done his work at school. The teacher reported to Charles's mother, however, that the boy had been given study assignments that he had failed to complete. This was a new attitude toward his school work; previously, he had at least tried to meet study obligations. He can give no reason for the change in attitude. He has been referred to the school guidance counselor.

On January 14, 1965, Florence Hecht submitted a charming poem to her teacher. This poem might well be attached to the permanent record and sent on to the junior high school in order that her special talent be known.

Value of anecdotal records. Anecdotal reports can be extremely valuable to you as a teacher and to other members of the school personnel. If your pupils know that that you keep pertinent records concerning them and their school performance, they realize that you regard them as individuals in whose strengths and weaknesses you are interested.

Children thrill to the knowledge that you recognize their cooperative behavior by recording it in writing. For a pupil to know that you have written an honest report about his lack of adherence to school regulations, his uncooperative behavior, or other misdeed may help deter him from engaging again in that form of undesirable conduct. Any subsequent improvement in his behavior should then be noted specifically in another anecdotal report, and he should be informed of this fact.

Anecdotal reports also have value in conferences with parents. A counselor or you as the teacher may be conferring with the parent of a child who is not achieving satisfactorily in his studies, in spite of his ability to do so. You can help the parent discover reasons for his poor work if you have available reports of his behavior—such as coming to class without having prepared home assignments, giving attention in class to something other than the lesson, and the like. Again, a parent may consult you about his child's plans for the future. Any records that you have on the child's interests might be helpful during these conferences.

Anecdotal reports also are valuable to members of the school who are charged with recommending pupils for special responsibilities or whose function it is to consult with parents and their children concerning the kind of secondary school in which it would be advisable for the young people to continue their education. An accumulation of such records can offer good evidence of a young person's habitual attitudes, interests, or observed behavior. In addition, secondary schools appreciate receiving from the elementary school as much information as is possible about a new student's attitudes and behavior habits in the lower school. Many appropriate and well-organized anecdotal reports can provide valuable informative material when sent to the secondary school.

The various uses to which anecdotal records can be subjected should convince you of their importance in the school life of individuals. Hence you need to be careful that you do not write an adverse report in a moment of anger caused by a pupil's display of a relatively insignificant uncooperative act. Be certain that you have viewed the incident objectively and unemotionally before you submit in writing something that may affect his reputation in the school and outside it.

The degree of value of anecdotal records depends on the attitude toward them of the teachers who submit them. Some teachers use them sparingly; others write many. The worth of various reports differs. Some teachers seem to observe and report only commendatory behavior; others appear to emphasize undesirable conduct. The alert teacher who is truly interested in all of his pupils tends, of course, to evaluate behavior intelligently and reports either praiseworthy behavior or behavior that needs improvement. In addition to reporting, this teacher also attempts to help the uncooperative pupil change his attitude, or solicits the services of school personnel and parents to bring about needed improvement.

Cautions in the use of anecdotal records. To help you in your use of anecdotal records, we shall summarize some of the cautions to be observed. The keeping of accurate anecdotal records is a sizable undertaking. Their value depends somewhat on the attitude of the school toward them. Even when the school administration is committed to them there are many limitations in their development and use. We present here some difficulties confronted by a teacher who conscientiously writes and uses anecdotal reports. In working with these records you may find it difficult:

1. To be accurate and to record information so that the record becomes more valuable than harmful.
2. To write reports objectively so that you avoid giving expression to your opinion—simply to record behavior.
3. To avoid using these records in defense of your own weaknesses.
4. To record all significant behavior incidents, good as well as bad.
5. To be alert to the danger of misinterpretation after you are no longer in the social setting in which the act occurred.
6. To write the kind of report that will not be damaging to the child if, later, it falls into the hands of irresponsible persons.

7. To follow up on discovered undesirable behavior practices.
8. To avoid submitting too many negative reports and too few positive ones.
9. To differentiate between a child's typical and atypical behavior.
10. To provide a set of anecdotal records that can be used by the entire faculty of the school or school system.

In spite of the limitations of anecdotal records, you will be able to function at a higher level as a teacher to the extent that you become skilled in the keeping of significant records. The greatest obstacle to the keeping of these records will be your attitude toward their worth. When you have faith in them you are likely to become proficient in their use.

Use of Autobiographical Reports

The autobiography is an effective device to obtain data directly from an individual concerning his attitudes, interests, and behavior habits. Youngsters in the primary grades usually are eager to tell their teacher about themselves, their interests, and their likes and dislikes. They may report what their parents and older brothers and sisters do and say (sometimes to the embarrassment of the teacher), and recount vividly incidents that occur in the home.

The teacher of young children can learn much about them and their home environment from their prattling to her or among themselves. Of course, you need to refrain from gossiping with other teachers about information you receive in this manner except as you report to your cooperating teacher what may seem to be undesirable home conditions that may need the attention of school people or a community agency.

Older children are less eager to report orally to their teacher about their homes and their activities outside of school. They do, however, like to write about themselves and their interests. They enjoy writing compositions on topics such as "My Favorite Pastime," "My Best Friend," "An Interesting Experience," "My Most Unpleasant Experience," "What I Did over the Weekend," "A Book I Enjoyed Reading," or any other topic that affords them an opportunity to write about themselves and their doings.

You must realize, of course, that children differ in their ability to express their thoughts in written form. Some compositions are likely to be short and tell little; others will be rambling and include more about the writer than the topic would seem to warrant; still others have value in that they omit material that you would expect them to contain, or give evidence of attitudes that you could not discover in other ways. You must be alert to the feasibility of the happening reported in a composition.

A child who is emotionally upset may write about an incident that never occurred. For example, a student teacher was reading a set of fourth-grade compositions on "My Most Unpleasant Experience." In her composition Mary Waters, one of the pupils, reported that her mother had locked her in a closet for a whole day and had refused to give her anything to eat or drink. Shocked by this story, the student teacher showed the composition to her cooperating teacher, demanding that something be done. Mary's regular teacher, who was acquainted with the girl's mother, realized that a situation of this kind was unlikely to occur. The teacher talked with Mrs. Waters about the composition and discovered that on the morning of the day Mary had written the composition, the girl's mother had not permitted Mary to wear a dress that was inappropriate for school. Mary, still emotionally upset by the denial of her wish, gave expression to her anger in this patently false story.

Some children have vivid imaginations that cause them to dream about exploits or other events in which they would like to engage and in which they would play the role of hero or heroine. Such was the experience of Harry Metz, a small, delicate fifth-grader. In a composition he described at great length a fist fight he had had with Jerry Brown, a tall, robust classmate. According to Harry, he had won the fight by knocking Jerry down. Upon investigation, the teacher discovered that no such fight had occurred. Jerry was a good-natured boy who was well liked by his schoolmates. When his teacher questioned him about the story, Harry's answer was—"Some day I'll beat all the boys."

The following three compositions, while not strictly autobiographical, do give insight into the personal characteristics of the children who wrote them. The compositions were written in class by fifth-graders to fullfill an assignment that each write about a recent interesting experience.

MY AQUARIUM
by A. F.

Since last year I owned an aquarium. In the aquarium I have different varieties of fish. In this report I will tell about my fish, how I got them and the reason I wanted an aquarium.

First I will tell about my fish. I have six fish in my tank, five gold fish and one catfish. I have three comet gold fish, one calico shubunkin, one water bubble eyed gold fish and one leopard catfish.

Now I will tell you how I got my fish. I got my first two gold fish (comets) last year. Also, last year I got the calico shubunkin and the third comet gold fish. Three days ago I got the water bubble eyed gold fish. Last year I got the leopard catfish.

Now I will tell why I wanted an aquarium. Well, my uncle and a lot of my friends had aquariums and I was getting jealous! So I started to save money for an aquarium. Finally I got it.

In some books they say once you catch the aquarium bug you can never get out of it. And I'll be happy if I keep it the rest of my life!!!

A SCARY EXPERIENCE
by M. F.

One night I was trying to go to sleep. But I just couldn't get to sleep, so I went downstairs. I was looking for my parents and I didn't find them anywhere. I kept looking for them. I looked upstairs and downstairs. Without realizing it I opened all the doors in the house. By that time I was scared and shaky. My parents said they would be home, but they weren't. Then my brother heard me and he called me to his room. Then I finally got to sleep. The next morning I asked my parents where they went. They said they went for a walk. Then they told me I left all the doors open and a robber could have come in and stolen everything. They said they were scared because all the doors were open. But they felt safer when they saw me in bed and I said I'm sure I'm as scared as you. Then I told them from now on if you are going out please tell me.

A ROMANCE IN CAMP
by G. S.

About two years ago when I was in camp, I met a boy, a very strange but handsome boy. His name is Henry—. Henry and I saw as much as we could of each other. On social or movie nights he would walk me back to the bunk. I felt like I was in a dream of heaven with Henry around. My dearest girl friend was Mary. . . . I felt very highly of her. One day when I had to go for the canary, I met an old boyfriend of mine, his name was Roy. I used to dream about Roy and I going steady. Roy probably dreamed about this too. But only one thing was wrong. Roy was Mary's boyfriend. I forgot about Henry for a while. Mary usually barged in on conversations that Roy and I carried on. Roy and Henry both asked me to the prom. Roy knew why I had to say yes to Henry. Roy lived only three blocks from my house.

Next Year: Roy and I met, Henry came back, but Mary didn't. Roy started to like another girl and paid almost no attention to me. He asked Randee to go to the prom with him. I felt brokenhearted. But this was my punishment!!!

Most children write truthfully about themselves. Sometimes they include things about themselves or their family that is for the teacher only. Hence you should never read to the class a child's autobiography (no matter how interesting and well written it may be) unless you have received the child's permission to do so. Even then you need to be careful about disclosing to other children something about the writer's home conditions that he has disclosed without realizing that thereby he might embarrass family members.

Significance of Sociograms

The dynamics of human nature are not easy to understand. The more aids we have at our disposal the better able are we to make value judgments on individual behavior. There are those who believe that any good teacher knows his pupils so well that an application of the principle of the sociogram will not reveal anything that he does not already know. Teachers who have used the sociogram in their classes are quick to point out that they can discover much about their pupils through the use of this device that otherwise would not have been discovered by them.

Before you attempt to utilize the principle of the sociogram you should have a purpose or problem in mind to which its application will help give you an answer. You may have observed that one of the children is behaving strangely among his peers and that he is not succeeding in his work. You may wish to discover by means of the sociogram the extent to which he is being accepted by the members of his class. This can be done in one of several ways.

You might organize a class project and ask each pupil to list the names of three children with whom he would like to work on it. Or you can use a more simple problem such as asking each child to write the names of three of his best friends on a sheet of paper. From this you might be able to obtain valuable information to enable you to gain insight into a young person's personality problem. The extent to which he is an *isolate* tends to be revealed through the use of the sociogram approach. It is important that the information obtained be kept confidential by the teacher. Figure 4 illustrates how a sociogram is constructed. Study it to determine how it can be of help to a teacher.

If you study Figure 4 carefully, you will discover that children differ in their attitudes toward their classmates. You will find that *E* (boy) and *K* (girl) are popular since they were selected by 6 and 13 children, respectively. *P* (boy) and *A* (girl) are isolates; the other children do not want them on their committee. How do you account for the different attitudes displayed toward these four children by their classmates?

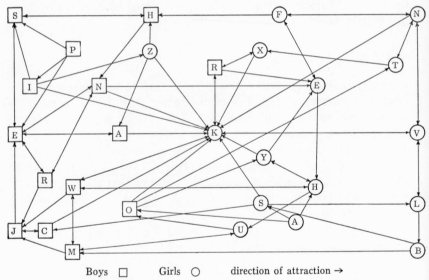

Boys ☐   Girls ○   direction of attraction →

Fɪɢ. 4.—Sociogram showing the choices of pupils to work on a committee on a social studies project (three choices).

Value of Individual or Group Projects

With our present focus on the full development of the individual and of ways and means of dealing with differences among learners, opportunities should be provided for children to plan and develop special learning projects on which a group can work together. The elementary school offers many opportunities for group work.

Whatever special project is approved must be within the capacities of the children involved. There also should be adequate materials and equipment for successful completion of the project. The teacher has the responsibility of giving the kind of supervision that encourages every pupil to participate in the project. When completed, the project needs to be evaluated. It should be presented to the class and be understood so that all members of the class will feel a part of what is being done by some of them.

It is through many of these well-planned projects that your pupils can be given opportunities to apply and reveal their special talents. Children need a variety of activities through which they can give expression to their creative urges. As you observe them at work on these special projects during your student-teaching experiences, you can learn much concerning ways in which different children attack such assignments. Thus, when you are a regular teacher you will be able to guide learning activities through the project approach.

Significance of Holding Informal Conferences

You often can make good use of a face-to-face meeting with a pupil. Technically, this is not considered to be a formal interview situation, but much can be achieved through its utilization. An informal talk can help you gain a better understanding of what motivates certain types of behavior by discovering more about the individual's interests, attitudes, and modes of thinking. What you gain from such an informal talk depends on your skill in interrelating with the child concerned.

The outcomes of the informal conference with a child usually depend on its underlying purpose, and whether it was sought by him or held at your invitation. If the child, because of his confidence in you, requests an opportunity to discuss an immediate problem that bothers him, the establishment of rapport between the two of you is easily achieved.

An informal conference might be held for the purpose of bringing greater understanding of his behavior to the child instead of scolding or berating him for some act. The discussion should represent a give-and-take relationship. If the conference is to be considered successful, the pupil should feel that he has been benefited in some way by it.

Older children and young adolescents sometimes tend to be secretive about themselves. They may have a tendency to respond with suspicion to a student-teacher conference initiated by the latter. If you wish an upper-grade pupil to reveal much about himself, it is up to you to convince him that you are sincerely interested in his welfare. You are likely to find the informal conference valuable as a result of asking significant questions and assuming the role of a good listener.

As a student teacher, you often are in a good position to talk informally with pupils. Through these experiences you can discover something of the value of this approach and, at the same time, get practice in the development of the technique utilized in these informal relationships with children. We now present some guiding principles that might help you during these face-to-face personal conferences. In an informal conference with a pupil, you are likely to find it important:

1. To meet in a place that provides privacy.
2. To assume a friendly attitude toward the child so that a free exchange of ideas may flow between the two of you.
3. To assume an attitude of learning from the pupil as well as imparting information to him.
4. To be concerned that the liking becomes mutual between the two of you.
5. To make a conscious effort to minimize your own talking in order that the child may reveal as much as possible of the problem that is under discussion.
6. To respect the confidences given to you during the conference.
7. To avoid any discussion of extraneous matters unrelated to the issue at hand.
8. To keep the conference within reasonable limits of time.
9. To help the child develop the feeling that he has gained something from this meeting.
10. To invite the child to talk with you whenever he has a problem on which you might be able to help him.

Much good can result from these conferences. As you develop skill in their use you will find that they are excellent teaching aids. You will find great differences among older pupils, especially concerning what they are willing to tell you during a conference. You will discover also that some children will tell you what they would not tell another teacher or that they will reveal to another teacher what they will not tell you.

Through face-to-face talks, you can discover many individual differences in the area of learning ability and in behavior patterns. Take care, however, that you do not attempt to help a young person solve a deep-seated personal problem but encourage him to seek the assistance of the guidance counselor. In fact, as a student teacher, you should not use the interview procedure for studying children without the approval of your cooperating teacher.

QUESTIONS AND TOPICS FOR DISCUSSION

1. List some of the values to you as a teacher of recognizing various differences among your pupils.
2. Differentiate between horizontal and longitudinal studies. Give an illustration of each.
3. As you examine the cumulative records of your pupils, note which items are not filled in. How do you explain these omissions?
4. What have you gained from observing your cooperating teacher and his class at work? Be specific.
5. Practice writing several anecdotal reports of pupil behavior. Submit them to your cooperating teacher for evaluation.
6. Have your pupils write autobiographical reports. Read them carefully. What do you learn about some that you did not know?
7. Ask your pupils to list the names of three classmates with whom they would like to work on a project. Arrange the results in the form of a sociogram. What information does this give you about individuals? What can you do for the isolates? Consult your cooperating teacher about this.
8. Set a simple project for small group participation. Observe pupils' attitudes toward the activity.
9. After you have had an informal conference with a pupil, review the important points of a conference presented in this chapter. Check those to which you adhered. Note those that you forgot. Try to remember them in your next conference with a pupil.
10. Why should you not hold conferences with children without first consulting your cooperating teacher?

RELATIONSHIPS WITH YOUR COLLEAGUES

You bring to your student teaching a personality pattern, a degree of individual ability, and a body of background of experience that differentiate you from every other student teacher. You want to prepare yourself to be a successful teacher. During this apprenticeship period you will experience many conditions peculiar to your student-teacher status in addition to those you will encounter when you become a regular teacher.

YOUR PROFESSIONAL RELATIONSHIPS

As a student teacher you perform in an educational environment that enables you to gain confidence in yourself so that later as a regular teacher you can work effectively with young people, and school and community personnel. You need to be helped to make a good social adjustment to the many differing persons with whom you will be associated—pupils, teachers, supervisors, and administrators, as well as other members of the school and college personnel. In addition, you will meet and work with parents and community leaders. Also, you will need to become acquainted with the social mores of the practice school and of the community.

Student Teaching as an Interacting Process

Your successful induction into student teaching is a two-way process. It necessitates the display of a spirit of cooperation between yourself and all others with whom you associate during the critical period of student teaching. You will respond favorably to any show of sympathetic understanding of your problems of adjustment by the members of the school to which you are assigned and by your college supervisor who is guiding your observational and teaching activities.

Your effectiveness in the classroom is strengthened to the degree that children and faculty members learn to respect you and cooperate with you. Consequently, you need to keep in mind that what you do or do not do affects the extent to which you are accepted by all of those with whom you are associated. The building of friendly attitudes of others toward you depends upon your attitudes and behavior toward them. At the same time, your attitude toward student teaching and the persons with whom you work affects the extent to which you are helped by them in practical ways to recognize the value to you of your various experiences.

Areas of Relationships

Your relationships with children were discussed in Chapter 3. These relationships stand at the top of the list of valuable interactions for effective teaching-learning conditions. Yet, of great importance also are the working relationships that you establish from the start of your practice experiences with all of the persons who, to a greater or lesser degree, are responsible for the extent of your success in your student-teaching activities.

You soon discover that this educational experience involves professional contacts with various people both within and outside the school or schools to which you have been or will be assigned. You realize that personal adjustments need to be made to the philosophy and practices of such individuals as your college supervisor, your cooperating teacher, the school principal, and other members of the school personnel.

You also will want to become acquainted with the educational ideals and the attitudes toward the school of the parents of the children and of the community as a whole. Your closest relationships probably will be with your cooperating teacher and with your college supervisor. There will, however, be occasions when you will need to interact in a constructive fashion with other individuals or groups. In this chapter we present concrete descriptions of some of the basic professional relationships that you will experience as a student teacher.

PROFESSIONAL HELP NEEDED

As we suggested in Chapter 1, your introduction into student teaching involves your assuming of new responsibilities and the changing of your attitude from that of a student to that of a teacher. This metamorphosis does not take place overnight, nor can it be brought about without the intelligent assistance of experienced and understanding professional associates.

You must be willing and able, of course, to profit from whatever help is afforded you in this critical phase of your teacher-education program. You also should know just what help you need in order to get a good start in this new experience and to continue to meet your student-teaching obligations effectively and successfully.

When you are ready for your student teaching, the college should prepare you for your new experience. An appropriate college instructor can acquaint you with the purposes of student teaching, point out the professional and personal values to you of participation in this area of teacher education, and brief you about your general duties and obligations as a student teacher. During your student-teaching period, college personnel, especially your college supervisor, can aid you in various ways to meet your responsibilities.

Most elementary school people recognize the importance of student teaching in the total program of teacher education. For example, in a brochure on student teaching prepared under the direction of the Division of Elementary Schools, Board of Education of the City of New York by the Coordinating Committee for Teacher Education, are found the following pertinent opening statements:

Student teaching is a series of laboratory experiences, carefully conceived and directed to develop a degree of expertness in teaching techniques and procedures. As apprentice teachers in the educational system, student teachers have problems peculiar to themselves in addition to those confronting regular teachers. An educational environment must be established that will enable them to gain confidence in themselves and to work effectively with children and school personnel. In this environment, students must have ample opportunity to engage in profitable experiences in observation, in sharing and participating, and in teaching, with the guidance and supervision of college and school personnel.[1]

[1] *Student Teaching in the Elementary Schools* (New York: Division of Elementary Schools, Board of Education of the City of New York), p. 1.

After you have received your school assignment and before you begin your responsibilities as a student teacher, you can profit from learning all you can about the school and its environment. If it is possible, you should visit the school and, with the cooperation of staff members, do the following:

1. Tour the building, noting the location of administrative and medical offices, teachers' rooms, library, cafeteria, and other special rooms.
2. Locate facilities available to student teachers, such as records, record forms, visual and auditory aids, and the like.
3. Procure informative materials, such as curriculums, courses of study, as well as the school handbook and other sources of information concerning the school's policies and practices.
4. Discover as much as you can about the community in which the school is located—socioeconomic status of its members, recreational and welfare agencies, the attitudes of the children and their parents toward school and learning, and anything else that might help you find a place for yourself in the community.
5. Have at least one conference with your cooperating teacher to find out what your definite responsibilities as a student teacher will be, to learn something about the pupils with whom you will be working, to receive materials that can be helpful in your observational, assisting, and teaching activities, and, in general, to overcome the normal fear you might experience as you begin this new adventure.

BUILDING PROFESSIONAL RELATIONSHIPS

From your first appearance in the school your displayed attitudes are important. Pupils and staff members constantly observe you in action and evaluate your teaching potentialities. Also, if the school is in a small community you make a favorable or unfavorable impression on people outside the school. To the pupils, to the school faculty, and to the community you are a teacher—not a college student. In all of these relationships you must assume a professional attitude.

As you go about the school in the performance of your various activities, your appearance, attitudes, and behavior are noted by those whom you meet or with whom you work. You impress them either favorably or unfavorably. They are quick to recognize your evidenced strengths and noticeable weaknesses, and they tend to treat you accordingly. You are being evaluated as a future teacher.

Most members of the school personnel, as well as your college instructors, are more than willing to meet you on a professional basis and give you whatever help you need to achieve success in your chosen lifework. In fact, it often happens that a cooperative student teacher is invited by his practice school to continue there as a regular teacher. The ability to build good professional relations can become one of your strongest assets.

Your Relationships with Your College Supervisor

The person whom you ultimately must satisfy for a final evaluation of your teaching effectiveness is your college supervisor. He serves as the link between the college and the school in which you work. Either he or a director of student teaching has the responsibility of assigning you to a school. He may have something to say concerning the cooperating teacher to whom you will be assigned. However, this usually is the duty of the school principal.

Importance of the college supervisor. The college supervisor has his theories of education and his own ideas about the teaching approaches to be employed by you. These can serve as background information for you. Yet, you must give careful attention to the plans and procedures utilized by your cooperating teacher. If you attempt to deviate widely from the methods utilized by the class teacher, you may confuse rather than help the pupils in their continued learning.

The college supervisor can be an excellent support-provider to you and to the cooperating teacher. To do this, he needs to help the cooperating teacher understand the purposes of student teaching and the need for providing you with at least a minimum of teaching opportunities. Your college supervisor should be available to you whenever he is needed. You should be able to go to him for help in planning your work as well as to discuss any problems that arise in connection with student teaching. You can benefit from his careful analysis of lessons that he observes you teach. You will want to know what he considers to be your strengths and your weaknesses. You will appreciate his suggesting ways in which you can bring about needed improvements rather than merely calling attention to your faults.

Functions of the college supervisor. In the performing of his duties, the college supervisor functions in the capacity of serving the student teacher, the college, and the school and its pupils. He acts as a kind of liaison between you, your college methods instructor, the school, and your cooperating teacher. You are likely to find that your college supervisor is concerned with most of the following functions:

1. Serving as the professional link between the school and the college
2. Acting as liaison between the student teacher and the cooperating teacher, between college instructors of education courses and your cooperating teacher, and between present educational policy and the way it affects your student teaching
3. Recommending the proper placement of student teachers
4. Assisting the procurement of professional materials for the student teacher
5. Critically evaluating the student teacher's classroom teaching
6. Facilitating various forms of communication between the college and the cooperating teacher
7. Alerting the cooperating teacher to the bases of selection of students for student teaching
8. Advising the cooperating school on personal strengths and weaknesses of individual student teachers
9. Keeping the cooperating school informed on the college courses in which a student teacher is enrolled during his student teaching
10. Providing the cooperating teacher with a tentative schedule of his official visits to a student teacher
11. Being sensitive to the interests and needs of the cooperating teacher and to the administrators of cooperating schools
12. Helping the student teacher plan his lessons for teaching
13. Helping the student teacher relate his experience to his teaching
14. Evaluating the student teacher's teaching based on personal observation of his teaching

15. Utilizing the cooperating teacher's evaluation of a student teacher in his own final judgment of teaching effectiveness

Your Relationship with the Administrators of the School

If you have not already learned it, you soon will discover that the principal is the most important person on the school staff. You perhaps have heard that as is the principal so is the school. This is more than an expression. The principal sets the overall tone of the school. He, with his staff, determines school policy. Whatever *esprit de corps* prevails in the school emanates from his influence.

An elementary school principal usually is deeply involved with the student-teaching program extant in his school. He is closely associated with all who are responsible for the progress of teacher trainees. With college personnel and members of the administrative and supervisory staffs of the school system he helps establish student-teaching policies and organize the training program. He selects, as cooperating teachers, those members of his staff who are interested in and especially qualified for such an assignment. He helps orient you, as a student teacher, to the school and to the community.

The principal may encourage you to participate in planning sessions for the conduct of assemblies or other whole-school activities. He is primarily responsible for making certain that you understand the philosophy that underlies school regulations, teacher assignments, and the like, and that you are treated as a member of a professional group. He gives recognition to any special contributions you make to the welfare of the school. Sometimes, he brings himself directly into the student-teaching experience by observing you teach and conferring with you about the lesson. You can be assured that he is aware of your presence in the building and is giving direct or indirect supervision to your activities.

The degree of friendliness that you meet in the school often rests with the principal. Many principals welcome the opportunity to be able to engage in the training of students. They believe that they have something to offer and do all they can to see that you are afforded every advantage possible in the school. These receptive attitudes enable you to build feelings of security and belongingness. They encourage you to want to teach.

Large elementary schools have other school administrators who

fill important roles in providing supplementary administrative relationships with you. These activities vary with schools, especially
with the size of the school. Probably, more than you realize it, all
administrators are aware of your presence in the school and are
devoting energy to the success of your student-teaching activities.
These are among the incidental professional values that accrue to
you without your being aware that they operate in your behalf.

Your Relationships with Your Cooperating Teacher

The cooperating teacher probably is the person with whom you
will work most closely during your student-teaching experiences.
You should realize that having a student teacher increases his already heavy load of duties. He must assume a double role, since
he is responsible for the successful progress of both his class and
yourself. His teaching effectiveness is evaluated in terms of the
success of his pupils in mastery of learning materials.

Responsibilities of the cooperating teacher. When a cooperating
teacher takes on the added responsibility of guiding your teaching
activities, he is faced with the need of devoting extra time and
energy to planning for his regular classwork and, at the same time,
to providing you with constructive and worthwhile activities. You
should keep this point in mind if you are tempted to think that
your cooperating teacher is not meeting your needs as well as he
might.

Whether your student teaching is being done in a college-operated
laboratory school or in a public school, your cooperating teacher
performs similar functions. He has the responsibility to make certain that the children are given good coverage in their curriculum
material. He becomes both a teacher of his pupils and a supervisor
of your activities during your stay with him.

Cooperating teachers in laboratory schools are selected because
of their ability to meet this dual role. Regular classroom teachers
in public schools sometimes are asked to perform this double function on short notice and without any special training for it. You
have the responsibility of assisting this person with whatever plans
are projected and to adopt a positive attitude toward what is being
done. This attitude should be one that will permit you to approach
your observation and teaching with an open mind.

Ways in Which the Cooperating Teacher Can Help You

The alert cooperating teacher recognizes your need for growth on the job and does what he can to help you use your special competencies to their best advantage. He attempts to enable you to grow in the process of relating to pupils and others in ways that are unique to you as a student teacher. Your induction into student teaching can be eased through the efforts of a sympathetic and understanding cooperating teacher.

The cooperating teacher can be especially helpful to you to the extent that he is willing and able to do the following:

1. Meet and confer with you before the first day of the term.
2. Acquaint you with the organizational structure of the school.
3. Arrange for you to meet other faculty personnel, especially other teachers of your grade.
4. Introduce you to the class in such a way as to help you feel important and needed.
5. Regard you as a member of the faculty.
6. From the start, provide opportunities for you to participate in class activities—a kind of team approach.
7. Alert you to the details of classroom management.
8. Assist you to discover the pupils' interests and abilities by giving you access to available records and by sharing with you his knowledge of the children.
9. Help you in your personal observation of learners and in your interpretation of gathered data.
10. Help you become aware of and meet learning differences among the children.
11. Explain his teaching approaches to you.
12. Acquaint you with his planning procedures and assist you in your own lesson planning.
13. Encourage you to participate in the evaluation of pupils' learning progress and in the recording of these data.
14. Make it possible for you to have special conferences with him whenever these seem desirable.
15. Evaluate your teaching activities critically and constructively.

Value of Conferences with Your Cooperating Teacher

You will find it valuable to confer frequently with your cooperating teacher. These conferences may be held during definite times set aside for them. If you wish a specific answer to a simple question, however, this can be taken care of at various times during the day.

You also will become involved in three-way conferences with your cooperating teacher and your college supervisor. In these, let the others take the lead, and try not to display a defensive or belligerent attitude. You are there to learn and to benefit from all the suggestions that you can receive from these two individuals. Even though you believe that you can justify your procedure, you should hear out the others before you present your views, unless you are invited to clarify the situation by presenting your ideas pertaining to it.

The cooperating teacher often will ask you for your opinion about one or another class procedure or about a pupil. If you have ideas based on observations, feel free to express them. You may be invited to give your opinion about a specific learning experience or to evaluate the learning progress of individual children. Do not hesitate to present your ideas, but do not force them into the situation. When you listen to the ideas of your cooperating teacher, you may find that you want to revise your judgments to conform more closely to those expressed by him.

It is through conferences with your cooperating teacher that you can receive such help as:

1. Discovering relationships between theory and practice
2. Developing an understanding of the role of the cooperating teacher and that of the school in the community
3. Growing in self-analysis and self-improvement
4. Developing a worthwhile professional attitude that serves you well
5. Learning to work with fellow teachers and other school personnel
6. Discovering that there is no one easy solution to many classroom problems
7. Learning to ask those questions that will enable you to grow in your profession.

Display a Good Attitude toward Your Cooperating Teacher

As a student teacher you need to be ever alert to ways and means by which your cooperating teacher is attempting to help you. You may have a tendency to accept many of his efforts in your behalf as routine activities. You may fail to appreciate the fact that he probably has devoted much time and thought to how best to help you grow in your profession. Often when your activities run smoothly you may not realize that they represent well-thought-through plans made by others for your benefit.

When your cooperating teacher gives evidence of respect for your personal integrity, his attitude should be reflected in your behavior toward him. When you are invited by him to seek his assistance and advice, take advantage of his offers. If he suggests your planning a lesson or working out a specific activity on your own, be sure to do so. He thereby is attempting to give you practice in meeting situations independently. He is trying to strengthen your self-confidence.

You must learn through observation of teacher-planning procedures how to meet classroom situations. You need experience in decision making in these situations. You will grow in making correct decisions under the guidance of your cooperating teacher and college supervisor. Hence keep an open mind and listen carefully to all suggestions offered rather than become defensive toward them.

You can improve your effectiveness as a student teacher when you display an attitude of willingness to discover new and better ways of dealing with learners and with subject content. Remember that it is one experience to observe an expert teach a lesson, but another to teach similar material as effectively as he does. Skill in the teaching-learning situation comes only with practice. Although you may believe that in your first attempts you performed well, it may be that there is more clumsiness in your approach than you realize. Fortunately, your beginning ineptitudes are likely to disappear as you continue to practice.

Do not hesitate to ask questions that will give you further understanding concerning teaching procedures and school routines, rules, and regulations. It is better to ask than to assume to know that about which you have only a vague idea. A careful study of the school handbook can be helpful. It gives you much information known to your pupils, which, if understood by you, reveals to learners the fact that you know what to do in various situations. This inspires them to have confidence in you. Many undesirable situations can be averted before they start.

The Importance of School Services

Just as a teacher is a member of the faculty and works on the school team, so must you become one of the group with functional relationships that reach beyond the classroom. You need to develop sensitivity to the working relationships that exist among the various personnel in the school. You also need to become a part of whatever extensions the school may have into the community.

The modern elementary school includes the services of many trained persons in addition to the administrative staff and the regular classroom teachers. During your student-teaching period in a school, you need to become acquainted with these services and utilize them as the opportunity arises.

As a student teacher you should maintain the attitude of a learner. Regard the various service personnel as experts in their field from whom you can gain much that will improve your teaching effectiveness. Your cooperating teacher is in the position of acquainting you with the services offered in the school and of encouraging your utilization of them and of those in the community with which the school has some dealings.

Your Relationships with Guidance Counselors

Most modern elementary schools have developed well-organized guidance services and include trained counselors among their staff members. You need to know these counselors and how they function in the school. You should understand the relationship of these counselors with classroom teachers and with pupils.

For a school-guidance program to be effective, there is needed close teamwork between counselors and teachers. It usually is in the classroom that individual needs become apparent. You become sensitive to these needs as you observe your cooperating teacher and engage in your own teaching. If a pupil seems to have a serious problem, his teacher needs to confer early with the guidance counselor to explore possible causes of the difficulty and to develop workable plans of action. You should participate in some of these conferences so that you learn about the services offered and also achieve a background of dealing with a particular problem.

Counselors need the cooperation of teachers in working with a disturbed or uncooperative child. They cannot and should not attempt to work alone. Guidance is a team approach in which the feelings and attitudes of the teacher are respected by the counselor. You will be fortunate if you are given an opportunity to participate in a conference between your teacher and a school counselor concerning members of the class. You need training in building these guidance interrelationships. Make certain that, before you complete your student-teaching assignment in a school, you become acquainted with its guidance facilities and learn something about what is being done to help in pupil adjustment.

You need to appreciate the fact that it is the function of the school counselor to bolster your teaching, not to undermine it. If you have an opportunity to work closely with a school counselor during your student-teaching experiences, you will come to understand that counselors have a definite role to fill in the school organization. Most teachers want to cooperate with counselors but need help to know how to work together. At first, you may regard consulting with a counselor to be a drain on your time; but, with practice, you will develop a good working relationship with him. Also, the help you receive from the counselor reduces your responsibility for trying, unaided, to solve a problem.

You may be fortunate enough to be assigned to do your student teaching in a school in which there is a good program of group guidance. If so, ask permission to observe in one or more of these classes. Here you will see practical applications of attempts to meet many of the personal needs of pupils. These group guidance classes have been more completely organized on the junior high school level than on the elementary school level, however.

Your Relationships with Other School Personnel

There are various other members of the school personnel whose services are needed to keep the school functioning as a well-organized, unified educational institution. You are likely to come into more or less direct contact with each of these groups. In so doing, you can gain some appreciation of their value in helping to keep the school a smoothly running organization.

The school secretary. You need to understand the precise functions of the school secretaries. They are responsible for taking care of teachers' attendance reports, sorting and delivering mail appropriately, preparing some reports and typing those prepared by other members of the school faculty, and caring for all the many other details that may need attention during the school day or week. You can lighten their work, for example, by submitting to them any documents about yourself that need filing and by recording promptly and accurately your arrival at and leaving of the school each day.

The custodial staff. The custodial staff is responsible for the care of the school plant. Their work includes the making of simple repairs and the daily cleaning of the building. You can help them by making certain each time you meet a class that any litter that accumulates during a school day is removed from desks and the floor before you and the class leave the room. Also, you should not remain in your room or keep pupils there so long after the day's school session is ended that you delay the staff in the task of preparing the room for the next day's session.

The school nurse. You should know where the office of the school nurse is located and the conditions under which you can make use of her services. You may find it annoying, on occasions, to have the school nurse or the dental assistant send for members of your class while you are in the midst of a lesson. You should cooperate with them graciously, however.

Workers in the school cafeteria. The workers in the school cafeteria are important members of the school's service personnel. The cafeteria is likely to be crowded during the scheduled lunch periods. Groups of hungry young people can be noisy and inconsiderate in their demands for immediate service. If you are asked to assist in lunchroom duty, you can be helpful by keeping the pupils in an organized line at the lunch counter, by trying to control any over-exuberant behavior, and by seeing to it that the pupils clear their tables properly after they have finished eating.

Your Relationships with Parents

Most parents of elementary school children are concerned about their children's progress in the development of good relationships both in and outside the home. Mothers and fathers tend to want to work with teachers in furthering their children's welfare. The National Congress of Parents and Teachers present the following as their common objectives:

1. To promote the welfare of children and youth in home, school, church, and community.
2. To raise the standards of home life.
3. To secure adequate laws for the care and protection of children and youth.
4. To bring into closer relation the home and the school, that parents and teachers may cooperate intelligently in the training of the child.
5. To develop between educators and the general public such united efforts as will secure for every child the highest advantages in physical, mental, social, and spiritual education.[2]

The National Congress of Parents and Teachers invites student teachers to attend P.T.A. meetings and become acquainted with their program at the cooperating school.[3] Regular P.T.A. meetings give parents and teachers an opportunity to become acquainted, to discuss in a friendly atmosphere the welfare of the children, and to consider ways in which they can cooperate in meeting a child's problems of adjustment. In an increasing number of elementary schools, mothers assist teachers during the school day in the school cafeteria and library and on trips to points of interest in the community. They also serve as "class mothers," and in other ways cooperate in a practical way with school people. Parents of elementary school children usually are more than willing to have individual conferences with the teachers of their children.

You will soon discover that you can learn much from parents. You also will learn that to confer with parents about a particular child's problem is not an easy matter. When no particular problem is to be considered, you may be able to carry on an informal conversation with most parents without any difficulty. Therefore, in

---

[2] *A Teacher's Guide to the P.T.A.* (Chicago: National Congress of Parents and Teachers, 1962), p. 47. Reprinted by permission.

[3] See *ibid.*, pp. 71–73.

order to promote growth in these functions, you need to be placed in situations that give you considerable contact with parents. If these situations are frequent and varied, your confidence in dealing with problems through them will be strengthened.

Your role with parents is likely to be indirect for most of the time you are doing your student teaching. Nevertheless, you can learn from parents how they feel about the school, the kind of education they want for their sons and daughters, and, perhaps, what their attitude is toward you as an inexperienced person leading their offspring in educational matters. These experiences can be invaluable to you.

You will want to share the responsibility of meeting parents and of preparing reports that go to parents describing the learning progress of their children. As a student teacher, you should not attempt alone to discuss a child's progress with his parents. Rather should you start by sitting in on a teacher-parent conference. The welfare of the pupil, the teacher, the parent, and yourself is involved. It sometimes takes long years of practice to avoid using expressions that give a negative effect to parents and to develop speech patterns that will give the more positive effect. The following expressions will illustrate this point: [4]

Negative Expressions	*More Positive Expressions*
Must	Should
Lazy	Can do more when he tries
Troublemaker	Disturbs class
Uncooperative	Should learn to work with others
Cheats	Depends on others to do his work
Stupid	Can do better work with help
Never does the right thing	Can learn to do the right thing
Below average	Working at his own level
Truant	Absent without permission
Impertinent	Discourteous
Steal	Without permission
Unclean	Poor habits
Dumbbell	Capable of doing better
Help	Cooperation
Poor	Handicapped

[4] *Conference Time for Teachers and Parents: A Teachers' Guide to Successful Conference Reporting* (Washington, D.C.: National School Public Relations Association and Department of Classroom Teachers, NEA, 1961), p. 13. Reprinted by permission.

Negative Expressions	More Positive Expressions
Calamity	Lost opportunity
Disinterested	Complacent, not challenged
Expense	Investment
Contribute to	Invest in
Stubborn	Insists on having his own way
Insolent	Outspoken
Liar	Tendency to stretch the truth
Wastes time	Could make better use of time
Sloppy	Could do neater work
Incurred failure	Failed to meet requirements
Mean	Difficulty in getting along with others
Time and again	Usually
Dubious	Uncertain
Poor grade of work	Below his usual standard
Clumsy	Not physically well coordinated
Profane	Uses unbecoming language
Selfish	Seldom shares with others
Rude	Inconsiderate of others
Bashful	Reserved
Show-off	Tries to get attention
Will fail him	Has a chance of passing, if

If you are invited to assist in the preparation of reports to parents, make sure that you understand the reporting system, and know what types of things to include and what to omit. Follow the practices of the school, not those utilized by the elementary school that you attended.

The following report cards are representative of those used in reporting to parents:

Your Relationships with the Community

In many communities you will find that the teacher's activities do not end when he leaves the school building. Varying with the size of the community, the professional status of the teacher receives differing degrees of recognition. You will find, however, that there is constant interaction between the school and the community. Often, what goes on in the community vitally affects the school, and school activities influence community plans and projects. You will want to become a part of that influence.

Seek opportunities to participate in those activities that are community centered and have significance for the pupils in the school.

PROGRESS REPORT[5]

INTERMEDIATE GRADES — 4, 5, 6

Message To Parents

The purpose of this report card is to help you to understand your child's progress in school. It shows the child's progress both in relation to his own ability and what is usually expected of a child in his grade.

Individual conferences between parent and teacher will be scheduled. Please make a special effort to attend. Your child's success and happiness depend to a large extent upon the cooperation between the home and school.

Name ....

Grade .... Year ....

Teacher ....

Principal ....

School ....

Parent's Comment

Parent's Signature ....

MARCH REPORT
Teacher's Comment

Parent's Comment

Parent's Signature ....

JUNE REPORT
Teacher's Comment

Parent's Comment

Parent's Signature ....

In September your child will be In
Grade ....
Room ....

[5] Progress Report for Intermediate Grades—4, 5, 6, Board of Education, Hartford, Conn. Reprinted by permission.

Progress Report — Grades 4, 5, 6

The checks on this page indicate your child's progress in relation to his own individual ability and effort

	Dec. Report			March Report			June Report		
	Very Good	Satisfactory	Unsatisfactory	Very Good	Satisfactory	Unsatisfactory	Very Good	Satisfactory	Unsatisfactory
ACADEMIC PROGRESS									
Reading									
Arithmetic									
Written Expression									
Oral Expression									
Social Studies									
CONDUCT									
Accepts his share of responsibility									
Obeys school rules and regulations									
Shows respect for authority									
Is a helpful group member									
Tries to improve himself									
Shows self control									
Is courteous in speech and action									
Shows respect for property									
WORK HABITS									
Effort									
Listens to and follows directions									
Works neatly									
Completes work on time									
Works with increasing independence									
Evaluates his work									
PRACTICES GOOD HEALTH HABITS									
OBEYS SAFETY RULES									
DAYS ABSENT									
TIMES TARDY									

Progress Report — Grades 4, 5, 6

The marks on this page indicate your child's progress in relation to what is usually expected of a child in this grade.

	Dec. Report	March Report	June Report
READING			
Reads clearly and with expression			
Is developing skills in silent reading			
SPELLING			
Spells assigned words correctly			
Spells correctly in written work			
Makes use of dictionary skills			
HANDWRITING			
LANGUAGE			
Speaks clearly and distinctly			
Expresses himself correctly in written work			
ARITHMETIC			
Understands number meanings			
Knows number facts and processes			
Applies basic skills to problem solving			
SOCIAL STUDIES			
Is increasing his knowledge of geography			
Is increasing his knowledge of history			
SCIENCE			
MUSIC			
ART			
PHYSICAL EDUCATION			

A = excellent
B = good (above average)
C = fair (average)
D = poor (below average)

No plus or minus signs will be used

Progress Report[6]
Primary Grades

An understanding between the home and school, based upon parent visitation and conferences, is necessary for the maximum growth and development of your child. You are urged to confer with the teacher and principal.

During the school year, four reports will be made to you to acquaint you with your child's progress. The first report, at the end of nine weeks of school, will be made through a parent-teacher conference. Printed reports will be issued at the end of the second, third and fourth nine-week periods, and will include the academic achievement and social development of your child and an estimate as to whether or not he is achieving according to his ability.

ROBERT D. MORROW
Superintendent

Tucson Public Schools
Tucson, Arizona

[6] Progress Report, Primary Grades, Board of Education, Tucson, Ariz. Reprinted by permission.

	First					Second					Third		
Marking Periods	Outstanding	Very good	Satisfactory	Needs to improve	Unsatisfactory	Outstanding	Very good	Satisfactory	Needs to improve	Unsatisfactory	Outstanding	Very good	Satisfactory

This report indicates by a ✔ the teacher's best estimate of your child's progress in relation to:

1. his ability as shown by the first evaluation in each subject.
2. others in his class as shown by the remaining evaluations in each subject.

LANGUAGE ARTS
Reading

	First					Second					Third		
Shows progress consistent with ability													
Reads with understanding													
Learns new vocabulary													
Applies word attack skills													
Reads well orally													
Reads for his own enjoyment													

Reads at the following level:

	1st.	2nd.	3rd.
Readiness			
Pre-Primer			
Primer			
First Reader			
Second Reader, Level 1			
Second Reader, Level 2			
Third Reader, Level 1			
Third Reader, Level 2			
Other			

Oral and Written Expression

	First					Second					Third		
Shows progress consistent with ability													
Is developing handwriting skills													
Writes legibly and neatly													
Expresses ideas well when speaking													
*Expresses ideas well when writing													
*Learns spelling words													
*Uses correct spelling in written work													

ARITHMETIC

	First					Second					Third		
Shows progress consistent with ability													
Understands meaning of numbers													
Knows and uses number facts													
Solves problems by reasoning													
Reads and writes numbers correctly													

*No grade after this statement indicates that children at this level are not evaluated in this area.

Marking Periods

	First					Second					Third				
e of Pupil	Outstanding	Very good	Satisfactory	Needs to improve	Unsatisfactory	Outstanding	Very good	Satisfactory	Needs to improve	Unsatisfactory	Outstanding	Very good	Satisfactory	Needs to improve	Unsatisfactory
AL STUDIES															
hows progress consistent with ability															
s developing a good attitude toward self & others															
NCE															
hows progress consistent with ability															
s growing in understanding of his physical world															
hows progress consistent with ability															
Expresses ideas in an original way															
C															
hows progress consistent with ability															
s sensitive to rhythm															
ings in tune															
Listens imaginatively															
SICAL EDUCATION															
hows progress in physical activities consistent with age and ability															

School ____
 her ____
Year

ONAL AND SOCIAL GROWTH

Accepts responsibility															
Makes good use of time															
Follows directions															
Works independently															
Listens attentively															
Uses materials and equipment wisely															
s developing self-confidence															
s developing self-discipline															
Shows initiative															
Works and plays well with others															
Practices good health habits															
Observes safety rules															

COMMENTS AND PARENT'S SIGNATURE

First Period

    Teacher's Comment (optional)

    Parent's Comment (optional)

    Parent's Signature _____

Second Period

    Teacher's Comment (optional)

    Parent's Comment (optional)

    Parent's Signature _____

Third Period

    Teacher's Comment (optional)

Your child will be placed in _____ grade

for the school year 19_____ to 19_____.

_____

                          Teacher's Signature

Tucson, Arizona

PUPIL PROGRESS REPORT – INTERMEDIATE GRADES[7]

— To —

Pupil's Name .... Grade ....

School .... Teacher ....

Principal ....

Dear Parents:

No two children are alike. Each grows and learns in his own unique way. We try to teach each child so that he may become his own best self.

This report includes both academic achievement and social development. You are urged to examine this card carefully and discuss it with your child.

This report is but one means of informing you about your child's development in school. Other means which the school uses and encourages are:

1. Pupil Progress Note to Parents
2. Teacher-Parent Conferences
   Pupil-Teacher-Parent Conferences
3. Visits to the School by Parents

Our common interest is to help boys and girls to be good citizens. It is necessary that we work together in order that this may be accomplished.

Sincerely yours,

ROBERT D. MORROW
Superintendent

PARENT'S SIGNATURE

1. ....

2. ....

3. ....

4. ....

5. ....

6. ....

Grade Next Year ....

TPS Form 25

[7] Progress Report, Intermediate Grades, Board of Education, Tucson, Ariz. Reprinted by permission.

Progress Report — Grades 1, 2, 3

The checks on this page indicate your child's progress in relation to his own individual ability and effort.

	Dec. Report			March Report			June Report		
	Very Good	Satisfactory	Unsatisfactory	Very Good	Satisfactory	Unsatisfactory	Very Good	Satisfactory	Unsatisfactory
ACADEMIC PROGRESS									
Reading									
Language Arts									
Arithmetic									
CONDUCT									
Ability to work with others									
Respect for authority									
Courtesy									
Self-control									
Responsibility									
Pride in personal appearance									
WORK HABITS									
Effort									
Attention									
Response to direction									
Completion of work									
Neatness of work									
Use of school materials									
Initiative									
OBSERVES HEALTH RULES									
OBSERVES SAFETY RULES									

	1st Report	2nd Report	3rd Report
DAYS ABSENT			
TIMES TARDY			

The marks on this page indicate your child's progress in relation to what is usually expected of a child in this grade.

	Dec. Report	March Report	June Report
READING			
Word mastery			
Reading for meaning			
Oral reading			
LANGUAGE ARTS			
Oral expression			
Written expression			
Handwriting			
*Spelling			
ARITHMETIC			
Understanding number meanings			
Knowledge of number facts			
Reading numbers			
Writing numbers			
***SOCIAL STUDIES**			
***SCIENCE**			
PHYSICAL EDUCATION			
MUSIC			
ART			

*Not every subject will be marked in first grade.

A = excellent
B = good (above average)
C = fair (average)
D = poor (below average)

No plus or minus signs will be used

If a child is failing and may have to repeat the grade it will

Social Progress

Name ....

	Six-Weeks Period						
	1	2	3	4	5	6	Av.
Is courteous							
Uses self-control							
Accepts responsibility							
Respects property							
Cooperates well							
Has good work habits							
Practices good health habits							
Observes safety rules							
Has good attitude							

Explanation of Marks Used

E – Outstanding
S – Satisfactory
U – Unsatisfactory

ATTENDANCE	Six-Weeks Period						
	1	2	3	4	5	6	Total
Days Present							
Days Absent							
Times Tardy							
Days Not Enrolled							

Academic Progress

	Six-Weeks Period						
	1	2	3	4	5	6	Av.
ARITHMETIC							
READING							
ENGLISH							
SPELLING							
WRITING							
SOCIAL STUDIES							
SCIENCE							
HEALTH							
PHYSICAL EDUCATION							
ART							
MUSIC							
INSTRUMENTAL MUSIC							

Explanation of Marks Used

1 – Outstanding;   2 – Above Average;   3 – Average;
4 – Below Average;   5 – Not Passing
R – After a mark refers to work below grade level

Your acceptance in the community will depend in part on your willingness to become active in one or another community project. Some of these activities can be provided in the school building itself, as in the case of parent-teacher meetings. Rather than to disregard these meetings, make every effort to attend them so that you know what is happening. Such meetings also can provide opportunities for you to meet and talk with parents and other community leaders.

Other activities in which you can participate are: attending meetings of neighborhood service groups with your cooperating teacher, helping with school-sponsored surveys of recreational facilities for children, working with welfare agencies and business and civic organizations that can provide resource material for teaching-learning purposes, and alerting children and their parents about community offerings that can be of benefit to them.

The better you understand the community and its goals and aspirations, the better will you be able to work with the learners and interpret the school to anyone who is interested in knowing about its purposes and offerings. There are many civic, religious, and cultural activities that might be commended to you. Become acquainted with them and associate with as many as your time permits.

EXAMPLES OF RELATIONSHIPS BETWEEN THE TEACHER AND OTHER SCHOOL PERSONNEL [8]

Teacher—Pupil

1. Maintain a sympathetic, understanding attitude toward each child
   a. Show an interest in the affairs, outside interests, and concerns of each child
   b. Recognize the worth and dignity of each child
   c. Treat each child with consideration
   d. Make every child feel that he belongs and that he is wanted
2. Discover and administer to the varying needs, interests, and abilities of each individual in the group
   a. Provide opportunities for, and recognize success
   b. Encourage a desire for progress
   c. Provide experience at each pupil's level

[8] Helen Bailey, *Classroom Management for New Teachers* (Philadelphia: Philadelphia Public Schools, 1962), pp. 12–13. Reprinted by permission.

d. Be patient and understanding in correcting pupil speech defects and peculiarities of accent or language forms

Teacher—Faculty

1. Recognize that there is a great deal to be learned from experienced teachers
2. Use professional ethics in discussing pupils and other teachers
3. Schedule your activities so that they will be least disturbing to your neighbors, and consult with them as you plan
4. Be punctual in returning materials that are shared
5. Show regard for others when using school facilities and equipment, such as the radios, television sets, the auditorium, the playroom
6. Be tactful in offering and accepting suggestions

Teacher—Supervisory Personnel

This group includes the principal, supervisors, collaborating teachers, and consulting teachers. These people have a service function, and are interested in your improvement. Only the principal has the additional function of rating your teaching efficiency.

1. Adopt a receptive attitude toward any help that is offered
2. Be sincere in trying out suggestions
3. Ask questions—requests for help are signs of growth

Teacher—Other School Personnel

The medical, attendance, and custodial services are necessary for the total success of the school program. Therefore they are worthy of co-operation, respect, and appreciation on the part of both teachers and pupils.

Teacher—Community

1. Take an active interest in Home and School Council affairs
2. Know and be willing to accept your neighborhood culture—strive to have children reach their highest potential—familiarize yourself with the neighborhood resources and resource people
3. Meet your children's parents on a friendly basis; do not wait for an unpleasant incident
4. The strongest link between the school and the parent is the Progress Report—therefore it should be used as an instrument to improve community relations (see Directions for Use of Progress Report, Grades 1 to 6, Form E 13)
5. What children describe to parents is one of the most important factors in public relations
6. Confer with principal regarding nature and amount of homework assigned

7. Permission for parents to visit a teacher or classroom must be granted by the office
8. Principals should be informed of teacher's requests for parental interviews

YOUR PROFESSIONAL RESPONSIBILITIES

Throughout this book, we stress the various approaches to your duties as a student teacher that are basic to your achieving a full and rich educational experience. Here we list some of the professional activities in which you can engage and some of the attitudes you can display in order to gain the approval and respect of your professional associates.

Ways in Which You Can Cooperate

It is essential that you begin your student teaching with the understanding that during your stay in the school you are there to serve in whatever ways you can. You should not assume that the responsibility for your success as a student teacher lies wholly with the persons who guide your activities. You need to take the initiative in discussing ways in which you can exhibit a cooperative attitude.

There are certain minimal activities in which you must engage. These include arriving promptly at the designated time, observing the cooperating teacher and his pupils at work, and planning and teaching a minimal number of lessons, some of which are observed by your cooperating teacher and your college supervisor. If your efforts do not go beyond these minimums, it is likely that you will not learn what is involved in carrying a full teaching load. You must be willing to help whenever, wheresoever, and however you can if you wish to grow professionally during your student-teaching experiences.

When you meet your cooperating teacher, indicate to him that you appreciate whatever he does for you and that you want to help him in as many ways as you can. The display of this attitude will get you off to a good start. As you participate in various class routines, you will get the feel of what to do as a teacher as well as how to perform these activities expeditiously.

At first, you probably will not know what you can do to help your teacher and will need to ask him to assign you odd jobs. If you are alert, however, you soon can find various ways to be helpful. For example, if you are assigned to the school sufficiently early to be present at the first meeting of the class, you can offer to prepare a seating chart for the teacher and another one for your use. Then, during the course of your stay in the class, you can assume much of the responsibility for the following aspects of a teacher's duties:

1. Record attendance
2. Monitor the bulletin board
3. Care for the cleanliness of the chalkboard
4. Regulate light and ventilation
5. Locate supplementary material
6. Distribute and collect materials
7. Set up demonstrations
8. At the end of a day, collect materials used and return to proper files or cabinets
9. Keep record of written material of the pupils and correct as much of it as the teacher encourages and your time permits
10. Supervise classroom study
11. Construct quizzes under teacher guidance, administer them and correct them, recording the results
12. Hold conferences with pupils
13. Supervise remedial activities
14. Assist with the preparation of report cards
15. Write evaluative reports of pupils' attitudes, behavior, and learning progress
16. Participate in fire drills
17. Conduct special class activities
18. Assist in supervising pupils in the lunchroom or cafeteria
19. Become active in meeting the school's organizational routines
20. Accompany your cooperating teacher and his class on trips to points of interest outside the school
21. Attend faculty meetings
22. Be present at as many parent-teacher association meetings as your college obligations permit

The foregoing are some of the activities in which you can participate. As you become increasingly aware, during your stay in the school, of the many differing duties of a teacher, you can find other ways in which you can give evidence of your cooperative attitude.

Do not try to undertake more jobs than your time or energy permits, however.

If you are combining student teaching with college study, you may be carrying a heavy load of work. It is not enough to be willing to assume extra duties. Whatever you do to assist your teacher must be done well. Otherwise, you will be more of a nuisance to him than a help.

Some schools prepare lists of available records or reports about their pupils. These can be valuable to you as a student teacher. Note the following material issued by the Rochester School system.

RECORDS AND REPORTS: ELEMENTARY SCHOOLS [9]

Pupil Information Form

The teacher should have a Pupil Information Form for each pupil in the class. If there is not a form for each pupil, consult the principal or school clerk immediately.

Class Record Book

Each teacher is supplied with a class record book at the beginning of the school year. The book is to be used to record class marks and test ratings from one progress card to another. This should contain all evidence to substantiate marks given on the progress card. Check with the school principal as to the kind of records to be kept. The school office will inform each teacher as to the disposition of the record books at the end of the year.

Register of Attendance

This *Register of Attendance* is the legal attendance record of every pupil registered during the school year. On the basis of the attendance record State aid is administered. It is vital that the register be accurate. The proper notations concerning a pupil's attendance must be entered each day.

Because of the changes that occur in pupil assignments at the beginning of the school year, a form called *Work Sheets for Attendance Registers* is provided. This form can be used until such time as the principal feels the pupil changes have ceased to be a major problem. The pupil information can then be transferred to the official *Register of Attendance*.

Before using the *Register of Attendance* read carefully the printed direc-

[9] Robert L. Springer, *Now That You Are with Us* (Rochester, N.Y.: City School District, 1963–64), pp. 25–26. Reprinted by permission.

tions and those provided by the school office. Any questions about marking and balancing the register should be referred to the school clerk or the principal. Sometimes asking to see a completed register from the previous year helps solve a problem.

No information relative to a pupil's attendance record may be given by a teacher to any person without the permission of the principal.

Attendance Reports

At the end of each 5-week period during the school year the classroom teacher is expected to balance the attendance register and supply the necessary information to the school office. If you have trouble, ask the school clerk, an experienced teacher, or the principal for help.

Cumulative Pupil Records

The Rochester Public Schools have a well-developed cumulative records system for collecting, recording, and using information about pupils. This system involves a set of cumulative record forms for each pupil. There is a Manual of Directions for each teacher.

New teachers are urged to become familiar with the record forms and the Manual and to make use of the cumulative records of their pupils. Questions concerning cumulative pupil records should be taken up with the principal.

Parent-Teacher Conference

The parent-teacher conference is a valuable technique used in clarifying the role of parent and teacher in understanding and guiding the child. When a teacher plans a conference, a note is written to the parents to suggest a convenient time for the meeting. Conversely, the teacher should expect the same courtesy in order to plan carefully for the conference. A meeting at the classroom door between bells or when children are present is not satisfactory except to answer a routine question. Parents or visitors to a school are expected to check through the office as a matter of policy.

Discussion with the principal preceding the conference may reveal important background information. When sending notes of importance home, it is wise to clear them through the principal and retain a copy for your files.

In talking with parents it may be helpful to remember:

Listen.
Respect parents' confidence.
Be honest.
Avoid getting into arguments.
Avoid "teacherish" language.
Be ready to explain what is done at school and *why*.
(Individual folders containing pupil's work are helpful.)

Progress Reports

Progress Reports are issued periodically according to a schedule set up by the Administrative Director. (Consult Calendar, page 3.) Teachers need to read the Progress Report Card Manual carefully before marking cards. Frequent evaluation and careful records will validate final summary marks. Teachers of special subjects will submit their marks to the classroom teacher for recording. In many elementary schools the principals check cards preliminary to their being sent home. Feel free to discuss any problems relating to marking with the principal or supervising teachers. Marks are also recorded on the Pupil Accounting and Classification Sheet.

Report cards are to be returned with parent's signature within a week. Check cards for parent's comments.

Transfer—Pupil

When a child is transferring to another school, it is important to check with the school clerk or adviser on the clerical routines to be followed. Regular transfer forms and all records need to be filled in accurately and completely.

ASSESSMENT OF YOUR STRENGTHS AND WEAKNESSES

You know that your cooperating teacher has the responsibility of evaluating your attitudes and behavior in light of your degree of displayed aptitude for teaching. He needs to recognize and report to the proper authorities your outstanding strengths and weaknesses. It might be helpful to you to know those traits that have been found to be the strong and weak points of student teachers.

Recently, Rachel D. Wilkinson published a report of the personal strengths and weaknesses of thirty-two student teachers as these were reported by their cooperating teachers. The number of persons involved is small. Yet, you probably can find much in the report that is applicable to yourself as a student teacher.

Strengths of student teachers. According to Wilkinson, the strengths seem to involve personal attributes, manners, and attitudes of the student teacher, evidence of planning, and teaching procedures. We present her findings: [10]

[10] Rachel D. Wilkinson, "Evaluation Based upon Observation of Reports of Supervisors of Student Teaching," *The Journal of Educational Research* (January, 1963), pp. 266–67. Reprinted by permission of Dembar Publications, Madison, 3, Wisconsin.

Personal strengths. With regard to personal strengths, pleasing personality, appearance, and voice were the main phases listed. The personality was described in the following terms: good appearance, attractive appearance, neatness, dress, attractive and friendly, and simply the word "appearance." The word "voice" was used alone to describe strengths along with "firm but friendly voice, voice and speech, tone of voice, good voice, and voice well modulated."

Some of the strengths depicting desirable manner and attitude were mentioned more often than others: mature, sincerity, enthusiasm, and rapport. Specific wording of these attributes is listed below, with similar items grouped together:

1. Cheerful, sense of humor, calm and happy, ability to joke, happy about work
2. Positive attitudes, use of positiveness and courteous manner, use of praise
3. Sweet and gentle, manner is gentle and assuring, gentle manner
4. Mature, poised, patient
5. Alert, industrious, willing, competent, capable, cooperative, works hard, seriousness toward work, hard worker, conscientious, willing and good natured
6. Manner, natural manner, sincere, professional manner, punctual
7. Enthusiasm for teaching, enthusiasm, curiosity about teaching
8. Gets along well with superiors
9. Likes children, respect for children, comfortable with children, and they with her, manner with children, well liked by children, understanding and sympathy, superior understanding, desire to work with children, rapport, ease with children
10. Patient, wonderful with children, warmth toward children
11. Willingness to accept criticism and learns quickly, willingness to learn, willing to follow suggestions, willingness to take suggestions
12. Self-evaluation, awareness of difficulties

With regard to the background of the students, the strengths noted included these: superior understanding of children, good background, writes well, artistic ability, expert pianist, command of subject matter, good at record keeping.

Teaching strengths. The descriptions involving planning for teaching indicated that the supervisor liked the planning techniques, careful planning, thorough planning, selection of teaching material, and charts and attractively prepared teaching aids.

The supervisors described the observed strengths in teaching as follows:

Excellent teaching, splendid, superb lesson, outstanding lesson

Fine motivation, creative, resourceful, original, and enthusiastic

Use of illustrative material, use of objective material

Routines, moved about, transition from one activity to another, thorough, reviews

Timing, alert to need for change of pace, adjustment to situation
Questioning, explanations
Ability to handle a class, no trouble with discipline
Character development, use of praise, mature judgment, sensitive to emotional problems, recognition of needs of children
Participation of children
Board writing clear, no errors

Weaknesses of Student Teachers

The improvements which the supervisors suggested that the student teachers needed to make were almost the opposite of the strengths which were observed by them. The improvements needed may be classified as weaknesses in personal qualifications, background, manner, and teaching techniques.

Personal weaknesses. The comments with regard to weaknesses in personal qualifications included: untidy appearance, overweight, poor health, and inadequate speech or voice defects.

The backgrounds were inadequate due to lack of information regarding teaching methods, poor handwriting, and a need of insight into how children learn.

Manner and attitude showed a lack of self-confidence, an unwillingness to accept suggestions, lack of poise and maturity, tardiness, irregular attendance, and inability to adjust to the children and to peers.

The complete list follows:

Manner, immature attitude, lacks spark and vitality

Lacks confidence, not assertive enough, negative approach, authoritarian, does not relax, tense, not sure of herself, feels inferior and lacks self-confidence, does not assume responsibility

Not punctual at school, attendance irregular, personal problems and illness interfered

Criticizes other teachers, an "apple polisher"

Unwilling to follow suggestions, unwilling to accept criticism

Sarcastic manner with children, emotionally involved with students

Too sensitive and reads trouble into situations where none exists

Teaching weaknesses. The weaknesses in teaching seemed to stem from these inadequacies: preparation for the lessons, use of teaching materials, motivation techniques, sense of timing, skill with questioning, routines, and adjustment to class and to individual children. The complete list of needed teaching improvements follows:

No plan, planning inadequate, duplicated material would have helped, does not plan for slow and bright students.

Tried to cover too many concepts in one lesson, poor timing, lesson too long, might use duplicated material to save time

Need to use concrete materials, techniques and methods, teaching skills, techniques of teaching

Does not know how to motivate, poor motivation, no ingenuity

Not challenging, does not require children to think

Directions not clear, questioning skills, questions and comments not suited to age level, vocabulary above children, repeats answers of children, does not allow children to talk enough, repeats what they say

Routines, untidy with classroom routines, does not adapt to rules and methods of class, attention to details, writes too low on board, careless habits with board work, overuse of O. K.

Participation of children, no participation by some children, needs to involve children in process, called on some children too often, some children too soft spoken

Did not have children put away objective material before going on

Discipline, getting attention of whole class, lets other groups get restless, does not get total attention, starting lesson without getting attention at the beginning

Insists on formal behavior

Maintains stationary position

The writer feels that the factors included under strengths and weaknesses found by the supervisors working in one term with 32 student teachers are revealing. Perhaps such a list might be made available to students as a check-list for self-evaluation. If over the years the same weaknesses are apparent in each group, it may mean that the screening process for the selection of student teachers is inadequate.

It was most interesting that the supervisors involved used similar terminology in describing the strengths and weaknesses of the student teachers. These comments were submitted without any previous discussion of what should be listed. Each comment was therefore an individual matter on the part of each supervisor.

General Comment

In the following chapters of this book, suggestions are offered for the overcoming of weaknesses common to beginning student teachers. You will find that to the extent that you throw yourself whole-heartedly into meeting the many areas of your professional relationships, you will increase your self-confidence and develop those attitudes and activities that will serve you well as you continue in your chosen life work.

QUESTIONS AND TOPICS FOR DISCUSSION

1. Indicate specifically how your college supervisor is helping you in your student teaching.
2. In what ways is the school principal supervising your activities?
3. What is your relationship with your college supervisor?
4. In what ways is your cooperating teacher being helpful to you?

5. Compare the report card used in your school with the models presented in this chapter. Of all of them, which one do you prefer? Why?
6. How effective is the guidance program in your school? Be specific.
7. Secure copies of all report forms used in your school. Report on their value.
8. In what special ways are you assisting your cooperating teacher?
9. Show your cooperating teacher Wilkinson's list of the strengths and weaknesses of student teachers. Ask him to evaluate you honestly according to the items listed. Do the same for yourself.

6

PLANNING FOR EFFECTIVE TEACHING

The primary function of the teacher is that of guiding children's learning activities. Insofar as their maturational growth permits, young learners acquire basic knowledge about themselves and the world about them, achieve some degree of competence in fundamental skills, and develop simple positive attitudes toward their social and civic responsibilities. Within the limits of their abilities and interests, they are attempting to prepare themselves for further educational attainments in light of their goals and ambitions and according to available educational offerings.

NEED FOR CAREFUL PLANNING

To the present, you have benefited from the learning guidance given you by many teachers. Some teachers seemed to you to be better equipped than others to help you master learning materials. You probably recognized differences among your teachers in their ability to handle subject content and to impart their knowledge of it to you. In some classes, learning proceeded smoothly and was pointed toward the achievement of specific purposes; in other classes little constructive activity took place. In other words, some of your teachers knew what they wanted to do and how to do it; others were not sufficiently prepared to guide learning activities.

Now, as a student teacher, you are beginning to realize that a successful teacher needs to do more than master the subject matter of his teaching and gain some understanding of children, important as these two aspects of his teaching responsibilities are. He must be able so to plan his work that every one of his pupils benefits from participation with him in the learning.

You are no stranger to planning. You constantly are making plans for your long-range and immediate activities. You are aware of the *what, why,* and *how* of your many life activities. So it is with the teacher. He should know *what* learning activities need to be planned, *why* he includes what he does in his teaching, and *how* the learning process can best be developed, term by term, week by week, and day by day.

IMPORTANCE OF PLANNING

Effective planning has many facets. It includes (1) an understanding of the general educational objectives of the elementary schools, (2) an appreciation of the contribution of a particular subject area to the general purposes of education on this level, (3) a comprehension of what is or should be included in a term's or a year's study of the subject, (4) a knowledge of the appropriate units into which the subject can be divided, and (5) facility in planning for short-range instruction.

Attitudes toward Planning for Teaching

At one time, a teacher had only to prepare elaborate daily or weekly lesson plans for all of the subjects included in his school grade. He often did not concern himself with what was happening in other grades except as he might believe (rightly or wrongly) that the previous teachers of his pupils had not prepared them adequately in one or more areas of study.

A teacher who has set high standards of accomplishment for his pupils may expatiate at length about the difficulties he encounters in bringing up to class level the children he receives from one teacher as compared to the background learning of those who came from another. Such difficulties often are rooted in the relationship between the complaining teacher and the teacher of the previous grade. For example, Miss L, a fifth-grade teacher, worked closely with Miss R, one fourth-grade teacher, but had little in common with Miss B, another fourth-grade teacher. Consequently, although Miss B's pupils were well-grounded in fourth-grade learning activities, they were not as ready for Miss L's approach to subject material as were the pupils from Miss R's class. They were at a disadvantage, at least during the early weeks of the fifth grade.

Although an ambitious teacher may be motivated to underplay

the effectiveness of other teachers in order to emphasize his own excellence, most elementary school teachers recognize the relationship of the work of their grade to the total curriculum, and cooperate with teachers of other grades to meet curriculum demands. The principal or a supervisory assistant, delegated by the principal to do so, is responsible for (1) providing all teachers with the approved course of study for every subject taught, indicating what shall be included in the work of each grade, and (2) ascertaining, through the utilization of various evaluating techniques, the degree of success each teacher has achieved in planning for and guiding pupil mastery of the learning material within grade limits.

Areas of Planning

Curriculum construction is a shared responsibility of teachers, supervisors, administrators, and boards of education. Working together as a team, the teachers of a particular subject area often with the help of other experts in the field, establish the educational purposes to be served by the subject, set broad limits to the content to be covered, and develop the teaching-learning units to be included, grade by grade. The individual teacher, preferably in cooperation with other teachers on his grade, determines appropriate approaches to the development of each unit.

Finally, the teacher, building on the foregoing basic aspects of planning, prepares his day-by-day lesson plans, perhaps bringing pupils into the planning process. In this chapter we consider the objectives of elementary education and the fundamental areas of curricular planning. The lesson plan is discussed in Chapter 7.

ELEMENTARY SCHOOL OBJECTIVES

In the past, the main purpose to be served by education on the elementary level was to guide children's development of skill in reading, writing, and arithmetic. Some lay people still seem to believe that elementary school learning revolves around the 3 R's. Educators, however, without minimizing the importance of skill development in these fundamental areas of study, recognize the significance in a child's developing behavior pattern of other learnings. Hence statements of elementary school objectives have expanded to provide for the meeting of the various educational needs of children.

Significance of Educational Objectives

Constructors of elementary curriculums are guided in their work by ever-expanding statements of educational objectives that are concerned with providing for the present and future personal, social, and civic needs of our children. Elementary school offerings are being geared to constantly changing economic conditions. During the present century, various sets of elementary school objectives have been and continue to be formulated.

Civic and educational associations, governmental leaders, boards of education and committees of school administrators, supervisors, and teachers are engaged in preparing educational aims and objectives that embody those areas of learning concentration that can help provide for every child the learning experiences that have value for himself and society. As an elementary school teacher, you need to know the purposes to be served by the subject areas that constitute the fundamentals of elementary education.

Cardinal Principles of Education

Early in the twentieth century, the Commission on the Reorganization of Secondary Education was appointed by the National Education Association to study the educational needs of young people, the social and civic functions of secondary schools, and the learning offerings of existing schools. As a result of their investigation, the Committee submitted its report, *Cardinal Principles of Secondary Education,* in which were included seven general objectives for education on the secondary level.

These are:

1. Health
2. Command of fundamental processes
3. Worthy home membership
4. Vocation
5. Citizenship
6. Worthy use of leisure
7. Ethical character

The objectives as stated are broad in their connotation. The Committee broke them down into specific areas of application to school offerings.[1] So widespread are these cardinal principles that, with the possible exception of Vocation, they have come to be accepted as applicable to elementary school education. In fact, since there is a growing trend to include some vocationally pointed material on the elementary school level, all seven of the cardinal principles are basic to education in the elementary school.

Follow-up Conference on the 1960 White House Conference on Children and Youth

A follow-up of the 1960 White House Conference was sponsored by the Elementary School Section of the Office of Education. The purpose of this conference was to consider suggestions that apply to elementary education. The participants in this follow-up conference stressed the need of making available "to all children and youth those educational experiences that will enable each to reach the fullest development of his potentiality." In light of this general educational purpose, the conference stated that the good elementary school—

Defines its role in the local community in the context of the home, other agencies and institutions in the community, and the specific conditions of the community.

Reflects the belief that the family is the basic unit of our society.

Reflects the society's belief in the worth and integrity of every individual.

Strives to provide equal educational opportunity for individual children and youth, recognizing both similarities and differences.

Plans a curriculum which initiates learning in keeping with known laws of child growth and development, and thereafter provides each individual with opportunities for continuity in his learning.

Plans curriculum experiences broadly to provide challenging learning opportunities for all children in all important areas of growth.

Helps children and youth develop intellectually, emotionally, socially, physically, and spiritually toward enabling them to function capably in their personal and social lives at home, in the community, and in the world at large.

[1] See *Cardinal Principles of Secondary Education,* Bulletin No. 35 (Washington, D.C.: U.S. Office of Education, 1918), pp. 5–10.

Discovers and nurtures the gifts and talents of *all* its children in whatever lines these attributes appear.

Seeks to discover and nurture creativity in every line of development.

Carries forward the significant learnings and values of our society.

Provides experiences to help children learn to function intelligently as members of a free, democratic society.

Fosters diversity of achievements among children.

Keeps up-to-date in content and in methods of teaching.

Facilitates in its organization, quality in the education of all children.

Provides kindergarten education.

Offers a strategic point at which to detect incipient needs and problems of children.

Seeks, through research activities, constantly to improve its ways of dealing with children.[2]

Other statements of aims follow:

The Fundamental Objectives of Education: New York City Schools

THE FUNDAMENTAL OBJECTIVES OF EDUCATION [3]

The fundamental aims and objectives of public education in New York City are in accordance with our democratic traditions and are based on the individual's needs for effective living. These general objectives of education are concerned with:

Character:

To develop the basis for rich, useful, moral, and ethical living in a society promoting the common welfare.

Our American Heritage:

To develop pride and faith in American democracy and respect for the dignity and worth of individuals and peoples, regardless of race, religion, nationality, or socio-economic status.

[2] *Implications for Elementary Education: Followup on the 1960 White House Conference on Children and Youth* (Washington, D.C.: U.S. Department of Health, Education and Welfare, Office of Education, 1961), pp. 13–14.

[3] Reprinted from *Grade Guide: 5–6* (A Guide to the New York City Curriculum Program), by permission of the Board of Education of the City of New York, Curriculum Bulletin, 1961–62 Series, p. 54.

Health:

To develop and maintain a sound body and to establish wholesome mental and emotional attitudes and habits.

Exploration of Ability:

To discover, develop, and direct individual interests, aptitudes, and abilities.

Knowledge and Skills:

To develop command, in accordance with ability, of the common integrating habits, learnings, and skills.

Thinking:

To stimulate the inquiring mind and sound thinking necessary for the development of reasoning based upon adequate hypotheses, supported by facts and principles.

Appreciation and Expression:

To develop an appreciation and enjoyment of beauty and to develop powers of creative expression.

Social Relationships:

To develop desirable social attitudes and relationships within the family, the school, and the community.

Economic Relationships:

To develop an awareness and appreciation of economic processes and of all who serve in the world of work.

WHAT WE BELIEVE: BALTIMORE CITY SCHOOLS [4]

It is the right of every child to experience a school program that will insure continuity of learning. The school will share with other institutions and organizations the responsibility for providing each child the opportunity to develop

[4] *Information for New Teachers* (Baltimore: Baltimore Public Schools, 1964), pp. 7–8.

physically, spiritually, mentally, emotionally, and socially so that he can live a full life, satisfying to himself and to society. In creating such a program the following principles should be kept in mind.

1. Each child should be helped to attain knowledge and to establish habits which will further his physical, mental, and emotional health.

2. Each child should develop competence, to his optimum ability, in the use of tools of learning.

3. Each child should have learning experiences, which will forward and promote optimum personal development in relation to his individual abilities, needs, and interests.

4. Each child should have the opportunity, through participation in good group procedures, to learn to live as a worthy member of a democratic society.

5. Each child should have the opportunity to participate effectively in citizenship projects concerning the school, the community, and the world at large.

6. Each child should have the opportunity to acquire knowledge, understanding, and appreciation of his own and other societies.

7. Each child should be helped to gain an appreciation for the arts which enrich life and should be given opportunities to develop his abilities in creative expression.

8. Each child should be guided to develop spiritual values which are basic to sound moral and ethical codes.

9. Each child should be guided in developing an understanding of family life and of his contribution as a participating member of the family group.

10. Each child should be aided in making wholesome adjustments in all human relationships.

11. Each child should be helped to develop interests and skills which may lead to satisfying and enjoyable use of leisure.

12. Each child should be encouraged to value and to aim for worthy accomplishment.

Summary Considerations

As you read and meditate on the foregoing sets of educational objectives and recall others with which you are acquainted, you no doubt become aware of the all-embracing nature of elementary education and its application to the life interests and activities of developing children.

Every child needs to master those knowledges and gain those understandings that are appropriate to his life pattern. He also must be helped to acquire such skills and competencies as will increase his proficiency in meeting his responsibilities as an active and constructive member of his family, of his school, and of his community group. In addition, if a young person is expected to become a worthy citizen of his country, he should be guided early toward the achievement of an intelligent outlook on world affairs, a constructive point of view toward life experiences, and a wholesome set of life values.

LONG-RANGE PLANNING

Before a teacher attempts to prepare plans for teaching children on any grade level, he needs to comprehend the aims and purposes of the curriculum in light of generally accepted objectives. He also should know how much and what content should be covered in his particular grade. He must be able to view the various learning areas in perspective—to recognize the significant aspects to be mastered by his pupils.

Curriculum Organization

The elementary curriculum is organized around those subject areas that can be expected to insure for the child the mastery of the basic knowledges, skills, and attitudes on which he can build his further learnings. The specific subjects included in most elementary curriculums are arithmetic (mathematics), reading, spelling, composition, speaking, listening, penmanship, history, geography, citizenship, science, health, art, music, and handwork. Some school systems have shop work for boys, and, in increasing numbers, elementary schools are offering a modern foreign language.

At one time the various subjects were taught more or less independently of one another. Educators now recognize that learning areas are not separate but that some subjects interrelate. For example, in many elementary schools the *Language Arts* include all or some of the following specific areas: speaking, listening, reading, composition, spelling, and penmanship. History, geography, and citizenship are included in *Social Studies*. Handwriting may be considered as one of the aspects of *Art*. Various other combinations of specific subjects are possible, such as the inclusion of physical activities and health education and guidance in the general field of *Health*. The long-range curriculum planning of a particular elementary school is dependent on its organization of subject matter.

Preparation of Courses of Study

Long-range teaching guides usually are called courses of study. They include the teaching-learning objectives and the topics or units to be taught, arranged in logical or psychological order. It is unlikely that during your student-teaching experiences you will be asked to participate in the preparation of a course of study. Moreover, you probably will find that one already has been prepared for each of the subjects taught in your school. Your cooperating teacher will help you become acquainted with and assist you in using these courses as you plan for your teaching under his supervision.

The course of study for a particular subject area may be prepared by statewide committees. In large cities, a committee of experts, selected from among members of the school system, often is responsible for the preparation of the document. In small school communities, the teachers may develop their course of study according to state-formulated curriculum objectives.

Application of Courses of Study

Most good courses of study are flexible. They allow for the meeting of specific pupil needs. During his years of working with children of differing abilities, the experienced teacher learns what in a given course of study needs special emphasis. He works out his own long-range plans in light of his background of experience. He is careful to achieve the specific learning goals of the various subjects and to include appropriate topics or units of the course of study. Your cooperating teacher will encourage you to work with him in making any needed changes in the planning for the particular group of pupils with whom you are working.

Not only are good courses of study flexible, they also are characterized by considerable interrelationship and, in some cases, over-lapping. For example, during the teaching of a unit in science, the teacher may include material that rightly is a learning area of social studies, health, arithmetic, etc. Moreover, regardless of the subject matter under consideration, the learning activities are likely to include one or more phases of the Language Arts. In the following chart are samples of the kinds of interrelationships that can exist among the subject areas comprising the elementary school curriculum.

CONTEXTUAL ASPECTS OF PLANNING

There is another aspect of long-range planning to which you should give attention. As a beginner, you may believe that you need to be concerned only with the work of the grade in which you are involved. This is not enough. You also should be cognizant of what your pupils have studied to the present and what lies ahead of them. For example, you are teaching a fifth-grade class. What have they had in the four previous grades and what is the course of study for the sixth grade? In brief, what learning experiences have your pupils had in preceding terms and what learning experiences can be expected to follow?

You probably have gained some understanding of long-range objectives and teaching approaches in your college methods classes. Now it becomes your responsibility to apply what you have learned in light of the philosophy and teaching approaches of the school in which you are student teaching. Your school may have a sequential pattern of learnings, from grade to grade, for each subject area. This can help you determine the teaching-learning materials on any one grade level. We present here the "Summary of the Elementary Curriculum" as it has been developed for the San Diego City Schools.[5] Study it carefully and, insofar as you can, compare it with accepted procedures in your school.

As you study the charts of interrelationships among subject areas in the San Diego City Schools, you will be impressed by the detailed treatment. This is all to the good. To provide a well-organized background of educational fundamentals for the child necessitates that

[5] *Elementary Program, San Diego City Schools* (San Diego, Calif.: 1963), pp. 18–34. Reprinted by permission.

CHART: THE INTERRELATED:

Read across ←→ the chart indicates how one curriculum :			
Read down ↓ the chart indicates how learnings fi			

	HEALTH	SCIENCE	ART	MATH.
HEALTH	Course of Study: Health Guidance, Health Teaching, Physical Activities.	Children find out how f o o d s are preserved.	Children design posters related to health learnings.	Children fig proportion time spent sleep, study, p
SCIENCE	Children learn the b a s i c food groups.	Course of Study: magnetism, earth in space, weather, etc.	Children prepare science bulletin boards.	Children le to interpret so on measuring struments.
ART	Children a p p l y art principles to decoration.	Children m i x colors. They learn how moisture affects clay.	Course of Study: drawing, painting, clay modeling, etc.	Children estin and compute cost of mater
MATH.	Children determine the cost of a day's meals.	Children c h a r t changes in temperature.	Children estimate length of materials needed.	Course of St concepts, r tionships, pri ples, system numeration.
SOC. STUDIES	Children learn about p u b l i c health agencies.	Children learn about Unesco.	Children visit a museum to see arts of other people.	Children th out relations for a Time L
MUSIC	Children c a r r y on rhythmic activities suggested in physical activities.	Children experiment with sounds on musical instruments.	Children interpret pictures after listening to music.	Children sense time. span notes — wh quarter, eigh
LANG. ARTS		Language activities go on in relation to the children's experience in all curriculum areas. Activities include listening,		

intcrrelated with the other six curriculum areas.

her curriculum arcas contribute to a specific area.

SOC. STUDIES	MUSIC	LANGUAGE ARTS		
		Communication	**Reading**	**HEALTH**
Children learn the dances of the early settlers.	Children carry on rhythmic activities.	Children use topics related to health for speaking and writing.	They read biographies of scientists.	
Children learn how climate affects peoples' lives.	Children learn how musical sounds are made.	Children observe and describe natural phenomena.	They read and follow science directions.	**SCIENCE**
Children learn about the crafts of other people.	Children make puppets for a musical production.	Children discuss famous pictures. They learn vocabulary related to art activities.	They read about the artist and his times.	**ART**
Children compare distances from one place to other places.	Children feel accent in rhythm and relate note values.	Children learn vocabulary and symbols of mathematics.	They read and solve "verbal" problems.	**MATH.**
Course of Study: citizenship, geography, history, etc.	Children learn songs of other people.	Children take notes. They develop discussion techniques.	They develop library and reference skills through reading.	**SOC.STUDIES**
Children sing American folk songs.	Course of Study: singing, listening, playing, etc.	Children write lyrics. They set poems to music.	They read words and music in texts.	**MUSIC**
telling, reading, and writing in science, art, music, social studies, mathematics, or health.		Course of Study: speaking, listening, composition, handwriting, spelling, reading.		**LANG. ARTS**

[6] Reprinted from *Grade Guide: 3–4* (A Guide to the New York City Curriculum Program) by permission of the Board of Education of the City of New York, Curriculum Bulletin, 1961–62 Series, pp. 54–55.

ARITHMETIC	Kindergarten	Grade One	Grade Two	Grade Three	Grade Four	Grade Five	Grade Six
Time Allotment	Taught in all daily routines	20 minutes per day			40 minutes per day		
Grouping	Very flexible groups to meet individual needs				Generally two flexible groups meet daily. Sub-grouping used to meet individual needs.		
Text	Basic State Text -- one per pupil (consumable in grades one and two) with Teacher's Editions. Extending booklets -- grades four - six.						
Acceleration	Able learners in grades two through five may work in the content of the next grade. Sixth graders who complete the State text may work in the Scott, Foresman supplementary text.						
Basic Grade Level Content	Counting -objects, people, happenings, etc., in actual classroom experiences. Addition -simple facts using concrete objects Subtraction -simple facts using concrete objects Quantitative Vocabulary The vocabulary of arithmetic is given major emphasis in kindergarten and the primary grades, and is further developed and extended throughout all grades.	Counting -to 100 by 1's, 5's and 10's. -to 20 by 2's Addition -the facts to 6 Subtraction -the facts to 6	Counting -to 200 by 1's, 5's and 10's -to 120 by 2's -using Roman numerals to XII Addition -the facts to 12 -3 place columns Subtraction -the facts to 12	Counting -Beyond 1,000 by 1's -to 36 by 3's -using Roman numerals to 39 Addition -facts to 18 -with carrying -columns with bridging tens Subtraction -the facts to 18 -regroups with 2 and 3 places Multiplication -2's, 3's, 4's and 5's and their inverses -with carrying -2 and 3 place numerals by one place number Division -up to three place numerals by 2, 3, 4, and 5, by long division	Counting Maintains and extends counting, use of Roman numerals, reading and writing numbers. Addition -4 and more place columns Subtraction -regroups with 4 or more places Multiplication -facts through 9 -4 place numerals by one place number -2 place numeral by a 2 place numeral Division -by the basic facts through 9 -up to a 4 place dividend by any	Addition Maintains and extends Subtraction Maintains and extends Multiplication -any number by a 2 place numeral Division -by any 2 place divisor any dividend	Multiplication -any number by 3 and 4 place numerals Division -by any 3 place divisor any dividend

144

Measurement -Learns concept of distance, amount, weight, time, and temperature	**Fractions** -understands that equal parts are equal -understands 1/2 and 1/4	**Fractions** -understands whole-part relationship -understands 1/3 and 3/4 -understands 1/2 of a collection	**Fractions** -understands fractions, show division relationships .. 1/3, 1/4, 2/3 and 3/4	**Fractions** -finds fractional parts of whole numbers	**Fractions** -adds like and unlike fractions -subtracts like and unlike fractions	**Fractions** -multiplies common fractions -divides common fractions
	Measurement -time on the hour -learns days of the week and months on the calendar -measures in inches -understands pound, liquid measures to quart	**Measurement** -time on half hour, quarter hour, and 5 minutes -60 min.=1 hr. 30 min.=½ hr. -months in order -measures to 1 gallon -measures in in., ft., yds., lbs., ½ lbs., and ¼ lbs. -12 inches to 1 ft., 3 ft. to 1 yd. -reads two-degree points on a thermometer	**Measurement** -time on the minute -measures in half inches -miles per hr.	**Measurement** Maintains and extends learnings and use of measure: linear, weight, liquid, time, temperature, and speed.		
	Decimals -positional value to 99	**Decimals** -positional value to 200	**Decimals** -positional value to 1,000	**Decimals** -learns system of notation through hundred thousand	**Decimals** -adds decimal fractions through hundredths -subtracts decimal fractions through hundredths	**Decimals** -multiplies and divides decimal fractions -interchanges with common fractions -rounds off
		Problem solving -related to classroom life. Solves orally problems related to work for the grade.	**Problem solving** -one step problems	**Problem solving** -one and two step problems	**Problem solving** -two step problems	**Problem solving** -two and more step problems

ART	Kindergarten	Grade One	Grade Two	Grade Three	Grade Four	Grade Five	Grade Six
Time Allotment	Daily art experiences				75 min. per week taught as a separate subject.	150 min. per week taught as a separate subject.	
					(Additional time used for special art-social studies projects.)		
Grouping	Opportunities are provided for team teaching, classwide instruction, and individual and committee interests.						
Acceleration	Because art recognizes and encourages the worth of each child's creative expression, it is expected that individual differences and less easily measured variations in expression will be normal. Provision for individual growth rates and levels of achievement must be a part of teacher planning.						
Basic Grade Level Content							

THREE-PART ART PROGRAM

Creative art expression is an integrative experience evolving through three phases:

AWARENESS, involving sensitivity to all forms of environment, gives vitality and depth to art experiences.

EXPRESSION, growing out of awareness, is the transformation of ideas, reactions, and feelings into visual form.

APPRECIATION, developing as judgments are made, increases awareness and subsequent expression.

BASIC AREAS OF ART ACTIVITY

There are six basic areas of art activity in which every child should participate. Continuity, variety and vitality in art expression may be achieved as each teacher selects, plans, and carries out specific activities with her class within the framework of these major areas. Basic areas include:

PAINTING   COLLAGE-MAKING   MODELING
DRAWING   PRINT-MAKING   CONSTRUCTING

Appropriate media or techniques for expression include:

powder paint
finger paint
water color
crayon
chalk
cut and torn paper
screen collage materials

vegetable, sponge and
  gadget printmaking
clay
papier-maché
paper sculpture
wood, cardboard, and
  box construction

Appropriate media or techniques include:

transparent water color
opaque color
fingerpaint
chalk
crayon
charcoal
cut and torn paper

monoprinting
block printing
screen printing
clay
papier-maché
paper sculpture
wood, cardboard

146

Time Allotment	Citizenship education is a continuous process extending throughout the school day. Opportunities for teaching citizenship are generally most readily found in social studies and language.
Basic Guides	Developing American Ideals in the Primary Grades Citizenship Section Curriculum Guides Outline for Education for American Citizenship
Basic Books	Selected by teacher from Classified and Open Shelf State social studies texts supplemented by Classified and Open Shelf
Basic Grade Level Content	<u>Citizenship education is a three-phase program maintained through:</u> --classroom organization and student government --study of the Constitution --patriotic observances <u>The goals of citizenship education are to teach the child to:</u> --accept personal responsibility for himself and for the welfare of others --respect the authority of parents, teachers, and other adults who supervise his activities --obey rules and regulations developed for the good of society --work democratically with others in the group --be honest, thrifty and persevering --have an appreciation of spiritual values --respect the rights and viewpoints of others <u>Children practice patriotism in school by:</u> --learning the Pledge of Allegiance and patriotic songs --celebrating our American holidays with class and school activities --learning how to express love of our country and respect for our flag --demonstrating loyalty to our country and to American ideals --learning about great Americans, our country's history, traditions, great documents <u>Emphasis</u> -Patriotism through the year, patriotic songs, special days and events, beginning history, poetry and literature -The Pledge of Allegiance, the flag of our country

<u>Emphasis</u>
-Preamble to the Constitution

<u>Emphasis</u>
-Bill of Rights

<u>Emphasis</u>
-Duties and responsibilities of citizenship

147

HANDWRITING	Kindergarten	Grade One	Grade Two	Grade Three	Grade Four	Grade Five	Grade Six
Time Allotment	10 minutes per day			15 minutes per day			
Grouping	Individual differences are met in small, highly flexible groups.						
Text		Teachers Manual		Basic State Text – one per pupil with Teacher's Manual			
Basic Grade Level Content		Manuscript -writes all letters, small and capital correctly -writes numbers from 1-12 -uses primary pencil	Manuscript -writes numbers to 100 -uses primary pencil	Manuscript -The skills of manuscript writing are maintained through the grades.			
				Cursive -makes transition to cursive writing -writes all letters correctly -uses number 2½ pencil	Cursive -emphasis on ending stroke -re-emphasis on correct letter size	Cursive -emphasis on checking and improving own work -uses ball point pen	Cursive -emphasis on compound curve letters and loop stem capitals
					Continued development and mastery of skills of cursive writing in the instructional period and at other times when writing is used.		

Time Allotment	Health education is integrated with all areas of the curriculum. Specific health units may be taught for short periods at the beginning or end of the school year or between social studies units.					
Grouping	Children may be grouped in lessons involving the text or committee work.					
Text	Basic State Text — one per two pupils — with Teacher's Edition	Basic State Text — one per two pupils — with Teacher's Edition			Basic State Text — one per pupil — with Teacher's Edition	

The goals of health education are:

–To motivate a desire for healthful living and a healthy body and personality.
–To develop concepts of the moral and ethical relationships of personal health to the health of the total community.
–To develop understanding and appreciation of the value of community health agencies and resources.
–To develop awareness and to teach knowledge of safety practices and principles.
–To teach methods and uses of scientific principles in reference to problems of health.

Basic Grade Level Content	Suggested Units	Suggested Units	Suggested Units	Suggested Units	Suggested Units	Suggested Units
–self-care experiences –begins to understand the importance of proper rest, diet	–Healthy Citizens –Dental Health –Care of Pets	–Care of Teeth –Healthy Eyes –Living Together Happily –Vacation Health and Safety	–Growth –Cleanliness –Sleep and Rest	–Growth and Measurement –Safety and First Aid	–The Eyes and Vision	–Bacteria as Friends and Enemies

Alcohol, Tobacco and Narcotics
–a legal requirement
Social Health
–with parent permission

149

LANGUAGE	Kindergarten	Grade One	Grade Two	Grade Three	Grade Four	Grade Five	Grade Six
Time Allotment	Language is taught as an integral part of all subject areas.			120 min. per week	150 min. per week	175 minutes per week	
Grouping	Individual differences are met in small, highly flexible groups.						
Text	Basic State Text - one per pupil with Teacher's Editions						
Basic Grade Level Content	Oral Communication A planned program in oral language is introduced in kindergarten and is extended through the grades. The program provides for planned progression for growth in:			−Correct speech −Conversation −Discussion −Reporting −Social courtesy −Choral speaking		−Telephone use −Voice quality −Storytelling −Dramatizations −Announcements −Giving directions and explanations	
	Listening Listening is the necessary counterpart of oral language experiences. Therefore, specific suggestions for teaching listening are included in every category of oral language experiences. Lessons are also planned to develop skills in listening, to:			−Gain information −Follow directions −Reproduce a message −Hear specific details −Discover main ideas		−Answer specific questions −Interpret new words through context −Evaluate (critical listening	
		Written Communication Practical Writing −dictates and copies composite letters −writes one or more complete sentences	Written Communication Practical Writing −writes an original letter in simple form. −writes two or more complete sentences	Written Communication Practical Writing −writes letters with correct heading, greeting, message, closing and signature	Written Communication Practical Writing	Written Communication Practical Writing	Written Communication Practical Writing
					Extends skills of writing friendly and business letters.		

150

-writes captions and labels -Capitalizes to begin sentences and proper names -uses periods and question marks correctly	-writes short messages -uses correctly capital letters, question marks, and periods -begins to proofread written work	-indents paragraphs -uses straight margins -keeps records of science experiments, etc. -writes news articles for class or school paper -proofreads own work	-writes reports, notices, and opinions -takes notes using abbreviations -outlines -summarizes -proofreads -uses dictionary and resource books	-writes book reviews -skims for information	-rewrites -writes informational articles -identifies adjectives, nouns and verbs
			Proofreads all written work to improve clarity of expression and to correct punctuation, sentence structure, spelling, etc.	Extends skills in note taking, outlining, summarizing, and using dictionary.	
Creative Writing -dictates and copies composite stories -writes short, simple poems and stories	Creative Writing -writes composite poems and stories -writes independent poems and stories	Creative Writing -writes original stories, poems and "word pictures"	Creative Writing Extends skills in writing original poems, stories, and descriptive paragraphs. Continues vocabulary development and the use of dictionary and resource books.		

MUSIC	Kindergarten	Grade One	Grade Two	Grade Three	Grade Four	Grade Five	Grade Six
Time Allotment		20 minutes per day			Instrumental instruction is given interested students 1 hour per week.		
Text	Teacher's manuals provided	Basic State Texts – two titles – ten per class		Basic State Text – one per pupil – with teacher's editions			

Activities and Learnings

SINGING – Purpose: to help each child to find enjoyment in singing, to develop his singing voice to the best of his ability, and to learn a repertoire of songs of permanent worth.

MOVING – Purpose: to encourage children to listen and to respond to music through creative bodily movement, in order to experience, recognize and gradually understand all of the concepts of rhythm and many of the other elements of music.

PLAYING INSTRUMENTS – Purpose: to provide another means of musical expression and to acquire the following skills and learnings:

For All Children

Percussion Instruments – to aid in accuracy of performance, and understanding of rhythm and tempo.

Melodic Instruments – to provide kinesthetic experiences with musical tone, and understanding of melody and harmony.

Chordal Instruments – to provide opportunity to accompany songs, and an understanding of harmony.

Orchestral Instruments – class instruction, and orchestra experience

LISTENING – Purpose: to acquaint children with a variety of music literature that is universally accepted as great and beyond their present performing ability. It includes vocal and instrumental music from classic, romantic, contemporary periods, as well as national idioms.

MUSIC READING – Purpose: to extend children's ability to enjoy, understand and perform music; (music reading is an integral part of all the above musical activities); to clarify musical elements that have been heard and performed (rhythm, melody, harmony, form); to improve accuracy of performance, and to use notation to learn new music.

	Grade One	Grade Two	Grade Three	Grade Four	Grade Five	Grade Six

Time Allotment

20 minutes per day.

Grouping

Individual differences are met in small, highly flexible groups. Children may be grouped in squads to provide more individual instruction.

Basic Grade Level Content

The physical education program is designed for guided play in the Kindergarten with activities structured for big muscle development and desirable social interaction. Throughout the ensuing years, the child grows in knowledge, abilities and skills. By the end of the sixth grade he plays team games, shows measurable growth in development of strength, endurance, flexibility, timing, rhythm and coordination.

The content of the balanced physical education program includes:

Games   Relays   Rhythms   Self-Testing Activities   Recreation Activities

Activities

-hollow blocks
-apparatus
-rhythms
-cycling
-ball
-sand play
-free play

Activities

-games
-relays
-stunts
-rhythm
-apparatus

Activities

Planned progression of the skills in the basic activities is extended through the grades.

Units

-kicking and batting
-circle and running activities
-net activities
-recreational activities

Units

-kicking and running
-net activities
-soccer activities
-recreational activities
-softball activities

Units

-soccer activities
-basketball activities
-volleyball activities
-recreational activities
-softball activities

153

READING	Kindergarten	Grade One	Grade Two	Grade Three	Grade Four	Grade Five	Grade Six
Time Allotment		120 min. per day	100 min. per day	80 min. per day	60 min. per day	40 min. per day	40 min. per day
Grouping		Children are divided by ability into three groups.					
Text		Basic State Texts - one per two pupils with Teacher's Editions. Supplementary State Texts - one per four pupils with Teacher's Editions. Supplementary Texts supplied by San Diego School District					

Basic Grade Level Content — Kindergarten

Reading Readiness
-speaks clearly.
-speaks in complete sentences
-retells a simple story in sequence
-makes up stories
-enjoys books, recognizes their use and importance
-hears minute differences of sounds
-sees likenesses and differences in objects
-classifies objects
-places objects or pictures from left to right
-recognizes colors

The content of the reading program provides for four types of instruction:

Basic Text Reading
--provides a continuity of learning experiences from grade to grade.
--provides a complete program for the development of fundamental reading habits, skills, and attitudes.

Supplementary Text Reading
--promotes fluid reading.
--strengthens the skill of comprehension.
--insures mastery of word-recognition skills.
--enlarges vocabulary.

Personal Interest Reading
--provides the opportunity for children to use reading skills.
--develops enjoyment in reading and a love of fine books.
--acquaints children with broad fields of literature.

Reference, News, and Reading in the Content Fields
--provides the opportunity to use reference skills developed in the basic reading program.
--provides the opportunity to use a variety of books, newspapers and magazines.

Objectives of the Reading Program are to develop comprehension and word analysis skills and appreciation of literature. As a result of reading instruction children:

--acquire word recognition skills
--develop independent study skills
--gain facts and ideas from

--develop reading skills, such as:
.comprehending and interpreting materials read
.reading efficiently, silently
.reading skillfully, orally
.reading with satisfactory speed

--read with efficient speed
--read well aloud
--appreciate literature
--begin to read library books
--build confidence in reading
--acquire word-attack skills

.mastering word-attack skills
.gaining power in word usage
.learning to read for different purposes

--develop reference reading skills, such as:
.using reference books for information
.using dictionary easily
.locating information quickly
.learning to use the library effectively

Developmental Steps in Reading

-Readiness period	-Review period	-Review period	-Review period	-Review period	-Review period
-Sight vocabulary building	.primer	.1st readers	.2nd reader	.3rd or 4th readers if necessary	.At level necessary for success
-Preprimer reading on several levels	.1st reader	.2nd readers	.3rd reader if necessary	-Fifth readers	-Sixth readers
-Primer reading	-Second readers L1	-Third readers L1 and L2	-Fourth readers	.basic and supplementary	.basic and supplementary
-First reader	-Second readers L2	.basic and supplementary	.basic and supplementary		
-Accelerated readers	.basic and supplementary	-Accelerated readers	-Accelerated readers	-Accelerated Program	
	-Accelerated readers			.Seventh Grade Readers	
				.Eighth Grade Readers	
				.Ninth Grade Anthology	
				.Assorted Graded subject set of 20 titles.	

SCIENCE	Kindergarten	Grade One	Grade Two	Grade Three	Grade Four	Grade Five	Grade Six
Time Allotment	Science related to the social studies units is taught during the social studies period. Science units are taught at the beginning, end, and between social studies units.						
Grouping	Children may be grouped in lessons involving the state text or committee work.						
Text		Basic State Text - one per two pupils with Teacher's Edition Supplementary State Texts (unitexts) one per class with Teacher's Manual			Basic State Texts - one per pupil with Teacher's Edition Supplementary State Texts (unitexts) three per class with Teacher's Manual		
Basic Grade Level Content							

The elementary school science program provides opportunities for children to become aware of scientific and technological advancements and to analyze their consequent influences. These opportunities help children to acquire and to develop a scientific attitude toward identifying problems, formulating hypotheses, and reaching conclusions based on truth.

The three basic approaches to science teaching are:
-science units
-science experiences related to other subject areas
-science related to special interests and events

The program is planned to provide a variety of experiences through active participation in discussing, planning, searching for information, experimenting, and evaluating.

The program is modified frequently to keep pace with scientific advancements.

The science program provides progressively advanced experiences at each grade in the following areas:

Living Things   Weather and Climate   The Earth   The Universe   Machines and Energy

Time Allotment	60 minutes per day – including art with related science and health.				60 minutes 60 minutes per day.		
Grouping	Flexible grouping – pupils work as individuals, in small and large groups, or as a class.						
Text	Unit sets provided by the district for each social studies unit.				Basic State Text – two titles – one per pupil with Teacher's Manual (except grade four). Supplementary State Texts – multiple titles from one per two pupils to one per six pupils		
Purpose of Social Studies	The content of the social studies is drawn from the social sciences, particularly history, geography, political science, and economics. The major purpose of the social studies is to develop competent, loyal American citizens. The social studies program develops: -knowledge and appreciation of our national heritage and way of life -pride and loyalty to American institutions and ideals -understandings essential to good citizenship -understandings of the importance of participation in the community, state, and nation -knowledge and concepts relating to the community, state, nation, and world						
Basic Grade Level Content	-experiences centered around the home, school, and neighborhood using block play, dramatic experiences, art construction activities, -the kindergarten social studies experiences are achieved through interest units such as: The Farm, Airplanes, Ships and Harbor	-studies how people live, travel, and work in the community; the importance of good family living, and the need for maintaining health and practicing safety	-studies how people communicate with each other and work to provide for the basic needs of food, clothing and shelter; the importance of animals to man	-studies how communities are dependent upon one another, how goods are interchanged, how communities are established, and the types of communities and regions found within our nation	-studies California's colorful beginning and the location and extent of our state's natural and human resources; learns about California's relationship to the nation and to neighboring countries	-studies historical events which depict the colonization of America; the contributions of early pioneers; the westward expansion; and the growth, progress, and problems of our country and Canada	-studies air transportation, Latin America, conservation and current affairs to gain a broad overview of our nation and its relation to the world

The goals of social studies are met through the study of prepared units.

SOCIAL STUDIES
Basic Grade Level Content (continued)

Units	Units	Units	Units	Units	Units
-Traveling in and out of the City	-Animals Around the World	-Pioneering Past and Present	-Living in Early California	-Our Nation Begins	-Living in Latin America
-Family and Community Life	-How We Communicate	-Ports and Cargoes	-Living in Mexico	-Our Nation Grows	-Air Transportation
-Working in the City	-How We are Fed and Clothed	-This Land of Ours	-Living in Our Country	-Living in Modern U.S. and Canada	-Conserving Our Nation's Resources
Unit Revision - completed 1961 1962 1963		Unit Revision -New units scheduled tentatively for 1965.		Unit Revision -Above units tentative for 1963-64.	Unit Revision -New units scheduled for 1964.

or

Combination Grade Units

(Optional science units may be used in lieu of one social studies unit.)

One and Two	Two and Three	Three and Four	Four and Five	Five and Six
-Farm Animals	-The Airport	-Living in Southern California	-Our Country's Colonial Days	-Exploring Africa
-Enjoying a Vacation	-Carrying the Mail	-Living in the Hawaiian Islands	-Our Country's Westward Expansion	-Communications
-Stores in the Community	-The Dairy Farm	-Living in a Pueblo Indian Home	-Modern Pioneers	-Trade and Transportation
-Traveling on a Train	-The Harbor			-Canada, Our Northern Neighbor

Skills, knowledges, and understandings are developed through the use of the following:

-locating, reading, organizing, and summarizing content material
-comprehending and interpreting factual materials
-recording and reporting information
-learning to work with others
-communicating ideas effectively to others
-thinking critically and creatively and solving problems in an organized fashion
-using maps, globes, and other geographical materials to increase understandings

SPELLING		GRADE ONE	
Time Allotment	Taught as an integral part of reading and language	20 minutes per day	
Grouping		Individual differences are met in small highly flexible groups. Often in grades 3 - 6 a portion of the class is involved with enrichment activities.	
Text		Teacher's Guide	Basic State Text (consumable)-one per pupil with Teacher's Edition

Basic Grade Level Content

The content of the spelling program includes:
-the words listed in the State speller for each grade
-the words learned in the previous grades and repeated in the review lessons
-the words given in the mastery list of the spelling series
-the words needed by pupils for individual and classwide activities

-spells and writes his first and last names -spells words in writing labels and sentences -applies phonics taught in reading -is alert to word beginnings and endings -makes own simple dictionary -uses variety of materials to find correct spelling -checks own spelling	-studies spelling effectively -associates sounds with letters -recognizes consonant sounds -recognizes vowel sounds -adds simple endings to root words -makes compound words -keeps personal record of misspelled words for study and mastery	-alphabetizes words by the 1st and 2nd letters -uses suffixes and prefixes to change meanings of root words -uses synonyms -proofreads words in tests and all written work	Continued development and mastery of: -the spelling lists by grade -spelling words to meet own needs -dictionary skills -use of phonics and word analysis skills -proofreading -vocabulary building through knowledge of word origins, multiple meanings of words, and the use of suffixes and prefixes to change meanings of root words

the various subject areas be well integrated. The elementary school graduate needs to possess a general understanding and appreciation of basic knowledges, skills, and attitudes upon which he later can build specific learnings. In other words he must have the tools of learning.

Elementary education cannot be segmented, but rather should represent a unified whole. This can be accomplished only through effecting a proper relationship among the various subject areas included in the elementary school curriculum. It is through curriculum adaptation that teachers attempt to meet fundamental educational objectives. In the chapter that follows, we indicate how the goal of integration can be achieved through the utilization of unit teaching and learning.

QUESTIONS AND TOPICS FOR DISCUSSION

1. Compare the educational objectives of the school in which you are student teaching with those presented in this chapter. Note likenesses and differences.
2. Try to recall the subjects you had as an elementary school pupil. Evaluate the knowledges, skills, and attitudes you possessed at the end of your sixth year in school.
3. How comprehensive are the courses of study available in your school in comparison with the curriculum design of the San Diego elementary schools?
4. In the school in which you are doing your student teaching, to what extent and how are the specific subjects included in broad curriculum areas?
5. Indicate the interrelationships that exist among the various curriculum areas for the grade in which you currently are student teaching.

7

PLANNING IN SUBJECT AREAS

With the help of your cooperating teacher, you probably have acquainted yourself with the following information: (1) the educational objectives of the elementary school in which you are a student teacher, (2) the curriculum design, and (3) the course of study for each of the subject areas included in the curriculum. Now you need to gain skill in organizing the teaching-learning material of your grade in such form that day by day and week by week the pupils gradually develop knowledge, skills, and attitudes appropriate to expected grade coverage. You also need to acquire skill in planning for the sequential teaching of each subject for which you are responsible.

Subject-area planning includes program scheduling, long-range or *unit planning,* and short-range or *daily lesson planning.* We shall consider program scheduling and unit planning in this chapter and daily lesson planning in Chapter 8.

PROGRAM SCHEDULING

A program schedule can be organized according to a weekly and/or a daily plan. In preparation for the week's or the day's teaching-learning experiences you should arrange the materials to be included according to time allotments recommended for each curriculum area.

Careful thought should be given to building the time schedule of classes in the elementary school. Among the points to be considered are:

1. Range and depth of skills taught
2. Mental and physical maturity of pupils
3. Alternating of activities
4. Time for and length of lunch period
5. Use of any audio-visual equipment and material

6. Use of special consultants, such as speech teacher, reading specialist
7. General philosophy of the school
8. Principle of flexibility
9. Focus on being functional
10. Principle of balance and variety
11. Principle of unity and continuity

It is believed that a schedule of time when flexibility is permitted is a great aid to the teaching-learning situation. The weekly schedule is used by some schools and the daily schedule is preferred by others. The weekly time schedule tends to allow for more flexibility in that the teacher may place first or earlier those enterprises or activities that are of greatest significance for the day. Then, too, a flexible schedule allows for the combining of lessons in language, in spelling, and in handwriting, for example. Also, social studies, science, and health may be interwoven, especially when the unit approach is used. We present time allotment schedules to illustrate both the weekly time schedule and the daily time schedule.

TABLE 3

Time Allotments in the Elementary Schools [1]

Kindergarten		
Daily Time Allotment		Weekly Time Allotment
10 min.	Opening exercise	50 min.
20 min.	Science Informal number work Planning	100 min.
50 min.	Worktime Choice Clean-up Evaluation	250 min.
20 min.	Music	100 min.
10 min.	Rest or Relaxation	50 min.
20 min.	Physical Education or Free Play	100 min.

[1] John H. Harris, *Elementary Handbook* (Des Moines, Iowa: Des Moines Public Schools, 1963), pp. 62–63. Reprinted by permission.

TABLE 4

TIME ALLOTMENTS (WEEKLY) IN DES MOINES

GRADES 1–5

	Grade 1	Grade 2	Grade 3	Grades 4 and 5
Homeroom (Opening exercises)	100	100	100	100
Recess	100	100	100	
Reading (Skills and Literature Appreciation)	650	550	525	275
Language (Oral and written instruction)	100	100	100	100
Spelling		75	75	75
Handwriting	75	75	75	75
Social Studies Science	200	200	200	275
Arithmetic	125	150	175	250
Health				70
Physical Education	100	100	100	180
Art	100	100	100	125
Music	100	100	100	125
Total	1650	1650	1650	1650

GRADE 6

Subject	Minutes
Homeroom	50
Language Arts	535
Spanish	100
Arithmetic	240
Social Studies and Science	300
Art	100
Music	100
Physical Education	200

San Diego—Grade 4: This schedule is based on the time requirements adopted by the Board of Education.[2]

TABLE 5

DAILY SCHEDULE

Time	Subject	Comments
9:00–10:00	Social Studies	Include science, health, and art * when appropriate and related to the unit.
10:00–10:05	Relief	This period is optional and may be handled according to school policy.
10:05–10:45	Arithmetic	Arithmetic grouping is recommended. See the Arithmetic Section in this guide for suggestions.
10:45–11:00	Recess	Softball is not recommended at this time.
11:00–11:20	Music	Plan a balanced program. See the Music Section in this guide.
11:20–11:45	Spelling and Language	Various combinations of these subjects are feasible. See the appropriate sections of this guide for suggestions.
11:45–12:00	Handwriting	See the Handwriting Section of this guide for suggestions.
12:00– 1:00	Noon	Supervise your own class until routine is established.
1:00– 2:00	Reading	The teacher works with three groups:
(1:00– 1:20)		—*At the circle*—Group 3. —Related seatwork or study— Groups 1 and 2.
(1:20– 1:40)		—*At the circle*—Group 1. —Related seatwork or study— Groups 2 and 3.

* Art will often be taught as part of the social studies program. However, beginning at this grade there will be the opportunity to plan for 75 minutes of art per week as a separate subject.

[2] *Elementary Program,* San Diego City Schools, *op. cit.,* p. 13. Reprinted by permission.

TABLE 5 (*Continued*)

DAILY SCHEDULE

Time	Subject	Comments
(1:40– 2:00)		—*At the circle*—Group 2. —Related seatwork or study— Groups 1 and 3.
2:00– 2:05	Relief	
2:05– 2:25	Physical Education	This is a teaching period. See the Physical Education Section in this guide for specific skills.
2:25– 3:05	Language or Art	Block time to provide more efficient learning situations (e.g., M-W-F, Language; T-Th, Art).

The teaching of phonics, dictionary work, and other word recognition skills are included within the framework set up by each teacher for reading, language, and spelling instruction.

INDIANAPOLIS:GRADE 1:
SUGGESTED FIRST GRADE SCHEDULE [3]

Recommendations by the state for allocations of minutes to subjects have been modified locally as follows:

Subject	*Average Number of Minutes per Day*
Opening Exercises, Pupil-Teacher Planning	15
Language Arts	150
Social Studies	25
Science	20
Physical Education, Health Needs, Health and/or Safety	35 (170 min. per wk.)
Music—Art	35 (170 min. per wk.)
Arithmetic	35
Evaluation and Dismissal	5
	320

[3] *Suggested Daily Schedule* (Indianapolis: Indianapolis Public Schools, 1963), p. 2.

The schedule *will be flexible* for the first week or until organization is definitely completed. Reading groups will be reorganized after children have been given the Metropolitan Test. The plans given here for the first eight days will give you time to get acquainted with the children, to determine to some extent their levels of maturity, and to make tentative groupings. After grouping more time will be given to reading readiness and reading and time allotments will follow more closely the suggested daily schedule.

Sample Daily Schedule

8:45 A.M.	Morning Exercises, News, Planning
9:00 A.M.	Social Studies
9:25 A.M.	Handwriting and Spelling
9:55 A.M.	Physical Education, Health or Safety
	(P.E.—20 min.—4 days
	Health or Safety—20 min.—1 day)
	Health Needs, Rest (10 min.—A.M.)
	(5 min.—P.M.)
10:25 A.M.	Reading
11:25 A.M.	Science
11:45 A.M.	Clean-up
11:50 A.M.	Dismissal
1.00 P.M.	Reading
2:00 P.M.	Health Needs, Rest
2.05 P.M.	Arithmetic
2:40 P.M.	Music (3 days—includes chorus)
	Art (2 days)
3:10 P.M.	Clean-up, Evaluation
3:15 P.M.	Dismissal

In some school systems teachers are expected to adhere closely to the daily time allotments and order of subject material included in the recommended schedule. Other school systems permit the teacher considerable leeway in the order of presentation, provided that he includes all required subject areas for his grade and allots to each the proper amount of time for the term or year.

THE UNIT APPROACH IN TEACHING

In the past, most teachers were accustomed to place major emphasis on day-by-day lesson planning. The many sequentially organized topics of a detailed course of study or the chapter contents of a textbook served as the bases of daily lesson plans. Following this procedure might result in segmented, unrelated teaching. The unit approach in teaching provides the teacher and his class an opportunity to center attention on a series of comprehensive learning wholes that, insofar as they represent the functioning of broad unifying principles, improve learners' retention of subject materials.

Interpretation of Unit Teaching

A unit of work can be interpreted as a series of teaching-learning experiences that are centered in and unified around an appropriate topic, a practical project, or a problem of interest to a particular group of pupils. Much of elementary school teaching centers around each of the various topics included in the course of study. However, more and more consideration is being given to the utilization of problem and project units that are developed by the teacher and pupils planning together.

Some subject materials, especially those in which sequential treatment is needed, such as arithmetic, lend themselves better to one approach rather than to another. Other areas of study, such as the language arts, the social studies, some aspects of science, and other materials that may have a direct bearing on children's experiences and relationships, can well include the problem approach.

The topical approach to unit planning is effective in the development of a skill. A textbook organized according to sequential steps of difficulty can be the basis of the learning process. For example, a course in arithmetic for the first term of the third grade is divided into four sequential units based on the content of "Arithmetic We Need."

Many elementary teaching-learning experiences are developed in the form of problem units. The problem may center around a particular subject area and be integrated with other areas of learning. The social studies area often is the nucleus of the unit with the inclusion of appropriate materials from other subject fields, such as the language arts, science, art, and music. To illustrate the organization of a unit plan we are presenting the following social studies unit to be used in the fourth grade.

SAMPLE UNIT PLAN [4]

Broad Topic: *How New Yorkers Make a Living (Social Studies, Grade 4)*
Possible Problem Title: *What Different Kinds of Work Do People in Our City Perform?*

Probable Duration: *3–4 weeks*
Suggested Sub-Problems to Be Discussed with Children:

1. Which people help to keep our city clean?
2. Which people help to keep us safe and healthy?
3. Which people provide us with food and clothing and supply other needs?
4. Which people help to transport persons? Supplies?
5. In what other ways do people make a living? (Arts, professions, banking, service, etc.)

Objectives of the Unit

A. Attitudes, Appreciations, Understandings

An appreciation of the many ways in which people earn a living and how they all help us

Growth in understanding the interdependence of people in New York City

Understanding that New York City is an important center of travel and trade

B. Skills

Growth in map skills: reading maps to locate New York City, the bodies of water, bridges, tunnels, airports

Learning how to mark on a map some of the important buildings and stores in the community

Planning and taking a trip on the subway and following the route on a map

Learning to use the index in a book

Learning to compare the information found in several social studies texts

---

[4] Reprinted from *Grade Guide 3–4* (A Guide to the New York City Curriculum Program) Curriculum Program Bulletin, 1961–1962 Series, by permission of the Board of Education of the City of New York, pp. 15–17.

C. Social Development

Learning how to plan and work together in groups

Beginning to assume responsibility for a group project

Beginning to evaluate group projects

Launching the Unit

1. Display pictures of New Yorkers at work
2. Show the filmstrip, "Story of a Great City," and note the people at work
3. Using a map, develop the concept of New York City as a port and center of world trade

Materials of Instruction (See references in *Social Studies 3–4*)
Trips to neighborhood places where people work, as: Ward Baking Co., supermarket, etc.
Filmstrip: *New York; Story of a Great City*
Books: *Big City Transportation, Big City Workers, Come to the City, This Is New York, We Live in the City, Men at Work*, etc.

Integration with Other Areas

Science:	Preserving foods, Handbook No. 3, p. 39–51
	The Water We Drink, Handbook No. 7 and *Operation New York*
Health:	People who handle food, work of the Department of Health, city laws for health and safety
Language Arts:	Listening to *Stories Round the Town* and *Know Your City, WNYE* (select appropriate programs from each series)
	Reading books about New York, reporting, preparing a list or display
	Telling about places visited with parents, the work of parents or other adults, demonstrating a process, etc.
	Using unit words: occupation, trade, business, harbor, bank, insurance, haberdashery, supermarket, etc.
	Writing letters of thanks, invitations; describing an experience in New York: writing on a topic such as: What I Want To Be When I Grow Up, etc.
Music:	Songs from *Music Round the Town*
Art:	Visit a museum of art to examine the work of artists or photographers
	Draw or paint scenes of people at work
	Arrange a corridor display of pictures showing New Yorkers at work

Possible Culmination

A dramatization or choral speaking about people at work

Evaluation

Give a test on knowledge, concepts, understandings
Observe how children use skills of research: using a table of contents, index, etc.
Look for desirable attitudes toward various kinds of work and workers
Observe changes in personal responsibility for keeping the city clean, observing amenities in public places, etc.

Value of the Unit Approach

Pupil interest is a prime motivator of learning progress. Since the unit approach is relatively flexible, it can be adapted to meet children's changing needs and interests. Also, practical learning outcomes can be stressed rather than only the mastery of subject content. Hence learning can become more meaningful. In addition, through the unit approach, the teacher can make provision for learning differences among his students. There is more opportunity for remedial work.

Planning for the Unit Approach

Planning for the unit approach to teaching requires a considerable amount of preliminary preparation. The term's or year's work can be divided into a series of related units. The preliminary step of dividing the course of study into appropriate units often is the responsibility of a group of teachers. Then, either the committee as a whole or the individual teacher organizes the aims, the materials, and the activities for each unit. The information to be mastered and the skills to be improved are noted.

Pupil participation in the determination of the activities to be included often is encouraged. Appropriate individual and group projects are planned and conducted by pupils under teacher guidance. Other activities may be dramatizations; demonstrations; oral or written reports based on reading, on other research, or on project construction; and whole class discussions. The final step is an evaluation by the teacher and pupils of the value of the unit of learning.

In planning unit activities with your class you serve as the chairman, giving the group intelligent leadership. The unit may be simple or relatively complex; but you know the aims that you hope to achieve, and you view these in light of pupils' interests and purposes. You attempt to motivate their thinking through questions that can arouse their interest or through involving them in challenging experiences, as you observe various children at work on unit activities. You thus can learn much about their attitudes and their strengths and weaknesses.

The extent to which a unit is an effective medium for successful teaching-learning experiences depends in good part on the care with which the unit has been selected. Here are guidelines for the selection of units that may be of assistance to teachers and committees:

1. The unit chosen should have value and significance (1) for the children, (2) to society, and (3) in the subject field of which it is a part.
2. Selectivity in unit selection is essential because the tremendous amount of knowledge generally and the explosion of knowledge in our times make it impossible for the learner to go into all aspects of a subject with equal thoroughness.
3. The unit area selected should be broad enough in scope to contain elements that will challenge the interest of every child in the group concerned.
4. The unit should be related to the scope and sequence which has been designated for the curriculum of the level or grade.
5. The unit should be appropriate for the age and ability levels of the children and suited to their interest and needs.[5]

CRITERIA OF A GOOD UNIT:

In constructing their own units, teachers should keep in mind the following criteria of a good unit:

A good unit will contribute to the growth of the child socially, emotionally, intellectually, and spiritually.

A good unit will challenge the child's interests.

[5] Wilhelmina Hill, *Unit Planning and Teaching in Elementary Social Studies* (Washington, D.C.: U.S. Department of Health, Education and Welfare, Office of Education, 1963), p. 18.

A good unit will continue the learning process, and through use of past experiences lead to broader interests.

A good unit will be adapted to the abilities of the child; it will meet individual needs and differences through the use of activities, materials, and oral and written expression.

A good unit will provide opportunities for research, working together, teacher-pupil planning, both group and individual creative expression, and reinforcing basic skills to higher levels.[6]

THE RESOURCE UNIT

Preplanning for the utilization of the unit approach to teaching and learning may include the preparation of resource units or collections of materials and activities that can be helpful in the actual development of subject aims. The suggestions included in a resource unit center around a specific topic, problem, or project that fits into the general outline of the course of study. In their preparation of a resource unit, individual teachers or committees of teachers differ somewhat in the format that they follow.

A comprehensive resource unit can include all or most of the following areas:

    I. Topic or problem

    II. Relation to objectives of the subject and students' interests

    III. Content or appropriate activities

    IV. Research to discover appropriate source material

    V. Developmental approach to the conduct of the unit

    VI. Possible media for evaluating worth of the unit

A well-organized, comprehensive resource unit probably contains much more material than can be utilized with any one class or group of children. For example, a planned resource unit may recommend the use of the following sources: much reading material, many community resources, and various audio-visual aids. A long list of possible learning activities also can be included.

[6] *Ibid.*, p. 31.

The teacher is not expected to employ every suggestion appearing in the outline of the resource unit. He is enabled, however, to select from the wealth of material at his disposal whatever would seem to be best suited for meeting the educational needs, interests, and abilities of a particular group of pupils. The resource unit is flexible. It provides ideas or suggestions upon which the teacher can build his teaching unit.

As a student teacher, you may be asked by your cooperating teacher to carry through a unit in a particular subject area. He may have available a resource unit that he will review with you, helping you to select those sources and activities that would seem best fitted for use with the class.

If your cooperating teacher does not have a resource unit, he and you can prepare one. He may permit you to do most of the work under his supervision. He probably will suggest some sources of materials that are in the school. You may be able to obtain others from books and other materials available in your college. Your college supervisor can be of considerable help to you in your development of the unit.

As an example of the contents of a resource unit, we present the following treatment of a unit in science for the intermediate grades.

A SAMPLE RESOURCE UNIT ON SPACE TRAVEL [7]

INTERMEDIATE GRADES

Generalization:

The universe includes all objects in the vastness of space.

Sub-concept:

Understanding and using the objects in the vastness of space present many problems and challenges to man.

Unit Objective:

To develop understandings about space travel.

[7] W. W. Dick, *Science Guide for Elementary Schools of Arizona* (Phoenix: 1962), pp. 29–31. Reprinted by permission.

I. PROBLEMS MAN FACES IN HIS EXPLORATION OF SPACE

A. *Hazards in Space Travel*

1. What particles from outer space may be dangerous?
2. What radiation from outer space may be dangerous?
3. How does a heat shield protect an astronaut on re-entry?
4. What is atmospheric drag?
5. What are gravitational oceans and sink holes?
6. What is a dyna-soar?

B. *Space Medicine*

1. What is the effect of acceleration and deceleration on the human body?
2. What is the effect of weightlessness on a human being?
3. Why are pressurized space suits and space cabins necessary?
4. How must space vehicles be constructed to insure physical and mental health of the astronaut?
5. What causes dysberism?
6. What causes anoxia?
7. What causes ebulism?
8. What happens to an astronaut's vision in space?
9. What are the problems involved in eating during space flight?

MATERIALS AND INSTRUMENTS FOR SPACE TRAVEL

1. What type of propulsion must be used in exploration of space?
2. What fuels propel rockets?
3. What materials are used in the rocket nose cone?
4. Why is the guidance system so important?
5. How does the escape mechanism work?
6. What factors influence the effectiveness of a rocket engine?
7. What is staging in a rocket?
8. How is re-entry into the earth's atmosphere accomplished?

ASTRONAUTICAL TRAINING FOR SPACE TRAVEL

1. To what stresses must an astronaut be conditioned?
2. What are the requirements for entering the astronautical training program?
3. To what kind of training is an astronaut subjected?

II. ACTIVITIES

A. *Demonstrate*
the principle of inertia (in connection with acceleration and deceleration)

    1. *Materials*
      A heavy book
      A sheet of notebook paper
      Two five-foot lengths of lightweight wrapping twine

    2. *Procedure*
      a. Place the book on the sheet of paper lying on a table.
      b. Pull slowly on the paper.
      c. Give the paper a quick jerk.
      d. With one length of string hang the book in a doorway. Tie the second string to the book and let it dangle.
      e. Pull down slowly on the dangling string until one string breaks.
      f. Repair the broken string and repeat the experiment. This time give the lower string a quick jerk sufficient to break the string.

    3. *Results*
      a. Does the book stay on the paper when the paper is pulled slowly?
      b. Does the book stay on the paper when the paper is jerked quickly?
      c. Which string breaks when the lower string is pulled slowly?
      d. Which string breaks when the lower string is jerked quickly?

B. *Demonstration*
of the principle of rocket propulsion

    1. *Materials*
      Several baseballs
      A pair of roller skates

    2. *Procedure*
      a. Put on the skates and stand on a smooth floor or sidewalk with feet parallel and close together.
      b. Throw one of the balls to a friend who is standing far enough away that you have to throw rather hard to reach him.
      c. Throw the ball still harder.
      d. Have a friend measure the change in your location each time you throw a ball.
      e. Throw several balls in succession.

    3. *Results*
      a. In what direction do you move after throwing the first ball?
      b. In what direction and how far do you move after throwing the second ball?
      c. What happens when you throw several balls in succession?

4. *Conclusions*
Throwing the ball is "action."
What do you observe about "reaction"?

C. *Demonstration*
of effect of color on heating

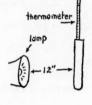

1. *Materials*
Heat lamp
2-Test tubes
2-One-hole stoppers
2-Thermometers
Black paint - white paint

2. *Procedure*
a. Cork each test tube with a one-hole stopper.
b. Place a thermometer in each test tube so that the bulb is inside the tube, but the thermometer can be read outside the test tube.
c. Paint one test tube black, the other white.
d. Expose each test tube to a heat lamp about twelve inches away. Record the temperatures after five minutes.

3. *Result*
Which color absorbed the most heat?

D. *Demonstration*
of propulsion

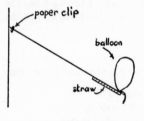

1. *Materials*
Paper clips
Thread
Drinking straw
Plastic tape
Balloon

2. *Procedure*
a. Tie paper clip one foot from end of thread.
b. Measure off fifteen feet of thread.
c. Slide drinking straw onto it and fasten each end to form support. Thread should be fairly tight and level.
d. Inflate balloon and attach it to drinking straw with plastic tape.
e. Let the balloon go.

3. *Result*
What happens to the drinking straw?

E. *Demonstration*
of propulsion

1. *Materials*
Block of balsa wood about 2″ x 2″ x 4″.

Two screw eyes
Carbon dioxide sparklet (available at drugstores)
Thirty to fifty feet of fine wire or nylon fish line
2. *Procedure*
   a. Carve one end of the balsa wood block to a bullet shape.
   b. Bore a hole in the other end just large enough to hold the carbon dioxide cartridge.
   c. Place the screw eyes at either end of the balsa block.
   d. Fasten the wire tightly across the room or in the hall.
   e. Hang the "rocket" so that the wire goes through the screw eyes.
   f. Puncture the CO_2 cartridge detonator and observe the motion of the rocket along the wire (a piece of sponge rubber at the end opposite the starting point will break the impact).
3. *Results*
   a. What happens to the rocket when the capsule is punctured?
   b. Why does the capsule feel so cold?
   c. What is the "action"?
   d. What is the reaction?

III. CONCLUSIONS

Children may develop these or other conclusions:

A. Space holds hazards for space travel such as particles, radiation, atmospheric drag and constant blackness.
B. A space craft must be built to protect the health and life of the astronauts.
C. Fuels must be developed for long space journeys.
D. Special persons are needed to become astronauts.
E. Special training is necessary for astronauts.

IV. EVALUATION

THE CRITERIA for evaluating this unit are in terms of reactions by the students. Were the students interested? Did they voluntarily do research and investigation on their own? Did the interest continue after the unit was completed? Have the students increased their knowledge related to their environment in the space age?

V. ENRICHMENT

A. Read and report orally on these fuels:
   1. Liquid propellants
   2. Bipropellants
   3. Monopropellants

B. Read and discuss books on rockets.
C. Read about and discuss jets.
D. Conduct oral class discussions.
E. Write a biographical paragraph about these men:
    1. Konstantin E. Tscalkovsky
    2. Robert H. Goddard
    3. Herman Oberth
    4. Wernher Von Braun
    5. Col. John Stapp
    6. Scott Crossfield
    7. Alan Shepard
    8. Virgil Grissom
    9. John Glenn
    10. Scott Carpenter
    11. Walter Schirra
    12. and other astronauts
F. Find out when artificial satellites are to be visible in your community. Try to observe them as they pass across the sky.
G. Make a diagram of a spaceship or space station. Include in your plans everything you think will be needed to make it possible for passengers to survive.
H. Report on recent rocket or satellite launchings giving such data as velocity, orbit, size of rocket, and information being gathered.
I. Have students collect pictures related to the unit and post them on the bulletin boards for observation and study.
J. Show any films, filmstrips, or slides available on unit subjects.
K. Try to find guest speakers or resource people.
L. Build model rockets.
M. Make a scrapbook of pictures collected or those drawn by student, newspaper and magazine clippings, and note date and source of each.

VI. GLOSSARY OF SPACE TERMS

Acceleration—The rate of increase of velocity.

Anoxia—Shortage of oxygen.

Apogee—The point at which a planet or another celestial object is farthest from the sun.

Astronaut—Any passenger of a space vehicle.

Astronautics—The science and technology of space flight.

Ballistic missile—One containing preset controls which determine the path.

Bipropellant—A rocket propellant in which both the fuel and the oxidizer are in the liquid state and are stored in separate chambers.

Booster—A propulsion unit used in the initial stage of flight.

Burnout—The cessation of burning in a rocket.

Centrifugal force—The apparent force tending to carry an object away from the center of rotation.

Centripetal force—The apparent force tending to pull an object toward the center.

Circular velocity—The speed required to maintain a body in circular orbit.

Deceleration—Negative acceleration; slowing down.

Dyno-soar—Dynamic soaring by a vehicle that can be controlled by activating wing surfaces after it has re-entered the atmosphere.

Dysberisms—Formation of bubbles in the blood stream when pressure is reduced.

Ebulism—Boiling of body fluids.

Escape velocity—The velocity which if attained by an object will permit it to overcome the gravitational pull of the earth or other astronomical body and to move into space.

Free fall—The motion of an unpowered body traveling in a gravitational field.

Fuel (of a rocket)—The liquid or solid part of the rocket propellant which combines with the oxidizer to produce the gases which propel the rocket.

Grain—The propellant mixture in a solid propellant rocket engine.

Inertia—The property of matter by which it will remain at rest or in uniform motion in the same straight line or direction unless acted upon by some external force.

Ion—An electrically charged atom formed by the loss or gain of one or more electrons without a change in the nucleus.

Ion rocket—One powered by a stream of ions.

Kinetic energy—The energy of motion.

Lunar flight—Space flight around or to the moon.

Mass—The quantity of matter in an object.

Missile—Anything which is propelled, no matter what the propelling force may be.

Monopropellant—A single liquid rocket propellant.

N A S A—National Aeronautics and Space Administration, a U. S. Government agency in charge of the space program.

Orbit—Path of a body relative to its primary.

Orbital velocity—The speed of the body following a closed or open orbit, most commonly applied to elliptical or near circular orbit.

Oxidizer—The liquid or solid part of the rocket's propellant which combines with the fuel to produce the bases which propel the rocket.

Paddles—The surface on space craft on which solar cells are housed.

Payload—Useful cargo.

Perigee—The point at which a moon or satellite in its orbit is closest to its primacy.

Photon—A light particle.

Primary body—The body around which a satellite orbits.

Propellant—A liquid or solid substance burned in a rocket for the purpose of developing thrust.

Retro-rocket—A rocket fitted on or in a vehicle that discharges counter to the direction of flight used to retard forward motion.

Rocket—An engine which can operate in a vacuum because its propellant is not dependent upon the oxygen in the atmosphere for combustion.

Space—That part of the universe between celestial bodies.

Space probe—Any vehicle traveling in space and sending back information.

Specific impulse—It is the amount of thrust derived from each pound of propellant in one second of engine operation. It is much like miles per gallon. A 200 second impulse means one pound of thrust for one pound of propellant for a duration of 200 seconds at sea level.

Supersonic—Beyond the speed of sound.

Telemetering—Technique of recording data associated with some distant event usually by radioing an instrument recording machine on the ground.

Thrust—Amount of push developed by a rocket.

Trajectory—Path described by a missile or space vehicle.

Weightlessness—Lack of resistance to the influence of gravity.

VII. BIBLIOGRAPHY

Adams, Crascib C., *Space Flight*, McGraw-Hill Book Co., New York, N. Y.

Asimov, Isaac, *Breakthrough in Science*, Houghton Mifflin Company, New York, N. Y.

Asimov, Isaac, *The Intelligent Man's Guide to Science*, Volume One. The Physical Sciences, Basic Books Inc., New York, N. Y.

Colly, C. B., *Count Down*, Coward-McCann, Inc., New York, N. Y.

Cox, Donald, *Stations in Space*, Holt, Rinehart and Winston, New York, N. Y.

Leonard, Jonathan N., *Flight Into Space*, Random House, New York, N. Y.

Ross, Frank Jr., *Space Ships and Space Travel*, Lothrop, Lee and Shepard, Inc., New York, N. Y.

Schneider, Herman and Nina, *Science in the Space Age*, D. C. Heath and Company, Boston, Massachusetts.

Trinklein-Huffer, *Modern Space Science*, Holt, Rinehart and Winston, New York, N. Y.

World Book, Vol. 16, Field Enterprises, Chicago, Illinois.

Booklets

Space exploration materials, National Aeronautics and Space Administration, Washington, D. C.

List of Periodicals, Aerospace and Aviation Periodicals for Teachers and Pupils: Circular #556, Revision 1959, U. S. Department of Health, Education and Welfare, Washington 25, D. C.

Specialized books on space flight and related disciplines: General Astronautics, P. O. Box 2151 Grand Central Station, New York 17, N. Y.

Pictures, pamphlets, and packets for airspace education. National Aviation Education Council, 1025 Connecticut Ave., N. W., Washington 6, D. C.

VIII. AUDIO VISUAL AIDS

Films

How We Explore Space, Film Associates of California, Los Angeles, California.
The Human Machine, Moody Institute of Science, Education Film Division, Los Angeles, California.
Man in Space: Man in Flight, Walt Disney Productions, Burbank, California.
First Men Into Space, Encyclopedia Britannica Films, Chicago, Illinois.

Film Strips

Man's Preparation For Space Travel, Jim Handy Organization, Hollywood, Calif.
Man Travels in Space, Eyegate Films, New York, N. Y.
Man In Space, Walt Disney Productions, Burbank, California.
Man In Space, Society For Visual Education, Chicago, Illinois.

You realize that this resource unit includes a tremendous number of possible approaches and activities. Within the time limit allocated to the development of a teaching unit it would be inadvisable, if not impossible, to utilize all or even many of the suggestions offered. The inclusion of all of this material in the resource unit affords the teacher an opportunity to select those approaches and activities that he deems to be best suited in light of the interests of his pupils and the teaching aids available for his use. In fact, the richness of the offerings makes it possible for the teacher to vary his presentation of the topics from term to term or year to year.

In many school communities, groups of teachers of respective subject areas participate in college- or school-sponsored workshops (often during the summer vacation) for the purpose of developing full and challenging resource units based on an appropriate course of study. The resource unit is not static, however. From time to time, it may need to be revised in light of newer subject findings, improved techniques, and the like.

QUESTIONS AND TOPICS FOR DISCUSSION

1. Distinguish among curriculum design, course of study, resource unit.
2. How strictly does your cooperating teacher adhere to a program schedule? Explain the reasons for any deviations you find.

3. List the activities your cooperating teacher has planned for the coming week.
4. State some of the values of unit teaching.
5. While you are a student teacher, plan several subject-area units in order to give you practice.
6. Why should you include more material in a resource unit than you expect to use with any one class?
7. To what extent is it desirable to permit your pupils to participate in unit planning? What might be some of the dangers of having children do too much of the planning?

8

PLANNING THE DAILY LESSON

The planning of an effective lesson is an essential skill of teaching. As a beginning teacher, you probably will find the making of an adequate lesson plan to be a difficult and frustrating experience. Hence during your student-teaching experiences you will need considerable practice in developing daily lesson plans under the guidance of your cooperating teacher and college supervisor.

THE STUDENT TEACHER AND LESSON PLANS

Planning procedures are much more flexible at present than they once were. This in no way detracts from their importance. The teacher needs to know exactly what he hopes to accomplish in a lesson and how he plans to develop the subject material. An experienced teacher may find it sufficient to prepare his written plan in the form of notes or a short outline. Much of his planning is done mentally. It is essential, however, that, as a student teacher, you begin to develop skill in the writing of carefully prepared lesson plans for the meeting of your daily teaching responsibilities.

Observation of Cooperating Teacher in the Utilization of His Plans

You can learn much about lesson planning by observing your cooperating teacher at work and by conferring with him concerning the concomitant aspects of teacher preparation as well as the specific areas of the daily lesson plan. You probably will find that a good teacher not only plans for teaching but also gives careful thought to the management of all of his daily duties. He is prepared for any eventuality that may occur.

If you are a careful observer, you probably will find as you watch and listen to your cooperating teacher and his class at work in any subject area that:

1. There is a purpose to the lesson that is made clear to the pupils.
2. The lesson is conducted step by step in such a way that good learning progress takes place.
3. If a discussion seems to veer away from the topic at hand, the teacher skillfully brings the thinking of the pupils back to the matter under consideration.
4. The lesson ends with a brief summarization of what has been accomplished.
5. An assignment for home study is definite and is given at that point in the lesson when it is most effective.

Your Responsibility in Lesson Planning

You cannot expect to be as proficient as an experienced teacher in conducting a smoothly running lesson. You can develop skill in planning and teaching, however. As you assist your cooperating teacher in conducting lesson procedures, some of your beginning activities in the classroom may be: helping to prepare and distribute materials, proctoring class tests, correcting test papers and recording their results, engaging in remedial work with individual pupils or small groups, and similar activities. After you have become acquainted with the total class situation, you will be given the opportunity to participate in the actual teaching of lessons.

Before you attempt to guide the learning experiences of the children, it is essential that you prepare a well-organized lesson plan. Your cooperating teacher can give you considerable assistance, but the plan itself must be yours. It should be based on your understanding of certain factors that are basic to good lesson planning and should incorporate those elements that have value in determining what shall be included and how teaching-learning experiences should be conducted.

In your college classes you probably have discussed lesson plans and perhaps have written some as a class exercise. You have seen some of your cooperating teacher's plans. As we suggested earlier in the chapter, you have observed this teacher put his plans into operation. All of these activities are helpful in that they acquaint you with fundamentals of lesson planning. They are only preparatory, however. No one of them is a substitute for the actual writing of a plan of procedure that you yourself will use as a guide toward stimulating pupil learning in the classroom.

Young people are quick to recognize whether you are well prepared for the day's lesson. Any hesitation on your part in getting started, any fumbling for materials, and the like, will cause them to give their attention to irrelevant matters. You have lost them, and may find it difficult to regain their attention. Hence there are various factors that need to be considered as you prepare your daily lesson plan.

Important Considerations

A specific lesson must fit into a sequential pattern of development. Rarely can you afford to have a lesson stand alone, unrelated to what precedes it or what will follow. As you plan a lesson, you need to review the material covered in the last lesson, decide what you expect to do in this lesson, and think ahead to what should be incorporated in the next lesson.

The inexperienced teacher usually has difficulty in adjusting his lesson plan to the rigid requirements of the time element. Either he has included so much in his plan that the time to be devoted to it has passed before he can complete half of what he expected to cover, or he has finished the lesson and has extra time that must be filled. The former situation is likely to occur more often than the latter. You are encouraged to prepare a *full* plan, but during the lesson period caring for extraneous matters such as reading notices, clarifying a special point in the lesson, and other unavoidable delays interfere with the smooth progress of the lesson.

Your lesson plan should be so clearly outlined that you are aware of the important points that must be considered and realize that certain details, worthwhile as they seem to you, may need to be omitted or given only passing recognition. You need to budget your material to meet your time allocation. As you gain in experience, you will achieve skill in budgeting your time in light of the activities to be included in the lesson.

THE COMPONENTS OF A LESSON PLAN

After you consider some of the important factors inherent in lesson planning, your next question is "What should be included in the plan itself?" The form of the lesson plan varies with teachers or schools. Your college supervisor probably has suggested a form that he favors. Your cooperating teacher may use another form. Eventually, you will decide for yourself the kind of plan that best meets your purposes. The following plan covers, in a general way, the various aspects of a lesson that you need to consider as you prepare to teach it:

A Lesson Plan

Subject   Date
School Grade
   Aim or Purpose
   Content
   Motivation or Introductory Approach
   Development or Procedures
     Activities
     Budgeting of Time
     Supplementary Materials
     Pivotal Questions
     Assignment
     Summary
     Evaluation or Comments

Aim or Purpose in a Lesson Plan

Aim or purpose is an extremely important aspect of the lesson plan. Your first consideration is to decide *why* you are planning to teach this lesson. How do you expect the pupils to benefit from it? In what ways does the purpose or aim of this lesson fit into the recognized objectives of the course of study?

State your aim simply and briefly. Here are a few examples of aims:

1. To create an interest in letter writing

2. To teach children how to read and interpret maps, globes, and charts

3. To develop basic economic understandings

4. To understand climate and climatic changes

5. To teach multiplication of numbers with two digits in the multiplier

Content in the Lesson Plan

It is not enough to have a definite, clearly stated aim or purpose for your lesson. You need also to include in your plan the subject matter upon which you expect to focus in your purpose in teaching the lesson.

In some plans, the content is included under the caption "materials." What is included in the content or material depends on the kind of lesson you are teaching. If your aim is to develop skill in changing common fractions to decimal fractions, it would be well to decide ahead of time the fractions that are to be changed and include these in your plan.

In dealing with a subject such as science, you should set down in your plan the subtopics that you expect to include. These should be arranged in logical or psychological order. For example:

Aim: To show how water gets into the air

Content: 1. Moisture in the air comes from puddles, lakes, rivers, oceans, etc., through evaporation
2. The rate of evaporation depends on:
   a. The temperature of the air
   b. The amount of moisture in the air
   c. The movement of the air

Motivation of the Lesson

You have learned from your own experiences and probably have often heard in your college education classes that interest is a prime motivator of activity. When interest is aroused in a project or situation, the learner tends to stay with it as long as his initial interest continues to function. This is a well-known psychological principle that applies to the teaching-learning process. Hence, as you plan each lesson, you need to consider ways in which you can "catch" your pupils' interest in the content of the lesson, so as to help them utilize their experiences in their struggle toward its mastery.

In planning your approach to a lesson, you must consider the present interests of your pupils (but you also should keep in mind the specific aims of your lesson and the amount of time available for its coverage). One motivating technique is to start the lesson by asking a challenging question that will encompass the material and be closely related to current child interest. Your task in motivating learners is to steer the discussion from pupils' responses to your question to the actual material of the lesson. The children may become so interested in discussing the question raised, however, that the inexperienced teacher finds it almost impossible to make the transition from the initial motivating effort to the consideration of lesson content.

Assume, for example, that your aim is to have your pupils learn about the responsibilities of citizens in a democracy. Most children like to take some responsibility for home management. Hence you might start the lesson with "How do you think you could best help your mother?" "Why?" These questions probably will lead to an animated discussion among the children concerning their special jobs in the home and the relative value of their activities.

How long shall you allow a discussion to continue? How well you go about transferring their attention to the broader concept of citizen responsibilities and yet maintain their interest is an important criterion. To do this successfully may require considerable teacher ingenuity.

A common mistake of an inexperienced teacher is to use motivation as a kind of "gimmick" to arouse pupil interest. As soon as the pupils are interested, he delves into the lesson with no further reference to the interest-arousing approach. In such cases, children are likely to fall into a kind of lethargy, showing little or no interest in what the teacher is trying to do. They experience a feeling of being "let down." To serve as a stimulator of learning progress, interest must not only be aroused, it must also be sustained and maintained throughout the conduct of the entire lesson.

Degree of pupil interest in learning depends on the presence of various factors. It is relatively easy to motivate children in those lessons that constitute progressive steps in the development of a unit of study in the planning of which they have participated. They are interested in seeing the project through to its conclusion. The extent to which individually, or in groups, they can share in its developmental activities predicates their continued interest in it.

Degree of maturity is also a factor of a pupil's interest in learning. It may be more difficult to encourage an upper-grade pupil to participate in learning activities than it is a young child. The preadolescent is concerned with himself and his present environment. He needs to be shown that what he is studying is associated with his current interests, ambitions, and activities. The child in the early grades enjoys activity for its own sake. His attention span is short, however. Hence his interest in a particular learning area wanes unless you change activities often.

Because of his more mature point of view, the older pupil is better able to project himself into the future and to recognize the possible value to himself of his formal learning experiences than is the younger child. Yet, regardless of the children's background of experience and degree of maturity, each lesson in a series of developmental steps needs to be so introduced and conducted that the learner regards it as a vital and stimulating learning experience.

The motivation of pupils in a lesson can take various forms. We have referred to the asking of a challenging question. In the upper grades the teacher can read, or have a pupil read, a brief, pertinent excerpt from a recent newspaper or a current magazine. A pupil may have been asked to prepare and read to the class a short report on a current incident or condition that refers directly to the subject of the lesson. The teacher or a pupil can present a simple and appropriate demonstration. An interesting picture or diagram, or a short film related to the subject matter, can be shown and discussed briefly.

Some teachers, in the upper grades, especially, occasionally administer a short objective review quiz that the pupils correct on the spot. The discussion of errors, if held to a minimum, can serve as the starting point of the day's lesson. An ingenious teacher can think of many ways to focus pupil interest on the lesson. Whatever technique he employs, his introductory motivation:

1. Should be geared to the experiences and current interests of the pupils.
2. Should lend itself to easy application to the content of the lesson.
3. Should not be accorded an undue amount of class time.

The Lesson Activities

A lesson devoted entirely to the question-answer technique is likely to induce daydreaming or the giving of attention to extraneous matters on the part of some pupils. There are times, of course, when a likely discussion of a topic of common interest is in order. You may have observed your cooperating teacher conduct just such a lesson. You probably noticed, however, that not all of the questions were propounded by the teacher. Pupil enthusiasm ran high; children asked questions of one another or disagreed among themselves. Part of the discussion may have taken on something of the nature of an informal debate. The skillful teacher encourages this kind of pupil participation. He is careful to lead the discussion in such a way that it does not become rambling or stray too far afield.

You can plan to include various types of activities in the conduct of the lesson. Some of these activities are:

1. Oral reports by individual pupils or by committees
2. Demonstrations by teacher or pupils
3. Reading aloud of pertinent material by the teacher or by children who read well
4. A short debate
5. Examination of illustrative material on bulletin board, etc.
6. Role playing or dramatization
7. Viewing of slides or short motion pictures
8. Radio listening or televiewing
9. Panel discussions
10. Construction of projects
11. Consulting reference material
12. Discussion of errors in a test previously taken by the children

13. Review drill
14. Supervised study

You probably can think of other activities that are appropriate to teaching-learning experiences. Whatever type of activity you select must be adapted to the maturity level of the group. Of course, we are not suggesting that you attempt to utilize all or even many of the foregoing types of activities in any one lesson. You may be surprised, however, to discover the extent to which you can vary the work of a lesson so that the interest of all the members of the class can be aroused and sustained.

The Budgeting of Class Time

Little need be said about the importance of budgeting time. As you list the activities that you expect to carry out during a day's work, note the approximate amount of time in minutes that should be devoted to each. Try not to depart from your schedule. Allocate some time to matters that deal with classroom management, but organize these matters in such a way that they can be executed efficaciously.

Arrange any materials to be distributed so that pupils can pass them out quickly. Keep your chalkboards clean and ready for use. Read important notices when requested. Do not discuss irrelevant matters with individual pupils during a school session. Maintain a businesslike attitude toward routine duties.

Preparation of Pivotal Questions

During the course of a lesson, you may need to ask many and varied questions that grow out of the activities being conducted. For example, after a pupil presents a report, you may need to ask a question in order to have him clarify some of the points of the report. Such questions usually cannot be formulated ahead of time. Hence it would be foolish for you to try to predict all of the questions that you probably will raise and to incorporate them in your plan.

You will find it helpful to include in your plan a short list of significant or pivotal questions arranged in sequential order. The content of the lesson revolves around these questions. Regardless of the various activities of the lesson, these pivotal questions should be included at such time and in such form that they will challenge the children to engage in reflective thinking as they discuss relationships and arrive at conclusions.

Inexperienced teachers often have difficulty in the formulation of thought-provoking questions. The "Yes" or "No" question should be avoided. For example, a fifth-grade class is reading *"Music on the Mississippi"* (Trails to Treasure). The question "Do you like Pete?" does not ask the children what they really think about Pete. Better questions would be "Why do you like or dislike Pete?" "What kind of a boy do you think Pete was?"

Questions dealing with facts sometimes are necessary, yet they tend to emphasize mastery of subject matter rather than critical thinking. Both content-oriented and thought questions may be included among pivotal questions. Note the following sets of questions.

1. Explain what is meant by habit.
   How important are motivation and practice in habit formation?
   What are desirable study habits?
   Why should you develop good study habits?
2. Explain how the colonies gained their independence.
   What were some of the reasons for the colonists' deciding to revolt against England?
   Why is the Fourth of July called Independence Day?
   What was the Declaration of Independence?
   What principles of the Declaration of Independence still hold true?
   Who were some of the heroes of the Revolutionary War?
3. Discuss foods and eating practices.
   Why should sweets be eaten in small amounts?
   What is a good lunch for a growing child?
   Why should a person rinse his mouth after meals?
   How is the eating of good food associated with growth and health?

As you were reading and thinking through the foregoing sets of questions, what were your conclusions about their value as pivotal questions? What might be the implied aims of the respective lessons? How clearly stated are the questions?

Value of Providing Supplementary Material

You may want to use various kinds of source material in order to illustrate or emphasize significant points of the lesson or to present additional information. Included among such materials could be: motion picture films; slide projectors; tape recorders; articles from newspapers, magazines, or reference books; charts, maps, or pictures; materials for an experiment; or any other form of resource material that can arouse pupil interest or help clarify subject content.

The utilization of resource material should not be a haphazard undertaking. Whatever is to be utilized during the presentation of a lesson should be prepared ahead of time for ready reference when needed. If you plan to use a story to illustrate a point, be sure that you are sufficiently acquainted with the story to tell it without hesitation and in such a way that it holds the interest of the pupils. Make certain that you can operate audio-visual machines correctly. If you plan an experiment, have all the needed materials available and follow the steps of the experiment accurately.

Care must be taken that all pupils can see any samples of visual material. Pupils also must be led to understand the relationship of source material to the subject of the lesson. If you have sufficient copies of the material for individual study, have them so arranged that they can be distributed quickly and efficiently. Use of the chalkboard by teacher or pupils for outlining points in the lesson, drawing diagrams, and the like also can be a valuable learning aid. Remember, however, that the utilization of supplementary aids has for its purpose the *helping* of children to improve their learning. Hence you must avoid devoting an undue amount of time to their presentation, lest consideration of them becomes an end rather than a means to an end.

Another important point concerning supplementary materials is that they should be collected and stored for future use. Materials used in an experiment are not always carefully cleaned and put into their proper cabinets. Teachers and pupils sometimes are careless about returning materials borrowed from the library. Excerpts from newspapers and magazines may become mixed with a teacher's or a pupil's other papers. A good plan is for the teacher to keep a working file of pertinent materials in which he replaces material when he has finished with it.

The Assignment of Homework

School people vary in their attitude toward homework for elementary school children. For some time there was a trend toward banning any homework, especially in the early grades. The trend now is toward requiring in all grades an appropriate kind and amount of study outside regular class sessions. Recently, New York City announced a new policy toward the kind, extent, and supervision of homework, including the responsibility of parents to cooperate with the school in making homework effective.

The stated purpose of homework is "to extend and reinforce learnings and to develop the sense of self-discipline, personal responsibility, and independent thinking." Homework should be given daily and checked and returned by the teacher. It should be related to classroom instruction; it should be definite and clear and adapted to children's needs, interests, and abilities. The time allotment for homework assignment is as follows:

Grade 1—about fifteen minutes

Grades 2–3–4—about twenty-five minutes

Grades 5–6—approximately forty-five minutes

A question often asked by a beginning teacher is "What assignment should I make?" Methods of assigning work for home study differ among teachers. Fortunately, relatively few elementary school teachers continue to assign "the next ten pages in the textbook." More appropriate and effective approaches are employed. Problems to be solved, pertinent questions to be answered, reports to be written, diagrams or charts to be constructed are among the many forms that the assignment may take.

To be effective, an assignment should motivate the interest of the pupil in continued learning. It is a part of teaching and serves as a transition from one lesson to the next. It never should be regarded as mere busywork. Whatever is included in the assignment should constitute a significant aspect of the total learning experience.

The assignment should be clearly and carefully explained so that every child clearly understands what he should do. If the class contains students of widely differing abilities and interests, appropriate assignments can be made on an ability and interest basis rather than assigning the same task to the entire class. The assignment becomes a challenge when it has meaning for the pupil and is within his limits of performance.

Consideration should be given to the time for making an assignment. It perhaps should be made at that point in a lesson where it seems best fitted. You should take care, however, that you leave sufficient time for its presentation and that whatever preparation is needed for it is done carefully. At times, the assignment can be a joint effort of teacher and pupils. In light of what has transpired during the lesson, the pupils themselves suggest further work that can be done outside the classroom. This is especially applicable when a lesson represents a teacher-and-pupil planned unit of study.

Teachers of upper grades who require their pupils to consult a public library about material for a homework assignment need to be careful in the use of the procedure. Too many teachers assign reference work to be done in the library without making certain that (1) the reference material is available and (2) the assignment is definite enough so that the pupil can find the material by using the card catalog without unduly involving the librarian. If you plan to send your pupils to the library for needed materials, first visit the library yourself to discover whether the material is available and where it is. Then be exact in your directives to the pupils concerning its location in the library and its use.

The Summarization of the Lesson

A successful lesson ends with a summarization of the points covered. As you prepare your lesson plan, review your stated purpose and decide whether you have developed that aim in the listed procedures. Then, in class, summarize what has been done.

A good summarization usually is brief. Perhaps, it may be no more than asking the class a question such as "What have we tried to do today?" "What have you learned in this lesson?" or "How has today's lesson helped you to _____?" Another possible approach to the summarization is for you to list on the chalkboard words or short phrases that cover the day's work with the comment "This is what we have done today. In our next lesson we shall try to _____." This might be a good point at which to introduce the next assignment, provided you have left sufficient time for its explanation. Your pupils' displayed attitude toward the summarization can give you an idea concerning the value to them of the lesson's activities.

Evaluation of the Lesson

You will find after you have taught a lesson that you have ambivalent feelings toward what happened during it. You may conclude mentally that some aspects of it were worthwhile but that, in some respects, you failed to accomplish what you had planned. At the end of the lesson, make appropriate evaluative comments of the lesson on your lesson plan. Include any reactions you may have received from the pupils, either expressed or implied. This is a useful habit to develop.

An honest evaluation of your performance, both in planning and in execution, can help you improve your worth as a teacher. As you gain in experience, you probably will find that you become your own most severe critic. This should not discourage you, however. A master teacher, no matter how long he has been in the profession, constantly discovers new ways in which he can approach teaching-learning situations and improve his practices and techniques.

A WORD OF CAUTION TO THE STUDENT TEACHER

A final word of caution to you as a student teacher may not be amiss. You probably are extremely interested in gaining experience in lesson planning and teaching. You are eager to "try your wings." You may be particularly enthusiastic about teaching elementary school children. You have developed a "feeling" about the way in which a lesson can be best planned and presented.

These are fine attitudes and probably indicate that you have the makings of an excellent teacher. You must keep in mind, however, that you are working with a cooperating teacher who is responsible for the learning progress of his pupils. The class is his, not yours. Consequently, it is your responsibility to follow his lead. For the duration of your student-teaching responsibilities, your lesson plans should be patterned after his. When you are permitted to teach, you must fit your lesson into his general organization. Your cooperating teacher may be willing for you to undertake the conduct of a unit of work that is of especial interest to you. You might ask him for the opportunity to do so; do not press the issue, however.

Be careful that you do not disrupt your cooperating teacher's established routines, even though you believe that your handling of them might be superior to his. Also, discourage any attempts on the part of pupils to make comparisons between your attitudes and activities and those of your cooperating teacher, especially if these comments seem to favor you.

QUESTIONS AND TOPICS FOR DISCUSSION

1. What is the value to you of observing and assisting your cooperating teacher before you begin your actual teaching experiences? Be specific.
2. Before you actually teach a lesson, ask your college supervisor to critically evaluate your prepared lesson plan.
3. If you have planned and taught a lesson, what difficulties did you encounter?
4. Select a lesson that you expect to teach. What will you do to arouse your pupils' interest? How much time do you plan to devote to the motivation?
5. In what aspects of your lesson can you expect pupils to be interested? Why?
6. Which of the various types of activities in the conduct of a lesson as listed in this chapter do you find to be most productive of pupil learning? Which of them do you employ?
7. As you are observing your cooperating teacher conduct a lesson, make note of his questions. How effective were they?
8. When and how does your cooperating teacher make homework assignments? Critically evaluate his procedure.
9. Why is it advisable to end a lesson with a summarization of what has taken place during the period?
10. Why should you follow the lead of your cooperating teacher in lesson planning? Be specific.

LEARNING NEEDS AND TEACHING APPROACHES

An important area of teacher education is to acquaint you with various teaching approaches that can serve as effective means of stimulating successful pupil learning. Hence, in your college classes, you probably have considered both teaching methods in general and those techniques that are appropriate for the guidance of learning in the elementary school. Here we are reviewing some of the teaching approaches to which you should give your attention as you plan the activities to be included in classroom procedures.

THE LEARNING NEEDS OF CHILDREN

Much of a young person's learning (perhaps more than we realize) is acquired informally. As he associates with other people, he tends to imitate their behavior. As he encounters new environmental situations, he attempts to adjust to them by various trial-error-trial-success activities. He constantly is engaging in one or another form of adaptive behavior. To leave the child to his own devices in the learning process would be a long and costly series of experiences, however. During his early developmental years, he might well acquire habits and attitudes that later would need to be revised in light of societal standards of correct behavior in the many aspects of individual participation in communal affairs.

Formal education, as exemplified by the many teacher-guided learning activities conducted in our schools, has for its purpose the acquisition by each learner of those competencies that have positive value in charting the course of his life pattern. Yet, unless an individual child is motivated to profit adequately from whatever instruction is provided for him, he achieves little that has value from his supposed participation in learning experiences. It is the teacher's function to utilize those teaching approaches that serve best to meet the learning needs of his pupils. Each pupil is expected, as a result of his schooling, to acquire appropriate knowledge, improve needed skills, and develop those attitudes, appreciations, and standards of behavior that, through their application, will benefit both himself and other people.

The Acquiring of Knowledge

The elementary school child needs to master a body of basic information about himself and the world about him that not only will be of current value to him as a developing individual but also will serve as the foundation upon which he can build further knowledge. Some items of information, such as correct spelling, certain health and safety rules, number combinations, significant historic dates and geographic locations, and simple scientific principles, are not matters of opinion. They need to be learned so thoroughly that they become a part of the child's habit pattern, ready for immediate recall. He needs to understand their significance and recognize their importance to himself.

In addition to *verbatim* memorization, the elementary school child engages in conceptual learning. From kindergarten on, he gradually develops a wealth of ideas concerning people, things, and relationships. Unless his thinking is well guided, he is likely to acquire misinformation rather than gain correct knowledge.

It is the teacher's responsibility to present informational material so that a pupil acquires accurate and clear concepts rather than merely memorizing words that possess little or no meaning for him. The child also should be aided in applying concepts to new situations. The body of knowledge acquired should have understandable application to the pupil's present and future life experiences.

We know that children differ in their ability to comprehend ideas. Because of a good experiential background and/or a superior intelligence level, some children can "grasp the point" much more quickly and easily than can their less favored classmates. Hence as you prepare your lesson plans in subjects such as the social studies and science, for example, make certain that you give thought to the individual differences among your pupils. This is a difficult task. You must be careful not to "talk down" to the brighter pupils; they thrive on meeting challenging learning situations. At the same time, you should not expect too much from less able children. If the class represents a heterogeneous group, try to fit your learning requirements to individual ability to perform successfully. For example, you can gear homework assignments and participation in class projects and the like to the differing needs, interests, and abilities among your pupils.

The Development of Skills

By the time a child is graduated from elementary school he has developed many different skills. He has acquired some of them with little or no awareness of the manner in which they have been developed; his mastery of others represents consciously engaged in learning activities. Every elementary teacher is responsible for guiding children's development of skill in learning areas such as arithmetic fundamentals, reading, listening, oral and written composition, penmanship, and the manipulation of appropriate materials.

Children must learn to express their thoughts, either orally or in writing, clearly, definitely, and in well-organized form. They should develop the habit of listening attentively to what other people say so that they comprehend what they hear. As important, if not more so, is their gaining of skill in the interpretation of the written word. In your college classes you probably have considered the various teaching approaches to be used in skill learning. Hence, at this point, we shall briefly call attention to some of the basic factors involved, excepting reading. So many children seem to have difficulty in developing skill in reading that we shall give attention to some of the specific difficulties experienced by children.

Factors in the development of a skill. As you help a child learn a skill you need to recognize his degree of maturational readiness to develop it, his attitude toward it, and the extent to which he is mentally and physically able to achieve adequate performance in it. You probably have developed so high a degree of proficiency in the skills you are planning to teach that you have forgotten your first fumbling attempts to master them.

You spell words and punctuate sentences as a matter of habit. Your penmanship is relatively legible. You can read with understanding. Unless you are careless, you handle number combinations correctly. In other words, as a teacher, you must understand the learning needs of your pupils at whatever stage of skill development they may be and proceed from that point toward improving their efficiency.

From the beginning of his mastery of a skill, a child should know what he is trying to accomplish. He is likely to progress more successfully in his learning if he understands and is helped to apply simple underlying principles to performance. For example, a boy who wants to play baseball learns to know the fundamentals of the game and a proper stance for batting. By the time a child reaches the fifth grade he probably has learned that good paragraph construction is based on the following of a format that includes a statement of the topic of the paragraph, details, and concluding statement.

You know that interest is a strong motivator of achievement. Interest in practice to improve a skill usually does not start suddenly, but is likely to be an accompaniment of active participation in the learning from the beginning. To arouse and maintain this kind of interest among your pupils may be one of your most difficult problems. In the introduction of skill learning, as in all other forms of learning, you need to stimulate the imagination of the children so that they can recognize the value of the learning experience to them. Each step of evidenced progress then is likely to be accompanied by feelings of pleasure in accomplishment and a desire to perform better. Some programmed learning machines help arouse and sustain interest in learning.

It is helpful for you to give evidence of your own interest in the skill you are attempting to teach and of the satisfaction you obtain from performing it. Your success can be measured by the extent to which you imbue your pupils with some of your own enthusiasm. Moreover, you must take care that (1) you do not expect too much from beginners, (2) you recognize their difficulties and are able and willing to help them overcome errors, (3) you are liberal with commendatory comments when these are deserved, and chary with discouraging remarks, (4) you encourage consistency in practice, and (5) you vary practice sessions in such a way that they do not become unduly routinized and boring.

Developing Skill in Reading

No one can question the thesis that much of an individual's successful achievement in most learning areas is determined by the effectiveness of the skill in reading that he develops during the early elementary school years. Unfortunately, too many secondary school and even college students are inadequate readers. Throughout the country, elementary school people are striving to find ways in which they can improve reading instruction. The Elementary Division of the New York City School System has developed an action program for the teaching of reading based on a set of objectives, the first of which has to do with *The Continuous Upgrading of the Teaching of Reading*. This objective is divided as follows:

OBJECTIVE ONE: THE CONTINUOUS UPGRADING OF THE TEACHING OF READING [1]

A. Develop a Lifetime Habit of Reading

Select material that will provide the pupil with lifelong cultural resources and interests, and provide frequent opportunities for pupils to exercise free choice of reading materials.

Raise the literary taste of pupils. Expand the child's literary heritage by introducing some of the appropriate classics. Choose from among stories, poems, myths, and legends selections appropriate to the children's maturity, interests, and abilities and which appeal to boys as well as to girls.

Strive for depth in interpretation of what is read so that the pupil may have vicarious experiences that will enrich his life and open broader horizons.

Extend the library program to encompass acquaintance with many different forms of literary expression.

Use literary works as a means of increasing vocabulary and enhancing appreciation of figures of speech and language rhythm.

B. Extend and Refine the Teaching of Functional Reading as Applied to the Content Areas

Give instruction in specialized types of reading involved in each content area.

[1] Reprinted from *Teaching 600,000 'Johnny's' to Read* by permission of the Board of Education of the City of New York, 1962, p. 26.

Teach the specific reading abilities needed for any content area when that area is being studied.

Encourage children to use the variety of reading materials related to the various content areas.

C. Sustain the Gains Made in the Upgrading of Reading Through the Improvement of the Reading Skills

Analyze the skills needed by each child in terms of an accepted list of such skills.

Include appropriate emphasis on phonics as one of the important basic word-attack skills.

Continue the teaching of reading skills *in all grades* in relation to individual and class needs.

Develop mastery of the reading skills by first teaching the skill and then providing the necessary practice in that skill.

D. Relate Reading to Other Phases of the Language Arts

Relate the upgrading of reading to improvement of spelling, creative writing, functional writing, handwriting, etc.

Relate the upgrading of reading to improvement in listening and speaking. Good enunciation, pronunciation, fine rhythmic speech patterns, and precision of communication are also basic to upgrading reading; these must be transmitted in part by the teacher through example, as well as precept. A child reads better the word he understands, the word he hears spoken correctly, the word he speaks correctly, the word he writes correctly.

Children differ in their ability to develop reading skill. By the time they reach the middle elementary grades some are one or more grades advanced according to standardized reading tests; some are very much retarded. Various interrelated factors can cause a reading lag. The child may have low mental ability and/or be a slow maturer. Poor eyesight or hearing also may interfere with a child's learning to read; he cannot see the letters of a word correctly or hear sound combinations properly. He may be the product of a culturally disadvantaged home or of a home in which a foreign language is used exclusively. Hence the child lacks sufficient impetus to learn to read. The situation is worsened if the child changes schools while he is in the primary grades. The teacher needs to discover the probable cause of a child's inadequate progress in learning to read.

Introducing children to the development of reading skill requires considerable training and much patience on the part of teachers.

There has been some controversy among psychologists and educators concerning the relative merits of the word method as opposed to the phonics approach. In an increasing number of schools both techniques are employed. The plan followed in Kansas City, Missouri, for the first grade illustrates this combination.

KANSAS CITY MISSOURI PUBLIC SCHOOLS
DEPARTMENT OF ELEMENTARY EDUCATION [2]

READING SKILLS INTRODUCED IN GRADE ONE

I. Phonetic Analysis

　1. *Rhyme*
　　—Visual-auditory perception
　2. *Consonants*
　　—Visual-auditory perception of initial consonants, ch, sh, th, and wh.
　　—Visual-auditory perception of final consonants.
　　—Silent consonant letters.
　　—Substitution of initial and final consonants in attacking new words.

II. Structural Analysis

　1. Recognizing words formed by adding s, 's, d, ed, ing to known root words.

III. Basic Interpretation Skills

　1. Interpreting the main idea.
　2. Recognizing emotional reactions and motives of story characters.
　3. Making inferences; interpreting ideas implied but not directly stated or pictured.
　4. Comprehending phrase and sentence meaning.
　5. Forming and reacting to sensory images (visual, auditory, kinesthetic, touch, taste, smell).
　6. Anticipating outcomes.
　7. Making judgments and drawing conclusions.
　8. Generalizing.
　9. Perceiving relationships, association through (use, class, general specific, part-whole, place or space sequence, cause and effect, time).

[2] "Reading Skills Introduced in Grade One," from *Suggestions to Teachers* (Kansas City, Mo.: Board of Education). Reprinted by permission.

10. Strengthening memory based on (observation, association, visual imagery, auditory imagery, logical relationships).
11. Summarizing and organizing ideas for the purpose of remembering.

The children of a heterogeneously organized class probably will differ widely in their ability to develop adequate reading skill. In such a situation the formation of reading groups is desirable. From cumulative record cards and the results of diagnostic tests in reading the teacher determines the reading status of each child, and then may form three reading groups according to ability level—top, middle, low.

You probably have discovered the reading group plan. It is customary to set up work for the first two groups that can be done independently, and then to work with the slow group—checking the previous assignment, developing new material, having the members of the group read silently or orally, and giving them a writing assignment on the developed materials. While this group is working independently, the teacher works with the middle and top groups.

You may find that trying to teach some children to read can become a frustrating experience. You need to have considerable ingenuity as you attempt to overcome the reading handicaps that are exhibited by some of your pupils. Yet, developing adequate skill in this area is possibly the most important phase of elementary education. The recognition of this fact has caused many schools and school systems to provide specially trained reading experts to work with those children who have severe reading difficulties.

The Development of Creativity

Young people tend to want to do things in ways that differ from accustomed routines. They constantly are seeking new approaches to the meeting of situations that are likely to arise in day-by-day activities. Most children have the urge to create. The success of their endeavors differs, of course, with their degree of creative talent.

As a teacher, you can utilize this characteristic. However, you may not always recognize the opportunities that are available to you in this area of learning motivation. Some subjects seem to lend themselves more easily than others to the development of creative expression. The teacher of a subject such as music, the dance, pictorial reproduction, imaginative writing, or science can encourage a talented child to achieve well in a special field. Even the child with mediocre artistic ability can be helped to produce something that is somewhat new and different.

The ability to create is not limited to children who have superior intelligence or who are especially mature for their age. Hence the teacher needs to be constantly on the alert for the expression of creativity by any member of the class. He recognizes what the pupils are trying to do and appreciates their potentialities. He realizes that effective creative expression must be built on a solid background of appropriate knowledge and skill, and he sees to it that his pupils acquire and maintain these as they go about producing the relatively new and different. In other words, the extent to which children adapt their creative potential to learning procedures depends in good part on the leadership of a sensitive, perceptive, and creative teacher.

The Maintaining of High Standards of Workmanship

The building of high standards of workmanship is among the most significant learning needs of children. The influence upon a child of the standards of those with whom he associates is all-pervasive. The child tends to imitate, either consciously or unconsciously, the effectiveness of older people whom he holds in high regard. At times, he is confused by differences he observes among the standards of individuals who are supposed to serve him as models to be followed. Eventually, in light of his experiences he sets personal standards of workmanship that influence his activities.

If you are satisfied with half-learned lessons, accept sloppily prepared papers, or condone lack of promptness in meeting obligations, you are not encouraging your pupils to achieve high ideals of workmanship. To the extent that you are careless about the management of class routines, come to school only partially prepared for meeting the class, or in other ways give evidence of low standards of efficiency, you are not a worthy model to be imitated.

You cannot expect perfection to be achieved suddenly by your pupils, but anything that is worth learning is worth learning correctly. Informational material must be accurate. Each step in the development of a skill should be performed correctly before the next step is attempted. One cannot build desirable work habits on a foundation of errors, or partially mastered learning experiences. Hence, in any area of study, constructive practice is needed to help learners attain high standards of workmanship that can be expected to carry over into their many areas of life activities.

TEACHING TECHNIQUES

Earlier, we referred to some of the activities you might include in your lesson plan that could serve as ways to achieve the objectives of your lesson. By so doing, you were noting teaching techniques that might be appropriate to the development of your lesson planning. There are various methods that can be used in teaching-learning situations. You need to know what these techniques are, how they operate, and to what extent each of them has value in helping you achieve your specific lesson goals.

The purpose of a particular lesson may be to increase your pupils' knowledge in a field of learning, improve their functioning of a skill, bring about changes in their attitudes, appreciations, or any combination of these. Your approach to the lesson will be the one that (1) seems best suited to its purpose, (2) takes into account the pupils' interests, abilities, and readiness for the learning, and (3) is suited to your particular teaching skills.

As you plan the various activities to be included in a lesson, you need to remember that your function is to guide the learning of your pupils. They make any changes that take place within themselves. It is a psychologically proven principle that one learns best by doing. Hence, whatever teaching techniques you employ, you need to involve your pupils mentally and physically in the learning experiences. We now shall review briefly various teaching techniques and the extent to which your pupils can be involved in the process.

Adaptation of the Lecture Method (Telling)

The lecture method as such is rarely if ever appropriate for use in the elementary school. There are occasions when "telling" by the teacher or a pupil has educational value.

Telling by the teacher. At times telling is needed. You are introducing a new topic of study. There may be certain background material that the children should have to prepare them for further study. You can acquaint them quickly and succinctly with those aspects of the material that can increase their understanding of what lies ahead. Or, the pupils might raise a question that should receive immediate attention if the lesson is to run along smoothly. It might be more advisable to talk briefly on the topic rather than to have the pupils themselves search for the answer.

To give a stimulating talk is not an easy task. Its content must be appropriate to the subject of study. It must be well organized and presented in an interesting attention-holding manner, since the attention span of elementary school children is relatively short. Hence you need to vary your talk by utilizing interest-arousing aids. You can use illustrative material, such as pictures or models. As you talk, you can place on the chalkboard, in outline form, the important points included in the talk. Another good device is to raise a few questions for the pupils to consider. You then can answer these questions and intersperse your talk with a few simple questions that can be answered easily and promptly. Give the pupils an opportunity to raise questions about those points that may not be understood by them. You can sustain pupils' interest in your talk by providing opportunities for them to participate.

Telling by pupils. Children enjoy sharing their experiences with adults and other children. You will find that many members of the class are eager to tell you and their classmates about a trip they have taken, a pet they own, a new baby in the home, and the like. You can utilize this childhood interest as the basis for training in oral composition by setting aside a period in the daily schedule during which the pupils are encouraged to talk on topics of common interest to the class as a whole. You must be careful, however, that you do not overlook some of the more timid children who are not so willing to talk about themselves as are their more aggressive, outgoing classmates.

A form of telling by pupils that is employed by many teachers is the "show-and-tell" technique. On specified days, individual children bring to class from home an object of interest that is exhibited and talked about by the child who brings it. This technique needs to be handled cautiously, however. The activity should be limited to the showing of simple objects that can be found in most homes. Your giving of special commendation to the child who brings something that is unusual or valuable may give rise to an unhealthful situation of which you may not be aware.

Children are competitive. In order to impress you and the class, a child may be tempted to take from the home a valuable object without parental knowledge or approval. Another child who believes he cannot compete with his classmates in the showing of interesting articles may develop a feeling of deep resentment toward his more favored classmates. If you utilize this technique for training in oral composition, be sure to give attention to the amount of skill displayed in the telling rather than in the unusualness of the object shown.

Value of telling. Whether the teacher or a pupil does the telling, the entire class can benefit from the activity. Children need training in attentive and thoughtful listening. Too many individuals are fluent talkers but turn a deaf ear to what others say. As you talk, you can help your pupils distinguish between details. You can do this by emphasizing the former through voice stress, significant voice pauses, and chalkboard notations. You can discover how well your pupils are following you by asking an occasional question during your talk. In the middle and upper grades the pupils can be encouraged to enter in their notebooks the important points of the talk.

The Recitation Method

The recitation method is a traditional teaching approach to the learning of subject matter. It usually is based on textbook material and may follow textbook organization. In the most commonly used form of the recitation method, the teacher assigns a chapter or section of the book for home study and then devotes most or all of the class time to an application of the question-answer technique. The questions asked may be more or less pertinent; individual pupils vary in their preparation of the home-study assignment; some of the material may not be fitted to the abilities and interests of individual pupils. The situation is worsened if the teacher calls upon each child, either alphabetically or according to a seating chart, and then enters a grade in his record book for the answer.

Importance of using the recitation method. Much of your own school learning may have followed the question-answer pattern. Now as a student teacher, you are tempted to employ the recitation method to the exclusion of other techniques whenever this is possible. You are accustomed to it. Basing your procedure on textbook coverage of the subject matter gives you a feeling of security. By adhering closely to it, you avoid the possible introduction of irrelevant material. The pupils are alerted to just what is expected of them in the way of study and, to a greater or lesser degree, attempt to fulfill required tasks.

When you use the recitation method, you supposedly have the entire class under your immediate control. Ideally, every pupil in turn takes part in the recitation. If one child cannot answer the question or gives an incomplete answer, you call on someone else, and continue this process until you receive a full or satisfactory response. If the material lies within the comprehension limits of all members of the class and is interesting to them, you might be able to conduct a relatively successful whole-class recitation. Unfortunately, even in a fairly homogeneous class, this situation is likely not to exist. Then you are faced with the problem of having your attention distracted from the matter at hand by those pupils who are engaging in activities of their own choosing, such as whispering among themselves, doodling, or daydreaming. An attempt on your part to recapture the attention of one of these pupils by asking him a question may be fatal. His response can be such as to disrupt the class completely.

What we have said to this point concerning the recitation method does not imply that material for home study should never be assigned. The pupils may need a background of factual material as a starting point for a lesson or series of lessons. The purpose for the study assignment and its content should be explained ahead of time. Then, some method must be found to discover whether the pupils have prepared themselves adequately. This can be done by administering a short quiz on the material or by a rapid oral review. Questions can be asked by the teacher and answered by volunteers. If you use this approach, be careful to include all of the children, the less able as well as the more able, the shy and retiring, as well as the outgoing and aggressive. Ask simple as well as more challenging questions. Do not allow the recitation to degenerate into a give-and-take between you and a small group of well-prepared, interested pupils.

As a culminating activity of a lesson or lessons, you may want to review some significant informational aspects of the study material. A good way to accomplish this purpose is to utilize a series of pertinent questions. Pupil interest is heightened if the activity takes on the nature of a contest. The children form themselves into two teams, and the questions are alternated between the two groups. Your purpose is not to discover which pupil can stay on line the longest but to keep everyone thinking. Hence a pupil who fails to answer a question correctly is not removed from the team. As a means of maintaining pupil interest in the activity, one child can keep an account of the number of errors made by each team. Through this quick review you can discover the areas of material that require remedial work.

The Socialized Recitation or Group Discussion

One of the disadvantages of the question-answer method is that even though a pupil may give a technically correct answer, what he is doing is merely repeating words that he has memorized. He may have little or no understanding of fundamental concepts. A significant purpose of a socialized recitation is to encourage reflective thinking on the part of every child who is participating in the discussion of a topic or problem of the group. The entire class may be involved in the discussion, with the teacher as a leader, or the class may be divided into small groups, each of which elects a pupil as its chairman.

Whole-class discussion. If the entire class participates as a unit, the teacher usually determines the topic or problem to be discussed. He can start the discussion with a provocative question and then "throw the ball" to the pupils. At times, they themselves may decide the aspect of a unit of study that they wish to discuss. The teacher, of course, must make certain that the pupil-selected topic or problem is relevant to the purpose of the lesson. He also needs to keep control of the situation, lest the children digress too much from the subject under consideration. If you attempt to utilize this approach, you may find it difficult to maintain a democratic attitude toward pupils' participation in a discussion and yet insure their concentration on the goal to be achieved.

Small-group discussion. A good procedure to follow sometimes is to have the class break up into small discussion groups. Movable furniture in the room allows for them to arrange themselves into intimate circles. Each group, with its chairman, can discuss the same topic or consider different phases of the same topic. While they are talking among themselves, the teacher moves from group to group, listening to what is being said and, perhaps, asking pertinent questions or otherwise helping to steer the group's thinking into appropriate channels.

After a sufficient amount of time has been allowed for the groups to arrive at some positive conclusions (usually not more than twenty minutes) each chairman reports to the class as a whole the reactions of his group. This procedure may result in further class consideration of the topic. The small-group process is an excellent way of encouraging the participation of those children who otherwise might remain silent.

Panel Discussion, Debate, and Dramatization

The small-group approach can take the form of a panel discussion or a debate. Some educators would also include the presentation of a dramatization in this category.

Panel discussions. In the panel-discussion approach, a group of children, preferably not more than five or six, prepare ahead of time and discuss in the presence of their classmates various aspects of a topic that is of special interest to them.

It is the chairman's function to bring all of the members of the panel into discussion and to limit in time the contribution of any one member of it. During the panel discussion, the other members of the class are encouraged to raise questions, to clarify moot points or to add appropriate comments at its end. The teacher must so guide the project that rambling or getting away from the topic is avoided.

The debate technique. The debate follows somewhat the same format as the panel discussion except that it involves only two teams of children whose function it is to discuss the pros and cons of a problem or situation that has interest potential for the entire class. The debaters must be well prepared, speak clearly and concisely, and present their material on the comprehension level of their classmates. Enough time should be available at the conclusion of the debate for the entire class to engage in a critical evaluation of the points of view presented. This can be accompanied by a further discussion by all of the significance of the material included.

The use of dramatizations. Dramatizations of appropriate study materials can afford young people opportunities to work together cooperatively in small groups as they plan for and take part in role playing. Care must be exercised that these dramatizations are short in length and that the same children, because of their dramatic abilities, are not the only ones selected to participate. The less vocal child can be helped to gain self-confidence by participating occasionally in this form of group activity.

Aims of Socialized Recitations

The conducting of an interesting and challenging socialized recitation requires considerable preparation on the part of the teacher. He must realize that the utilization of this technique serves a dual purpose. The aim of the lesson should be to further learning in the subject matter under consideration. At the same time, the children receive training in working cooperatively with others as they exchange ideas, share one another's thinking, and learn to respect the points of view of classmates. It is a socializing experience that can help young people gain facility as members of committees or of other group activities, both in and outside their school experiences.

Appropriate materials for discussion. Some learning materials can be adapted to the utilization of the socialized recitation better than others. The mastery of factual material, for example, requires that the pupils not only understand but also memorize appropriate content. Let us face the fact that before an individual can apply knowledge to current or future life situations, he must be thoroughly grounded in it. It is the teacher's responsibility so to guide the learning that his pupils recognize the value of the learning and are willing to submit to the task of achieving a solid and accurate mastering body of facts.

At the same time, there are many areas of learning to which the discussion approach is admirably suited. These include situations in which the purpose or goal is to stimulate children to deal with significant issues (such as in the social studies), to achieve commendable social interrelationships, to determine important policies concerning school or out-of-school activities, to participate in problem solving, or, in general, to gain skill and confidence in individual or group thinking.

Conduct of the discussion technique. In any form of group discussion, the pupils are encouraged to express their attitudes, judgments, and points of view. These then are critically evaluated by their teacher and other class members. Petty arguments among a few children must be avoided, however. The teacher needs to know when to step into a discussion that is pupil chaired, for example, and bring it back to a consideration of vital issues. In this connection, it is important that class or smaller group discussions be based on an adequate knowledge of pertinent subject matter. Reflective thinking cannot take place in a mental vacuum. Expressed opinions based on emotional attitudes rather than on facts have no educational value.

As a student teacher, you may want to experiment with the socialized recitation or discussion technique. You probably should not attempt to employ it until you have had an opportunity to become acquainted with your pupils and can recognize their strengths and weaknesses. You also must have earned their respect so that they will accept your leadership and cooperate with you in working out the details of the discussion. Your cooperating teacher and college supervisor can help you in your preplanning for the lesson.

Problem Solving

One of the main objectives of education is to help an individual acquire a body of ideas that he can apply in his attempted solution of the many problems he constantly encounters during his life course. If he is to interpret accurately and intelligently what he hears and reads about local, national, and world happenings, he needs a broad knowledge that may cross various fields of study, such as science and the social studies. In the conduct of his affairs as a home member, a worker, and a citizen of his country, he faces problems of adjustment that can be resolved effectively only to the extent that he can apply to them the basic principles of human interaction.

School people realize that they cannot prepare any young person specifically for the meeting of all of the various problems that he may experience in the future. They do recognize, however, their responsibility for trying to teach him how to attack problems that may arise in his current experiences in various learnings, thereby equipping him with an appreciation of those principles and generalizations that may have continued value for him. It is hoped that the kind of intelligent and accurate thinking encouraged in the classroom may have transfer value in that it helps the learner function more efficiently in his out-of-class life.

The problem-solving approach. You probably are well acquainted with the steps in John Dewey's analysis of problem solving.[3] Dewey's steps apply to a complete act of thought and include:

1. Becoming aware of a felt difficulty
2. Identifying the problem
3. Assembling and classifying data and formulating hypotheses
4. Accepting or rejecting the tentative hypotheses
5. Formulating conclusions and evaluating them

Whenever you motivate your pupils to engage in reflective thinking, you are attempting to help them follow Dewey's stages in an act of thought: preparation, readiness, and mental interaction. Problem solving should not be regarded as one of many teaching techniques. Rather is it a mode of approach that is characteristic of various methods of teaching.

You can begin a lesson with a question that is appropriate to the subject of the lesson, such as "How does water get into the air?" "What can we do to protect school property from damage?" "Why do we keep milk in a refrigerator?" "What does our government do for us?" You have posed a problem situation that probably can be resolved during the class period by the use of one or more teaching techniques: lecture, discussion, demonstration, and experiment.

Throughout the aforementioned learning experience, you are encouraging the children to engage in reflective thinking. You help them follow Dewey's steps as you motivate them to define the problem, apply knowledge already mastered or discovered, construct possible solutions, evaluate them, and finally agree on what may seem to be the most appropriate conclusion. The actual testing of the accepted hypothesis may or may not be possible during the lesson.

The problem-solving approach usually is basic to the development

[3] John Dewey, *How We Think* (Boston: D. C. Heath & Co., 1933), chap. 6.

of a larger unit of study. The sequential steps in the procedure may be somewhat as follows:

1. The problem is located and defined.
2. Under teacher leadership, the pupils decide on desirable approaches to be utilized, and individual and group projects are determined.
3. The children, either individually or in groups, engage in supervised study and research.
4. The various pupils share their findings with the class by means of individual or group reporting; dramatization or role playing; showing and explaining of illustrative material, such as diagrams, charts, or models; carrying on of experiments, and the like.
5. The class as a whole conducts socialized recitations in which possible conclusions or hypotheses are considered, and the most appropriate generalization is selected.
6. The learning outcomes from participation in the study of the unit are evaluated.

Each of these steps in the development of a unit probably will include several days of classwork, but there is evidenced a sequential pattern of activities that build up into a logical and psychological whole. This procedure is likely to hold the interest and attention of the learners.

Important aspects in problem solving. You will have many opportunities to apply the problem-solving approach. The problem may be a relatively simple matter of deciding the best way to attack a particular bit of subject matter, to decide on a course of action; it may represent a complex situation that necessitates the amassing of considerable research material for its solution. In either case, you need to make certain that the problem has interest appeal and is suited to the children's ability to profit from participation in the activity. The problem should not be so easy that it provides no challenge to the ingenuity of your pupils, nor should it be so difficult that many of them are unable to comprehend what is to be done.

The problems you set for your pupils or that you help them solve should be related to their experiences to the extent that they recognize the value to themselves of dealing with them. At the same time, you need to be careful lest they become so involved emotionally that they are unable to consider the problem situation objectively rather than from a biased point of view. One of the purposes of utilizing the problem-solving approach is to give young people practice in applying the scientific method in arriving at solutions of the many problem situations they are likely to encounter throughout life.

The expression of personal opinion has a place in problem solving as children seek to find possible answers to questions raised in their attempts to find a solution. Their opinions, however, must be based on known facts. For example, a group of children cannot decide by vote the present composition of the United Nations, the geographic location of Iran, the process of osmosis, the function of the red corpuscles in the blood. Facts such as these need to be discovered through research, if they are not already known, in order to solve a problem that involves the utilization of such factual source material. Moreover, knowledge gained as a means of helping in the solution of a problem often is learned more effectively than if it were acquired in the form of more or less unrelated facts to be memorized.

Your attitude toward and the nature of your participation in problem-solving situations are very important. The classroom atmosphere should be free and friendly. Intelligent guidance on your part is necessary all along the way. Your pupils will need your help not only in setting up appropriate problems but also in defining them clearly and accurately. It is your function to procure source material for them or be able to tell them where they can find it.

The children should receive training in collecting and organizing data in such a way that it is easily available when they need it. As they deal with a relatively difficult problem, they may need help in dividing it into its respective units for research purposes without losing sight of the basic problem. You also have the task of guiding their critical thinking as they consider the various possible solutions, each of which should be stated clearly and definitely.

The selection of the final hypothesis or conclusion can be a challenging class project. You need to keep the children's thinking focused on the requirements of the problem and the extent to which the possible solutions meet these requirements. This is a good point at which to stress the need for objectivity of judgment in light of existing conditions. A consideration of the various ways in which the selected hypothesis can be tested offers opportunities for discussion of cause-and-effect relationships. An ingenious, imaginative teacher can stimulate much exciting and worthwhile learning experience among his pupils through the utilization of the problem-solving approach.

The Laboratory Technique

Simple forms of the laboratory technique can be used, especially in the upper grades. The conducting of experiments is a common approach to the teaching of the sciences. The laboratory technique also can be used as a means of providing opportunities for children to work alone or in small groups in the process of carrying on projects in an area of study that appeals to their current interests. The laboratory experience is a form of problem solving. As groups of pupils work on the same or different laboratory exercises, the teacher, acting as a consultant, moves among the members of the class and offers help wherever it is needed.

If you plan to utilize this teaching technique, you need to make certain that the problems to be solved are within the ability range of those who participate in them. Considerable flexibility is possible in that you can set up activities of varying degrees of difficulty and assign them in accord with the particular abilities of individual children or groups. Also, appropriate equipment should be available and prepared ahead of time so that needed materials can be assembled without delay. Discussion should accompany the activity. At the beginning of the activity, the pupils can discuss what they expect to do and why. Toward the end of the period, they should be given an opportunity to summarize their findings and compare the value to them of what has been accomplished.

The laboratory technique has various advantages. Through participation in the experience, the pupils can build desirable generalizations or principles. They are learning by doing. They are gaining practice in working together in small cooperating groups, thereby furthering the process of socialization in a friendly and relaxed classroom atmosphere. As the teacher confers with individual pupils about their activity, he is enabled to become better acquainted with them, their strengths and weaknesses, and can arrange for remedial work appropriate to their respective needs.

The Place of Practice in the Learning Situation

Psychologists and educators are placing so much emphasis (and rightly so) on the interest factor in learning and on the children's essential need to comprehend and understand learning materials that it is believed by some people that practice or drill has no place among learning experiences. Nothing could be further from the truth. Adequate mastery of learning content is not possible without well-organized practice. A child needs to engage in intensive repetition of an item of information, a form of skill, or an aspect of attitude in order to enable him to give correct automatic responses when they are needed.

Unfortunately, in the recent past, some school people came to regard drill as a useless, boring activity that is much disliked by young people. High schools and colleges complain that many entering freshmen come to them poorly prepared in such fundamental areas of learning as reading, written composition, and arithmetical computation. Some college entrants have brilliant ideas and mature understanding in various areas of knowledge, but they are woefully lacking in the fundamentals, such as spelling, grammatical structure, handwriting, arithmetical operations, and the mastery of simple matters of fact. Hence the lower schools have begun to assume greater responsibility for providing opportunities for young people to practice intelligently those learnings that are essential to adequate mastery of significant aspects of any of their fields of study.

The Conduct of Effective Drill

Unmotivated drill can be boring. Children tend to enjoy practicing mental and motor skills, however, when they (1) understand the material that they are practicing, (2) recognize the need for repetitive activities, (3) can check their progress in improvement, and (4) come to appreciate desired outcomes of their practice. In other words, children usually are more than willing to submit to intensive drill if they are motivated to see its value to themselves.

Children differ in the amount of practice needed to fix certain learning materials adequately. You can keep this in mind as you plan drill sessions. Those who require less drill activity can be given other interesting and challenging assignments while the slower pupils continue their drill activities.

You probably have learned about the spacing and duration of practice periods. Keep these points in mind as you arrange your practice lessons. Be alert to whether the pupils' interest in the drill process is waning. If so, change the activity. In most practice sessions there is a point of diminishing returns.

Before practice starts, make sure that the children are ready to repeat correct responses. It is better to begin by having the pupils practice simple elements in the total situation to which they know the correct response than to start them on a more complex operation in which errors may occur that they will incorporate in their practice. To be functional, drill should be specific.

As is true of other teaching approaches, you must prepare carefully for practice sessions. You need to take care that your pupils know what the correct response is that they are to practice. Do not allow so much time to elapse between practice periods that your pupils have forgotten what they are to practice. Insist on accuracy of performance. Be alert to those children who have specific weaknesses or disabilities and give them opportunities for special drill.

We hear much these days about the great need among secondary schools and colleges for the application of remedial learning techniques. This is an admission of insufficient or poorly organized practice experiences during the original learning situations. As teachers, we cannot disregard our obligation to make certain that children practice learning materials in those ways that will serve them and future activities. Also, we should keep in mind that forgetting sets in as soon as practice ceases. Hence we should not be satisfied merely to see to it that a motor or mental skill has been mastered. We should provide for periodic reviews of practice materials so that the habit is maintained and strengthened.

SUGGESTIONS FOR TEAM TEACHING

The concept of team teaching is more than a professional fad. It is based on the theory of utilizing the competencies of each member of the staff to the fullest. The idea is to give more pupils the benefit of the professional training and experience of more than one teacher during a current term or year. Team teaching is not a plan that automatically becomes a better way of guiding the learning process. In order to be successful, the teachers involved must learn how to function in this new medium. It calls for a new kind of cooperation and planning.

A great deal of effort already has gone into planning for team teaching. We present the following hypotheses and elementary school team models that have been suggested by John A. Brownell and Harris A. Taylor.[4]

HYPOTHESES

. . . we offer certain general and specific hypotheses regarding teaching teams. To a greater or lesser extent, all types of teaching teams possess common advantages and create similar difficulties. These common, hypothetical advantages, as compared with regular classroom organization, might be stated as follows:

Practical and effective in-service education through frequent team meetings.

Marked success in inducing new teachers into school systems as a result of interns as team teachers.

The use of aides to release teachers from routine duties.

Teacher involvement in planning and developing team curriculum because of team structure.

Through selection of team teachers and election of leaders, recognition for outstanding teachers.

Because of team structure, the ability of the team to form large and small groups for instruction, from one teacher to one student, to one teacher for 200 students.

Because of team structure, the ability to vary the length of instructional period to suit content and interest span.

Because of team structure, the ability to group and re-group frequently by achievement or ability levels.

At the elementary level, the ability to develop exchange teaching opportunities amongst the team teachers in order to exploit teachers' special talents, knowledge, and training.

Improved guidance from the planned exchange of information about students and the intimate atmosphere within the team.

Improved correlation of subject matter because of cooperative planning in team meetings.

Through team leaders and team meetings identification and use of community resource persons.

4 John A. Brownell and Harris A. Taylor, "Theoretical Perspectives for Teaching Teams," *Phi Delta Kappan* (January, 1962), pp. 151–53. Reprinted by permission.

The planning of field trips for team students in team meetings and less interference of field trips with other teachers' classes.

Because of their children's common experiences, increased interest and involvement of parents.

Because teams can be kept together for more than one school year, the organization to develop sequences of content and intellectual processes.

Improved climate of motivation because of accent upon individual identity and team spirit.

Because of team structure, the best use of teacher talent.

Because of varied groupings and presentations, greater student interest.

Under typical school conditions the common difficulties might be expressed as follows:

Finding teachers who can function harmoniously as a team.

Finding strong team leaders.

Scheduling team classes in secondary schools and organizing flexible groupings in the elementary schools.

Irritating effects of teams on existing departmental and grade level organizations.

Creating new and different administrative roles and problems.

Forcing independent and creative teachers into groups which inhibit their freedom.

Lowering the morale of non-team teachers.

Locating, training, and supervising teacher aides.

Many of the assumptions listed initially are clearly apparent in the elements and hypotheses, though some must be inferred. As we turn to the analysis of team models, we shall find additional evidence of these ideas.

REPRESENTATIVE TEAM

We propose a series of team models. Because not all of the elements set forth in the definition section would necessarily be represented on any one team, several different combinations of elements are possible. More elaborate combinations would occur when the factors of subjects or grade levels were introduced. Indeed, so many combinations are possible that no complete explication can be made. We hypothesize, therefore, that certain representative combinations are most fruitful in the development of theory. If we establish continua of *theoretically* possible combinations for elementary schools and high schools, we can choose representative combinations at the extreme and the midpoint for each continuum to indicate the scope of possible combinations.

ELEMENTARY SCHOOL TEAM MODELS

Inasmuch as the elementary school is most frequently organized into grade levels, let us suggest a continuum with grade levels. We shall use a six-year, 600-pupil school for our model.

Model I

grades	1	2	3	4	5	6
classes			team			

At one end of the continuum, a team consists of all classes of a particular grade level. Such a team can be formed for each grade. In a very large school, more than one team per grade could be organized.

Model II

grades	1	2	3	4	5	6
classes						
	team					

At the other extreme, a team comprises one class from all grade levels. As many teams can be formed as there are vertical arrangements of classes.

Model III

grades	1	2	3	4	5	6
classes						
					team	

In a middle position, a team contains classes from two grade levels. In a six-grade school, three teams can be formed; in a very large school, more than one team per pair of grades could be organized.

Simple variations of Models I and II merit attention. In any grade, two teachers with complementary talents can form a team; at adjacent grade levels, any two such teachers can form a team.

Hypothetically, a different continuum can be described for elementary schools not organized into self-contained classrooms. While these models are theoretically possible, most educators would seriously question their desirability and feasibility. The principle of this continuum is still grade levels, but the unit of organization is content rather than self-contained classes.

Model Ic

grade	6				
classes	A	B	C	D	E
language arts	team				
science	team				

At one extreme, a team consists of one content area and pupils from one grade level. As many teams can be formed as there are major content areas in the curriculum.

Model IIIc

grades	1	2	3	4	5	6
language arts	team					
social studies	team					
mathematics	team					

At the other extreme, a team comprises one content area and pupils from all grade levels. As many teams can be formed as there are similar content areas at all grade levels.

Model IIc

grades	1	2	3	4	5	6
science				team		
language arts	team					

In a middle position, a team comprises one content area and pupils from two or three grade levels. A team can be formed for each major subject area.

The value of these last three theoretical models lies in the modifications which come to mind. Content areas might be broadly defined to include combinations of subject matter such as mathematics and science, language arts and social studies, fine and practical arts (physical education, home economics, industrial arts), or various "core" arrangements. In an eight-year elementary school, or in a junior high school, with such a definition of content, three seventh-grade core teachers, each with a complementary specialization, might combine to form a Model Ic team.

ENGLISH	SOCIAL ST.	MATH
social studies	English	English
mathematics	mathematics	social studies

Any one of the teams described above could in turn be modified by the inclusion or exclusion of certain categories of teachers and auxiliary personnel.

For example, consider the following modifications of a Model I elementary team:

The existence of certain preconceptions about the elementary school seem to recommend the Model II team for experimentation. This team, comprising classes from two grade levels, appears to have the fewest weaknesses. It is realistic with respect to present teacher preparation, yet it propels teachers in new directions. It offers pupils a means of moving ahead as their abilities permit, yet it retains some homogeneity of age. It moves the elementary school into a new mode of organization, yet it keeps those features which provide for security during a time of change.

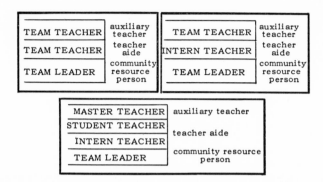

OPERATIONAL DESCRIPTION

If the advantageous hypotheses regarding teams were being confirmed, how would elementary school teams probably be functioning? We propose this description:

The faculty teams consist of several teachers, each with certain talents and training. Each team meets regularly to exchange ideas, to develop common policies and purposes, and to share information regarding pupils on their teams. By having each teacher assume responsibility for specialization in subject matter and in supporting activities such as remedial instruction, the faculty teams become self-sufficient units. By specializing, each team teacher can assist the other team members in planning curricula, in developing appropriate instructional techniques, and in meeting demands for increasingly specialized knowledge. When the faculty team deploys pupils into small and large groups for instructional periods, the specialists handle these groups as planned in team meetings. In schools organized into self-contained classrooms, exchange teaching (in which a team teacher takes the class of a colleague or perhaps several classes in a large group situation), brings to bear the specialization of one teacher upon all team pupils. Because team teachers meet regularly, they work not only on organization of material and high quality instruction, but also on problems confronting individual pupils, such as poor reading skills, low motivation, poor study habits, unwholesome behavior. Such interchange among team members will help to establish a professional faculty spirit and will deepen the regard for individual teacher talent. Inevitably, more responsibility for curriculum development will be in the hands of qualified classroom teachers.

We cannot predict what the future of team teaching may be. At present, it is an interesting experiment in the teaching-learning approach with which you should be acquainted and for participation in which you should be prepared. It is a fact that some teachers are better suited than others for this kind of cooperative activity. Perhaps beginning teachers may gain greater facility in working with their colleagues and learn how to maintain a closer relationship with students than now is apparent in the group-teaching approach. Then we can expect real values to accrue from the adoption of team teaching.

QUESTIONS AND TOPICS FOR DISCUSSION

1. What specific skills need to be improved by elementary school children?
2. To what extent and how do the subjects provide opportunities for creativity?
3. Evaluate your attitude toward high standards of workmanship as evidenced by your habitual performance of tasks assigned you.
4. What have been your reactions as a student to your teachers' utilization of the telling method?
5. Distinguish between a regular recitation and a socialized recitation.
6. Give an example of small group discussion that would be appropriate to language arts.
7. Suggest at least five problems associated with your pupils. Have them present solutions for the problems.
8. Show how you could guide pupil thinking in one of the problems suggested in question 7.
9. Describe at least two interesting approaches to practice or drill in various subject fields.
10. In what ways does your relationship with your cooperating teacher resemble team teaching? Be specific.

TEACHING GIFTED AND RETARDED LEARNERS

Teaching-learning approaches in the elementary school are pointed toward helping pupils master curriculum materials that have been developed in light of generally accepted educational objectives or goals suited to this school level. The teacher's task would be relatively simple if all of his pupils possessed equal ability to benefit from exposure to learning situations in his particular subject. As you know, this is not true, however. Individuals differ widely in the extent to which they are mentally fitted to profit from instruction that does not take into account the presence of these differences.

No two pupils are exactly alike in their power to deal effectively with learning materials. Ideally, every child would be given an opportunity to proceed in mastery of learning materials at his own rate of successful achievement. Since public education must, perforce, be conducted on a relatively large-group basis, the best that we can hope to accomplish is so to organize our planning procedures that we provide in a general way for at least three categories of mental differences—the gifted learner, the average learner, and the retarded learner.

THE IDENTIFICATION OF INDIVIDUALS WITH MENTAL DIFFERENCES

In your preteaching courses to this point, you probably have learned about individual differences. You know that there is no sharp line of demarcation among learners' mental capacities. Rather does each individual have a place somewhere along the line from mental retardation to high mental superiority. Hence school administrators need to establish lists of criteria in light of which they can determine the extent to which some of their pupils perform academically more effectively than so-termed average pupils and others who are inferior in learning achievement.

Commonly used criteria are the results of standardized testing instruments such as group and individual intelligence, special aptitude, and achievement tests. The results of intelligence and aptitude tests combined with measures of achievement can serve as indicators of what may be expected of a young person in respect to future academic performance. Yet, we cannot accept test results alone as our sole criteria of ability range. Other means for identifying the gifted include such methods as observation, school marks, work samples, age-grade status, interest inventories, interviews, rating scales, autobiographies, and sociometric studies.

Another source of information is the recorded history of degree of successful achievement in various learning areas as this is noted on a pupil's cumulative record card. Much also can be learned about a young person's mental status through teachers' and parents' observation of his behavior and attitude toward school learning. The individual himself may be able to evaluate his learning potential in comparison with that of his fellow classmates.

One pupil realizes that he finds studying easier than do some of his friends. Another struggles to master a unit of subject material and decides that he is "dumb" because he is less successful in his study than others, in spite of his efforts to achieve desired learning goals. In addition, children are quick to recognize differences in learning effectiveness among their peers. By utilization of a combination of these media, it is possible to differentiate, in a general way, among the mental capacities of individual students.

Characteristics of Intellectually Gifted Children

The gifted learner can be expected to have a high intelligence quotient. The normal or average IQ's range from 90 to 110. Since individual ratings on various intelligence tests may vary somewhat, an IQ of 115 to 120 is supposed to be characteristic of the fast learner. The mentally superior or gifted individual is expected to achieve an IQ of at least 140. Hence, although the intelligence quotient is a commonly used criterion of superior learning ability, its use as a criterion should be evaluated in light of other displayed qualities or traits.

Mentally superior children tend to have intensive and extensive interests. They can analyze complex relationships and arrive at original solutions to complex problems. They can deal with abstractions and excel in independent thinking. They enjoy engaging in research, not only to achieve a learning goal but also to participate in the activity itself. They like to read, often delving into difficult reading materials beyond study requirements.

Gifted children usually can express their ideas clearly and succinctly in both oral and written form, and have a rich vocabulary. They master factual information easily and apply creatively what they have learned. Such pupils offer a definite mental challenge to their teachers and are a joy in the classroom.

According to one analysis of the characteristics of the gifted, superiority seems to show itself in one or more clusters of traits: (1) the intellectually gifted who excel in most scholarly activities, (2) the talented and creative in areas such as music, art, and mechanics, and (3) those who have special ability in self-direction and social leadership.

Comparison of intellectually gifted children. Intellectually gifted children when compared with children in general often give evidence of the following characteristics:

1. Maintain a longer attention span
2. Display greater initiative
3. More able to make logical associations
4. Use an enriched vocabulary
5. Greater degree of social adjustment
6. Keener powers of observation
7. Greater ability in conceptualization
8. Greater ability in retention
9. Greater ability to express ideas
10. Greater intellectual curiosity
11. Greater self-reliance
12. More sensitive to viewpoint of others
13. Greater ability of self-criticism and self-checking
14. More creative and inventive
15. Greater power of concentration
16. Usually more persistent in pursuit of goals
17. Greater energy and alertness

18. More independence in work and study
19. Greater diversity of interests
20. Greater versatility
21. Taller, and stronger and healthier than average for age
22. More mature physically and better coordinated than average for age

Characteristics of intellectually gifted children suggested by the New York State Department of Education. They include the following:

The highly intellectual child, then, is likely to be:
The youngest in the class
Independent and able to keep ahead
Attentive to detail
Responsive to humor
Imaginative and creative
Responsive to the feelings of others
Versatile

He has:
Great intellectual curiosity and need for creativity
A high capacity for listening to directions and responding to them
A greater range and intensity of interests
Great sensitivity
A high capacity for self-direction

He learns:
More and more quickly than the average
By "figuring things out" more than by imitation and repetition
From vicarious experiences as much as a slow learner learns from immediate experience

He prefers:
Older children for intellectual stimulation
Learning situations that require generalizations at a higher level than other children of his age
Subjects like science, history, economics, English, and mathematics
The abstract and general to the concrete and piecemeal
Informational books, if accessible

In general, he:
Employs less overt trial and error in problem-solving than do other children
Assumes leadership in solving group problems
Is not easily distracted from problems under consideration
Completes assignments quickly and has more spare time, which, if encouraged, he will use in purposeful activities
Finds distant goals motivating

Can carry through prolonged projects for several weeks at an earlier age
than most children

Gains early mastery of reading skills and has strong interest in books

Scores extremely high on achievement tests

Appreciates subtleties, and understands mood, tone, and intent of poetry

Probably does best in reading and language, poorest in handwriting and
spelling

Dislikes routine and repetitive tasks

Requires less detailed and repeated instructions

Is usually large for his age in terms of his family type, physically well
developed and well adjusted

Will be found in all races, religions, socioeconomic backgrounds [1]

Characteristics of Retarded Learners

As is the practice in screening rapid learners, standardized tests
are used in attempts to discover those pupils who can be expected
to encounter difficulties in mastering learning materials. The intelligence quotient is a commonly utilized criterion.

The validity of a low intelligence quotient is a moot question. An
individual may score low on an intelligence test because of his
unfamiliarity with the language or because he is unacquainted with
the background knowledge needed to interpret verbal test items
correctly. It is a fact that children's ratings on these tests have
improved as they have been exposed to better cultural conditions.
However, consistently low results on a series of performance as well
as verbal tests probably indicate low mental alertness.

The retarded learner is likely to exhibit characteristics that are
basic to his inability to master learning content effectively. We must
remember that, like the gifted learner, the retarded learner differs
from so-termed normal learners in degree of ability rather than in
kind. The below-normal child can think, but he is weak in abstract
thinking. He needs to be stimulated by concrete situations and ideas.
His study habits probably are poor. He does not know how to attack
study materials quickly and efficiently. Also, his attention span is
relatively short. He finds it difficult to concentrate on the task at
hand and is easily diverted by distracting elements in his environment.

---

[1] *Curriculum Adaptations for the Gifted,* Bureau of Elementary Curriculum Development (Albany: New York State Department of Education, 1958), pp. 13–14.
Reprinted with permission but not copyrighted.

Since a retarded learner is deficient in viewing situations and conditions in their proper perspective, his ability to find solutions to any but the simplest problems is weak. He does not always recognize appropriate relationships, and, therefore, is unable to achieve valid conclusions or generalizations. The slow pupil sometimes can memorize material by rote, but he may fail to understand what he has memorized.

One of the most serious problems of a retarded learner is his low reading ability. By the third grade the child needs to have facility in reading in order to get ideas from the printed page. If the child is unable to read he cannot keep up with the other members of the class who have achieved the ability to read on grade level. The teacher must give special help to the slow learner in order to enable him to develop skill in reading. It is possible to teach a slow-learning child to read.

A few mentally retarded individuals (IQ below 70) can be found in the junior high school, but they rarely are able to continue through the senior high school years. Some slow learners, individuals with intelligence quotients between 75 and 90, are able to complete a modified secondary school curriculum. Their degree of moderately successful achievement depends partly on their own efforts and partly on the effectiveness of teaching approaches. Based on early studies of intelligence of school children, about 5 per cent of an unselected school population have an intelligence quotient of 78 or less, and about 2 per cent have an IQ of 73 or less. However, according to Elsie H. Martens, Chief, Exceptional Children and Youth of the Office of Education:

Intelligence tests, however, are not infallible, nor is the rating of a child on an intelligence scale the only thing that should be known about him. Emotional conflict, physical condition, or the environmental situation may interfere with the full expression of his intelligence. When circumstances change, he may be better able to respond and thus to rate higher on an intelligence scale. Moreover, a child may be intellectually retarded, even to a rather serious extent, and still have enough social competence to get along in the world fairly well. No child should be called "mentally retarded" or assigned to a special class for mentally retarded children without full consideration of all these facts.[2]

[2] Elsie H. Martens, *Curriculum Adjustments for the Mentally Retarded,* Bulletin 1950, No. 2, reprinted 1957 (Washington, D.C.: U.S. Department of Health, Education and Welfare, Office of Education, 1957), p. 5.

WHAT CAN THEY DO?

All pupils can deal with things, persons, and abstract symbols, but in vastly different degrees of complexity. Theoretically, a retarded child of any chronological age can acquire the information related to school subjects which normal 7-year-olds acquire when his "mental age" is 7, as determined by standardized mental tests. Theoretically, too, it is possible by means of mental measurement to tell to what extent a child is capable of mastering abstract symbols such as numbers, letters, and words. Actually, however, this principle applies to groups rather than to individuals, and here, as elsewhere, exceptions occur that must be treated in keeping with the needs of the individual case. Factors of physical health, personality, and environment may be responsible for a seeming deficiency in intellect that disappears when the causal factor is removed.

Because a deficient child can by the time he is 16 years old learn a little of a given school subject, it by no means follows that such learning should become the goal of his education. It would be a far wiser investment of time to center his education on the activities which will be of greatest use to him. Mentally retarded children and young people are not equally deficient in all directions. Most of them can learn to work with concrete materials and objects better than they can learn to work with symbols or abstract ideas. A great many different kinds of useful work can in fact be mastered by them. Education should, therefore, take account of these facts: (1) That mentally retarded pupils can work more succesfully with objects and materials than they can with the tools of literacy (words, numbers); and (2) that in the realm of symbols they can, *as a group,* learn about as much as their "mental age" may indicate, in terms of what average children of that age accomplish.

As for emotional experiences, the mentally retarded share the ordinary human emotions. They "have feelings," and their feelings are much more like those of ordinary persons, apparently, than their intellectual abilities are. They hunger and thirst just as others do; are made glad or sad, as their desires are gratified or not; are capable of affection, discouragement, and all the other emotional experiences common to man. These observations apply to all above the extreme of idiocy, where mental life is at a low infantile level.[3]

You need to understand that for a retarded child to compete with his brighter classmates is an extremely discouraging situation. He often gives up trying to succeed in his work. He is the pupil who may become a disruptive influence in the classroom. He may become a truant or wait impatiently for the day when he will be old enough to drop out of school.

[3] *Ibid.,* p. 6.

TEACHING APPROACHES FOR MENTAL DEVIATES

The fundamental goal of the elementary school is to prepare all of its pupils for a useful and personally satisfying mode of life. School people long have tried to meet the problem of providing more or less appropriate learning situations to meet the needs of slow learners. Appreciating the mental handicaps of these pupils, they have attempted, although not always successfully, to offer modified programs of studies through participation in which these children might become reasonably well fitted to earn a livelihood and become constructive citizens. In large urban communities, special programs have been established to meet the learning needs of the less academically minded pupils.

Concern for the mentally superior is a more recent development. At one time it was believed, erroneously, that the bright could take care of themselves. It was assumed that, given the opportunity to participate in learning activities, these children would be self-motivated to achieve successfully in light of their superior interests and abilities. Community and school leaders are now realizing that modern technological and social advances demand the services of an ever-increasing number of well-trained experts in various fields of endeavor. We cannot afford to waste whatever mental superiority can be found among the youth of the land. Hence it is the function of our schools to provide appropriate learning situations that develop fully the individual powers of gifted children.

Administrative Responsibility for Meeting Individual Differences

What is done for the rapid and slow learner, respectively, depends in good part on the educational philosophy of school administrators and their policy toward making special provisions for meeting the educational needs of their young people. Elementary school principals' efforts in this respect are limited, of course, by the size of the school or school system, and the money available.

TEACHING GIFTED LEARNERS IN THE ELEMENTARY SCHOOL

Various approaches are being used in modern schools to motivate rapid learners to achieve successfully. As we have suggested, the procedures utilized are in keeping with administrative policy, the percentage of the pupil body that can be identified as mentally superior, and available materials and equipment. The purpose of the differentiated program may be *acceleration* or *enrichment*, or a combination of the two. The "gifted" may be taught in special classes (homogeneous grouping) or in regular classes (heterogeneous grouping).

Value of Acceleration

School people are becoming increasingly interested in providing opportunities for acceleration of mentally superior children. Acceleration can be justified for at least two reasons. First, since the bright child can master learning materials more quickly than is possible for less able individuals, he is likely to be bored in class or "get by" with a minimum of study effort. He may develop habits of laziness and fail to utilize his full study potential. Secondly, many of these pupils plan to enter a vocational field that requires five or more years of academic preparation beyond graduation from high school. This causes a delay not only in his participation in gainful work activity but also in the establishment of a home of his own.

The Value of Enrichment

In its most general connotation, the term *enrichment* as applied to curricular offerings includes any learning materials and experiences that go beyond the minimal essentials included in a course of study. Actually, however, by enrichment we usually mean the extent to which the superior pupil is provided opportunities to engage in study experiences that are in advance of what normal or average pupils are expected to master. "Enrichment, in whatever form, is effective only when it provides for a broader scope of activities, when it challenges and encourages special interests, and when it fosters talent, creativity, and originality." [4]

In special classes, superior pupils can benefit from participation in enriched curriculums. In regular classes, the teacher can encour-

---

[4] *Administration: Procedures and School Practices for the Academically Talented Student in the Secondary School* (Washington, D.C.: National Education Assoc., 1960), p. 87.

age rapid learners to engage in more intensive and extensive study projects. It must be kept in mind, however, that able pupils differ in their individual interests. Enriching experiences, therefore, need to be encouraged in light of particular interests. For example, one pupil may respond to special challenge in the sciences or mathematics, another's concern may be that of social problems, while still another's chief interest lies in the field of the language arts.

As the members of a class select their special projects in the development of a unit of study, the more able pupils can be motivated by the teacher to choose those requiring the greater amount of research. They also can be encouraged to prepare and report on aspects of study material that demand the utilization of special books and equipment. Since bright children are likely to complete assigned classroom tasks more quickly than do the others, they can devote the extra time at their disposal to one or another form of advanced work.

Suggestions for Curriculum Enrichment for the Gifted

Numerous procedures are being used to help the child within the regular classroom enrich his experiences. We present here curriculum adaptations suggested by the Division of Elementary Education of the State of New York.[5]

CURRICULUM ENRICHMENT

1. Giving children many opportunities for:
   a) Expressing feelings and emotion in art, music, dancing, and creative writing of poems, stories, and plays.
   b) Participating in dramatics.
   c) Exploring areas of interest.
   d) Reviewing interesting books that are too difficult for the average child.
   e) Creating book interpretations through drawings or miniature scenes set up in the classroom or library to stimulate others to read.
   f) Developing contributions to current events discussions.
2. Providing challenging materials.
3. Promoting the desire to help others in the classroom.
4. Providing positions of responsibility.

[5] *Curriculum Adaptations for the Gifted,* Bureau of Elementary Curriculum Development (Albany: New York State Department of Education, 1958), pp. 13–14, and 24–27. Reprinted with permission but not copyrighted.

5. Calling attention to opportunities to write creatively and to enter general scholastic competition such as spelling, essay, art, and writing contests and to participate in science and current citizenship experiences.
6. Encouraging development of hobbies.
7. Alerting children with special talents to opportunities for further development.
8. Encouraging joy and personal satisfaction in work well-done.

ACTIVITIES IN THE AREA OF SCIENCE

1. Build, operate, and maintain a simplified observatory and weather station, such as keeping weather records, reading weather maps, or using a can to catch and measure rainfall.
2. Study weather reports from stations throughout the country. Using their own blank maps, pupils indicate areas of high and low pressure, cold and warm fronts, and learn to make actual forecasts.
3. Plan and operate a school museum.
4. Study telegraphy (simple blocks of wood, a piece of metal, wire, magnet, and a dry cell).
5. Construct a radio.
6. Make reproductions to show the development of an invention.
7. Study the production of sound from a phonograph.
8. Study the school public address system.
9. Make a xylophone.
10. Make a working model of some piece of simple machinery of interest to the child and his group and demonstrate its principle to the group.
11. Identify rocks and minerals through scratch tests, cleavage, and Geiger counter.
12. Make a soilless garden, using a sponge, gravel, moss basket, and sawdust.
13. Make a magnetic stage, using a cardboard carton in which figures pasted to bits of iron are moved by a magnet held under the figures. Explain the principles involved.
14. Prepare a primary science file in which simple experiments written on large file cards are placed according to areas of study.
15. Make a fall seed collection in which seeds are collected, classified according to mode of travel, and placed on a chart with proper headings.
16. Make a satellite demonstrator. Thread a string through a spool, tie a small stone on one end and a larger stone on the other; by holding on to the spool and whirling the smaller stone around, the larger stone will be pulled through by centrifugal force. Explain the principle involved.
17. Make a steam turbine. Attach the lid of a tin can to the top of a closed coffee can, the top of which has a few holes, and partly fill with water; place the can over heat and the steam escaping through the holes of the can will turn the wheel, illustrating the steam turbine. Explain the principle involved.

18. Make a water turbine, by having water falling from a faucet turn a simply constructed wheel with paddles. Explain the principle involved.
19. Make and explain an electromagnet.
20. Make a blinker light (constructed like a telegraph except that a light replaces the sounder).
21. Demonstrate rain by heating water, making the steam come in contact with ice and condense; observe the droplets fall from the glass tube.
22. Assemble a small electric motor with the help of a resource person.
23. Collect and analyze samples of soil.
24. Study ways of purifying water.
25. Study animal tracks.
26. Review new sample science tests.

ACTIVITIES IN THE AREA OF LANGUAGE ARTS

1. Read or tell stories to younger children.
2. Scan and classify reading materials for the school library.
3. Interview resource persons.
4. Participate in a debate or panel discussion on a current issue (with children of higher grades if the topic is beyond the interest of the gifted child's classmates).
5. Read books on advanced levels.
6. Write scripts for radio programs.
7. Write dramatizations of historical events and stories.
8. Express orally or in written form feelings about music, paintings, etc.
9. Evaluate children's magazines (set up evaluative criteria and make a recommended list for the library).
10. Survey pupil reading habits to determine extent of magazine reading as compared to book reading.
11. Document research using bibliographies, footnotes, and quotations.
12. Analyze pictures having fine expressions of human emotion; stress joy and happiness.
13. Trace the derivation of a word.
14. Study a foreign language, after age eight, twice weekly.
15. Write plays.
16. Write unfinished stories to be completed by others.

ACTIVITIES IN THE AREA OF ARITHMETIC

1. Draw to scale.
2. Study a problem, such as the cost of building a house (involving kinds of materials, fixtures, construction, installation, and labor costs).
3. Compute the cost of traveling a given distance in early days and at present, and show the findings in chart or graph form.
4. Compile budgets for a pioneer family and present-day family of comparable size for a given period of time; compute increases in percentages.

5. Estimate answers to addition examples in new ways.
6. Discover various ways of verifying sums and differences.
7. Employ short methods in solving multiplication examples.
8. Make a time line of historical events.
9. Reduce foreign money to our values.
10. Calculate comparative costs of cash payment versus credit buying.
11. Keep a record of family buying of special sales versus regular purchases, and calculate economies effected by taking advantage of special sales.
12. Study the history of numbers.
13. Study other number systems, i.e., dyadic, duodecimal, etc.
14. Play number games (i.e., write any number you like, multiply by 2, add 18, and then divide by 2, now subtract the number with which you began; the answer will always be 9).
15. Construct riddles. (An example of a gifted fourth grade child's riddle is as follows: $\frac{3}{4}$ of Jane $+ \frac{1}{2}$ of us $+ \frac{1}{3}$ of Ann $+ \frac{2}{3}$ of rye $=$ January.)
16. Prepare a display of banking forms, insurance forms, mortgage forms, etc., with an explanation of each.

ACTIVITIES IN THE AREA OF CITIZENSHIP EDUCATION

1. Trace a series of historical events.
2. Study the origin of our food supply, laws, governments, etc., as a basis for understanding the evolution of our culture.
3. Make a map showing early travel routes in a particular area and the highways and rail and air routes now in use.
4. Compile a list of special skills used by employees in industry.
5. Make a chart showing the designs of early coins and contrast them with present-day coins.
6. Write and help produce plays and puppet shows on topics in the citizenship program.
7. Make scrapbooks, posters, paintings, murals, etc., on topics of particular interest.
8. Prepare special reports, going more deeply into topics or events than the rest of the class.
9. Do independent research into the causes and effects of selected events on topics in history and geography.
10. Prepare short biographies of the lives of famous people.

ACTIVITIES IN OTHER AREAS

1. Form a chess club.
2. Observe school plant operation and maintenance.
3. Serve as head of school drives (i.e., Red Cross, March of Dimes, etc.).
4. Organize and plan a school hobby show, bookfair or folk dance festival.
5. Devise new games; give instructions and direct the game.
6. Survey community resources for field trips.

7. Study and interpret the history of classical pictures.
8. Assist in the organization of school clubs.
9. Play question-and-answer games. (The gifted make up a "panel of experts," children of average ability select questions to ask, slow children use open books and judge whether answers are correct.)
10. Study and prepare menus of different countries.
11. Help other children in his own grade or those below, under careful guidance, to see that the practice is not carried to the point of exploitation; such help may include science demonstrations, crafts, and games.

Types of Grouping for Effective Learning

You probably are acquainted with the two generally accepted forms of grouping pupils for instructional purposes: *heterogeneous* and *homogeneous*. The former term applies to that type of class organization whereby all of the pupils in a subject area, regardless of their degree of mental ability, are taught together as a group. In the latter type, some provision is made for different ability levels to be placed in classes in which they supposedly are receiving instruction with pupils similar to themselves in ability to profit from learning stimulation.

All of the pupils in a special class are not homogeneous in every respect. The teacher is dealing with individuals in this type of class just as surely as he is in a regular class. Even though the members are supposedly relatively similar in scholarship ability, they may be very different in degree of emotional maturity. Hence they do not respond similarly to motivating devices. Moreover, some teachers attempt to apply the normal curve of distribution in comparative evaluation of study success. As a result, some of his pupils earn lower grades in this class than they would in a regular class. Ability grouping has definite advantages. At the same time, other factors may interfere with the success of its functioning. Much depends on the leadership abilities of the teacher.

The Teacher and Special Instructional Provisions for Gifted Learners

A question often raised is "What kind of person should teach the mentally superior learner?" The answer might be that this teacher should possess those qualities of leadership that are desirable in all teachers but perhaps a little more pronounced. Enthusiasm for teaching, sympathetic understanding of the problems of the gifted in a world consisting (for the most part) of less able individuals, and ingenuity in providing challenging learning situations are among the qualities that should be possessed by men and women who attempt to guide the learning of these learners. Some of his pupils may possess a higher degree of mental ability than he does. This is no detriment provided he can recognize and respect their superiority.

FIFTY SUGGESTIONS FOR TEACHERS OF GIFTED BOYS AND GIRLS [6]

1. Individually help each child accept himself.

2. Privately praise the child for performance achieved at superior level.

3. Through example to the class, provide a climate which is accepting of the child who is different, the bright as well as the others.

4. Provide opportunity for individual book reports.

5. Provide opportunity for individual dramatizations.

6. Provide opportunity for individual performances, musically.

7. Provide opportunity for individual demonstrations.

8. Provide opportunity for individual student teaching explanations.

9. Permit the child to help grade papers.

10. Permit the child to be class librarian.

11. Permit the child to be in charge of visual and auditory aids.

12. Permit the child to teach slower children in the class.

13. Permit the child to be helping teachers in other classes.

14. Permit the child to maintain class bulletin boards.

15. Permit the child to take class attendance.

16. Permit the child to arrange for class trips.

17. Provide record player with earphones to be used with French and other languages.

18. Provide record player with earphones to be used with social study records.

19. Provide record player with earphones to be used with music.

[6] Ann F. Isaacs, *Guiding the Growth and Development of Young Gifted Children* (Cincinnati, Ohio: Pamphlet of the National Association for Gifted Children), pp. 7–10. Reprinted by permission.

20. Provide record player with earphones to be used with English.

21. Maintain art appreciation reproductions with self teaching manuals. (Current Met. Mus. Reproductions.)

22. Maintain self teaching instructions in various media of art.

23. Maintain science kit materials which children can pursue sans individual attention.

24. Obtain an old typewriter and manual that the child may teach himself to type.

25. Encourage them to write poems.

26. Encourage them to write plays.

27. Encourage them to write stories.

28. Encourage them to direct plays and assume responsibility for other production details.

29. Encourage them to write autobiographies.

30. Encourage them to help teacher maintain an enrichment file card index of things to do when work is completed.

31. Let them give daily weather reports.

32. Let them give news reports.

33. Let them give science reports.

34. Let them give current events reports.

35. Let them give United Nations reports.

36. Make full use of the psychological services your school system has available for the gifted.

37. Provide workbooks for areas that may require remediation, or that will encourage advance progress, seek additional help when needed.

38. Excuse children from regular classwork to visit experts in their fields of interest.

39. Excuse children from regular classwork to visit the library.

40. Excuse children from regular classwork for extra lessons.

41. Excuse children from regular classwork that they may work on their own pet projects.

42. Provide books at an advanced level, being careful not to supply tests that will be specifically used in next grades.

43. Alert the children's teachers for the coming year of their talents.

44. Work closely with the parents.

45. Encourage the parents to become familiar with the literature on the gifted that they may become more successful in guiding the child's talents.

46. Work closely with administration.

47. Strive to find the child's special interests and abilities.

48. Be active in your local gifted child chapter of the National Association for Gifted Children. If none exists in the community, do your part to initiate one, tell parents and colleagues about the organization.

49. Keep abreast of latest research in the field of education and psychology of the gifted.

50. Encourage your school system to provide a supervisor for the gifted.

TEACHING CHILDREN WITH CREATIVE ABILITY

You will find that even bright children differ in their degree of creative ability. Yet, all children should be provided with opportunities to express whatever latent creativity they possess. We quote from Irene McKee who indicates ways in which children can be motivated to engage in creative activities.

CREATIVITY IN THE CLASSROOM, CANTON [7]
IRENE MCKEE, TEACHER, BELLE STONE SCHOOL, CANTON, OHIO

Creativity Is a Way of Thinking

Creativity involves: self reliance, independent thought, motive power, inner drive or desire, ability to continue in face of difficulties, patience, persistence; working without constant direction, supervision, or praise; knowing how to fail intelligently (Research is 99.9 per cent failure); studying and using what is already known; appreciation of the contributions of others; critical attitude toward own work; recognizing what is good and what needs improvement.

[7] From a special report on *Creativity in the Classroom,* Canton, Ohio, in Lester D. Crow and Alice Crow, *Educating the Academically Able: A Book of Readings* (New York: David McKay Co., 1963), pp. 263–66.

Developing Creative Ways of Working and Thinking

Children are developing creative ways of working and thinking when they:
1. Begin work without being told.
2. Find answers to many of their own questions.
3. Look at own work with critical eye and make revisions.
4. After finishing one task, decide what to do next and do it.
5. Have courage of own convictions (backed by proof and reasons) even though it means standing alone.
6. Look for and develop constructive differences rather than sameness; express individuality.
7. Consider many ideas and solutions, never sure there is just one right answer.
8. Do not give up easily; are willing to check and correct many times until a high standard is reached.

Creativity of Children Difficult to Identify

The best-dressed, most artistically decorated classroom does not always prove that its students are creative. The "creation" may have been largely teacher-planned and produced. A fluently given oral talk or a well-organized cleverly written composition may easily fool even a very discerning teacher when in reality much of the effect has been parent engineered. However, these situations may well be used as an introduction or springboard for creativity on the part of children themselves if everyone concerned is willing to identify and accept rather crude beginnings. Anyone versed in identification realizes that creativity like any other skill requires practice and that first clumsy attempts are steps to learning. These attempts are identified as creative, are accepted, and are criticized *constructively*.

Creativity Increases with Practice

In the classroom

Assignments that provide opportunity for creativity:

Each child chooses a different way of reporting what he has learned.
Write other titles for story, chapter, or topic.
Express an emotion in many ways—voice, facial expression, actions, posture, words, picture (art), music.
Round robin story; one child begins and each child adds.
Show picture to class; child imagines situation and in limited time writes his idea.
Give phrase; child lists as many events or plots as he can in allotted time. Examples of phrases: "How wonderful!"—"Having Trouble?"—"I hardly know where to begin."

We work each day the creative way:

Group selects topic; works out display for classroom or bulletin board and puts it up.

Each child chooses or is assigned a different topic. He locates information, takes notes, organizes material, writes about topic, and makes illustration or chart. This is all done at school.

Work an arithmetic problem in all the different ways possible. Discuss merits of various methods.

Find out how different children solve problems mentally. Compare and practice ways others suggest.

Write letters to pen pals throughout the United States.

Assign questions in social studies. Make sure that some answers may: necessitate search beyond text and encyclopedia; depend on reading map, picture, graph, or chart; require arithmetic computation; be controversial; be matter of opinion; depend on reasoning; be found in newspapers or magazines.

Biographies afford excellent examples of creative thinking in action. How was each person creative and what characteristics helped him to succeed?

Make a special study of one scientific topic. Give demonstration and share extra information with class. Explain value of this principle to our lives.

Every day a different child plans opening exercises and is chairman for the day.

Other creative activities used in our classroom are oral, written, drawn, pantomimed, or sung. They may be fanciful, factual, or fictional, and include: original stories, poems, newspapers, plays, essays, songs, puppet shows, assemblies, models, murals, riddles, posters, letters, news, stories behind the news, rhythmic interpretations; evaluation of books, films, radio or television programs, biographies; quiz programs; vocabulary games.

TEACHING RETARDED LEARNERS IN THE ELEMENTARY SCHOOL

As we have suggested, the mentally retarded (IQ's below 70) are segregated in special classes and taught by specially trained teachers. You probably will not have these children in your classes, unless you are teaching classes for mentally retarded children. You will find in your regular classes, however, some slow-learning boys and girls who experience difficulty in meeting successfully their learning requirements. Teaching-learning approaches for slow learners are different from the procedures usually found to be effective in dealing with rapid learners.

Organizing Curriculum Materials for Retarded Learners

Curriculum guides for severely retarded learners usually are organized around numerous related activities and procedures. A detailed list of such activities has been prepared by H. M. Williams and is presented here for your information.[8] Williams believes that these activities can be used successfully in classes of children who are in the "middle-range" retarded group, provided appropriate teaching materials and facilities are utilized.

I. SELF-HELP

    a. Personal grooming

        1. Dressing
            Putting on shoes correctly
            Tying shoe laces
            Buttoning
            Zipping zipper
            Fastening snaps
            Fastening belt
            Putting on and taking off clothing
            Caring for clothing properly (using hangers and hooks, putting away shoes, overshoes and rubbers, keeping locker or closet neat, putting away soiled clothing)

        2. Personal appearance
            Washing hands and face, keeping lavatory neat and clean
            Combing or brushing hair
            Cleaning fingernails
            Brushing clothes
            Brushing teeth
            Using handkerchief, napkin
            Polishing shoes

II. PRACTICAL ARTS

    Practical arts deal largely with home and housekeeping tasks in which the children can learn to be genuinely useful, and which contribute to their feeling of worthiness and belonging, in ways in which they can justifiably take pride.

[8] Harold M. Williams, *Education of the Severely Retarded Child: Classroom Programs* (Washington, D.C.: U.S. Department of Health, Education and Welfare, Office of Education, 1961), pp. 34–38.

1. *Housekeeping*
   Setting table properly
   Cleaning up after meals; putting away dishes
   Sweeping or using vacuum cleaner
   Making beds, arranging linen
   Putting proper things in refrigerator
   Dusting and polishing furniture
   Preparing simple foods

2. *Other activities*
   Caring for house plants
   Weeding
   Trimming borders
   Washing blackboards and windows
   Answering telephone and doorbell
   Mailing letters; carrying messages
   Doing simple shopping errands
   Hanging up laundry
   Folding linen
   Keeping room neat
   Picking up and putting away materials

III. LANGUAGE

Because of these children's language deficiency, special attention should be given to language development. All situations should be verbalized as far as possible. Communication through language should be encouraged, not only in teacher-pupil contacts but also in contacts between the children. Oral communication is an essential aspect of adjusting conflicts.

1. *Increasing vocabulary*
   Learning names of persons and things, articles of clothing, familiar objects, foods, common animals
   Learning action words
   Listening to and following directions
   Listening to stories

2. *Improving speech.* Based on individual analysis, and with the help of a person skilled in speech correction, such activities as the following may be introduced:
   Learning to make correct sounds through imitating position of organs of speech, games, rhymes, etc.
   Eliminating baby talk, omissions, substitutions, etc.
   Learning a pleasing voice placement

3. *Encouraging oral expression.* (Have a morning conversation period.)
   Telling experiences, etc.
   Telling stories
   Participating in dramatic plays
   Learning rhymes
   Playing games which emphasize oral communication

IV. SOCIALIZATION

The controlled group situation in the school provides opportunity for one of its major contributions to the development of those children. Since socialization is particularly dependent on learning by doing, every opportunity for social participation should be used.

1. *Simple good manners and appreciation of others*
   Making appropriate use of "thank you," "please," and the like
   Greeting and responding
   Listening while others are talking
   Using good table manners
   Addressing others by the proper forms

2. *Respect for the rights of others*
   Sharing, taking turns
   Helping others in tasks
   Respecting property rights
   Taking responsibility for a social role

3. *Group activities*
   Playing with others at as socialized a level as possible
   Carrying on a conversation
   Developing a desire to please others
   Carrying one's share of responsibilities

V. MOTOR SKILLS

Since these children typically show retardation in motor development, considerable emphasis should be put on development of coordination.
Playing rhythmic games
Walking, running, skipping, going up and down stairs, hopping, use of tricycles, jungle gym, etc.
Throwing, bouncing, catching a ball
Using balance boards
Doing simple folk dances
Stringing beads, weaving, pasting, cutting with scissors, doing simple woodwork, drawing, doing craft paper work

VI. SAFETY

Safety education involves recognition and proper behavior with respect to the many potentially dangerous situations that surround us. Among these are, proper behavior with respect to:

Hot or sharp objects
Stairways
Electrical outlets
Poisons and harmful chemicals
Street safety
Playground equipment
Safety in group situations; refraining from tripping, striking, and pushing others, throwing objects, etc.

VII. HEALTH

Health education is primarily, for this group, development of simple understanding and habits.

Simple understanding of how disease is transmitted
Proper habits regarding use of handkerchief when coughing, sneezing
Habits of cleanliness, washing
Proper toilet routines
Reporting accidents, and getting help when skin is injured or when there is bleeding
Proper habits for care of the teeth
Avoiding medications in bottles, etc., except under direction
Simple understandings and habits regarding food, drinking fountains, etc.
Understanding need for rest
Daily inspection routines
Knowing the appropriate attire

VIII. PERCEPTION TRAINING

Perception training means something similar to the old "sense training" but recognizes that the processes involved are more complex than are implied by that phrase. Much of the work in kindergarten and the early grades involves training in comparison, discrimination, and recognition.

Matching colors and forms; discrimination
Learning color names
Sorting beads or cards
Making letters and numbers
Finding colors and objects in pictures
Copying simple designs

Coloring
Playing imitation games
Matching pictures, numbers, words
Listening for changes in rhythm
Matching pitch of tones

IX. CONCEPT DEVELOPMENT, MENTAL GROWTH

Learning simple concepts of quantity, such as bigger, smaller, heavier, etc.
Counting, recognizing numbers
Learning simple concepts of money and making change
Learning simple concepts of space, such as over, under, tall, short, etc.
Learning concepts of time, such as before, after, morning, afternoon, month, day, week
Knowing time to the hour
Repeating from memory
Developing imagination through games, dramatization, drawing, make-believe
Problem solving—making choices, decisions, deciding when work is finished, finding out what is wrong with something, deciding where things should be put, working puzzles
Following directions.

X. ACADEMIC SKILLS

The academic skill will necessarily be limited, but opportunity should be offered to learn as much along these lines as the individual children show capacity for.

1. *Reading*
   Copying letters or words
   Writing names
   Labeling pictures
   Making signs
   Finding own name card
   Recognizing names of children
   Recognizing and interpreting signs
   Passing out name cards to the children
   Matching word cards
   Reading days of week from calendar
   Doing flannel board activities
   Speaking in unison
   Saluting the flag
   Repeating nursery rhymes
   Saying words of a song
   Reading pictures

Giving names of objects in pictures
Looking at books and magazines

2. *Science*
Knowing about care of pets
Growing plants, including caring of house plants, growing things
from seed
Knowing about farm animals, what they eat, how they are cared for
Talking about zoo animals after field trips
Recognizing some birds—keeping a bird feeder
Studying bees and other insects, including harmful insects
Observing and recording the weather

3. *Social studies*
Knowing about police and their duties
Discussing community news
Using simple geographical concepts; giving directions; knowing the
neighborhood, transportation
Knowing how we get our food and about the farm
Looking at pictures of factories and what is made in them; going
on field trips
Knowing about the mayor and council, the city, the State, the
National Government, the name of the President, etc.

XI. EXPRESSIVE ACTIVITIES

1. *Arts and crafts*
Using crayons
Coloring outline pictures
Cutting and pasting
Poster-painting
Finger-painting
Making collages
Loop-weaving
Lacing
Using stencils, tracing patterns
Folding paper
Working at simple woodcraft, driving nails, glueing, sandpapering,
assembling ready-cut materials, varnishing
Doing simple serving

2. *Music*
Learning nursery and seasonal songs
Singing games
Listening to music
Playing in a rhythm band, with blocks, triangle, or drum
Marching to music
Interpreting rhythms, walking, skipping, etc.

3. *Dramatic play*
   Learning parts in a play
   Participating in free dramatization
   Acting out parts in stories

4. *Manipulative skills*
   Playing games
   Using a marble board
   Using a sand box
   Participating in free group play
   Doing exercises

Curriculum Provisions for the Retarded Learner

Children with mental retardation must be considered first as children who are growing up, and second as being mentally retarded. The curriculum offered them must be one to fit their learning needs. They need to learn as much as they can about living in their society. This will include the *basic skills, fine arts, physical education,* and a core of *health, science,* and *social studies.* Since they are usually placed in a special group for their training, the core approach seems to be the type of curriculum that will serve them best.

In a primary class the teacher might organize the activities according to a time plan that approximates that suggested in Table 6.

TABLE 6

SUGGESTED WEEKLY DISTRIBUTION OF TIME (ASSUMING A FIVE-HOUR DAY)

Activities	Distribution of Time in Percentage
Basic skills (reading, arithmetic, language arts)	30
Fine arts (music, creative drama, storytelling)	30
Core work (health, science, social studies)	30
Physical education	10

It might be noted that for the intermediate group Practical Arts should be included to the extent of about 10 per cent. This time would be taken from the Fine Arts, thus reducing it to 20 per cent. To be of value to them, the learning of slow children needs to be practical in that it helps them meet simple everyday situations. Hence teaching procedures are so organized that the various subject areas are presented according to a unit approach. An example of the unit applied to home life follows.

TABLE 7

Topic: Foods as a Part of Daily Life

Chrono-logical Age	Mental Age	Social Characteristics	Experiences
1	2	3	4
6 to 12.....	Below 6......	1. Preschool and kinder-garten characteris-tics. 2. Individualistic play. 3. Individualistic desires. 4. Random and seeming-ly unpurposeful ac-tivity. 5. Manipulistic play—with obects. 6. Unfinished products in work.	1. Daily trip to market or store with older group to do buy-ing. 2. Carrying basket home and arranging pur-chases on shelves. 3. Washing vegetables and fruits. 4. Dramatic play—par-ties, home and store situations.
6 to 12.....	6 to 9........	1. Primary or intermedi-ate characteristics. 2. Desire for companion-ship in play. 3. Purposeful activity in that the product satisfies own de-sires. 4. Beginning of forma-tion of small groups.	1. Setting tables. 2. Pouring milk, cutting bread and butter for tables. 3. Making bread and muffins. 4. Making butter. 5. Cooking simple des-serts. 6. Clearing tables and stacking dishes.

[9] Elsie H. Martens, *op. cit.*, insert between pp. 20–21.

TABLE 7 (*Cont.*)

Trips	Social Science Concepts and Activities	Reading Activities
5	6	7
To stores in company with older groups: (a) Bakery. (b) Dairy. (c) Market. (d) Grocery. (e) Farm.	1. Articles of food as part of own meals. 2. Immediate source of food: Farmer or store. 3. Health values of food. 4. Table habits. 5. Identification of foods by name. 6. Mother's part in preparation of foods. 7. Child's part in helping mother.	(Prereading in nature.) 1. Representation of food objects seen at store —modeling, drawing (size, shape, and color). 2. Stories and games. 3. Development of vocabulary through oral conversation. 4. Identificatioin by name and classification of food, as fruit. 5. Dramatic play: parties and home situations. 6. Oral directions.
1. To— (a) Stores. (b) Warehouse where food comes in. (c) Vegetable and fish markets. (d) Dairy plant. (e) Bakery. (f) Freight cars, refrigeration cars. (g) Farm. 2. Fishing trip.	1. Experiences on play level: (a) Growing of food on farm. (b) Selling of food at market. 2. Kinds of food. 3. Uses of food. 4. Home cooperation in use of food.	1. Experience reading about excursions to farm and store. 2. Oral conversation. 3. Poetry, stories, games. 4. Chart reading of child's original stories. 5. Free painting to illustrate stories.

TABLE 7 (*Cont.*)

Arithmetical Situations	Related Spelling	Nature Study and Science
8	9	10

1. Buying articles of food at store.
2. Counting objects.
3. Liquid measure: Glass, pint, quart (milk).
4. Building of arithmetical language: Near, far; heavy, light; some, many, few; hard, soft; round, long, short.
5. Play with pound and half-pound weighted bean bags.
6. Sense of balance: Use of balance bar, scales.
	None.	1. Informal acquaintance with growing things in environment:
		   (*a*) Helping to water plants.
		   (*b*) Helping to weed garden, etc.
		2. Informal experience with elements as talked about in daily living: Stars, clouds, rain, snow, bugs, pets.
		3. Identification of food.

1. Identification of coins to 25 cents. 2. Making change to 10 cents. 3. Weights: Pound and one-half pound. 4. Liquid measure: Quart and pint. 5. Counting measure: Dozen and one-half dozen. 6. Continuation of counting. 7. Continuation of arithmetical language.	None.	1. Discussion of how elements make food grow. 2. Classroom garden. 3. Picnics: Outdoor cooking; building fires.

TABLE 7 (*Cont.*)

Health	Manual Experiences	Physical Activities and Recreation—Not Necessarily Related
11	12	13
1. Establishment of habits of cleanliness by practice. 2. Handling of food utensils. 3. Slow eating with correct mastication. 4. Washing foods: Fruits. 5. Establishment of regular eating habits—no eating between meals. 6. Brushing teeth after meals. 7. Establishment of correct habits of elimination.	1. Free play with large saw, hammer, nails. 2. Making crude toys needed in own play.	1. Individual play to promote acquaintance with environment; exploration. 2. Toys: Wagon, ladders, apparatus. 3. Sand play. 4. Large blocks. 5. Free rhythmic response to music. 6. Rest periods.

1. Continuation of habit establishment.
2. Cleanliness of dishes.
3. Attractiveness of served food.
4. Scrubbing of food before cooking.
5. Care of burns and cuts obtained in kitchen.
6. Correct posture at table.
	1. Making:
	  (*a*) Large boxes for vegetable bin.
	  (*b*) Holders.
	  (*c*) Mats for table.
	  (*d*) Garden markers.
	2. Activity in cooking and washing dishes.
	3. Painting, stimulated by trips.
	4. Cleaning, waxing, polishing furniture.
		1. Singing and simple circle games.
		2. Free rhythms.
		3. Dramatic play: House, trains.
		4. Block play developed in groups.
		5. Active games of simple type.
		6. Story playing.
		7. Sensory games.
		8. Relaxation.

General Classroom Procedures for the Mentally Retarded Child

Harold M. Williams, Specialist for Exceptional Children and Youth of the Office of Education, outlines classroom procedures for the severely retarded child for a school day. He suggests:

The school day.—The organization of the school day revolves to a large extent around the question of how closely the program should be structured or reduced to a regular routine. It has been urged that a closely structured daily routine gives additional security to this type of child. It has also been suggested that their probable future status of dependence or semidependence will tend to require them to follow imposed routines more closely than other children.

The following is a fairly representative sequence of activities. No specific time schedule is suggested since completion of an activity is generally considered to be preferred to too strict adherence to a time table.

Activity	*Comments*
Period I. Arrival greeting and morning routines.	This first period offers opportunity for oral communication, practicing social skills, and habituating such routines as putting away outer wraps and personal grooming.
Period II. Group conversation and planning period.	A "good morning" song; name recognition, discussion of events of the previous day; discussion of weather and timely topics; assignment of routine duties, including appointment of children to be on the various committees to water the plants, set the table, and preview the days activities.
Period III. Routines, group activities such as music, rhythm, toilet, and snack.	Completion of planned routine activities, followed by toilet routines, group activity, and snacks. A brief rest period may also be inserted here, if needed.
Period IV. "Large muscle" activities, group games, rhythms, outdoor activities.	In this period, group games, socialization, and other physical activities may be arranged. The actual programing depends largely on the maturity and readiness of the group.
Period V. Individual or small-group work on projects or units.	This period may come closest to "academic" school work, as planned by the teacher in relation to the group's maturity.

Period VI. Quiet period, listening to music, singing, or stories.	This period is planned in part to precede lunch or dismissal.
Period VII. Lunch or dismissal.	A lunch period provides excellent opportunities for teaching social competencies and skills.
Period VIII. Individual or group work.	For those classes which continue after lunch, an additional activity period may be used.
Period IX. Quiet period preparation for dismissal.	This period may be comparable to Period VI in classes which dismiss before noon.[10]

Since slow learners tend to be retarded in reading, each of their teachers must be a teacher of reading. He has the task of finding reading materials for them that are within their comprehension limits. He also may need to give them extra help in gaining an understanding of reading content. The utilization of audio-visual aids has value as a means of stimulating interest among these children.

The retarded learner is discouraged by the fact that his achievement does not measure up to that of his classmates. The teacher can encourage such a pupil by helping him compare his present performance with past performance. To the extent that improvement is evidenced, he can be stimulated to compete against himself, thereby attempting to better his record.

QUESTIONS AND TOPICS FOR DISCUSSION

1. Describe ways in which we can identify the mental deviate.
2. Select one of your pupils who is supposed to be mentally superior. Watch him at work and try to determine to what extent his behavior exemplifies those characteristics of the academically superior person listed.
3. Select a retarded learner and compare his characteristics with those listed.
4. Differentiate between acceleration and enrichment. Which approach do you prefer? Why?
5. List at least three examples of enrichment for each of the grades 2, 4, 6.
6. Compare the instructional provisions for gifted and retarded learners cited in this chapter. Note specific likenesses and differences in approach.
7. What provision does your school make for meeting mental differences?
8. If your class is grouped heterogeneously, how does your cooperating teacher care for the needs of gifted learners? Retarded learners?
9. Which group would you prefer to teach (gifted, average, retarded)? Why?

[10] H. M. Williams, *op. cit.*, p. 48.

11

UTILIZATION OF TEACHING AIDS

The success of teaching is closely allied to the extent that the teacher knows his subject, understands the learner's educational needs and abilities, and recognizes and is enthusiastic about his many teaching responsibilities. No matter how well he is prepared to do a good job, however, he can improve the teaching-learning situation by utilizing the various teaching aids that now are available for his use.

You have had experience with supplementary learning materials. Your own teachers have applied some of them, and you probably have studied about them in your college classes. Here we are reviewing many of these aids to good teaching, their availability, and their proper use. As a student teacher, you can become better acquainted with them, so that you can make intelligent use of them in your teaching procedures.

GENERAL CONSIDERATIONS IN THE USE OF TEACHING AIDS

It is generally agreed among educators that learning is facilitated by the use of learning aids, such as textbooks and other reading matter, projected materials, nonprojected materials, and other resources that can be found in the school's community. Certain general principles of usage need to be kept in mind as you plan to incorporate the utilization of them among your learning procedures.

Purposes to Be Served by Supplementary Aids

Regardless of the type of material, you need to consider its usage in light of the purpose it can be expected to serve. You must keep in mind your instructional aim and your approach to the realization of this objective. Whether your goal is to increase subject-matter mastery, skill improvement, or attitude development, you must make certain that the learning aid is suited to your purpose. Although it can arouse and help maintain pupil interest, your intent is not merely to amuse or entertain. Your pupils need to recognize this fact.

Unless children are properly guided, they may become so involved in an attention-getting experience that they lose sight of its educational significance. For example, a fifth-grade instructor was accustomed to begin his class sessions with a short film appropriate to the discussion. He overheard one of his pupils comment on the fact that attending this class was a very enjoyable experience—that all one had to do was to relax and be entertained. Since this pupil rarely participated in the discussion, the instructor wondered to what extent this procedure was stimulating the pupil toward learning activity.

A learning aid should not be utilized as a kind of busy work. Too often, a teacher is tempted to assign book material to be read or workbook exercises to be completed in order to free himself for another activity. During the "busy work" period, the teacher corrects papers, prepares assignments, and the like. Pupils soon discover that the assigned task does not have a significant educational purpose. Consequently, they give it minimal attention.

Importance of Aids in Providing for Learning Differences

We know that children differ in learning interests and in their ability to profit from learning experiences. Hence you need to vary learning approaches so that individual pupils can benefit from the activities in which they participate. Some pupils can learn much from the printed page, but many profit more from dealing with concrete materials. In fact, actual and vicarious experiences have strong learning potential for most individuals. One field trip may be worth more than the reading of many pages. A good motion picture or a series of slides can point up details that might be missed if they were the subject of an oral discussion. A chart, a map, or a diagram can present quickly and accurately facts or conditions that would take many words to describe or explain.

As you plan for the inclusion of teaching aids in your class procedures, be sure to evaluate their usefulness in light of your pupils' interests, learning needs, and readiness to profit from the use of particular aids. You must know something about the pupils' background of experience and their likelihood of regarding an aid in its proper perspective. The time element also is important.

Supplementary material must be appropriate to a specific learning experience and presented as a significant aspect of the total situation so that its relevancy can be recognized by the learners. It may be difficult for them to appreciate the significance of an audio-visual aid that is presented out of context. Used correctly, supplementary materials can (1) increase motivation toward effective learning, (2) provide for individual differences, and (3) serve to make learning more permanent.

Availability of Supplementary Learning Materials

You will find that schools and school systems differ in their policies toward the use of learning aids. For example, among the more often used audio-visual aids on the elementary school level are films, slides, and filmstrips, although some recent devices, such as tape recorders, television programs, language laboratories, and teaching machines are beginning to receive attention. The greater use of all of these aids is projected for the future.

Schools seem to differ in their use of these aids not only in light of available money for their procurement, but also in their willingness to give them financial support. Some materials are kept in the library or other convenient place in the school itself. Others, such as films, for example, are stored in a central depository and loaned to the individual schools. Still others are housed in community centers from which they can be obtained. More will be said about the availability of these materials as we discuss the various types of aids.

Utilization of Instructional Resources

Your teaching should be so organized that you can make full use of all instructional resources available to you. These resources often are greater than many teachers are aware. We present a list of materials that can be easily found if not readily available in your school.

Reading Materials

Clipping file
Library books
Newspapers
Periodicals
Pamphlets
Reference books
Textbooks

Audio-Visual Materials

Bulletin boards
Chalkboards
Charts and graphs
Dioramas
Filmstrips
Flat pictures
Globes
Motion pictures
Posters
Radio
Record player
Slides
Specimens and models
Table displays
Television sets
Tape recordings
Transcriptions
Wall maps

Manipulative Aids

Abacus
Arithmetic materials
Bead board
Bead string
Compass
Counting units
Domino cards
Fractional units
Games of various kinds
Magnetic board
Number strips
Pocket chart
Protractor
Science material
Science table
Specimens

Resources in Community

Field trips
Interview opportunities
Resource visitors
Surveys

In the remainder of the chapter, we consider each of the more or less commonly used teaching-learning aids. Before we do this, however, we wish to add a few cautionary comments. Do not regard the utilization of teaching-learning aids as a means of relieving you of teaching responsibilities. Contrariwise, they add to your duties but are well worth the time and energy expended. Keep these points in mind when using a supplementary aid:

1. Select an aid in light of the learning interest and ability of your pupils.

2. Use an aid only for educational purposes.
3. Be sure that the material is integrated into the learning situation for which the aid is intended.
4. Prepare thoroughly for using the aid by familiarizing yourself with its operation and by making whatever arrangements for its use that are needed.
5. During the use of the aid, keep the pupils alert to its significance.
6. Engage in an appropriate form of follow-up.
7. Evaluate the use of the aid for future application.

READING MATERIALS AS AIDS

To the present and, probably, for a long time to come, the written word constitutes the one most important aid to learning. The value to the child of printed material depends, of course, on the appropriateness of its content in a particular area of learning, the appeal of the style and format of the material to the reading ability and interest of the reader, and the way in which the teacher uses the material in motivating the learning process. Reading materials commonly used in the modern classroom include textbooks, supplementary books, workbooks, magazines, pamphlets, bulletins, brochures, and newspapers.

The Textbook as an Aid

Publishers of textbooks are becoming increasingly aware of the factors that combine to produce a good, usable textbook as a learning guide. They select authors who know their subjects well and have had experience in teaching the subject matter of the material covered. Attention is being given to improving a book's organization and format. Much pertinent and interesting illustrative material is included. Attempts are made to adapt the style of writing to the reading comprehension level of the learners for whose use it is intended. Size of type and kinds of illustrations are important for the elementary-school child.

The selection of textbooks. In the past, textbooks usually were selected by state educational officials or by administrative officers in individual schools. The trend now is to have available textbooks examined by a committee of teachers, either on the state or local level. Selection of the basal text is then made in light of accepted educational objectives.

Various factors are important in the selection of textbooks. In the selection process, it is suggested that the teachers involved give attention to the following points:

1. Course objectives
2. Apppropriateness of text content; readability
3. Suitability to planning and teaching procedures
4. General makeup of the book—style of writing, quality of paper, size of type, illustrative material, etc.
5. Author's reputed competence in the field
6. Recency of publication

Teachers in public elementary schools do not have freedom in the selection of textbooks. The school provides the books for the pupils. Because most textbooks are costly, they are used over and over again, often to the point that they are outdated. Current materials are omitted or presented inadequately. The teacher then needs to supplement the content or, in other ways, make certain that learners do not receive inadequate or inaccurate concepts. Perhaps the growing popularity of paperbacks may some day eliminate the use of outmoded texts.

The use of the textbook. A good text contains much material that has value to the learner and should be mastered by him. Few teachers now assign textbook reading by chapters or pages without giving needed explanation. You probably will find, even in a relatively homogeneous bright class, that your pupils need some help in attacking reading material. Technical terms and unfamiliar words may need to be interpreted ahead of time. A few key questions on the content of the reading unit are helpful. Recognize the fact that some members of the class may have reading difficulties that require special assistance if textbook study is to benefit them.

Be discriminating in your choice of textbook material to be used. Do not believe that you must have your pupils read the book from cover to cover; at the same time, be careful lest, because of time pressure, you omit significant material. Finally, remember that a good textbook is your most valuable teaching aid if you use it intelligently rather than abuse it.

Teaching-Learning Aids in Printed Material Other Than Textbooks

Appropriate reading materials can be obtained from various sources. Most textbooks include a bibliography of related readings. Some of these books may be found in the school or public library. Various bibliographies are available for your use.

A good school library usually includes various books for each of the subjects taught in the school. These can be read in the library or borrowed for class or individual use. You may have developed a library of your own that contains books appropriate for pupil reading. You also may find that the parents of some pupils have interesting books that they are willing to lend you for class use. Whatever may be the source of available books, you need to make certain that you approach their utilization with the same care that you exercise in selecting material for study from the regular textbook.

The use of pamphlets and bulletins. Much interesting and worthwhile material can be found in current pamphlets and bulletins. Common sources of such materials are public service organizations, government agencies, and various fields of industry. They usually can be acquired at little or no cost. If used intelligently, they can help in bringing subject matter up to date and in adding interesting details. Some of these can be found in a well-stacked school library. You can obtain others by writing for them to the proper source. For example, you can contact agencies such as the American Library Association, Chicago, Illinois; the Superintendent of Documents, Government Printing Office, Washington, D.C. 20402; and similar organizations.

Before you place pamphlets or bulletins in the hands of your pupils, you should read them carefully and evaluate their usefulness. You should evaluate supplementary aids by asking yourself such questions as:

1. Does the aid add anything to material already available?
2. Is the content of the material within the pupils' reading and comprehension range?
3. Should the content of the material be considered by all of the members of the class or limited in use to the more able pupils?

4. Does the material contain details that go beyond the educational purposes to be served at this stage of learning?
5. Is the material up-to-date?
6. Has the material been written to advertise a particular product or service?
7. Is the content of the material compatible with your teaching goals?

The use of newspapers and magazines. The use of clippings from newspapers and magazine or other periodicals can serve two purposes. Not only does it bring into the classroom some valuable up-to-date material, but it also encourages the habit among your pupils of reading worthwhile current materials with a definite purpose in mind.

Newspapers and magazines are easily available as sources of supplementary study materials. Most school libraries subscribe to various monthly and weekly periodicals, and keep copies of the better newspapers on file. These can be referred to by you and class members. You probably are alert to anything that appears in the daily newspaper or appropriate periodicals that are pertinent to a subject. Committees of pupils can be assigned the task of finding interesting material in magazines or newspapers that you supply them, or they can be encouraged to bring appropriate clippings from home.

Children need training in looking for pertinent material and in their treatment of it. You need to teach them to be discriminating in their selection of valid material. School and public libraries find that some pupils are not careful with the books and reading materials they use. They sometimes clip excerpts from them. Do not place so much emphasis on the desirability of pupils' bringing interesting clippings to class that you, unintentionally, foster this bad habit.

The use of the library. The school, college, and local public libraries are invaluable sources of supplementary reading materials. You need to acquaint yourself with their offerings and use them. Especially should you become acquainted with the library facilities of the school in which you are teaching so that you can help your pupils become more proficient in their use of it. Too many children hesitate to avail themselves of library services because they do not know how to find the materials they need.

In an increasing number of schools, pupils are escorted to the library by their teacher, given instruction by the teacher or the librarian in its use, and given opportunities for practice. In some schools, supervised study periods are conducted in the library. There, either the pupils are permitted to browse around the room in search of material of interest to them, or they follow a prearranged plan of consulting the catalog file for assigned material, locating it, reading the assignment, and returning the material to the proper desk or stack. This is excellent training in library usage. When you request pupils to consult library materials on their own, be sure that you have first offered suggestions that will help them locate the material and use it properly.

Building a file of supplementary reading materials. For you to need to search for appropriate material each time you wish to use it in connection with the presentation of a particular topic can involve the expenditure of much time and energy. Many teachers begin early in their teaching career to build a valuable file of pertinent materials. Now would be a good time to start this procedure. In your own study, you probably have accumulated much such material. Start a working file. Be constantly on the alert for pamphlets, bulletins, and magazine and newspaper articles that may have value to you as a teacher, and file them.

Several cautions are needed. File the materials in such a way that they are readily accessible and grouped according to specific topics. Date all clippings. Remove from the file any materials that are outdated. Use the materials with discrimination. Some articles may be suitable for consideration with one class but not with another. A specific bit of information may be of interest to some pupils or suited to their learning ability but inappropriate for others. A good workable file of reading material is a boon to the teacher of any elementary school subject.

COMMONLY USED VISUAL AIDS

Some materials are utilized so generally in classroom procedures that we tend to take them for granted, failing to recognize their value as teaching aids. Included among visual aids are: the chalkboard, the bulletin board, duplicated material, pictorial material, maps, charts, diagrams, graphs, the so-called realia, and exhibits. You probably are acquainted with the use of these materials. Here we are presenting some suggestions for you to consider as you employ these resources in your teaching.

The Use of the Chalkboard

In most classrooms, the chalkboard is used constantly. The teacher uses it to fulfill various purposes. He may use it to:

1. Write important notices to be brought to the attention of the children.
2. List the important points of a discussion.
3. Present graphs, diagrams, charts, sketches, and other illustrative material.
4. Give pupils an opportunity to express themselves.
5. Note homework assignments.
6. Call attention to special items of information, summarizations, and the like.

Children also can be trained in the proper use of the chalkboard. One member of the class, for example, can be selected to place a brief summarization of the points developed during the course of a discussion. Pupils can work out the solution of a problem or other aspects of written work, such as a paragraph on pertinent material or an outline of the significant topics in a lesson. The work placed on the chalkboard can then be evaluated by the teacher and the other members of the class. Needed corrections of work placed on the chalkboard by pupils should be made in such a way that everyone in the class sees and understands them.

When you use the chalkboard, be sure to comply with the following suggestions:

1. Make certain that all pupils can see the chalkboard. Permit them to move around the room in order to get a better view of it.
2. Take care that the writing is legible and large enough to be read easily by all pupils.

3. Check the lighting of the room lest there be reflected light or glare on the board.
4. Keep chalkboard and crayon trays clean.
5. Refrain from cluttering the board with much writing; organize the material in such a way that it is easily read.
6. Practice standing to the side of the board as you write so that you can watch the class as you write and avoid obstructing their view of what you are writing.

The Use of the Bulletin Board

At one time it was customary to have a classroom equipped with a small bulletin board on which were posted important official notices. The modern trend is toward having in each classroom a large permanent bulletin board, sometimes extending along the length of one wall. The board usually is made of cork or covered with magnetized material, in order to facilitate the posting and removing of materials. The function to be served by the bulletin board is to present appropriate learning aids, such as pertinent clippings from magazines or newspapers, diagrams, charts, pictures and other appropriate illustrations, and various materials prepared by the pupils.

The care and arrangement of the bulletin board is important. A teacher can organize the board to meet the particular needs of his classes. Material placed on the bulletin board should be (1) pertinent, (2) well arranged, and (3) removed as soon as it has fulfilled its purpose.

Pupils can assist in keeping bulletin board material well organized and up to date. They usually experience much satisfaction from participating in a project of this kind. To the extent that the pupils themselves share in providing materials for showing, they are likely to watch for new items, read them, and benefit from them. Of course, the teacher should not place material on the board without directing the pupils' attention to it and explaining the reason for its being there.

The Use of Pictorial Representations

Included among pictorial representations are single pictures, posters, postcards, and illustrations appearing in books, pamphlets, magazines, and travel brochures. Pictured material is abundant and much of it can be obtained at little or no cost. Moreover, children usually respond to their showing with much interest. Appropriate pictures can be used to motivate learning. Publishers of textbooks recognize this fact. Many modern textbooks are well illustrated.

Magazines like the *National Geographic, Look,* and *Life* contain pictures that serve as excellent media for the arousal of interest in various learning areas. Good pictures also can be obtained from numerous agencies, such as chambers of commerce, government departments, tourist agencies, commercial and industrial organizations. You will have little difficulty in collecting interesting and appropriate pictorial material.

The showing of pictures is a relatively simple matter, but you must be sure that everyone in the room can see a picture sufficiently well so that he can note specific details to which you direct the class's attention. The picture also can be passed around the room or projected on a screen. Be careful that you select pictures for viewing that are related to the topic or lesson being discussed and see to it that the children recognize the relationship. Encourage the pupils to give attention to pictures that are in their textbook by asking questions about them or by commenting on their significance.

Appropriate pictures and posters can be mounted attractively and used as room decorations or exhibited on the bulletin board. Even though you like certain pictures or posters very much, do not leave them in view for an entire term or year. After they have served their purpose, remove them, substituting others for them. Pictorial materials have value in arousing pupil interest and clarifying ideas, if these suggestions are followed:

1. Utilize pictures that present accurate images
2. Use only those pictures that are pertinent to the topic of study
3. Interpret the meaning of the picture
4. Allow sufficient viewing time for each pupil to comprehend the meaning, without wasting time

5. Assign certain pictures to selected pupils for their special study and report
6. Encourage pupils to contribute to the class collection of pictures from newspapers and their own magazines and to supplement class reports with illustrative material
7 Motivate specially talented pupils to prepare posters for class use

The Use of Maps, Globes, Graphic Materials

You probably have used these types of materials in your own study activities, and are relatively well acquainted with them. Your responsibility as a teacher is to train your pupils in their proper use, and motivate them to refer to the appropriate aid when the occasion arises.

Various kinds of maps, globes, atlases, and gazettes are indispensable teaching aids for the teacher of the various areas of the social sciences and science. Pupils need to learn how to interpret these media correctly. Pupils can be encouraged to prepare their own graphic material. Such material must be correct in every detail, of course.

Good maps, charts, diagrams, and other graphic materials can be found in many modern textbooks and other reading matter. You should encourage your pupils to study these carefully as they read contextual material. You also can place appropriate graphic representations on large cardboards ahead of time, in preparation for class discussion; detailed construction of charts, graphs, and diagrams should not be overemphasized.

The Use of Realia

Certain supplementary materials often are referred to as realia. They include (1) objects, such as a plant or insect, a piece of furniture (colonial, for example), or a kind of military weapon; (2) models, such as a model of the Parthenon, the human skeleton, or a spinning wheel; and (3) specimens or samples within a general classification (types of igneous rocks, of deciduous plants, or of Greek architecture).

Some teachers are ingenious in helping their pupils collect or make various types of realia. A field trip is an excellent medium for gathering specimens for study in science, for example. Visits to museums enable children to become acquainted with objects with which they otherwise would have little or no experience. Many elementary school pupils are interested in building models of various kinds. The building of model airplanes, spaceships, and the like seem to have a particular fascination for some boys. There is one caution here, however. The construction of a model may become a class project, but it should not be given an undue amount of class time; neither should the fundamental purpose for the model be lost sight of.

Some suggestions for the use of realia are:

1. If possible, pupils should have direct experience with objects and specimens.
2. The telling and showing technique should be used if only one specimen is available.
3. If there is a sufficient number of specimens available, they should be studied individually by each class member.
4. In dealing with models, the teacher should call attention to differences between an actual object and its model.

OTHER FORMS OF AUDIO-VISUAL AIDS

Among more complex teaching aids can be included motion pictures, filmstrips, slides, opaque projectors, and machines used in programmed learning. We shall discuss each of these aids briefly.

The Use of Motion Pictures

A motion picture probably is the best substitute for firsthand experience with people, situations, processes, and places removed from the immediate environment of pupils. Many good motion pictures are now available for use with most of the subjects taught in the elementary school. Since films are expensive, the building of a film library is not possible except in large city school systems. Schools can borrow appropriate films, usually for a small fee, from college or university film libraries, commercial circulating libraries, and some state departments of education. Film catalogs that can be obtained from sources such as these give specific information concerning available films and directions for ordering them. McGraw-Hill Text-Films and Coronet films are popular sources of teaching films.

Pupils enjoy watching motion pictures. It is your responsibility to make certain that a film you select for viewing is pertinent to the learning situations for which it is intended. You must help the pupils recognize the purpose to be served by its showing, and direct their attention to its important points. Unless the pupils are guided in their viewing, they may attend to details that are relatively insignificant.

The following suggestions may be helpful for film showing:

1. Preview a film to decide what it is about and whether it is appropriate to your purpose.
2. Arrange to have the projector, screen, and film ready for showing without unnecessary delay.
3. Make certain that you can operate the projector smoothly.
4. Explain ahead of time the purpose of the showing and to what the pupils should be alert. Give them several pivotal questions to consider while they are viewing the film.
5. Refrain from interrupting the showing with questions or comments.
6. Discuss the film with the class as soon after the showing as possible. If you wait too long, details may be forgotten.

The Use of Filmstrips

Filmstrips are available in black and white and in color, and come in the form of stereopticon films and film rolls. Some filmstrips have accompanying records that are synchronized with the pictures, and others are accompanied with text material. They can be run with or without sound. Sometimes a teacher prefers to run them silently and give his own explanation or call attention to specific points. The equipment is relatively inexpensive and is simple to operate. Hence film strips are used more frequently than motion pictures.

Like motion pictures, filmstrips should be previewed by the teacher. He should be well acquainted with the teacher's manual that accompanies the filmstrip to make certain that he knows the purpose to be served by showing the filmstrip and that it meets his purpose. The pupils need to be prepared for the showing. While the filmstrip is being viewed, the teacher can make appropriate comments in order to direct the pupils' attention to important points. After the viewing, its contents should be discussed for the purpose of giving clarification to the ideas in it.

The Use of Slides

The utilization of slides is similar to that of filmstrips. A series of related slides can be helpful in bringing the attention of the class to concrete aspects of a lesson. They are available for many different kinds of learning materials. Commercially prepared slides usually are mounted on glass, but you can prepare your own pictures mounted on cardboard.

Arranging for the showing of slides follows the general pattern used for the viewing of other projected materials. Preview the slides and prepare the pupils for the experience. During the viewing, you can raise questions, make comments, and answer pupils' questions. Use a pointer to note any specific details. One advantage of using slides is that you can keep any one or more of them on view while you discuss specific points to be noted. Of course, either during or after the showing, apply what has been learned from the viewing to the topic under discussion.

The Use of the Opaque Projector

The opaque projector is a valuable and handy teaching aid. Since it projects opaque material by the use of reflected light, you can project suitable materials on a screen, the chalkboard, or a wall of the classroom. Various types of materials that can be projected are a page from a book, a chart or map, a cartoon, a song, a clipping from a newspaper or magazine, and similar illustrative material. It is advisable to have the material properly labeled for showing and filing.

TEACHING MACHINES AND PROGRAMMED INSTRUCTION

A recent innovation in the use of teaching aids usually is referred to as programmed instruction or programmed learning. In this form of learning, a series of related problem materials is presented to the pupil. He is required to respond to each step in the series. He is apprised immediately of the correct response and can evaluate his performance. In its fundamental concept, programmed instruction is similar to the purpose of the workbook technique (except that in the latter procedure, the pupil usually does not have the correct response immediately available but must seek it in a textbook or other source of information).

The Essentials of Programmed Instruction

Programmed instruction has made great strides, especially in our large cities. Much thought and experimentation already has gone into meeting the various types of problems that arise in connection with its best implementation. The following not only describes the process but also gives insight into how it can be developed and utilized in the teaching-learning process:

THE ESSENTIALS OF PROGRAMMED INSTRUCTION [1]

The essentials of programmed instruction are (*a*) presenting the student with a series of logically related problem materials; (*b*) requiring the student to make a response to each step in the series; and (*c*) immediately apprising the student of the correct response.

Together with the student the programmed material comprises a teaching-learning system with immediate feedback. The rate of learning is determined by the student's ability to absorb new bits of information.

Linear and Intrinsic Programs

There are two kinds of programming systems in current use. The *linear* method utilizes a step-by-step procedure of learner-constructed responses. Progress through the program depends on the learner's making correct responses. Incorrect responses are immediately corrected.

The *intrinsic* method of programming is also known as *branching*. It presents the student with a number of multiple-choice items. Wrong responses are corrected through branching. While in a linear program all students must read every frame in an identical sequence, intrinsic programs provide for skipping items or taking an abbreviated track.

Advocates of intrinsic programming regard the teaching-learning act as a communication process. For example, according to N. A. Crowder, the

---

[1] Reprinted from *Curriculum and Materials* by permission of the Board of Education of the City of New York, XVII, No. 2 (Winter, 1963), 4–5.

response primarily serves the purpose of informing the student as to whether or not the initial communication process was successful.

If the response is wrong the program assumes that the error in learning occurred somewhere before the response was made, and therefore directs the student into a remedial or corrective sequence. Schematically, the items (or frames) in an intrinsic program may be arranged as follows:

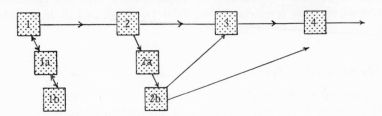

B. F. Skinner and other advocates of linear programming maintain that the act of responding tends to cause learning. This necessitates breaking-down and ordering information into small steps so that the student can always answer correctly. Each item in a linear program is presented in an ordered sequence. Schematically, the items in a linear program may be arranged as follows:

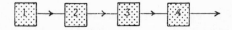

Programmed instruction makes it possible to achieve some of the critical functions of the teaching-learning process through self-instruction. It has the following advantages:

1. Each student progresses at his own rate.
2. It provides the learner with immediate feedback and reinforcement.
3. It can free the teacher from some of the less creative aspects of teaching.
4. It provides a method for the controlled study of teaching and learning.

Teaching Machines and Programmed Instruction

Until recently, the proliferation of teaching machines has overshadowed the concept of programmed instruction in the popular mind. However, it is important to indicate that a significant difference exists between the two.

Teaching machines are inherently stimulus devices and as such can be considered audio-visual aids, similar to film projectors or tape recorders. On the other hand, programmed instruction is a particular method of presenting learning material. While teaching machines are the "hardware" (with varying degrees of complexity), programmed instruction is the implementation of a number of theoretical principles of learning.

Programmed material can conceivably be presented by any number or types of machines, including film projectors and/or tape recorders. In another sense, programming can be compared to careful teaching which thoroughly analyzes materials and presents them to pupils in small, progressive steps.

The utilization of programmed instruction and/or teaching machines presents two distinct problems. The acceptance of programmed instruction in education will depend, at least in a good measure, on its theoretical soundness and practical implementation. The choice of the particular vehicle or vehicles (teaching machines) for the presentation of programmed instruction will depend on factors of economy and mechanical efficiency.

Implications for Curriculum

Programmed instruction has numerous implications for curriculum research and development. In the evaluation of curriculum materials one of the greatest sources of error is teacher variation. Porter suggests that "mechanical devices can go far toward eliminating the 'teacher effect' in educational investigations." [2]

The development of curriculum under programmed instruction becomes subject to specific principles which in turn are directly related to a theoretical system. Stolurow suggests that programmed instruction offers a method of reexamining the instructional process itself rather than, as is usually the case, shoring up existing procedures by adding additional activities.

Most persons associated with teaching machines and/or programmed instruction feel that they are here to stay. It would be unfortunate, however, if the educational possibilities of programmed instruction were to go the way of all too many suggested innovations.

The most significant contribution that programmed instruction may be able to make to education is that of providing educators with a sound theory of teaching and learning.

Some of the ramifications of programmed instruction, and its implications for curriculum, may be seen from the flow chart.

Values of Programmed Instruction

Learning material that is carefully and completely programmed enables the child to progress at his own rate of speed. A bright pupil is not held back, and a slower pupil can work as slowly as he finds it necessary for mastery and understanding of the particular learning material. This approach also enables the student to vary his speed of progress in terms of his interest and special talent.

[2] D. Porter, "A Critical Review of a Portion of the Literature on Teaching Devices," in A. S. Lumsdaine and R. Glaser, *Teaching Machines and Programmed Learning* (Washington, D.C.: National Education Assoc., 1960), p. 126.

LEVEL 1. INFORMATION AND EXPLORATION

| Investigation of area by and through:

Literature
Speakers
Commercially prepared materials and demonstrations
Visitations
Workshops
Committees | → | Decision making for development and/or utilization | → | Establishing machinery for:

Administration
Implementation and evaluation
Control
Teacher training for use and/or development | → | Definition:

Why? (rationale)
Need, interest
Where? (placement)
Curriculum area
Grade level
Pupil population (kind)
How? (design)
Program length
Time allotment
Pupil population (size) |

LEVEL 2. PROGRAM SELECTION

| Criteria for selection:

Subject matter
Authorship
Technological
Sampling
Statistical analysis | ← | Curriculum outcomes:

Behavioral objectives
Knowledge
Skills
Attitudes |

LEVEL 3. RESEARCH AND DEVELOPMENT

Completion of program — Revision of items — Writing of items

Final Editing — Training of programmers — Selection programmers

Testing of program with sample of pupils — Retesting of items with individual pupils — Pretesting of items with individual pupils

Utilization of selected or developed program

LEVEL 4. EVALUATION AND EXPERIMENTATION

Evaluation of program in terms of: Curriculum objectives Scope Sequence Time Error rate		Adaptation to curriculum pattern
	Decision making for future utilization	Modification of curriculum content and/or methodology
Research on programmed instruction related to: Curriculum Learning process Teaching process Pupil characteristics Other related problems		Approved
		Disapproved

Fig. 5.—Programmed instruction activities flow chart.

The challenge to the teacher is to discover how best to use this new teaching aid in the teaching situation. Although it is an aid that has been constructed by educators, it is tested by pupils in the teaching-learning situation. Both teachers and pupils need to perfect ways of utilizing this new tool for the purpose intended—that of helping the learner in his pursuit of an education.

Teaching machines and audio-instructional methods and devices never can serve as a substitute for teachers. They may have value, however, to the learner in various ways. Programmed instruction, for example, can be helpful to the child through attempts at self-instruction. He thus can be motivated to formulate his own plans of learning activity (*self-teaching*) ; he can work at his own rate (*self-pacing*) ; he can score his own answers (*self-testing*) ; and he can discover his own errors (*self-diagnosis*). Helpful learning possibilities are inherent in this approach. The actual educational worth is an unknown factor, and will vary with individuals. There is concern also that many learning needs will not be met and that undesirable rote rather than functional learning will result.

RADIO, RECORDINGS, AND TELEVISION

School people are becoming increasingly alert to the value of radio broadcasts, recordings, and television programs as teaching-learning aids. The utilization of these media for educational as well as entertainment purposes among people at large has done much to enhance their worth within schools as well as outside the school. You probably are acquainted with their use as educational media. Hence we shall offer only a few suggestions for their application.

The Use of the Radio in Education

The radio probably can be used most effectively by teachers of music, language arts, science, and the social studies. Some commercially sponsored radio programs, for example, are excellent media for helping pupils (1) improve their knowledge of current happenings and other news events, (2) gain an understanding of scientific advances, (3) learn to appreciate artistic production, and (4) become acquainted with leaders in various fields as the latter relate their experiences and expound on their points of view.

Some of the larger school systems have instituted their own radio systems. The Cleveland school system was the first to experiment with radio broadcasting on a large scale. During the school year, Station WBOE operates daily from 8 A.M. to 4 P.M. Programs are broadcast for the purpose of giving demonstration lessons and for bringing to young people many stimulating and enriching programs. Other school systems also have access to radio programs throughout the school day. Some of these are broadcast by the school system, and others are commercially produced.

Many elementary schools have a sufficient number of radio sets so that they can be used in individual classrooms. Teachers need training in their utilization, however, in order to become proficient in selecting appropriate programs and in preparing pupils for participation in them. One advantage of the radio is that it affords pupils an opportunity to learn how to listen thoughtfully so that they benefit from the experience. A good radio listener gives active attention to what he hears, especially if the material included in the broadcast is discussed immediately after the listening and associated with the specific purposes of the lesson under consideration.

An effective learning aid is the presentation of pupil-planned and pupil-conducted radio broadcasts. These programs can include dramatic presentations, panel discussions, a survey of pupil activities, musical programs, quiz programs, reports of sports events, and many others. Some of these pupil-sponsored activities are disseminated over the school address system; others are broadcast to interested persons outside the school by way of the cooperation of the local broadcasting stations.

The Use of Recordings

Commercially transcribed or school-prepared recordings have considerable value as learning aids. Often, it is not possible for a particular group of pupils to listen to the original broadcast. A wire tape or disc recording then can be played at an appropriate time. At present, many commercial radio companies make recordings or transcriptions of programs that are suitable for school use. Some schools maintain a library of pertinent materials that can be borrowed by individual teachers.

As the need for it arises, an appropriate recording technique can be used as a teaching aid in various subject fields. Of particular value to the teacher of music is the recording of a musical composition. The learners are motivated to direct their attention to specific musical qualities, such as rhythm, tone quality, cadence, and theme. In the teaching of a foreign language, recordings are used as the bases of instruction in the proper use of the language, voice quality, pronunciation, and organization of ideas. The language laboratory is becoming a fixture in the teaching of foreign languages in many schools.

The Use of Television Programs

At present, the utilization of television programs for educational purposes is receiving considerable attention from school people. In their attempts to tie in this popular medium of mass communication with school needs, educators are encountering several problems. Telecasts vary in their educational value. The installation of adequate sets is expensive. Arranging for the viewing during school hours of worthwhile programs, such as eyewitness reports of important happenings, legislative sessions, significant conferences, holiday celebrations, and the like, may disrupt scheduled class activities. Teachers need training in the proper use of this teaching aid.

Young people are avid television viewers, but they are not always discriminating in their selections, however. Exciting programs, such as Westerns and mystery stories, and variety shows seem to have popular appeal. These often conflict in time, especially with after-school programs that teachers wish their pupils to view. It often is difficult to convince a child that he should give up watching a particularly engrossing program for one that may have educational value for him but that he finds much less interesting.

In spite of high costs and difficulties of operation, some civic organizations and schools are experimenting with this medium. Closed- and open-circuit television is coming into some use. An extremely interesting experiment in educational television was begun in 1961. Known as the Midwest Project on Airborne Television Instruction, this project brings televised educational materials into hundreds of school systems in states such as Indiana, Illinois, Kentucky, Ohio, Michigan, and Wisconsin. The cost of the experiment has been carried by the Ford Foundation and various contributors from industry.

Various agencies are providing schools with appropriate televised materials for school use. For example, television cameras are now so constructed as to make it possible to project the field under a microscope onto a TV screen in such a way as to show an enlarged plant cell. Through this approach, it is possible for everyone, at the same time, to view it and for the teacher to interpret what is being observed. This is likely to be more effective than having each pupil in turn observe through the eyepiece of the microscope.

Regardless of whether meager or rich televised material is available for your use, you need to follow suggestions for its viewing similar to those indicated for the use of motion pictures. Insofar as possible, acquaint yourself with the purpose and content of the telecast; prepare your pupils for its viewing; and discuss its implications with them as soon after they have seen it as is possible.

THE USE OF COMMUNITY RESOURCES

In the preceding pages, we have discussed the value in the teaching-learning process of pupils being exposed to various audio-visual aids. Good as these media of instruction are, young people still need to experience actual situations such as they encounter in their life outside the school. Within the school's community there may be many resources that can add zest to learning. Provision should be made for pupils to know about and work with them.

The utilization of community resources can be handled in one of two ways. Resource people and materials can be brought into the school, or the pupils can go out into the community and learn about conditions and activities at firsthand. As a student teacher, you probably will have little opportunity to participate in the organization of community-pointed projects, but you can become alert to the many learner opportunities that are available in a school's community.

QUESTIONS AND TOPICS FOR DISCUSSION

1. Endeavor to discover what supplementary learning aids for your subject areas are available in your school. Consult your cooperating teacher about the extent of their use.

2. Evaluate the textbooks in various learning areas from the point of view of coverage, reliability, authenticity, and recency. Which ones seem to be most suitable to your needs?

3. How well are you acquainted with available teaching materials in your school library? Neighboring public library?

4. Look through any supplementary reading material you have collected. Appraise their value in light of the questions on pages 265–66.

5. To what extent and how does your cooperating teacher use the chalkboard?

6. List appropriate uses of graphic material in teaching.

7. Which do you prefer to use: films, filmstrips, slides? Give reasons for your opinion.

8. How much training have you had in the use of teaching machines and programmed learning? What purposes do you think are best served by their utilization?

9. What difficulties can you encounter in attempting to utilize radio and television as teaching aids?

10. To what extent and how does your school take advantage of community resources as teaching aids?

12

CLASSROOM MANAGEMENT AND OUT-OF-CLASS RESPONSIBILITIES

By this time, you probably have discovered that teaching, in its broadest connotation, includes the assuming of responsibility for various other activities that have educational implications in that they can enhance learning outcomes. In this chapter, we discuss briefly the problems that confront the teacher in classroom management and the teacher's out-of-class responsibilities.

PROBLEMS ASSOCIATED WITH CLASS MANAGEMENT

In other chapters, we refer to ways in which you can assist your cooperating teacher in caring for certain routines that can facilitate learning. Here we review the significance of the various items that are generally included under the heading of classroom management.

As you observe your cooperating teacher and his class in action, you may be impressed by the fact that the room appears to be a pleasant, comfortable place and that class activities proceed smoothly and with little or no confusion or loss of time. This is not an accident; rather does it reflect the teacher's recognition of the need to provide for the management of routines in such a way that they do not interfere with the primary purpose of the class session—the mastery of specific learning materials.

Purposes Served by Good Classroom Management

The proper conduct of class routines not only frees the teacher and pupils for teaching-learning activities, but has educational value to the extent that thereby the pupils are helped to develop constructive work habits. Some routine activities may have to be performed by the teacher. Others can be delegated to the pupils. In either case, they should be definitely organized at the beginning of the term or year, with the pupils participating, insofar as possible, in their planning. Then, in order to develop good habits of work, whatever procedures are selected should be followed consistently so long as they serve the purposes for which they have been selected.

Much has been said and written about the educational value of stimulating young people's interest by presenting them with the new and the different. This psychological principle does not apply to those details of management that serve as the bases for getting things done quickly and efficiently. An orderly, businesslike atmosphere in the classroom encourages the pupils to devote their energies to study activities and helps them maintain an attitude of desirable control of their behavior. To the extent that pupils understand the purposes of certain classroom procedures and have assisted in setting them up, effective and well-established routines can set the stage for a high degree of efficiency in the conduct of teaching-learning activities.

Types of Routine Activities in the Classroom

The master teacher seeks to achieve an attitude of freedom and informality in the classroom that is conducive to interested and active learning experiences on the part of the pupils. At the same time, certain practical routines need to be more or less formalized in order to avoid waste of time and energy. The following list of items can be regarded as routine matters. Using this checklist as a guide, evaluate routine procedures in the classroom or classrooms in which you are having your pupil-teaching experiences. Also, keep this list in mind when you yourself become a regular teacher.

As a student teacher you need to develop certain routines that will enable your teaching to run smoothly. There are many activities that can be more or less routinized so that the children will know what to expect. The activities that warrant your attention and that have a bearing on routinized plans include attention to such activities and procedures as (1) the physical condition of the room, (2) the tidiness of the room, (3) the movement of pupils, (4) the seating of pupils, (5) the handling of materials and supplies, (6) the making of records and reports, and (7) the system used in classroom procedures.

Many school systems give helpful suggestions to new teachers on the aforementioned points. As an aid to getting started effectively and of knowing what to do in their school system, Kansas City, Missouri, for example, provides its teachers in the elementary school with "Routines and Habits," which they are encouraged to learn and to work into their general plans. We present them here.

ROUTINES AND HABITS [1]

Establish Standards for Routines and Habits

A. Give specific directions for each activity.
B. Be certain the group knows exactly what is expected.
C. Check after the activity to see if expectations were met.
D. Remind the group of these expectations before each future activity.

Plan and Carry Out Routines

A. Enter and leave the room quietly.
B. Move group from place to place in orderly lines: to drinking fountains, toilet rooms, cafeteria, auditorium, and playground.
C. Send children in small groups to cloakroom, then form lines in the room for dismissal.
D. Use drinking fountains and toilet facilities at times provided for the group, except for emergencies.
E. Sharpen pencils at a definite time.
F. Teach children how to use the type of desk provided.
G. Keep orderly desks, inside and out.
H. Put away materials used in one activity before taking out those needed for a new activity.
I. Allow time for changing activities in a quiet and orderly manner.
J. Have desks cleared when the group leaves the room for a brief time, unless the same materials are to be used immediately after returning.
K. Collect all art supplies and keep in storage space.
L. Pass and collect materials according to some organized plan.
M. Have children remain at desks except at approved times.

Develop Habits

A. Listen attentively in all audience situations.
B. Take turns in conversation, with one person speaking at a time.
C. Follow individual and group directions quickly.
D. Start work immediately; make good use of time.

[1] *Routines and Habits* (Kansas City, Mo.: Board of Education), mimeographed. Reprinted by permission.

E. Complete assigned work before undertaking self-chosen activities.
F. Use a standard form for all written work. (See mimeographed sheet for Written Work, Grades 4–7)
G. Use a small check (√) to indicate an error and no mark if the work is correct.
H. Leave all papers in tablets unless a reason is given for removing them.
I. Use social courtesies such as "thank you," "please," and "excuse me" at appropriate times.
J. Show courtesy when other children make obvious errors.

SUGGESTIONS FOR PERFORMING CLASS ROUTINES

The need for the establishment of classroom routines is great. A few suggestions concerning their nature and use are presented for your attention.

Physical condition of the room. It is important that there is sufficient light in all parts of the room so that no child suffers from eyestrain. According to the direction of the sun, those pupils who sit near the windows may be exposed to a glare, necessitating the drawing down of the window shades; but doing this may prevent children who are removed from the windows from having enough light by which to read or write. Hence artificial lighting may be required. You can assist your cooperating teacher by caring for this detail of class management. Watch the direction taken by the sun and adjust the shades so as to avoid glare or shadows. Regulate the artificial light as needed. Also, when the class leaves the room, make certain that the electric light is turned off. Teachers' carelessness in this matter can cost the school community a considerable amount of money.

The proper regulation of the room's temperature and its ventilation are matters that should be a primary concern of the teacher. As he and the class become involved in lesson activities, they tend to be unaware of the fact that the room is becoming overly warm and "stuffy." The temperature should range between 68° and 72° F., and the humidity should be about 40 to 50 per cent.

The teacher needs to consult the thermometer occasionally and see to it that the room is well ventilated. Care must be taken, however, that no pupil sits in a draft. It may be advisable to ventilate the room at the beginning of a period. If the room has regular double windows, the top one should be opened, rather than the bottom one.

In many schools, the opening and closing of windows is the teacher's responsibility. Pupils are not permitted to handle window poles.

Children tend to differ greatly in height. The seats in the classroom must be so adjusted to their needs that their feet can rest comfortably on the floor. This is taken care of in most schools by having furniture of different sizes. The teacher should so seat the pupils that the seating arrangements are satisfactory. If this is not possible with the desks and chairs already in the room, proper adjustment of furniture may be needed.

Neatness and attractiveness of the room. You are responsible for the neatness of your room. Pupils can be delegated in turn to pass a wastepaper basket around the room and to gather scraps of paper or other materials from the desks or floor. This can be done quietly as a matter of habit, with a minimum of interruption of regular class activity. Children should be discouraged from leaving waste materials in their desks. An occasional inspection and cleaning out of pupils' desks may be necessary. The teacher should set a good example by keeping his own desk uncluttered.

The storing of needed materials also requires constant attention. Pupils can be trained to take care of this routine. Classroom storage space often is inadequate. Books, maps, equipment, and other materials should be returned to their storage space after they have been used.

Each teacher should make certain that (1) all chalkboards are cleaned at the end of every lesson, and (2) bulletin boards are attractively arranged and contain only pertinent material that is removed as soon as its purpose for being displayed has been fulfilled. Pupils can be delegated to attend to the care of chalkboards and bulletin boards.

Distribution of material. Much time and energy can be saved if books, supplies, and other materials can be distributed according to a preplanned system of procedure. Certain pupils can be named as monitors of various materials to be used during the day. At a directive from the teacher, they can obtain the materials from the closet and distribute them, and then collect and return them to the closet at the appropriate time.

If written homework has been prepared for reading by the teacher, these can be *collected* by the first pupil in each row. This procedure usually saves more time than having the papers passed down the line. Some pupils, as they pass papers, stop to compare what other pupils have done with their own contribution. The teacher also can work out a timesaving plan for *returning* papers. Rather than calling each child by name, he can have the papers arranged according to rows, and have them returned to appropriate pupils by someone in each row. There is one slight objection to this mode of returning corrected papers. A child may be sensitive about having other pupils see the mark he earned on a test, for example. He would prefer to keep this a matter between his teacher and himself.

Movement of pupils in the school. Some schools have relatively strict regulations about pupils wandering around the building. You need to acquaint yourself with the rules of the school in which you are working, and follow whatever its policy may be. In some schools, there is a pass card in each classroom that must be shown by any pupil in the halls upon request by a teacher or monitor. Except in an emergency, a teacher should not permit more than one pupil to leave the room at a time.

The teacher needs to alert his pupils relative to what he expects of them in his classroom. Early in the term, he can make known that he expects them to enter the room in good order, take their seats promptly, and talk among themselves quietly until the signal is given for the start of the lesson. The procedure for leaving the room should be similar to that of entering it.

The seating of pupils. Teachers differ in methods of assigning seats to pupils. Some teachers still employ an alphabetical arrangement. This has an advantage in that it may help the teacher learn the names of his pupils more quickly than he otherwise might. It also has several disadvantages. It places the pupils in relatively the same position in every grade classroom, especially if most teachers place the pupils alphabetically by beginning with *A*'s and continuing through to the *Z*'s. No provision is made for the suitability of the furniture to individual pupils' sizes, or for the meeting of hearing or sight differences. Too many seating changes may need to be made after a seating chart is arranged according to this alphabetical order.

The following is an approach to seating arrangements that has proved itself to be successful with some teachers. For the first few days of the term, the pupils are permitted to select their own seats. Each of these days, the teacher calls the roll for attendance. Generally, roll-calling is regarded as a waste of time. At the beginning of the term, however, it can serve at least two useful purposes: (1) the teacher can learn how to pronounce individual names, and (2) both the teacher and the pupils have an opportunity to associate names with individuals.

One difficulty associated with having pupils select their own seats is that two or more close friends may elect to sit together and are tempted to communicate with one another excessively. The teacher needs to be alert to any such situation, and warn the pupils involved that they must desist from continuing this practice. If the warning brings about no behavior change, he may have to separate them by changing the seat of one or more of them.

The use of systematic procedures. The items under this heading need little further consideration. You already have been alerted to the value of beginning and ending each learning session promptly. Every child should be encouraged to feel that he has a significant share in class activities. If the lesson is well organized and is conducted in an interesting, businesslike fashion, few children will find time to engage in daydreaming or other irrelevant activities.

Study tasks should be assigned in light of individual ability to perform them. Moreover, whatever is assigned for class or home performance should be worthy of the teacher's giving it his attention. Written work, either as a class or a home assignment, should never be destroyed by a teacher before he has read and evaluated it. In fact, pupils like to have all of their written contributions, tests, reports, and the like returned to them with some notation (perhaps no more than a check mark) to indicate that the teacher has looked at it and has recorded something about it.

Handling materials and supplies. You know that when you are planning your work, you need to prepare for the use of any materials. You also realize that you should order supplies such as paper, pencils, paper fasteners, and the like far enough in advance so that you have them conveniently stored and on hand when they are needed. We already have considered such matters as distributing and collecting papers and providing for display of teacher-learning materials.

Your school probably has a uniform policy for the labeling of written work. Discover from your cooperating teacher what this policy is and make certain that your pupils follow prescribed formats. Also, many teachers require their pupils to complete and submit notebooks that contain research material appropriate to the study material of the course. These notebooks should be well organized and neatly prepared. Do not encourage your pupils to spend an undue amount of time on the preparation of elaborate covers. Also, warn them against including any illustrative material that represents the cutting up or otherwise defacing of books or magazine articles that do not belong to them. Some young people are so eager to submit an unusually attractive notebook that they will devote to its preparation time that could be used to better advantage, or include pictures, for example, that have been cut out of library books or taken from materials belonging to their parents.

The making of records and reports. You must be accurate in checking attendance. The class roll book is a document that, on occasions, is needed in court to verify data about a young person's presence in school on a certain day. Considerable embarrassment can be caused the school when or if teachers' records are not correct.

One of a teacher's important functions is the assigning of achievement grades or marks. These must be based on sufficient evidence so that they can be rechecked when necessary. Parents sometimes insist that their child has been treated unfairly, that he has been given a low grade because of personal prejudice, etc. You need to be able to substantiate your evaluation of a pupil's work by having available a series of marks that he has earned during the particular marking period under consideration. Some teachers keep samples of their pupils' written work until the end of the school term or year. They may return them to pupils to examine corrections noted, but then re-collect them, and file them for showing to parents and administrators as needed.

You probably do not need to be reminded that any reports requested by the administration should be submitted promptly and in good form. Negligence on the part of even one teacher can interfere with the smooth running of administrative routines. As a student teacher, you may not know that much paper work must be prepared almost daily by the principal and his staff. The central facility of a school system constantly needs to be alerted to what is going on in the schools. Much of the required information must come from individual teachers. Hence it is essential that you accept this responsibility cheerfully and, in every way that you can, co-operate with your administrative officers.

The use of courtesy in the classroom. To the extent that you display a courteous attitude toward your pupils you are encouraging them to be well mannered in their relationships with one another. Older children usually treat their fellow classmates courteously.

Children also need to receive training in being courteous to visitors. It sometimes happens that the class is interrupted by the entrance into the room of another faculty member. The teacher should not need to do more than excuse himself to the class, perhaps suggesting that they continue the discussion, go on with a project with which they have been working, or consult their books. Upper-grade pupils probably will not need such a reminder, but younger children tend to talk more or less noisily among themselves unless they have been taught to behave courteously.

In their many visits to the classrooms of elementary schools, the authors have been impressed favorably by pupils' courteous treatment of them. A child sitting nearby is likely to alert a visitor to what is happening in the classroom, to give him a copy of the book or other material that is being used, and in other ways make the stranger feel at home. To the extent that our schools are encouraging the development of courteous manners, they are to be much commended.

CLASSROOM MANAGEMENT PROBLEMS

School people of the Philadelphia Public School System have outlined in considerable detail the various aspects of good classroom management. You can profit from reading the suggestions carefully and incorporating them into your own classroom procedures.[2]

CLASS CONTROL

Control varies from authoritarian to self-directing. The teacher must find the control level of the class and begin there. It is especially important that he should not overestimate this level. For detailed guidance, see Administrative Bulletins 22 and 22A, DISCIPLINE FOR CONSTRUCTIVE CITIZENSHIP. Some things to consider are:

[2] Helen Bailey, *Classroom Management for New Teachers* (Philadelphia: Philadelphia Public Schools, 1962), pp. 14–21. Reprinted by permission.

Class Sense

a. Be conscious of every child at all times
b. Be aware of and make provision for individual differences in interests and abilities
c. Watch for signs of fatigue (yawning, restlessness)—introduce a new activity
d. Watch for "high energy output" children—channel them into useful activities
e. When distractions occur, turn them into teaching situations if desirable
f. On certain days in a term that are accompanied by a high degree of excitement, such as stormy days, play days, excursion days, etc., schedule quiet activities—on returning after active experiences, plan to have the children talk about these experiences
g. Gain the attention of the group as a first step in starting a new activity—insist that all desk tops be cleared when activities do not require use of materials

Language and Speech

a. Use a friendly conversational tone which at the same time carries conviction
b. Resist trying to talk louder than the class
c. Adjust the speed of your speech and choice of vocabulary to the maturity level and background of your children
d. Directions are wasted when given to an inattentive class—first make certain everyone is looking and listening; then give the directions step by step, making sure each is understood before going on to the next—use as many sensory channels as possible—for example, use the blackboard along with verbal explanations
e. Avoid talking too much
   (1) Do not make a habit of repeating the child's answer
   (2) Develop co-operative discussion rather than pupil-teacher dialogues
   (3) Avoid lecturing

Class Movements

Loss of control is more likely to occur when the children are moving about; therefore, teacher supervision is essential. All activities which are to be performed regularly and in the same manner should be routinized as soon as possible. Point out the need and develop the routine procedures with your children in accordance with your planning. Then be consistent in using the plan adopted.

a. Entering the Room

(1) Greet the children as they enter

(2) Allow only a portion of the class to go to the coat room at one time

(3) Take a position which will enable you to supervise the coat room and classroom at the same time

(4) Have planned before-school work—as control is established this can be less formal

b. Leaving the Room

(1) Dismissal—Escort children to the place indicated by your principal in a prompt and orderly manner

(2) Adjust time allowance required for dressing to weather conditions

(3) Lavatory privilege—Consult your principal for local rules and the nurse for individual cases

(4) Teacher—If for any reason the teacher must leave the room, arrangements must be made for the class to be supervised by another teacher

c. Movement Within the Room

(1) The beginning teacher must insist that the children remain in their seats until granted permission to come to the teacher. Learn not to answer the child who disregards this requirement.

(2) Pencil sharpening requires regulation and supervision. Ask your helping teacher for the local practice. A proper attitude toward an orderly procedure is the key to the elimination of disorder. Some teachers have the class use school pencils with two central storage boxes. Pencils with broken points are put in one box and sharpened pencils taken from the other.

(3) Use of the waste basket also requires supervision. Some classes may be able to use the basket on an individual basis. More often the teacher will find it more orderly to have fixed times for collections. For example, a helper may carry the basket through the aisles just before recesses and dismissals.

(4) Changing seats for regrouping must be done in an orderly manner if the children are to arrive in their new seats in a state of readiness to work. Any movement must be planned with the children so as to avoid having them pass in opposite directions or having lines cross. It may be best to send one group at a time. In rooms with movable furniture, the new teacher would be wise to limit regrouping to the movement of chairs.

(5) Helpers, to be of real value, must be briefed on their work. Jobs should be rotated. By discussion with the class, standards of performance can be developed.

(6) Use of the classroom library, centers of interest such as the science table and display boards, activities for children who finish their work before others, etc., also require planning and supervision.

d. Passing Through the Halls

    (1) Pupil leaders must be advised of route and stopping places
    (2) Usually a teacher can control a line best from the rear
    (3) Consideration of others requires quiet movements

e. Safety Drills—Air Raid and Fire

    (1) Consult the principal for your school policy
    (2) Generally speaking, automatic response and absolute quiet are minimum requirements
    (3) From the first day, teach procedures and practice performance

BEHAVIOR CONTROL

Behavior in school is conditioned by the level of control in the home and community. Fewer behavior problems arise if our work is geared to the achievement levels and interests of the children.

Improper Methods of Behavior Control—Negative methods of dealing with children, even when seemingly effective, should never be used. The most common of these are:

a. The use of subject material as a disciplinary measure—for example, the repeating of a sentence 100 times, the assignment of numerous arithmetic examples, etc.
b. Frequent detentions
c. Sarcastic comments
d. Forced apologies
e. Personal indignities
f. Sending a pupil out of the room where he will not be under supervision
g. Sending a pupil to a lower grade
h. Placing a pupil in the corner
i. Encouraging the class to shun or reject a child
j. Corporal punishment—use of physical force of any kind to secure obedience is *absolutely forbidden* in Philadelphia

Proper Methods of Behavior Control

Your class reflects you. "Be self-controlled, for this is the foundation on which you develop control over others." Develop standards of behavior with the children and be consistent in following through. Let the child know in advance you will accept him even though you will not accept his misbehavior.

a. Signal Interference—A nod, frown, or raised eye-brow to the offender
b. Proximity Control—Move close to the child who seems about to cause trouble
c. Planned Ignoring—Some situations are best ignored at the time for the

best interests of the class—however, the teacher must make a note of them for a later conference

d. Separation—There are times when a change of seating will help both child and group—isolation should be a temporary measure—teacher and child should work on mastery of control so that the child may be restored to the group

e. Deprivation—Deprive the child of the privilege of taking part in the lesson when his behavior has obstructed group progress—subsequently this child would make up the assigned work

f. Group Control—Be sure the limits of control are co-operatively formulated and are understood—then the child should feel responsibility to the group for living up to the standards

g. Praise and Encouragement—Praise and encouragement for acceptable behavior is more effective than nagging

h. Emergency Action—The teacher is responsible for seeing that the safety of the children is not endangered by a pupil's misconduct—the teacher should take whatever reasonable and practical steps are necessary in such exigencies

i. Help from the Principal—Usually a good teacher handles his own discipline, but there are times when the best teachers have individual problem cases. Such conditions are not to be considered personal failures. Go to your principal for advice if a discipline problem is becoming acute.

j. Other Help—If the teacher feels the need of help from other school personnel such as the home and school visitor, school nurse, or counseling teacher, he should consult the principal

GENERAL PREPARATIONS

Know Your Children

a. Learn their names quickly—use seating chart and/or name plates
b. Study records for abilities, interests, and physical condition
c. Become aware of reading, arithmetic, and spelling levels
d. Consider the home background; make a tour of your school community
e. Recognize leaders, followers, and friends

Know Your Teaching Materials

a. Guides—Consult your principal for the guides you should have (Music, Health, and Physical Education guides are written for specific grades)—familiarize yourself with them
b. Books—Consult your principal (see page 10)
c. Illustrative Material (see page 10)
d. Teaching Equipment (see page 9)—Learn to use before utilizing in a lesson

e. Supplies—Have needed materials prepared and on hand in the classroom and not in the hall closet; pencils sharpened, paper cut, books handy, crayons and paints ready, etc. Many a lesson has been ruined, the interest lost, and disorder created because the teacher had to seek materials (see page 10)

THE ROOM

Factors concerning the health, comfort, and control of the children are:

Seating (rooms are equipped with two or more desk sizes)

a. Fit the desk to the child in order that:
   (1) Feet are placed flat on the floor
   (2) Knees clear the under side of the desk
b. Seat children with eye and ear disabilities in the best vantage points
c. Seat small children where the view of the chalk board is unobstructed
d. Children should not sit facing direct light for long periods of time—the teacher should stand in such a position that children are not forced to face the glare from the windows
e. Consult your publication on GROUPING for basic seating patterns if the room has movable furniture (be sure the desk and chair match in size)

Lighting

a. Shades should be adjusted by the teacher to:
   (1) Provide maximum daylight
   (2) Eliminate glare and reflections on the chalk board and pupils' desks
b. Electric lights
   (1) Supplement daylight with electric light only when necessary
   (2) Turn off lights when not needed
   (3) Conserve electricity—turn lights off when leaving room

Ventilation and Temperature Control

a. When the room needs ventilating, ascertain from your principal the procedure you should use (recess time, noon, etc.)
b. Check on removal of excess clothing

Appearance

The room should reflect the daily activities of the class; also, it should be attractive and stimulating *a.* Decoration

   (1) Display boards should be the result of co-operative planning (this should be a teaching-learning situation)—the effectiveness of the display boards can be judged by the active interest of the children
      (*a*) Change the board as new activities replace the old
      (*b*) Use harmonious background colors
      (*c*) Anything worth displaying is worthy of a caption
      (*d*) Use rules of composition for arrangements
      (*e*) Display "improved work" as well as "best work"
      (*f*) Put smaller displays at the eye level of the children
      (*g*) Set aside an area for the teacher's use (a model display)
   (2) Window sills (not a storage space)
      A colorful protection will enhance the setting for your plants and flowers

b. Housekeeping

   (1) Walls and woodwork—avoid using nails, thumb tacks, or adhering tape
   (2) Pupils' desks—teach orderly arrangement—provide for periodic cleaning—the teacher's desk should be a model of orderliness
   (3) Floors—a clean floor is a reflection of your health program—develop a plan for the time and method of using the waste basket
   (4) Dressing room and storage areas—maintain a neat and orderly appearance
   (5) Clean-up—during the day, the teacher must plan to allow time in the program for a clean-up at the end of any activity
   (6) At the end of the day—see the principal for procedures to be followed in regard to:
      (*a*) Placement of classroom furniture
      (*b*) Disposal of trash
      (*c*) Arrangement of shades and windows
      (*d*) Care of erasers and chalk boards

GROUPING

At the very beginning of the term, the new teacher will normally work with the whole class as one group. When the teacher thinks the class is ready for group activity, group procedures may be introduced gradually. Grouping is necessary for effective modern teaching. It requires much planning and preparation; first, by the teacher, and later, by teacher and pupils together. Some requirements for successful group activity are:

1. The teacher must have full control of the whole class before attempting group activity.
2. The activity must have within it different levels or areas suited to the needs of the children.

3. The teacher must have the necessary materials on hand and in condition for the children to use (in the room itself—paper cut, pencils sharpened, etc.)
4. Some children must work more or less independently while the teacher is directing the activity of others. Therefore, the independent group must know how to do the work without help. This means the particular activity must be taught to the whole class before it is assigned for group activity.
5. The first part of each lesson in which there is group activity must be given over to a discussion of exactly:
    a. What is to be done
    b. Where the child is to do it
    c. Who is to do it
    d. What materials the child is to use
    e. What outcomes are to be expected
    f. What is to be done by those who finish early
6. The last part of each lesson should usually be devoted to checking outcomes:
    a. What did we get done?
    b. What should we work on next time?
    c. How well did we work?
7. Consult Curriculum Office publication, GROUPING.

RESPONSIBILITIES OUTSIDE THE CLASSROOM

The responsibility of the elementary school teacher for pupil welfare and for other professional obligations goes beyond his regular classroom duties. These various phases of teacher responsibilities are listed by the Des Moines Department of Elementary Education as follows: [3]

SUPERVISION OF CHILDREN

The work of the elementary school teacher is concerned with the total growth and development of the pupils under his guidance. Learning occurs outside of the classroom as well as within it. To plan effectively for the total needs of children, a teacher must be aware of their activities in the halls, in the lunchroom, on the playgrounds. Thus, supervision is part of the teaching job.

Young children need careful, continuous guidance in developing desirable patterns of behavior. Responsibility for that guidance rests with each member of the faculty. Supervisory duties are planned at the building level to meet building needs. The duties may vary somewhat from building to build-

[3] Robert R. Denny and Sarah M. Page, *Elementary Handbook* (Des Moines, Iowa: Department of Elementary Education, 1963), pp. 57–59. Reprinted by permission.

ing but, in general, they provide for the supervision of children from the time they come to school until they leave for home.

COMMITTEE WORK

There will be opportunities for you to grow professionally through participation in committee work. Though these activities require time, they reward the participant through: (1) the satisfaction of contributing to the building, the system, and the community; (2) the stimulation of the exchange of ideas; (3) the formation of friendships with co-workers from other schools in the system.

PROFESSIONAL MEETINGS

Pre-service college education is the beginning of preparation for teaching; it is not the end. Growth within the profession continues through each day of experience. There are no hard-and-fast rules for solving the problems that arise. Much of the learning takes place when the teacher faces the actual situation. In-service professional meetings are planned to aid you in solving the problems and to help you develop your ability to teach. They may have various names (faculty meetings, area meetings, sectional meetings, general meetings) but they have one purpose in common: to help you "grow on the job." Thus, they are part of the teaching job.

There are several types of in-service meetings. They may be for buildings, areas, sections, or the entire instructional staff. They involve a representative of a building or a grade level, or teachers from a grade level or department. They may be called by the superintendent, directors, supervisor, or principals.

Faculty Meetings

Wednesday nights are reserved for faculty meetings except in cases where a principal supervises two buildings. In such instances another time will be designated.

These meetings are devoted to discussing items that are of concern to the immediate faculty.

If a meeting is called outside the building at any time when there is a faculty meeting within the building, the teacher should always consult the principal before making a decision in regard to which meeting he is to attend. Effort is made to avoid conflicts, but they do occur sometimes.

Area Meetings

To expedite the transmission of information, it is necessary at times for the faculties of schools near each other to meet at a central location. These are called area meetings.

Sectional Meetings

Sectional meetings are composed of several area groups in the same general vicinity. Sectional meetings are held at a central location and are used as a means of contacting many faculties at one time.

Supervisors Meetings

Thursday is reserved for meetings called by supervisors. If circumstances are such that a teacher must be absent from a meeting called by a supervisor or director, he should make previous arrangements with the person who called the meeting.

Planned Observations

Principals may plan for inter-school or intra-school visitations.

The directors of the different departments may arrange for teachers to observe a textbook consultant demonstrate or discuss the use of a guidebook or text. They may plan workshops to help teachers learn how to use materials and equipment, how to make permanent seatwork materials, etc.

General Meetings

General meetings involve the entire instructional staff and are usually listed in the general bulletin issued from the Superintendent's Office each Tuesday.

The large-group meetings are scheduled as needed. There is no definite day for them as there is for faculty meetings.

Television In-service Meetings

Some meetings are telecast over KDPS-TV to be viewed by school personnel.

QUESTIONS AND TOPICS FOR DISCUSSION

1. As a result of your observation of your cooperating teacher's classroom routines, note any that could be improved. What changes would you recommend?
2. List at least five classroom routines that could be performed by children in Grade four and above.
3. Why should children not be permitted to use window poles?
4. What type of seating arrangement is utilized by your cooperating teacher? How well does it function?
5. What is the attitude of your cooperating teacher toward written work submitted by his pupils?

6. Keep a list of reports your cooperating teacher submits to the administration. For each report note its purpose and the time required to prepare it.
7. Cite examples of courteous behavior on the part of the children in your classroom.
8. How does your cooperating teacher handle instances of discourtesy among the pupils?
9. List the out-of-class responsibilities of your cooperating teacher.
10. To what extent are you, as a student teacher, given an opportunity to participate in classroom management and out-of-class responsibilities?
11. Does your school allow for any club or out-of-class activities for the children? Describe and evaluate any that are available.

13

THE DISCIPLINE PROBLEM

The ultimate goal of an individual is to develop the kind of behavior that will enable him to become an accepted member of his societal group where that may be and whenever it is necessary. The achievement of this goal represents a long road of learning and behaving. A person is not born a self-disciplined individual nor does he achieve that self-controlled behavior without many experiences in working with others. He literally grows into the kind of behavior that he comes to utilize in his everyday activities.

In the classroom, the teacher is concerned with the kind of behavior, both individual and group, that will enable the teaching-learning process to continue in such a way that optimum results can be obtained. Often unknown to the learners, the teacher is trying his best to provide good learning conditions for his pupils.

GENERAL CONCEPTS OF GOOD DISCIPLINE

Although a well-disciplined individual is the pride of the family, of any school, and of society, we are concerned here with what has happened to that individual to make him the behaving person he is and what can be done to train him to be an effective social unit in his group, regardless of its size or purpose, or whether it is within the school or outside the school.

Discipline in the school implies behavior in some form. Various types of behavior become a part of an individual as he lives day by day, week by week, and year by year in his home, his school, and his other social settings. The teacher usually has two general concerns in coping with the problems of discipline: (1) he wants sufficient quiet in his classroom to enable him to discharge his function as a teacher, and (2) he wants each of his pupils to become the kind of person who can function as a democratic citizen wherever he may be and whenever called on to set an example to others.

Impact of Earlier Training

The function of the school is greater than that of making Johnny conform to expected behavior. Parents sometimes have the notion that the development of needed inner behavior controls is the function only of the school. The parent of the preschool child often is heard to remark, "When you go to school, your teacher will make you behave." Although we are interested in the discipline problem of the elementary school, we must not lose sight of the fact that the child comes to his teachers with habit patterns of behavior that are partly formed in the home. The parents in the home do more than they realize in the way of giving direction to the ultimate behavior of the growing child. There is general agreement that the child learns more during the first five years of life than during any other comparable period. The relative weight may be even greater in the area of behavior outcomes.

Goal of Behavior Development

As our understanding of child psychology increases, we are learning that there are forces at work on individuals during their developing years to determine the kind of behavior they will exhibit at any stage of their development. No longer are we attempting to impose a forced obedience; rather are we trying to encourage the development of self-discipline under sympathetic guidance. The child who is encouraged in the home to practice self-control comes to school ready to live cooperatively with others in his new environment.

The ultimate goal of the individual is to develop the kind of behavior that will serve him well in all situations—the classroom, the social situation, and the home. He is then self-disciplined. He exhibits self-control. He is under less tension when he has these inner controls that constantly work for him. His emotions work for him because he possesses the behavior habits that are of value to him in his relationships with other people.

The individual who is able to change habitual behavior that interferes with his welfare and the welfare of others in his struggles for social acceptance becomes the kind of person who is easily accepted by others. He demonstrates traits of self-control and of self-discipline. Thus the development of self-control and of self-discipline becomes one of the most important goals toward which an individual can strive.

Need for Adjustment to Specific Situations

Any individual, of whatever age, who enters a social situation must learn to meet the needs of that situation. He soon discovers that he must adjust to the habits, thinking, and mores or general habit patterns of the group. As he enters into the activities of the group, he learns to give and take in his struggles toward self-realization. He becomes sensitive to the wishes and behavior of those with whom he associates. He often defers to the interests and wishes of the members of the group.

A child's going to school is a common practice, but the school to which he goes is a particular school and different from every other school in the country. Likewise, each classroom is different from every other classroom, not only in the country as a whole but also in the building in which it is located. Many factors account for this difference. Among the important considerations are the attitudes of the teacher and of the particular learners who inhabit the room.

In his attempt to achieve what he seems to be there to achieve, each child learns to cooperate with the other learners present and with the leader—the teacher. To provide a good working situation and establish good working relationships, it becomes necessary to know what is expected of every member of the class. Hence there is a need for the formulation of rules to govern behavior for effective learning conditions. Not only should each learner know the rules that should govern his behavior but he should help, insofar as possible, to set them up so that he understands them and knows why their enforcement is necessary. Then, too, he should know who is given the responsibility to apply the rules whenever necessary to bring his behavior or that of others in line with established practices.

Need for Concern with Drives of Individuals

It is normal for a child to strive to satisfy his drives and urges in a way that may give him the greatest pleasure. If he were the only person involved, the behavior displayed might be of little concern, but it must be realized that he functions along with other human beings in a situation. Each of the other individuals also has personal drives and urges that he is interested in satisfying. Hence a clash of expression of individual drives may ensue unless some adaptations are made in the behavior displayed by everyone. The responsibility then falls to each to inhibit any personal drive or activity that may interfere with the approved activity of others. This attempt at self-control is needed if learning conditions are to be worth while.

A great concern of pupils and of a beginning teacher is associated with the problem of discipline. The student teacher may exhibit considerable fear that he will have difficulty in achieving good discipline in his class. This is not an unfounded apprehension. No matter how extensive and intensive your subject matter mastery is, you soon discover that your teaching success rests heavily on your ability to control your class to the extent that you and the pupils can participate in the teaching-learning activities that you have planned.

The urge on the part of an older child to test the teacher is great. The urge to give a student teacher a difficult time may be even greater. Two attitudes often prevail among children: (1) they want to provide the best teaching conditions possible for you as a student teacher and hence cooperate to their best ability, or (2) they set about to make it difficult for you and give you what they call the full treatment. They practice all the tricks of teacher testing.

Need for Self-Discipline Rather Than Discipline in the Classroom

The implication of discipline is that obedience prevails in the classroom but that it is predicated upon the direct reaction to superimposed authority displayed by the teacher—the authority figure. Human behavior needs to be controlled either from within or from without. When the control force is from a source outside the individual, he may display disciplined behavior. However, when he responds to a force that directs his behavior from within himself, he is considered to be self-disciplined.

A child needs disciplined behavior for his own life adjustment. How to achieve that kind of behavior is most important to him and to those who attempt to help him gain commendable behavior controls. Until recently, educators regarded discipline as referring to what is done in the classroom to force learners to redirect their behavior to conform to those rules and regulations as set forth by the school and/or the classroom teacher, and rigidly enforced by way of one or another drastic overt means. The ability of the teacher to gain overt obedience to his commands was believed to be evidence that a class was well disciplined.

Today there is greater emphasis on other factors in the classroom situation that contribute to disciplined behavior. We are more concerned about the teacher's attitude toward pupils' behavior and the effect of their behavior on the learning process. The cause of any noise in a classroom is more important than the fact that there is noise, or the amount of noise that may be present. We are especially concerned that the learning situation is conducive for every member of the group to be able to progress toward the achievement of his educational goals.

Basic Principles of Discipline

As a student teacher or a beginning teacher, you rightly can be interested in the problem of discipline. You may not have received help along these lines in your other college courses. You may not have been informed of many of the problems that you will face in your initial teaching. Hence some guiding principles here may help point the way for your thinking and planning in coping with many of the problems that are likely to arise.

You need to discover much about the policy of the elementary school in which you are doing your student teaching, the nature of the children, and what is expected of the teacher. Of equal importance is the cooperating teacher. You need to learn how to work with him and to be given the kinds of opportunities that will enable you to cope with discipline situations on your own. Unless you have some knowledge on these points, you may find it difficult to adapt your teaching to the needs of the school, the teacher, and the learners.

The following general principles may be helpful to you in the development of self-discipline among your pupils. They embody elements of good teaching. When carefully followed, they may help not only you as the teacher but also your pupils, whose behavior you are stimulating toward the kind of self-discipline that will be good in the classroom as well as in other group situations. In your attempt to guide the behavior of your learners, strive to:

1. Stimulate each learner to adopt a plan of action that will enable him to attain a worthwhile goal.
2. Follow the lead of your cooperating teacher.
3. Interpret all rules and regulations so that they are understood by all learners.
4. Make clear to your pupils that an infringement of rules warrants a penalty.
5. Offer teaching leadership so that your pupils are not expected to remain quiet for the sole purpose of being orderly.
6. Have classroom conditions reflect out-of-class life situations.
7. Help pupils establish habits of behavior essential to self-discipline.
8. Provide forms of activity that enable the members of the group to participate actively without the need for complete silence at all times.
9. Provide effective learner activity during each classroom session.
10. Provide for individual differences.
11. Enlist the cooperation of the class in achieving good learner conduct.
12. Deal with the misdeed rather than making it personal.
13. Establish classroom routines in class management.
14. Help each learner consciously develop self-discipline.
15. Display the kinds of attitudes that will invite cooperative behavior.

BASIC BEHAVIOR DIFFICULTIES OF CHILDREN

During the early years, unless care is taken, a young child may develop behavior habits that are unwholesome. The young child meets his needs by displaying behavior that is aggressive and selfish. He has not yet learned that he should be polite. When he wants something he reaches for it and may grab it. Likewise, when something is taken away from him and he does not understand the reason for this, he may object vociferously. This is his way of communicating his feelings. The older child's attitude may be similar, but he is learning to use more subtle ways of expressing his feelings.

Why Children Misbehave

All young people have drives of aggressiveness and self-interest. These drives continue throughout life, but, as they grow older, children come to control these urges and socialize them or give acceptable direction to them. The young child may be jealous of his baby brother or sister as the mother seems to focus most of her attention on caring for the helpless infant, and he displays attention-demanding behavior.

Need for understanding. The young child needs to be helped to understand why he cannot be allowed to harm the baby and why the baby needs much care. During these experiences, the feelings and attitudes that later operate in his life are being set. Jealousy will take on different forms during later years, but it still is rooted in the factors of love, fear, and hate. The young child experiences jealousy because he desires the affection of his mother and believes that he is losing it or has lost it; the older child experiences jealousy for similar reasons, but the adored object is likely to be found outside the home, among his peers.

There are times when young children and even adolescents or adults must obey immediately without waiting for reasons. In most instances, children deserve to know the reason for requiring certain behavior and denying others. There are few instances, however, when reasons for required behavior should not be given to children in the elementary school. If we wish to build into the individual those attitudes that direct proper behavior, we must help him understand why he is expected to behave in one way rather than in another in a given situation.

Love and attention. Children engage in active behavior to attract attention to themselves. They love the limelight. Often they do things deliberately to attract attention, knowing that they are likely to be reprimanded. To them disapproval is better than being ignored. Sometimes it is necessary to give a child the kind of attention that he *thinks* he should have. In the classroom, this is fraught with danger. His peers may expect the same treatment, or they may come to believe that the child so favored is teacher's pet.

The factor of boredom. A good program of activities tends to stave off the feeling of boredom. Idleness promotes mischievousness.

Many pupils misbehave because they either have too little to do or dislike what they are doing to such an extent that they develop a feeling of boredom. The teacher can introduce interesting activities to overcome this feeling. An activity in which the pupils are interested often is the key to the establishment of a needed change of attitude that will bring about desired behavior in the situation.

The factor of frustration. The child meets many situations in his home and school life that tend to frustrate him. He needs to discover that he can resolve these and move on to the mastering of more difficult problems. It is a slow process for him to learn to channel his drives into socially acceptable patterns. Yet, he is faced constantly with the choice of doing either what he pleases or what he believes will please others. Although the latter may be somewhat frustrating to him, they serve as important socializing experiences.

The factor of anger. When things go wrong it is easy to display angry behavior. The young child learned early that he could control his environment when he used this form of behavior. In some instances he went so far as to engage in temper tantrums. These experiences aggravated the problem of developing proper attitudes toward behavior during his later growing years. Nevertheless, these attitudes and behavior patterns need to be reckoned with and plans laid to eradicate them.

The angry older child displays the kind of behavior that tends to avoid a direct attack on the individual who arouses his anger; he may grab the first thing in sight and throw it, or engage in an entirely different form of activity. If his anger is in the form of a temper tantrum, he may speak loudly in the presence of others, give the "silent treatment," attempt the use of sarcasm, or perhaps express deep self-pity and display antisocial behavior of one kind or another. He prepares himself mentally to reveal to those at whom his anger is directed that he does not like the behavior displayed toward him.

CAUSES OF BEHAVIOR DEVIATIONS

The display of deviant behavior may be rooted in a variety of causes. The child may have developed many socially nonacceptable attitudes. He may have experienced numerous emotional tensions. He may have had many frustrating experiences to which he had difficulty in adjusting. No matter what the nature of the experience, the chances are that any displayed deviant behavior can be traced to physical, personal, or social factors associated with the kind of behavior the individual displays.

Usually the interaction among the various factors that cause unacceptable behavior is so subtle that we are seldom aware that one dominates others or that all are exerting an undesirable influence at any one time. It is difficult to pinpoint the physiological, the social, or the personal as the sole cause of maladjusted behavior. Any one of them may be reinforced in its effect on individual behavior by the active influence of one or all of the others. For example, glandular disturbances may alter a child's overt behavior so as to reveal his inner state.

Influence of Physical Factors

Children differ in their rate of physical development. Parents' attitudes toward a growing child often are influenced by this factor. The small, slowly developing child may be unduly coddled. Because of his apparent immaturity he is permitted to engage in self-aggrandizing behavior and is not expected to meet rightful responsibilities. A rapidly developing child may be regarded as more mature for his age than he actually is and demands are made on him for the exercise of self-control that he is not yet ready to assume. This parental attitude may cause considerable resentment in a younger, rapidly developing child who recognizes the fact that his parents expect greater self-control on his part than they do in the case of an older, more slowly developing brother or sister.

Also, as the older child approaches the pubescent years, his behavior is influenced by the physical changes that are beginning to occur. His attitudes toward adults and peer associates are changing. Childish interests are giving way to new needs and urges. During these in-between years, many young people's accustomed behavior no longer is satisfying. They begin to demand rights and privileges that cause adults to wonder what has happened to conforming behavior patterns.

Physical defects. The child with physical defects of any kind may indulge in behavior that seems to be different from that of boys and girls who do not have these physical defects. Every child wants to participate in activities enjoyed by his peers. Denial of this participation may cause him to become embittered and resentful. He may resort to teasing and tormenting, to temper tantrums, and to making excessive demands on others. He is unhappy and strives for attention from others in devious ways.

Influence of Personal Factors

The relative strength of a child's inherent drives and urges gives direction to the overt behavior that may be displayed in the classroom. As he lives and develops, each individual progressively acquires attitudes and action patterns that serve him in his school and social situations. There is a constant temptation to engage in behavior that deviates from the expected norm in any situation. The individual's self-interest, his interest in the imitation of the behavior of others, or his disinterest in or unawareness of consequences of his acts often causes a display of nonconforming behavior.

The factors that constitute the personality of the teacher are most important in the teaching-learning situation. The interests and attitudes displayed by him stimulate one or another form of behavior in the situation. The behavior of children often is directly related to the behavior displayed by the teacher. It is not comforting for a teacher suddenly to discover that what he has been doing and/or the attitudes he has been displaying are the determining factors of behavior displayed by his pupils.

Factor of self-interest. Personal factors are very important to the child in the development of behavior patterns. The older child is aware of himself as a person and of his real or imagined personal limitations. He is sensitive to the attitudes of his peers toward him and to the nature and extent of his learning achievement. His emotions are attuned to his ability to rate among his fellow classmates.

Pangs of suffering are experienced by the pupil who cannot get himself to take part in class discussions largely because he believes that what he has to say is not worth while and that what is said by others is said so much better than he can say it if he should try. He retreats toward becoming an isolate largely because he has the difficulty of recognizing in himself the fine qualities that he finds and admires in others of his age group. He suffers further if he is extremely sensitive to adverse criticism of his behavior expressed either by his peers or by his teacher. This child gives evidence of too great concern with self; not enough thought or energy is directed toward the welfare of others.

Self-interest is a worthy goal when it is accompanied by a sincere interest in the activities of those with whom one is associated. The very young child is expected to display self-interest. However, as the individual grows, and develops social values, he tends to outgrow the need for self-satisfaction. During these years he learns to modify his self-centered interests; he becomes more and more aware of the interests of others and varies his conduct in such ways as to earn the approval of others.

An extremely self-centered child can use many and devious means to satisfy his selfish interests. He may "apple-polish" the teacher, "torment his friends," or "hoodwink" his parents. Behavior of this kind does not set well with the other members of the group, and often leads to the rejection of this type of person from the inner circle of the group. Too many such experiences may encourage him to become a "bully" unless he is given proper guidance toward social cooperation.

Teachers can do much to give direction to a child's self-interest. He should be helped in such ways that:

1. His extreme self-interest does not dominate his behavior.
2. He becomes aware of the consequences of his behavior at all times.
3. He does not give the impression that he is stubborn or uncooperative as his displayed self-conscious behavior often suggests.
4. He controls his desire to imitate undesirable behavior.
5. He is encouraged to emulate wholesome, outgoing qualities evinced by his teacher or other adults.

Social Factors in the Environment

A child's overt reactions in social situations often reflect home influences. His attitude toward the teacher, the classroom, the learning materials, and his classmates is rooted in the home. He comes to the elementary school with well-established effective attitudes toward the school and all that it connotes. He has a history of learning success or of a lack of it. His behavior patterns are ready to continue as they have in the past.

Attitude toward school. If the child is relatively unsuccessful in his learning he may be driven by his need for activity to do things that will overcome the boredom experienced; he is likely to participate in the kinds of activities that yield immediate satisfaction, disregarding both teacher and class disapproval. He may be tempted to throw spitballs, tear up his written work, carve his initials on his desk, or engage in similar disapproved behavior. He prefers disapproval of his behavior to being ignored.

Desire for approval of behavior. An individual of any age needs to be secure in the affection of another or of others. This is especially true of the elementary school child. If he admires his teacher, he puts forth great effort to cooperate with him. If he is sensitive to the interests and wishes of others, he makes an effort to cooperate with his classmates. He wants to belong.

PREVENTIVE DISCIPLINARY MEASURES (GENERAL)

The good classroom teacher is the key to preventive discipline. This is not the entire story, however. What the child brings with him to the teaching-learning situation either predisposes toward socially acceptable behavior or has built-in patterns that are conducive to uncooperative behavior. Both teachers and pupils know the need for and the value of correct behavior. Proper attitudes toward discipline become a powerful preventive measure.

In the following pages we direct your attention to significant aspects of teacher characteristics and procedures that can encourage smoothly running learning experiences, relatively free of disciplinary disruptions. Much of what is suggested here is discussed at length in other chapters.

Importance of Teacher Activity

Pupil behavior is responsive to the behavior traits displayed by the teacher during his teaching function. The teacher, through good lesson planning, knowledge of pupils, proper use of time and equipment, and the recognition and commendation of good achievement and progress on the part of learners, does much to prevent misbe-havior in his classroom.

The student teacher needs to observe what the successful teacher does to make the teaching-learning situation run so smoothly. When everything goes well, it is not easy to discover precisely what has been done to make everything so effective. You are likely to find that the successful teacher knows his subject matter, understands the capabilities and attitudes of his pupils, utilizes workable pro-cedures in class management, and actively leads the discussion so that there is a realization of progress or achievement.

The beginning teacher and especially the student teacher needs to be realistic. You must work with existing conditions. These may be a crowded classroom, a child who has immediate personal prob-lems that are home centered, or inadequate material. The preventive aspect of discipline is (1) to study the records so that you know the individual pupils, (2) to organize your work so that you can cope with large classes, and (3) to plan to utilize supplementary material when and if these are available.

Importance of Teacher Assets

In your evaluation of preventive measures do not forget to inspect your own assets. What you bring to the classroom in yourself and your personal equipment might be your strongest means to establish predisposing attitudes toward desirable behavior. If you know what you expect to do and proceed to carry it out, your pupils are likely to gain the kind of respect for you that will encourage them to follow your lead and thereby avoid getting into trouble.

Misbehavior often starts when your pupils begin to feel that nothing worth while is happening; they are bored. Good motivation of the learning process gives the learner the mental stimulation needed for thinking and learning. Most pupils prefer to be active mentally rather than to be forced to sit idly by while a teacher makes up his mind as to what he will do next.

Children are keen observers of their teacher's behavior and of teaching procedures. They become outspoken critics of ineffectual teaching. Since they are likely to emulate your behavior, try to set the kind of example that is worthy of imitation. Give your admin-istrator the kind of cooperation you expect from your pupils. If reports are due at a definite time, have them prepared and submit them by the date due. Expect the same from your pupils. Do not, however, expect your pupils to be prompt with study assignments and written reports if you have sloppy habits. Pupils have a way of discovering how you perform in these matters. Set a good example.

Importance of Getting the Right Start

Student teachers often decide that they are going to revolutionize discipline by treating learners like human beings and by being a good fellow from the start. They have been learners in the classrooms for many years and believe that the teacher has been too rigid. They intend to demonstrate that the teacher is and can be more human than he often is thought to be.

Student teachers often believe that the teacher can become a friend among his learners from the start. Unfortunately, they may discover that it is far easier to relax one's control than to recapture a loss of it. They usually find that once the situation has gone beyond their control they have to exercise rigid authority in order to provide acceptable teaching-learning conditions.

As a student teacher, you need to become aware of the fact that there always must be a difference between your position and that of learners. You must discover that you need to establish in the minds of the learners the fact that you are the recognized leader of the group and that your authority needs to be respected at all times, regardless of the extent of friendship that may be established between yourself and each member of the class.

Professional Factors That Can Prevent Discipline Problems

Your duty as a student teacher is that of advising and guiding pupils in your class. The manner in which you discharge most of the following responsibilities will determine the extent to which your discipline problems will be reduced. You are likely to find that your teaching will be more effective when:

1. You discover that a child learns best when (*a*) his mental and physical activities are appropriate for his ability and he feels confident that he can accomplish what is expected of

him, (*b*) his efforts are appreciated by you and his classmates and he is free from personal distractions, and (*c*) he likes and respects you and appreciates your use of corrective measures to help him learn.

2. You observe and encourage the educational and emotional growth and progress of each of your pupils.
3. You provide opportunities for the development and improvement of the child's social relations.
4. You understand the individual pupil's role in the group, his interests, abilities, behavior patterns, goals, and family problems.
5. You use classroom practices that will further good pupil-teacher relations.
6. You are alert to changes in the pupil's pattern of behavior, work, or attitudes.
7. You utilize in a professional manner knowledge obtained from standardized tests, cumulative records, interviews, informal discussion, and observations.
8. You maintain a relaxed atmosphere that avoids tensions yet encourages each pupil to work to his maximum capacity.
9. You insist on respect for authority and the rights of others and of property, as well as on fair play, courtesy, and respect for established rules and policies.
10. You obtain the help of counselors and supervisors as needed.

Importance of Good Motivation

The arousal of learner interest in the learning material stands high as a preventive of misbehavior. Good teaching cannot be achieved without motivating the learner. The teacher who knows his learners is able to gear his teaching to their experience levels. Motivation is more directly associated with this fact than it is, for example, with the utilization of a story or novel situation to interest the learner. Some of these attempts may actually be distracters rather than motivators. If you begin each lesson with a novel approach, be sure that, as soon as possible, you direct the thinking to the problem situation with which you will be concerned during the lesson.

The good teacher begins promptly so that his learners become so interested in what is going on that few evidences of misbehavior are detected. This type of teacher plans his lessons on the experience level of his learners. His learners then are able to understand what is happening and get enjoyment from the learning experience. The good teacher avoids the spectacular in arousing a desire on the part of his pupils to learn. He challenges their thinking because he has learned to ask thought-provoking questions rather than merely factual ones.

PREVENTIVE DISCIPLINARY MEASURES (SPECIFIC)

Since the teacher is the key person to preventive discipline, what he does becomes most important. The suggestions that follow do not guarantee the elimination of discipline problems, but they can reduce the number of such by anticipating what might happen if these practices are not utilized. Read these preventive procedures carefully. To as great an extent as is possible for you to do so, try to apply them during your student teaching experiences. In some instances you will need to consult your cooperating teacher and/or your college supervisor concerning your utilization of a particular procedure. Since you are not in complete charge of the class, you do not want to do anything that goes counter to the regular teacher's disciplinary approaches. In general, however, you should find most of these suggestions helpful to you as a student teacher.

Display an Attitude That Anticipates Pupil Cooperation

Teachers and pupils must learn to live together and to work together in the classroom situation. This is a goal that should consciously be in the minds of all concerned. The teacher must assume the role of the leader since it is within him that authority is vested for the guidance of behavior. The wise teacher uses this authority to stimulate cooperation between himself and his pupils. He can impose his authority or he can invite cooperation. The same overt behavior may result in either approach; but the behavior responses that result from *a request* are more likely to be based on a cooperative attitude and hence become more functional in the lives of the pupils.

Your pupils sense the extent to which you expect them to be orderly and quiet. Once you decide that quiet must prevail in your classroom and that you will not countenance foolish or noisy behavior, this decision will be conveyed to the members of your class through the tone of your voice, your manner, and your general attitude. The pupils then know that you expect attentive cooperation and intend to get it from them. This attitude convinces them that you and they are there for the business of learning.

You should not beg for quiet; you should insist on it. You need to show in your voice, manner, and readiness to start teaching that there is work to be done and that you have a plan for completing it. You cannot afford to be indecisive. You need not scold or even raise your voice as you give the members of your class the kind of mental orientation that will enable them to engage in active thinking about the study material. You must mean what you say. The will to carry through is important in the situation, and the members of the class need to discover that you are fair and just, but ready to follow through until behavior conforms to good classroom conditions.

Speak Clearly and Distinctly

The voice of the teacher is important and should be clear and distinct. It should have enough volume to reach all parts of the classroom, without being sharp or shrill. The teacher can use his voice to alert individuals to active thinking or he can use it to lull them to sleep. The teacher with a faltering voice or a timid approach is the one whom elementary school pupils "ride." Both through his speech and manner he should exhibit an attitude of confidence in himself so that he commands the respect of others.

Be Prepared for the Entire Day

A student teacher as well as a regular teacher must be prepared to continue the teaching for the entire day. There is nothing so conducive to disorderly behavior as not being prepared to move smoothly from one learning situation to another. Experienced teachers usually are able to meet all emergencies, but the student teacher or the beginning teacher should be prepared to fill every minute lest he invite disorder in his class. It is too much to ask pupils to sit quietly when you have nothing further to offer. When you do not give the pupils something to do, they will turn to their own activities.

Use the Names of Your Pupils from the Start

The proper identification of pupils can easily be accomplished by means of a tentative seating chart. It might be advisable to invite the members of the class to help you prepare this chart at the first meeting of the class. You can ask each to write his name in the proper space on your prepared chart form. This is easily done by passing it to each pupil. Some of the names may not be written as plainly by the pupils as you will need for your use. However, you can use this chart to call on a pupil within the first few minutes of the first day. The pupils gain the impression that you know what you are doing and begin to develop a positive attitude toward you.

Delegate Class Routine to Members of the Class

What you do in class management will set the pace for orderly activity. Each teacher has his own way of dealing with the matter of daily routines of class management. During your observation of teaching give special attention to what is done by your cooperating teacher. Decide on a satisfactory procedure for class management, and use it. A fluctuation of practiced routines, even of method of passing out papers, may be upsetting to some members of your class. Decide on a method of collecting work and follow it, thereby avoiding any confusion that results from pupils not knowing what to expect. Also, give your pupils instructions on how to head written work and follow that plan constantly.

Pupils can be trained to be responsible for many class routines. When they know what is expected they are willing to cooperate in helping with many activities of class management. All pupils can participate in keeping the room tidy by learning to pick up paper, and the like. One trustworthy pupil can, under supervision, help in taking attendance. Responsibility for cleaning the chalkboard can be rotated among the pupils of the class on a definite schedule basis.

Practice Emotional Control

There are times when elementary school pupils seem unreasonable and unruly. These are trying times and will tax you to retain your emotional composure. There are occasions, however, in every classroom when you need to express disapproval of undesirable behavior. You must learn to deal with such situations without losing emotional control. This does not imply that you should attempt to disapprove misbehavior with a smile. It is difficult, if not impossible, to disapprove asocial behavior with a smile and be effective in the classroom.

As a student teacher, it is appropriate for you to experience the feeling of anger as you deal with behavior problems, but you should show the members of your class that you can control your temper and refrain from angry blasts or temper-tantrum behavior. If you shout verbal disapproval at your pupils they resent you or inwardly laugh at you. Pupils have profound respect for the teacher who, in difficult situations, gives overt evidence of emotional control expressed in patient consideration.

Children know that misbehavior is to be corrected, and usually do not object to having you give the leadership needed to change their behavior for the better. They object less to the fact that you disapprove their misbehavior than they do to the fact that you lose your temper in so doing. Your attitude should be objective, and you should direct your disapproval toward the offense rather than make it personal. It is not easy to disapprove only offensive behavior and avoid having the offender feel that it might be personal. A silent look of disapproval often is effective, especially if the behavior is corrected thereafter.

The teacher is expected to practice emotional control in all situations. He is the leader in any emergency, such as the sudden outbreak of fire or an unfortunate accident to one of his pupils. His approach in meeting accidents, illness, or fire should serve as a calming influence on those with whom he works. A focus on his responsibilities usually helps him practice emotional control in trying situations. Also, although it is easier said than done, a teacher should be equally calm in the presence of his superiors. His supervisors have no more right to use fear as a disciplinary measure in dealing with him than he has in dealing with his pupils.

Remember the Human Relations Factor

Older children are individualistic and need to be treated as persons who can think for themselves. They are outgrowing the mere acceptance of orders simply because these are given by someone in authority. They are concerned with the reasons that govern the request. They have a strong pull toward wanting freedom, yet they desire the protective guidance of an understanding teacher.

Boys, especially, enjoy teasing and tormenting. They find many ways to annoy or torment their teacher and constantly tend to tease the members of their group. The teacher who recognizes the presence of these urges and acts accordingly earns the sincere admiration of his pupils. Most children are ready to cooperate. The teacher needs to establish the kind of relationships between himself and his pupils that will enable them together to function at a high level in the teaching-learning situation.

Be Able to Locate the Guilty Person

If you know your pupils and a disturbance occurs, you should be able to identify the guilty person as soon as you locate the point of disturbance. Each member of your class is deterred somewhat from engaging in uncooperative behavior by his knowledge of the fact that you are alert to everything that takes place in class. Your attention to any and every distracting influence is paramount. This does not mean that you make an issue of each one, merely that everyone knows that you understand what is happening.

Plan to Keep Every Child Busy

A resourceful teacher finds ways to keep all members of the class busy. He keeps an eye on incipient troublemakers and arranges to keep them occupied. There are some pupils who cannot be reached by you when you are doing your student teaching. In these cases you should enlist the help of your cooperating teacher and, when you are a regular teacher, the help of the guidance counselor.

Give Attention to the Seating of the Pupils

Much continued disturbing behavior can be prevented by reseating those pupils who have too much to say to each other and who may have less to talk about if seated alongside another pupil. It is known that one pupil may have a bad effect on another and excite him to excessive talking. When you discover this, you can rearrange your seating plan to alleviate some of the problems that seem to be arising in the existing situation. Often, one pupil will become mischievous if he is near a friend; if he is removed to another section of the classroom, he will be quiet.

Practice Calling on the Less Attentive

It is satisfying to carry the discussion on the level of those who are eager to participate and are raising their hands. You need to stimulate the thinking of all, especially those pupils who give evidence of daydreaming, show an interest in friends, engage in excessive doodling, and the like. With careful planning, it is easy to bring them into the discussion. It will not happen, however, unless you do something about it. Be aware of the less vocal, and direct questions to them that they probably will be able to answer.

Make Constant Use of Your Eyes and Ears

It is interesting to study the behavior of pupils in a classroom. Usually when one of them wishes to engage in deviate behavior he first takes a quick look at you before he starts his act. You can do much at this moment to alter the pupil's behavior by "catching" his eye and continuing to look at him. You thereby are letting him know that you suspect what he is about to do. He then is likely to desist from a planned bit of mischief, an attempt to cheat on a test, or any other form of undesirable behavior.

As you move your eyes around the room, the members of your class begin to realize that you are aware of them and of what they are doing. You will find that this is more easily done when you are standing or moving about in the room, rather than remaining seated at your desk. You need to develop skill in writing on the chalkboard so that you do not lose contact with the class. Your recognized ability to see and hear what is happening in your classroom enables you to prevent much deviant behavior from starting.

Display a Sense of Humor

Amusing incidents are likely to occur in the classroom. Consciously or unconsciously, a pupil may say or do something that arouses laughter among his classmates. Show that you are a good sport by joining briefly in the merriment. If a pupil seems to be baiting you deliberately, ignore it at the time and direct the attention of the class to an activity that they will find interesting. Avoid a sharp retort, or any indication of the fact that you have been hurt or angered by what he has said. Later, in a private conference with him, you can attempt to discover why he acted as he did and bring about a better relationship between him and yourself.

Avoid Public Conflict with Pupils

Try to avoid criticizing a pupil or arguing with him in the presence of other members of the class. Display patience and show the poise that is expected of a teacher. When suggestions for improvement are necessary, make them to as great an extent as possible in a private personal conference. Always be as supportive as possible to the pupil. Whenever it is possible give him the benefit of a doubt.

Help Pupils Who Tend to Interfere with Others

When a pupil interferes with the study or learning of his classmates, request his cooperation by a quiet approach. Whatever you do should be done with calmness, dignity, and firmness. Try to help the individual before you decide to send him to a counselor or administrator for assistance in dealing with his problem.

Display a Personal Interest in Pupils

Children like to believe that their teacher is interested in them as persons. Getting this idea over to them works wonders in gaining their cooperation with you. Attend as many of their school meetings as your time permits. They appreciate your cooperation with their special assembly programs and their school events. Also, pupils develop a warm feeling toward you if you listen sympathetically when they tell you about some of their problems and if you respect their confidences. They also thrill to receiving a short message of sympathy—a telephone call or, perhaps, a visit when they are ill.

Be Well Organized and Businesslike

When you are well organized, it implies that you know what you intend to do and that you have a plan to implement your purpose. If you have worthwhile material for each lesson you can provide your pupils with a program of action that tends to deter the start of most behavior problems. Make it a point to display enthusiasm for each subject.

You have responsibilities for discipline both in and out of class. You should supervise the behavior of pupils assigned to you. If there is crowding in passageways, let your presence and influence be known. It is your duty also to keep a careful record of attendance and tardiness and to submit this record to the administration when due. Laxity in these matters may be a causative factor of your own discipline problems.

Encourage Pupil Cooperation

You will find it helpful to involve the pupils as much as possible in class activities. The extent to which they know what is expected of them and what procedures are to be utilized will determine the nature and willingness of their cooperation. Bring the pupils into your planning. They like to carry out procedures they have helped to plan. This was discovered many years ago when the junior high school pupils in New York City were invited by the Superintendent in charge of Junior High Schools to draw up a "Code of Behavior" for their group. This became an excellent experience for them. However, it has no more value to present junior high school pupils than a code of behavior drawn up by educational experts. For such a code of behavior to be most effective, each generation of pupils needs to develop one of its own. As the young people work on it, they achieve an understanding of its purposes and a willingness to live by its provisions.

Strive to Be Impartial

You need consciously to try to avoid a display of favoritism toward one or more members of your class. Although you want to be impartial in your attitude toward your pupils, human nature is such that partiality may tend unconsciously to creep into your teaching-learning situation. Sometimes pupils are aware of your behavior long before it occurs to you that you may have given one or more pupils the kind of attention and/or consideration that you have not given to the others.

You wonder how it is that partiality tends to creep into your practices. One child reacts toward you in a way that another does not. This starts a chain of human interactions that is different from what it is between you and another or even every other member of the class. You must guard against displaying greater interest in this individual as a person than in others in the class. You need to evaluate fairly the attitudes and behavior of your pupils and treat each according to his personal needs and his ability to meet his responsibilities. Individual differences exist and should be reckoned with, but not to the extent of giving excessive attention to the interests of one or two pupils.

Pupils have the right to expect fair treatment at all times. You are wise to examine, from time to time, your relationship with the members of your class. If you find that you are giving undue attention to one or more of your pupils or if several of them are taking an overabundance of your time after class, you might try to bring this into line with what you do for and with other members of the class.

Need to Cooperate with Parents

Parent-teacher relationships are closer on the elementary level than they are in the higher schools. Most elementary schools have actively functioning parent-teacher associations. In an increasing number of communities, the parents of elementary school children follow with interest and understanding the learning activities in which their children engage and assist in every way possible toward furthering pupil progress. It also is becoming customary for each class on a grade to have a "class mother" who serves as a kind of liaison officer between the class teacher and the other mothers of the children in the class or grade.

A plan recently developed in New York City is to employ available mothers, at a small honorarium, to help school people for several hours daily in the management of school affairs, such as helping in the office, cafeteria, and the like. Although parents sometimes attempt to assume too much authority in influencing school management, they usually are extremely helpful in their relationships with the elementary school staff.

The personal relationships that develop between an individual teacher and parents depends in good part on the teacher's attitude. Parents do not relish being requested by a teacher to come to school only when Johnny or Mary has gotten into difficulties. A parent resents hearing only about his child's poor study habits or mischievous behavior. No child is all "bad." You may find it necessary on occasions to discuss with a parent one or more undesirable characteristics of a child. When you do this, be sure that you also call attention to some of the boy's or girl's good qualities. By so doing, you are more than likely to gain the wholehearted cooperation of the parent. In fact, the parent whom you are interviewing may be willing to tell you about some of the child's mischievous acts—which of course, according to the parent are inherited from the other parent's family!

Another way to encourage good personal relationships between yourself and parents is to report to parents, by letter, telephone, or personal interview, any especially fine behavior traits or activities of their children. You will find through the utilization of well-considered approaches that your relationships with your pupils are improved to the extent that your associations with parents are friendly and cooperative.

Learn to Work with the Guidance Counselor

The relationship between the teacher and the counselor should be a reciprocal one. Some teachers have not yet developed the confidence in counselors that should prevail in our schools, but most teachers want to cooperate with guidance counselors. They are unhappy, however, when the guidance counselor has information about a learner that is not made available to sympathetic and understanding teachers.

Teachers are handicapped by the pressure of time and crowded classrooms. Counselors must be sensitive to these facts and try to make it easy for the teacher to work with them. They must be ready to help the teacher eliminate such causes of arguments as "I do not have the time to give to that extra work for one pupil." They need to convince teachers through tact, diplomacy, and artful persuasion that the guidance function can go forward only when both teacher and counselor work together for the good of the pupil.

The counselor can help you realize that there are some children so emotionally disturbed that they cannot be given sufficient help in the classroom. With this reassurance from the counselor, you are encouraged rather than discouraged when he attempts to provide satisfying and enriching experiences for this kind of pupil. You then are willing to accept the assistance of the counselor.

QUESTIONS AND TOPICS FOR DISCUSSION

1. Present an actual discipline problem that has arisen in your class and indicate what was done either by you or your cooperating teacher in solving it.
2. List at least five rules or regulations that are intended to govern pupils' behavior in your classroom.
3. What is your cooperating teacher's attitude toward any pupil who fails to respect such class rules?
4. Differentiate between discipline and self-discipline.
5. To what extent do discipline problems arise when you are in charge of the class? How do you handle such situations? How should you?
6. Study those pupils in your classroom whose behavior is undisciplined. Try to discover the reasons for their lack of cooperation.
7. List some of the frustrations often experienced by children.
8. Cite examples of displayed self-interests among the pupils in the class. How does your cooperating teacher handle such situations?
9. List teacher characteristics that are effective in encouraging good discipline among pupils.
10. Which of the procedures for preventive discipline listed in the chapter do you consider most significant? Give reasons for your choices.

14

THE DEVELOPMENT OF SELF-DISCIPLINE

Constructive discipline is concerned with motivating the utilization of correct behavior at all times and in all situations. A pupil's classroom behavior should be judged on the basis of his reasons for behaving as he does, and the effect of his behavior on other children in the learning situation. For example, the cause of noise in a classroom may be more important than the fact that noise is heard. What may be considered to be confusion in one situation may represent orderly procedure in another. Most important is whether all members of the group are busily progressing toward the goals they have set for themselves.

NEED FOR STANDARDS OF BEHAVIOR

Children need standards to govern their conduct. They want to know the general principles that are to be used to guide their behavior. They are entitled to understand the rules and regulations that are to be used to govern their behavior. These serve as stabilizing influences for them.

Each child should be stimulated toward the achievement of a particular goal. He should work under a set of rules that he understands, and he should know that an infringement of these rules will result in some form of penalization. Quiet should not be expected for its sake alone but for the purpose of getting on with the work of the day. Classroom conditions should be conducive to thinking and, insofar as possible, reflect life situations.

Desirable behavior habits should be trained into each individual to such an extent that they become habitual. Each child should be encouraged and expected to participate actively in every learning situation of which he is a part. The nature and extent of his self-discipline is evidenced in group situations in which there is a minimum of teacher supervision.

Pupil behavior should be a joint function and responsibility of both the child and the teacher. The person with the authority, the teacher, should transfer the responsibility for behavior to the pupils individually and collectively whenever they demonstrate ability to use the responsibility intelligently. This approach helps children function effectively in all social or group situations in which they find themselves.

Constructive discipline is based on active participation, cooperation, and social awareness, as these operate to bring about changes in child behavior. The aim is not to have a classroom in which nothing ever goes wrong, but rather one in which the pupils and the teacher alike know when something has gone wrong and are able and willing to effect needed changes for good social living.

PRACTICES FOR CONSTRUCTIVE DISCIPLINE

Elementary school pupils enjoy working at worthwhile tasks. You should work with ideas in such a way that all learners in the class gain in understanding of the material under consideration. There is deep satisfaction that comes with doing high-quality workmanship if it has a purpose. This does not imply that a child always should be permitted to do only that in which he is interested at the moment. Rather does it mean that the teacher has an obligation to motivate the learning in all situations to the extent that interest may be aroused in each and every worthy learning activity. This may be facilitated by providing a variety of functional activities. Lessons can be individualized or respective pupils can be assigned a responsibility for a particular phase of a unit of study.

The teacher is one unit or cog, but an important one, in the class and school setting. What each teacher does individually becomes important collectively in building what is known as *esprit de corps*. The rapport and spirit that permeates the school is something that is built up over a period of years.

The standards of a school help build the reputation of the school; the school's tradition, in turn, works for the benefit of the school. It is easy to develop self-discipline in situations in which, for years, good behavior has been the accepted practice. The going is rough if the school develops a reputation of laxity; it is difficult also for a teacher who has the reputation that children have excessive freedom in class.

Sensible approaches to constructive discipline are especially important in the kindergarten and early elementary grades. Unless they have had nursery school experience, youngsters beginning their school life bring with them various attitudes toward adult authority. Many children come from homes where they have been trained to accept fair and just controls of their immature behavior patterns. However, some school entrants have been reared in homes where adult controls were so rigid that they have become either timid and fearful or resentful of any disciplinary measures. Others have been permitted so much permissiveness of behavior in the home that they have come to regard the fulfillment of any whim or fancy as their rightful prerogative.

The teacher in the primary grades, especially in the kindergarten and first grade, needs to develop facility in handling these various types of children. She must be able to avoid tugs of war over toys and other materials between aggressive youngsters, prevent the demanding child from overwhelming his timid classmates, and make certain that well-trained children do not learn bad habits from less disciplined pupils. This is not an easy task and is one that requires considerable ingenuity on the part of the teacher to perform.

As a student teacher, observe carefully the practices of the cooperating teacher. Note that she maintains a certain, pleasant attitude regardless of any disturbing incidents that may occur. She rarely scolds. She does not meet temper tantrum with temper tantrum. Yet, as she proceeds with the various activities of the day's schedule, she is aware of what each child is doing and is quick to enter any situation that requires her guiding influence.

Fortunately, young children usually are malleable. Also, their attention span is short. If two children are "fighting" for the possession of a toy, for example, the teacher can shift the interest of the aggressor to another activity. She also needs to be aware of the tendency of the fearful child to withdraw from group activity and encourage his or her participation. Occasionally, the teacher needs to meet a child's undesirable behavior with a firm but kindly spoken "No," and make certain that obedience is forthcoming.

In general, praise for conforming behavior rather than reprimand should be employed. Even young children give evidence of the competitive spirit and want to receive approval. The ingenious teacher of young children can find many ways in which to help youngsters develop respect for constructive authority. Of course, parents should be urged to participate in whatever can be done to encourage the development of good discipline among young children in order to prevent later behavior difficulties.

REMEDIAL MEASURES FOR IMPROVING PUPIL BEHAVIOR

We can all agree that misbehavior should be corrected. The means by which this is accomplished is less clear. There is no one panacea or recipe for correcting misbehavior of individuals. As a student teacher or a beginning teacher, you may express the desire to be furnished with a simple formula to help you meet disciplinary problems. It will not take you long to discover that general principles are all that can be supplied. Their application almost always needs to be modified to meet the particular needs of the individual and the situation in which the misbehavior arises.

Suggestions for Correcting Misbehavior in the Classroom

The measures to be used to correct misbehavior are never simple and are never the same for two teachers or for two different classes in the same school, nor for two individuals in the same class. A teacher may be able to apply one technique effectively and be unable to get satisfactory results from the use of another. It seems that, although a method works in one situation, this does not, in and of itself, make the method a psychologically good one. Merely to change overt behavior does not insure effective behavior patterns; much depends on the nature of the new behavior and how it was brought about.

Indirect control is usually the better approach, yet there are times when direct control is necessary. A technique used effectively with one pupil in one situation may fail when used by the same teacher to achieve its purpose with another pupil or in another situation. Hence you will find it necessary to vary your methods of dealing with uncooperative children. The effectiveness of a measure depends on the way it is used and on the extent to which it applies to the behavior pattern and attitudes of this individual and his particular offense.

Be Impersonal in Your Approach

The teacher should make any disciplinary measures he uses as impersonal as possible. It should be a matter of correcting the offense and not abusing the pupil who has misbehaved. Whatever measures are used should be understood by the child and should be accepted by him as reasonable. It is important that extreme measures be administered in private and that they be adjusted to the nature of the offense. When administered, the teacher should not be in a state of anger or displaying a temper tantrum. All measures should be effective, yet not be physically harmful to the individual.

The guilty person should be penalized in such a way that there is no interference with the learning opportunities of the members of the class. Care should be taken that the entire class is not penalized for the misbehavior of one or two misbehaving members of the group. The important consideration is to enlist the cooperation of the class in developing desirable behavior practices among all the members of the group.

If an entire class is punished for the misdeeds of one or two wrongdoers, they are not likely to want to cooperate in developing a good spirit in the group. When you get the members of the class to laugh at, rather than with, the culprits, you are making headway in having the members of the class help in providing conditions necessary to good learning.

Use Praise When Warranted

You will find it most helpful if you use the positive approach in whatever you do. Think constructively. Do not criticize your superiors. Be careful of your criticisms of your pupils. Your words get back to your pupils in ways you little expect. Practice using praise whenever and wherever you can. This applies both to your pupils and to your colleagues. Be fair, generous, and willing to ask pupils to display acceptable behavior.

Many behavior problems that develop might have been avoided if you had made wise use of approval and given recognition to respective individuals and their achievement. When they fail to win approval for acceptable achievement, children often turn to other less desirable approaches as attention getters and become problems to their teachers. They prefer your disapproval to lack of recognition of what they have done or are doing.

You are likely to find it profitable to evaluate the achievement progress of each child and thus convey to him the fact that you are interested in what he is doing. If your evaluation is meaningful to him, he then understands that you appreciate whatever difficulties he may be encountering with it.

Behavior problems often arise when there is conflict between teacher and pupil. The giving and receiving of desired approval is a continuous process that enlists the interests of both the teacher and the pupils. You should learn early to make judicious use of this effective means of directing pupil behavior. Praise based on evaluation and disapproval directed against all misbehavior without favor are helpful factors in the development of those attitudes that govern good social behavior.

Remedial Measures Based on Definite Causes

The behavior of children is affected by many factors of influence such as physical, social and emotional, home and community, and society in general. Remedial measures to be used in the redirection of behavior based on any one or more of these factors can go a long way toward helping the individual adjust his behavior for good social living.

Physical factors. If a determination has been made that the cause of misbehavior has a physical base, suggestions for possible remedial action might include such as:

1. The giving of a thorough medical examination in school
2. The provision of a minimum of medical and dental attention
3. The provision of food and rest in school
4. The reporting of health status to parents by nurse and physician
5. The enlisting of the assistance of outside agencies
6. The provision for corrective therapy for physically handicapped children
7. The provision for individuals having physical disabilities

Social and emotional factors. Action that can be taken to remedy behavior caused by social and emotional factors includes such procedures as:

1. The giving to the pupil by the teacher of affection and sympathy
2. The provision of guidance services
3. The giving of responsibility to pupils in light of their ability to use it
4. The provision of group projects to develop group morale
5. The giving of praise to children for work well done
6. The provision of outlets for pupils with excess energy and for those with high ability

Factors originating in the home and community. Action recommended to treat causes of behavior problems that may have their origin in the home and community include such procedures as:

1. Visits to the home by teachers or social workers
2. Conferences with parents either at school or at home
3. Provision of recreational facilities in the school to supplement those in the community
4. Cooperation with various out-of-school agencies
5. Utilization by the teacher of good mental hygiene principles

Factors originating in the larger social order. There is a tendency to hold the school responsible for the development of adequate behavior, in spite of the ills of society. The home and community exert a potent influence on the behavior of the developing child. Hence much of a child's behavior needs to be redirected through the influence of the school. The school accepts the child where he is and attempts to help him develop those attitudes and behavior practices that enable him to be self-disciplined. Remedial approaches for the correction of behavior resulting from causes originating in the larger social order include the need to:

1. Teach children to cooperate with teachers and schoolmates
2. Teach children obedience for school rules and regulations
3. Teach children to participate in school activities

4. Teach children to respect school property
5. Teach children freedom of controlled expression
6. Teach children to accept disapproval of misconduct
7. Teach children to accept school obligations such as completing homework, etc.
8. Teach children good sportsmanship
9. Teach children proper social skills
10. Teach children good manners
11. Teach children how to work on a team
12. Teach children to develop to the extent of their capacities

SPECIFIC REMEDIAL SUGGESTIONS FOR TEACHERS

Different approaches have been tried in the past with varying degrees of success to effect a change in behavior. The more common corrective or remedial measures include a long list of practices. Among those often used can be mentioned: change of seat, apology, demerits, deprivation of privileges, detention, assigning extra work, ignoring, isolating the offender, scolding, time for meditation, providing incentives, payment for property damage, appeal to members of class, advice of experienced teachers, personal conferences.

You help establish the attitudes and habits in your classroom. You must learn to live with them. It is helpful to have rules to guide your own conduct and decisions in matters of behavior control and the development of self-discipline. For example:

1. You should avoid publicizing offenses and parading them before your class. This is likely to create more problems than it deters.
2. You should avoid punishing the entire class for misconduct of a few members.
3. You should avoid the use of ridicule or sarcasm as a means of punishment.
4. You should not make threats. You must carry out all plans that you announce. Idle threats are of no value to anyone.
5. You should not assume authority that is not yours. For example, you should not announce a make-believe suspension. It can only be an unrealistic, undesirable threat since you do not have such authority.

You should avoid making an issue of situations or of undesirable behaviors that are trivial. You must decide what behavior is permissible for good teaching-learning procedures and what needs to be corrected. You need to know what is going on, but you also need to decide when and where to defer what is happening. As you gain confidence in the situation, you will become attuned to this and realize better what ought to be done in each situation. For example, neither permit pupils to congregate around your desk during class time, unless you invite them to do so, nor allow uncontrolled movement of them in the classroom.

Value of Changing Pupil's Seat

If two or more pupils indicate by their behavior that they cannot work quietly when seated together, you might find it helpful to change the seat of one or both of them. The individual pupil must be aware of the reason for your changing his heat.

Pupils who are close friends often have a great deal to talk about. They may have developed habits of teasing one another when out of class, and this may carry into the classroom unless you do something to terminate its continuation. Separation is helpful since it enables these pupils to give attention to what is happening in class rather than to each other. It is good for the other pupils since it has removed one of the irritants in the situation and has subtly put them on notice that action will be taken when needed.

Factor of Using Apology in Correcting Behavior

The use of apology with children to correct misbehavior is fraught with danger. A child should never be forced to apologize for his misdeeds. Of course, your interest is to bring about a change in the attitude and behavior of the individual. Your motivation should be that of helping him *want to behave properly*.

You want to help a child achieve more than an expression of regret—you want him to mean what he says. It is so easy to verbalize the words in a statement of regret. The expressed regret is of little value unless it is accompanied by deep feelings of regret and a resolution that such behavior will not be repeated. You are succeeding in correcting misbehavior only to the extent that the child actually regrets his mischievous behavior whether he utters a formal apology or not.

Factor of Denial of Pupil Privileges

Behavior changes for the better can be achieved through the denial of certain school privileges to individual pupils. If a pupil does not perform his duties efficiently, he can be helped immeasurably by calling on another pupil to take them over at the time. For example, if a pupil is assisting the teacher with lateness and absence records and is either late himself or, in some other way, inefficient, he should be replaced by another pupil who will discharge his duty faithfully. If a child cheats to gain a higher standing in class, he should be denied the recognition that accompanies the higher achievement.

Care must be exercised to utilize only those forms of deprivation that are valuable to improvement of behavior without injury to health or safety. An uncooperative child should not be deprived of organized health-giving exercise that may be planned for all pupils. To deny him the needed physical activity may further aggravate behavior problems.

Deprivations that may encourage the child to engage in other and perhaps more serious misbehavior should not be used. Corrective measures that temporarily deny a misbehaving pupil his rights and privileges in a particular situation may be applied if the individual is helped to understand the relationship between the denials and his uncooperative behavior.

The Factor of Requiring Extra Work

Seldom, if ever, should additional work be assigned to change undesirable behavior into desirable behavior. This approach is likely to instill more negative attitudes than any possible good that can result from the work completed. If you wish to reward a pupil, give him the *privilege* of doing extra work or study; never *impose* extra study on him as a penalty for misbehavior.

You are interested in having your pupils learn as much as they can. You need to do what you can to activate the learning process. Although you may believe that you are requiring added exposure to new learning material, you should be concerned with those learning outcomes that may result from enforced extra study as a correction for disciplinary problems. If you use this technique, you are likely to arouse dislike of the subject.

Factor of Awareness of All Behavior yet Separating It from the Personal

You need to detect all misbehavior but to be careful that you do not make your disapproval of it personal. To the extent that you can separate the misbehavior from the individual and focus on it when you reprimand him, you are likely to succeed in working with children. It is a fine line between the two that can be appreciated by the learner when he realizes that you are willing to accept him as a functional member of the group so long as his behavior is in line with acceptable class standards. He then realizes that you will not discredit him because of his misdeeds, but that you will not countenance any nonconforming behavior either.

The pupil should be helped to realize that any misbehavior is not acceptable in a particular situation. As the teacher, you have many ways of acquainting him with this fact. You may disapprove with your eyes; you may deny him the privilege of participating in the discussion by not giving him an opportunity to enter into it; you may openly reprimand him. Most of these are positive and dynamic acts, although the denying of privileges is an overt expression of ignoring him. There are other extreme measures that can be taken in the ignoring process.

The Factor of Isolation of Offender

There are various ways in which the child can be isolated from the members of the class. He can be physically removed, or he can be denied the opportunity of participating in any group activity that may be in progress. When a child is isolated, he should be denied special privileges until his case is settled. If the span of time between the offense and the final settlement is long, he may need to be readmitted into class activities during which time his problem is being considered.

The Factor of Scolding

Scolding implies oral reprimand in the presence of peers. Take care that you do not become a nagging teacher. Petty faultfinding is an indication of a lack of self-confidence. Children dislike this approach. The overly faultfinding teacher loses the respect of pupils. Moreover, too often, scoldings are not followed by constructive action. If they continue, regardless of the school rules that have been broken, children soon become insensitive to their application. Whenever it is necessary, however, call attention to any infraction of school rules, but be judicial. Use the question approach. It is better to have the child tell you what he intends to do to correct his behavior than it is for you to thrust it at him.

Misbehavior among children often is the result of a striving to gain approval from members of the social group. Every child has a strong desire to belong and to have his behavior approved by both his peers and his teachers. If you can so direct the influence of the class as to cause a child's misbehavior to be made a matter of class disapproval, you will be spared the need for scolding or reprimanding. Genuine changes in behavior are the result of such social pressures. The skillful teacher learns how to make effective use of this corrective measure.

Value of Lapse of Time before Dealing with Penalty for Offense

When it is known that the individual has committed an act that warrants corrective action, it often is wise to give the offender some time to think it over before you attempt to resolve the problem. When an offender has an hour or more, for example, to meditate on his wrongdoing, he is likely to resolve that he will try not to repeat the offense.

Incentives That Stimulate Change in Behavior

Not all pupils go to school because they want to go. Some are sent to school. As you realize the importance of the implied difference, you come to appreciate the fact that your job of motivating the learning process for all of them is a sizable one. It is not enough to hope that the success achieved in gaining knowledge, skills, and attitudes will furnish the momentum for your pupils to want to continue in the learning situation. Many of them will need special incentives to spur them to greater study activity. You can help them acquire the desire of self-improvement. This in itself can be an intrinsic reward that will give direction to individual behavior.

The age and the interests of the pupils are important to the form of incentives that may be useful for them. Learning for the sake of gaining an education is an intrinsic reward of great value. Many pupils, however, need incentives that are extrinsic in nature. Our system of grades or marks represents a type of reward that serves as an incentive for some pupils, but not for all.

A slow-learning pupil often finds it difficult to compete with his more able classmates in study activities that go beyond his ability to master. Hence he is likely to receive lower grades than the others. Your emphasis then should be on this pupil's attempts to improve his achievement in comparison with his own past record rather than in comparison to the grades earned by other pupils. In addition, you should set learning tasks for him that are in accord with his intellectual level. You also should attempt to discover any phase of the learning situation in which the child may display interest and for which he has some aptitude, and then reward his efforts in this area by words of approval. A fundamental educational principle, of course, is to avoid exposing less able children to unfair competition with those who are much more able than they are.

The bright underachiever poses a problem of adjustment. For one or another reason, he displays little or no interest in his schoolwork and performs inadequately. The offering of extrinsic awards may fail to improve his attitude toward study. It is then the responsibility of the school people involved, in cooperation with parents, to attempt to discover the cause of the pupil's failure to conform to learning requirements. This may be a difficult task, requiring patient working with the pupil by teachers and counselors. If they persist, however, they usually can bring about a change of attitude that will result in the young person's devoting his energies toward achieving academic success that will serve as an intrinsic reward for his efforts.

Value of Appeal to Members of Class

If you are not able to identify the guilty person you might wish to appeal to the entire class for a solution of the problem. In so doing, you may shield the guilty person and gain his cooperation by saving his face and at the same time setting the class against the repetition of that particular kind of activity. You will find that there are times when you need not identify the wrongdoer.

Value of Getting Advice of Experienced Teachers

In your observation of teachers, you are afforded an opportunity to discover how various situations are handled by them. Yet, you know that, when you are teaching, the class reacts differently under your leadership than when another person is guiding the learning process. You discover that the pupils are the same pupils but that they behave differently when you are in charge. This is characteristic of all learners; they behave differently in the presence of different teachers. More than they realize, teachers are responsible for differences in pupil behavior in the classroom.

You might make it a point to ask teachers about ways to develop self-discipline in pupils. Ask them what they do to deter problems from arising and what their attitude is toward various types of behavior problems. Sometimes, teachers find it difficult to advise you. They have developed certain habits of dealing with such difficulties and now use them almost unconsciously. They may tell you that they are alert to all that transpires in the classroom but that they avoid being petty about it. They avoid making an issue of something that is trivial. You will discover after a talk with a teacher or teachers about dealing with discipline problems that the best way for you to learn to deal with misbehavior is for you to develop these skills in the classroom.

Experienced teachers will tell you that the problem of discipline is one that is ever present. They know that they must be alert to the problem at all times and not "let up" on their standards lest confusion begin in class. Recently about 3,400 classroom teachers were asked about this problem in a study made by the National Education Association. It was revealed that the problem of discipline continues to be their major concern. The beginning teacher also places discipline high on his list of classroom situations to master, but the kind of discipline problems he meets are often somewhat different from those met by the experienced teacher.

When you are in doubt about how to handle a particular discipline situation, it is wise to seek the counsel of an experienced teacher, guidance counselor, or administrator. First you should use your own resources to correct the behavior. Do not hesitate, however, to enlist the assistance of more competent persons in the resolution of behavior problems. Avoid letting the situation get out of hand before calling for assistance. You may find that suggestions coming from experienced teachers or from other trained experts are most helpful.

Value Associated with Holding a Personal Conference with a Pupil

Most student teachers do not get sufficient training in the use of the personal conference with individual pupils. When skill is developed in the use of a personal conference, it can become one of the most effective means of bringing about a readjustment of recalcitrant behavior. In a face-to-face talk with a pupil before or after the regular school day, during the lunch period, or at any other convenient time, much can be accomplished by way of having the learner understand what is meant by good classroom attitudes and behavior. To be effective, these talks need not be formally planned but may grow out of a need that arises in the classroom. Your preparation for them should be based on an acquaintance with whatever information may be available about the habits and record of the pupil.

The personal conference should not be used as a scolding session. If properly conducted, you as well as the pupil can gain from a personal conference. For you, it can enable you to gain insight into the pupil and his problem; for the pupil, it affords an opportunity to strengthen his self-confidence and his urge to belong.

If you talk privately with a pupil who has been extremely uncooperative, instead of scolding him publicly, you gain in stature— the members of the class respect you for it. Sometimes, during these face-to-face conferences, the pupil tells you things that you otherwise would not be able to discover but that are pertinent to his displayed behavior. At the same time, you find that you are more successful with some pupils than with others in these conferences, since some pupils tell you many things that other pupils tend to withhold from you.

In these personal conferences, you should learn to listen and to ask the kind of questions that will elicit information pertinent to the child's problem. Your role should be that of establishing a warm, permissive, informal atmosphere that will promote the flow of personal information. Once obtained, this information should be treated as confidential.

THE STUDENT TEACHER AND DISCIPLINE

Many student teachers and beginning teachers claim that the most difficult aspect of teaching is the maintaining of good discipline among their pupils. You should be concerned about discipline, but you should not be afraid to meet the problems that arise. Perhaps, more than you realize, your own attitudes are potent instigators of the kind of behavior evidenced by the members of your class.

Student Teachers Learn by Practice

Because of your inexperience, you are likely to make mistakes in dealing with your pupils that later you will know how to avoid. You are likely to find that your own errors tend to contribute to the discipline problems that arise in your classroom. A primary purpose of your engaging in student teaching is to learn from your mistakes at this time when you have help in overcoming them rather than when you are on your own as a full-time teacher.

More often than many beginning teachers realize, they provide the stimuli that are basic to the chain of misbehavior that ensues. For example, a student teacher was teaching reading to a third-grade class. In her preparation of the lesson, she attempted to learn all about the picture on which the reading was based. While inspecting the contents of the picture with the class, one child reported seeing something in the picture that had escaped the student teacher during her preparation. Unconsciously, the teacher said "Gee! I didn't see that!" Some minutes elapsed before the child bouncing in her seat, called out, "Gee! Gee! Gee!" She was promptly reprimanded. Yet, the teacher actually was responsible for stimulating this behavior. Until her college supervisor told her what she had said, she was unaware of the fact that she had said "Gee! I didn't see that!"

There are various mistakes that are made by teachers that account for a child's misbehavior. We already have referred to some of these. They include:

1. Coming to class unprepared or poorly prepared for the lesson
2. Failing to use motivating procedures
3. Wasting time trying to locate materials that should be at hand
4. Repeating an indistinct answer rather than requiring the pupils to speak clearly
5. Oversimplifying explanations or stating them in terms beyond pupils' ability to comprehend
6. Wording questions vaguely or indefinitely
7. Utilizing inappropriate motivation
8. Failing to adjust lighting and heating conditions and seating arrangements according to pupil needs
9. Interrupting a lesson to harangue a pupil for misconduct
10. Engaging in emotionalized behavior or "throwing a temper tantrum" when things go wrong
11. Assigning the class "busywork" in order to complete reports, etc.
12. Failing to return pupils' written work that has been properly evaluated
13. Standing with back to class while writing on chalkboard
14. Assigning work for home study hurriedly or without proper explanation
15. Failing to provide for ability differences among the pupils
16. Employing the question-answer technique of recitation to the exclusion of other more interest-arousing approaches
17. Caring for all class routines personally rather than delegating some of them to pupils
18. Permitting pupils to leave the classroom at will

You should try assiduously to refrain from falling into any of the foregoing errors. Moreover, your whole classroom manner exerts a powerful influence on your pupils' attitudes. They react unfavorably toward a teacher (1) who indicates by a low voice and hesitant manner that he is afraid of the group, or (2) who, by the use of loud tones and an aggressive attitude, seems to give evidence that he expects trouble and is ready for it. Try to assume an attitude of self-confidence and of a belief in your pupils' desire and ability to cooperate with you in achieving worthwhile learning outcomes.

Special Suggestions for Dealing with Factors of Poor Discipline

You know that slides to be used as teaching aids usually are accompanied by study guides to assist you in their presentation. One such guide is presented here. It contains pertinent suggestions concerning discipline.[1]

I. Recognizing Danger Signals
   A. Inattention
      1. Making-up in class
      2. Comic books
      3. Daydreaming
      4. Boredom
   B. Teacher faults
      1. Remains seated at desk
      2. Permits pupils to congregate around desk
      3. Tolerates uncontrolled movement by pupils
      4. Lacks direction
      5. Ignores physical factors that contribute to misbehavior

II. Contributing Factors to Poor Discipline
   A. Poor lesson planning
      1. Starting classwork late
      2. Absence of directions
      3. Lack of motivation
      4. Monotony of presentation
   B. Lack of pupil participation

III. Setting Up a Trouble-Free Classroom Climate
   A. Procedures set up cooperatively by pupils and teacher
   B. Pupils comply with procedures they helped to develop
      1. Entrance and exit from room
      2. Distribution and collection of materials
      3. Proper disposal of litter
      4. Initiating activities
      5. Controlled pupil movement

[1] Allen Wetter, *Discipline Study Guide* to accompany slides on "Discipline in the Junior High School" (Philadelphia, 1961). Reprinted by permission. (Allen Wetter is Superintendent of the Philadelphia Schools.)

    C. Teachers share in responsibility
        1. Plan good lessons
            a. Be interesting and detailed
            b. Use a variety of techniques
            c. Follow courses of study
        2. Know your pupils
        3. Use your time and equipment efficiently
        4. Use praise and recognition
        5. Assign responsibilities to pupils

IV. Treating Trouble Immediately
    A. Pause and look at person(s) meaningfully
    B. Gestures
    C. Move closer to disturbance
    D. Confiscate material
    E. Separate offenders
    F. Isolate within room
    G. Deprive pupil of privileges
    H. Admonish or reprimand
    I. Confer after school
    J. Refer to other school personnel

V. Getting Help
    A. Keep records
    B. Study previous records
    C. Ask other teachers
    D. Refer for counseling and other specialized services
    E. Contact home
    F. Confer with vice-principal.

The Building of Good School Spirit

It should be comforting to you to appreciate the fact that you are not alone in your attempts to develop well-disciplined behavior among young people. In reality, pupil discipline is the responsibility of every member of the school staff—the principal and assistant principal, the guidance counselors, and the teachers. Building pupil morale is an important function of the school's personnel who work with learners. Some principles that should characterize the building of good school spirit and, in turn, of acceptable behavior are summarized below. As they apply to you they include:

1. Your awareness of a pupil who has a problem and who needs help; opposed to here is a problem child.

2. Your acceptance of the immediate problem as a learning experience that can be used to help the pupil meet his future problems effectively.

3. Your eagerness to get the pupil's side of the story, including listening to his ideas regarding what should be done about it.

4. Your willingness to display an attitude of acceptance of the pupil even after he has violated regulations.

5. Your fairness, consistency, firmness, and understanding.

6. Your willingness to commend a pupil for partial success rather than to condemn him hastily for failure to achieve.

7. Your ability to build or to restore a pupil's self-respect rather than to destroy or remove his feeling of security.

8. Your desire to assist a pupil to work out a plan that may ameliorate the immediate situation, preclude the occurrence of unfavorable responses, or find constructive activities that give direction to his behavior.

9. Your willingness to give a child a vote of confidence by giving him a second chance in the form of new responsibility.

10. Your interest in providing favorable conditions that will enable a pupil to achieve successful performance.

11. Your willingness to discuss established ground rules with your class.

12. Your willingness to keep records of disciplinary infractions for future reference as a means of helping individual pupils improve their behavior.

THROUGH DISCIPLINE TO SELF-DISCIPLINE

Throughout this discussion we have stressed the value of your employing constructive techniques that have as their primary purpose the restraining of pupils from engaging in various forms of misbehavior. To the extent that you are achieving your goal, you are building habits of control among children that can function when your pupils are removed from your physical presence. Your own well-disciplined behavior can serve as a model that they are likely to imitate more or less consciously. Your encouragement of pupil cooperation can carry over to situations outside the classroom.

Some people seem to believe that the well-disciplined person does not fear the consequences of asocial behavior. This is an error. We all tend to avoid engaging in socially unacceptable acts because we are unwilling to face the aftermath of such behavior. The difference is one of motivation. The child refrains from being "bad" because he fears that a penalty for his deed will be administered from the outside in the form of physical punishment, loss of privileges, isolation from his group, and the like. The administration of such penalties probably is needed in the beginning stages of his training. Gradually, however, he can be guided to think through the effects on himself and others of his displayed attitudes and behavior. This broadened concept of discipline motivates him to behave toward others as he would like them to behave toward him.

As you, in your dealings with your pupils, give approval to evidences of controlled behavior and show disapproval, with reasons, of uncontrolled activity, you are helping the members of your class recognize the value of cooperation. Especially, as you commend improved behavior on the part of former recalcitrant children, you are assisting them in developing those inner satisfactions that are experienced by well-disciplined individuals.

One of the chief areas of learning for the child is the acquisition of ideals and standards of behavior that shall enable him to meet present and future responsibilities constructively so that he is a worthy participant in the activities of the various groups of which he is or will be a member. If he is to earn the respect of his associates, he needs to exercise control of his emotions and appreciate the rights of others as well as his own. In other words, he becomes a self-disciplined individual in all of his various relationships. To the extent that you can help a child develop such self-control or self-discipline, you are fulfilling one of your most important teaching functions.

QUESTIONS AND TOPICS FOR DISCUSSION

1. Present various causes of behavior difficulties of children.
2. To what extent should you as a student teacher be alert to the behavior of each child in class?
3. Outline the difficulties involved when there is excessive teacher domination or when the class has too much freedom in connection with the development of self-discipline.
4. Carefully read the rules presented in this chapter for guiding your own conduct. How well are you succeeding in applying them to your own class behavior? Note the ones that need improvement.

5. How can you ascertain the sincerity of a child's verbal apology for a misdeed? Illustrate.
6. List constructive deprivations that would have value in helping your pupils achieve self-discipline.
7. Give the psychological factor involved in avoiding the requirement of extra work for misbehavior.
8. What are some examples of the "ignoring" process in dealing with a child's lack of cooperation?
9. How can your cooperating teacher assist you in developing self-discipline among your pupils?
10. Reread the list of teachers' errors and check those that you tend to commit. Try to avoid them.
11. Summarize the ways in which you can help your pupils develop self-discipline.

15

EVALUATION OF PUPIL PROGRESS

Everyone in the school is interested in and concerned with the evaluation of the pupil and his progress. The teacher, however, is the school person who is most directly involved with the responsibility of measuring and evaluating individual achievement. He is better able to assess this progress when he knows something about each pupil's capacity to learn, and the extent to which each has mastered significant concepts or skills basic to an understanding of the next learning unit. In other words, the effectiveness in evaluating extent of learning is helped to the extent that the teacher knows his pupils.

It is important to know the objectives of education that are to serve as the base of evaluation of teaching-learning outcomes. It is as these are known by you and your coworkers that your teaching will be directed toward meaningful purposes and that you will know what learnings are to be evaluated. Evaluation is the final step in the educative process.

Objectives of education of which you were aware prior to the period of instruction serve as guides against which to measure the extent of learning resulting from your teaching efforts. Too often these objectives are assumed rather than set forth or even consciously conceived. You might refer to the goals of elementary education that we presented in Chapter 6. These can serve as possible educational outcomes against which to measure educational or learning progress.

EVALUATION OF PERSONAL QUALITIES

Various types of well-organized tests have been constructed to yield results that give one or another measure of pupil ability, competence, or personality. Intelligence tests, both individual and group, are widely administered. Some of these yield results that give information concerning both abstract and mechanical ability. Individual and multifactor aptitude tests also provide helpful data for the teacher.

Various other tests have been standardized to measure such qualities as personal traits and interests. These include numerous self-administering tests as well as those in which an individual is rated by others. Some personality and interest tests are locally constructed and do not have norms available for comparative purposes. Projective techniques such as the *Thematic Apperception Test* and the *Rorschach Inkblot Test* have norms that add to the worth of these tests.

We shall consider the various types of standardized tests that are available for the evaluation of pupils' personal qualities. Many of these tests have been in use since the beginning of this century. Their worth depends on the extent to which you are able to make professional application of available scores or upon the accuracy of the data obtained by their administration.

Intelligence Tests

During recent years, many instruments have been devised to measure the mental capacity of learners. The general intelligence of individuals is variously referred to as mental ability, academic aptitude, or scholastic aptitude. The index that roughly represents level of mental ability is the IQ. This index is obtained by dividing the mental age of an individual as obtained from a standardized intelligence test by his chronological age, and then multiplying by 100. The IQ is relatively constant throughout the developing years of the individual. Many valid and reliable tests (both group and individual) have been devised to measure mental ability. An intelligence test with high reliability is one administered to one student at a time (individual intelligence test), such as the 1960 revision of the Stanford-Binet or one of the several Wechsler tests of intelligence such as Wechsler Intelligence Test for Children (WISC).

Personality Evaluation

Any effort to measure an individual's interests, drives, and behavior is an attempt to evaluate personality. You must not be misled, however, into thinking that personality can be measured by a compilation of scores obtained from tests of intelligence, aptitude, and achievement. The measurement of any one of these traits represents only a phase of personality. It is the integrated functioning of all the aspects of the individual that represents his total personality pattern. Hence personality evaluation is concerned with the measurement of all qualities that reveal the individual as a unique functioning entity.

There now are available numerous measuring instruments that give some indication of an individual's attitudes toward himself and others; his fears and worries; his likes and dislikes; his degree of adjustment as revealed on pencil-and-paper tests; his understanding of socially acceptable behavior in general. Observable evidence of an individual's behavior suggests something concerning (1) the ways in which he behaves in school or other social situations, and (2) the extent to which he is liked by others. If he displays a cooperative attitude and other pupils seek his company, he appears to have desirable personality qualities adequate for the social needs.

You must keep in mind that personality patterns, although somewhat stable, are not static but continue to respond to influences within and outside the individual. Hence some personality measurement may yield personality ratings that vary with the time and conditions of the testing. Factors such as the emotional state of the individual and his attitude toward the administrator of the test may influence his responses at the time of its administration. In spite of other limitations, such as deliberate falsification of responses or inability to recall past experiences, it is possible from the results of personality tests to discover certain inherent attitudes, emotional states, and behavior patterns that otherwise might not be revealed to you or another person.

EVALUATION OF LEARNING PROGRESS

The individual most directly affected by evaluation procedures is the pupil. He feels more at ease in his study when he has confidence in the approach that is used in judging his learning achievement. An evaluative system that is fair and is administered uniformly to all pupils tends to give each child security and helps him become more certain about his progress. The kind of measuring instruments you use and the way in which you utilize the results obtained are the concern of every learner in your class.

During the term, you are likely to utilize many evaluating devices such as oral recitations, short quizzes, written reports, teacher-constructed short form and essay examinations, and standardized achievement tests. Your success from the viewpoint of your pupils will be determined, in part, by your skill in using effectively these instruments in evaluating their learning progress.

Daily Oral Recitation as an Evaluative Instrument

Although there are advantages to entering a mark in your class record for pupil responses during the daily recitation, the disadvantages seem to outweigh the advantages. The pupils come to class presumedly prepared to participate in the discussion. When you make it a point to evaluate in written form every remark made by them during their attempt to answer questions, you provide conditions that are threatening and not conducive to the production of creative thinking. You should attempt to develop ideas based on the background of your pupils, and thus stimulate the thinking process. To the extent that you provide thought-provoking questions, you will stimulate the kind of thinking that is likely to enable them to arrive at solutions of problems that you pose.

Several factors militate against the value of recording grades for participation in discussion. The questions that you ask respective pupils to answer are likely to vary in difficulty. Also, some pupils become so involved in guessing what the next question will be that they fail to listen to what is being said by a pupil who is discussing the present question. Then, too, the shy child is at a disadvantage in comparison with the more aggressive or outgoing child who often talks without having much to say on the topic.

Written Reports as Evaluative Instruments

You have a responsibility to evaluate all written work that you require pupils to submit to you. This includes such written materials as compositions, project reports, and notebooks. As a student, you probably always have looked forward with anticipation to the return of your written work. You have appreciated a teacher's evaluating and grading it carefully and fairly. Now you have the responsibility of returning written work as quickly as time will permit your careful evaluation of it.

In some subjects, workbooks and notebooks are necessary. When either is used, it is your duty to encourage your pupils to keep them neat and to make careful entries in them. A workbook or notebook is for the pupil's use, but you need to supervise the writing to insure its accuracy of content and usability at a later date. Encourage pupils to make only those entries that have a bearing on the subject. An elaborate cover design may satisfy the ego of the pupil but does not contribute to worthwhile content. The nature of the material and its applicability to the topic are of prime importance. You become skilled in helping pupils prepare worthwhile notebooks by giving time and attention to this kind of project during your student teaching experiences.

The Use of Tests in Measuring Achievement

The tests with which you are likely to have the closest relationship from the point of view of application are the various forms of tests that are used to measure extent of achievement. You will use many short quizzes and either prepare or help prepare questions for administration to evaluate small units of study. You also will be involved in the preparation of end-term or final examinations.

You are likely to use the results of certain standardized achievement tests that were administered earlier. Scores made by third-, fourth-, fifth-, and sixth-grade pupils in such learning areas as reading and mathematics will be found on most cumulative records. In addition, you may participate in the administration of standardized tests that are devised to measure extent of achievement in the subjects that you are preparing to teach or are teaching. You should be acquainted with reliable tests in each subject area and know how to interpret the results of their administration.

The use of short quizzes. Rather than rate each oral contribution of your pupils, it might be a better policy to plan short quizzes that cover the assigned work and, using no more than five or ten minutes for each, get weekly statements that can be rated and recorded. You need to encourage home study and to know something about the extent to which it has been completed. Some time then can be devoted to the solution of problems that challenge the thinking of your pupils and, at the same time, make them feel more at ease in the learning situation.

You need to develop skill in using a procedure that will enable you to check on homework assignments. In the upper grades you can enlist the help of the pupils in the administration of this technique. An elementary teacher, for example, gives the responsibility of quizzes on assigned home study to rotating pupil committees. Each of these committees (numbering three pupils) in turn prepares appropriate short-form questions or one essay question, and administers them. Sometimes the committee corrects the papers; sometimes the pupils exchange papers and rate them; at other times the teacher collects the papers and marks them. A record of the pupils' performance is kept in a special notebook for the teacher's use. Of course, a project of this kind requires careful teacher supervision, but the pupils' participation in testing procedures helps them recognize the difficulty of preparing adequate questions and of rating them accurately and honestly. Most fifth- and sixth-grade pupils enjoy participating in these projects.

Teacher-made Tests and Examinations

You will want to make use of many types of written tests to measure pupil achievement, since you will need much information to assist you to determine the mark to be placed on a report card. Of course, these paper-and-pencil tests serve purposes other than that of aiding in the determination of grades. They can be regarded as devices that reveal something about the success of the teaching-learning process. You should not lose sight of the fact that effective teaching as well as extent of learning are reflected in these measurements.

Objectivity in testing. Teachers need measuring instruments that will help them measure learner achievement more objectively than can be done by using only the essay-type questions. Numerous experiments have been made that reveal the wide range of scores assigned to answers on essay questions even when they are evaluated (marked) by experts. This holds not only in subjects like the language arts and the social sciences but also in the physical sciences and mathematics. For example, 142 teachers rating one English paper assigned scores that ranged from 64 to 98; 118 teachers who rated a final examination paper in mathematics gave scores ranging between 28 and 92. Objective-type tests tend to correct this fault even though they have faults of their own.

Good objective test questions are difficult to formulate. The challenge to the test constructor of the short-form objective type test is (1) to select questions that completely cover the material to be tested, and (2) to prepare questions that are clear, thought provoking, and ranging from the simple to the relatively difficult. A variety of objective-type tests are in wide use. Included among them are true-false tests, multiple-choice tests, completion tests, matching tests, identification tests, and controlled essay-type tests. We present sample questions of each type from several learning areas.

Examples at Elementary School Level

Examples of true-false questions. Directions: Place a plus sign (+) before each statement that is true or essentially true; place a zero (0) before each statement that is false.

1. Plants need animals in order to survive.
2. A magnet has both a North and a South pole.
3. The earth is smaller than the sun.
4. Dams help to control floods.
5. In the United States shadows are longest at noon.
6. Animals that sleep throughout winter are said to hibernate.
7. The annual interest on $200.00 at 4% annually is $80.00.

Multiple-choice questions. Directions: In each question, select the best ending and place its identifying letter before the number of the question.

1. The eggs of frogs hatch and develop into (*a*) fish, (*b*) clams, (*c*) toddlers, (*d*) tadpoles.
2. Magnets attract (*a*) zinc, (*b*) silver, (*c*) aluminum, (*d*) iron.
3. Water power comes from (*a*) frozen water, (*b*) falling water, (*c*) heated water, (*d*) distilled water.
4. The Pacific Ocean was discovered by (*a*) Balboa, (*b*) Lewis, (*c*) Boone, (*d*) de Soto.

Matching questions. Directions: On the line before each object in the left column, write the letter of the right-hand column that describes its use.

Object	*Used to Measure*
___ 1. barometer	*a.* distance
___ 2. thermometer	*b.* weight
___ 3. scale	*c.* liquid
___ 4. yardstick	*d.* temperature
___ 5. microscope	*e.* air pressure
___ 6. quart jar	*f.* small objects

Identification questions. Directions: On the lines below, write the names of the states for the numbers given.

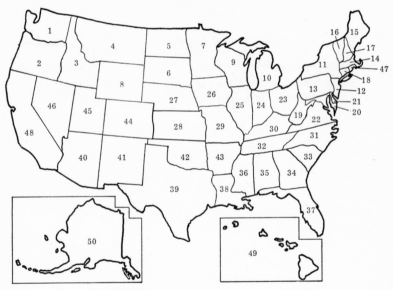

FIG. 6.—States in the United States.

44	_____	3	_____
32	_____	33	_____
22	_____	16	_____
38	_____	6	_____
8	_____	25	_____

Examples at Level of the Student Teacher

Same or different meanings. Directions: Differentiate between *Same* or *Different* meanings of words by placing an *S* or a *D* before each set in this list.

___ 1. maturation—learning   ___ 5. projective test—*TAT*
___ 2. diagnostic—prognostic   ___ 6. motive—purpose
___ 3. test—scale   ___ 7. character—personality
___ 4. mental age—IQ   ___ 8. norm—standard

Controlled completion. Directions: In the blank space provided, place the proper word from those given below.

1. When learning takes place _____ are produced in the

_____.

curves   changes   plateaus   retention   organism   diagram

Controlled essay. Directions: Answer each question as indicated in the space provided.

1. Five characteristics that describe child behavior are:
   a.
   b.
   c.
   d.
   e.

2. State three advantages of the cross-sectional study approach over the longitudinal approach in the study of individuals.
   a.
   b.
   c.

Principles of Test Construction

When you construct questions to measure the achievement of your pupils, you can be guided by some basic principles such as:

1. The questions should be drawn from the material learned without attempts to use trick questions.

2. The questions should be stated clearly so that they can be comprehended by each pupil.

3. The questions should become progressively more difficult in the test, especially if it is a short-form test.

4. Most of the questions should be geared to the ability level of the less able, but a few should be difficult enough to challenge the mentally superior pupils.

5. The test should be long enough to keep the pupils busy during most of the time set for the test.

6. Each pupil should be given a copy of the questions. When questions are placed on the chalkboard, you must make certain that they can be read easily by every pupil in the room.

7. If for any reason you need to read the questions to the class, your reading must be clear, distinct, and slow enough for each pupil to grasp the meaning of the question.

8. The questions should be so worded that they permit of only one correct interpretation.

9. The pupils should be given the correct answers to the questions they missed on the tests. This can best be accomplished by returning corrected papers and discussing them.

10. Evaluative judgments of pupils' success in the test should be made by you in relation to the relative performance of each member of the class.

Special Considerations

You should make certain that material included in the test is based on the material that was to be learned. As you correct test papers you can note such things as (1) the errors that are common to the majority of the learners, and (2) errors made by various individual pupils. The first procedure will help you evaluate your teaching effectiveness; the second is diagnostic in that it gives you insight into individual weakness.

As you go over test papers with your pupils, you may find it advisable to assume the responsibility for the common errors made by them and have these errors become the bases for further class discussion. Each child should recognize his errors and understand the correct answer when it is supplied to him. Often a child will need additional instruction before he comprehends sufficiently so as to make the material useful in his educational progress. You will find that if you use test results constructively, pupils do not fear tests but are glad to have them administered so that they may know the extent of their achievement in the subject.

STANDARDIZED ACHIEVEMENT TESTS

Standardized achievement tests are usually of the short-form type. Most of them have multiple-choice questions with four or five options from which to select the *correct* or *best* answer. These tests are constructed by test experts who follow definite rules of construction. When the term *standardized* accompanies a test it means that, after wide administration of the test in a particular learning area, norms have been established for the test. A manual usually is provided that offers carefully prepared directions for the administration and scoring of the test.

During the process of standardization, the preliminary form of the test contains more items than will be included in the final form. Through proper elimination of questions and rearrangement of those retained, the test usually is scaled—i.e., the least difficult questions are placed near the beginning and the more difficult ones toward the end of the test.

The worth of a standardized test depends on its *validity* (measures what it is supposed to measure) and its *reliability* (yields consistent results after repeated administrations). A test that has high reliability is one that gives comparable results when used to test the same group of pupils after an interval of time or that yields consistent results whenever administered.

Standardized achievement tests are not to be used to measure achievement in learning units as you progress in your teaching of a subject, but rather for comparative purposes with other pupils who have completed the study of the subject for which the test has been constructed. Results obtained from the administration of standardized achievement tests can be used properly to compare the achievement of your pupils with established norms. Note that standardized tests other than achievement tests are administered to evaluate individual pupils in comparison with large numbers of same-age groups in areas such as (1) intellectual capacity, (2) interests, and (3) emotional adjustment. Standardized tests should not be administered as a kind of busywork. Once administered, the results should be studied and serve as a basis for adjusting teaching procedure to learner difficulties.

EVALUATION FOR PURPOSES OF MARKING AND GRADING

One of the most difficult responsibilities of a teacher is to determine a mark that represents extent of achievement, record it, and perhaps justify it to the child. More and more, teachers are coming to realize that teacher-assigned marks are not as absolute as once had been believed. At best, marks represent no more than a teacher's estimate of pupil achievement. Usually, they are indicative of the extent to which, in comparison with others in the class, an individual pupil has succeeded in the learning of assigned material in the course.

Need for Competence in Marking

You will need to develop skill in the use of various kinds of tests so that you can use the results obtained in your assessment of a pupil's standing in his work. This necessitates (1) the construction of valid short-form tests and (2) the using of acceptable procedures in the marking of essay-type papers. You know about the variability among the marks from one teacher to another. You also need to realize that, during your marking process, you should maintain the same rating standards for all pupils. For example, it is better to complete a set of essay papers for a class once you start marking them so that you use one standard for all the papers. It is known that marking standards are likely to vary, on the same question, from one marking period to another.

Scores obtained from the administration of classroom tests and examinations serve as a significant basis for marks or grades to be entered on report cards. These assigned marks will be as valid and as reliable as are the scores obtained from the tests used. In a short-form test, for example, the number of items included, the extent to which they cover the subject matter, and the care exercised in its construction are factors that influence school marks. Essay questions should be so worded that pupils understand exactly what they are expected to include in their answers. Children are interested in the marks they receive and the basic considerations used in their determination.

Method of marking important. The index that you use to evaluate the extent of pupils' learning is the mark that you give, whether it is in the form of a *percentage* or of a *letter*. The former represents, in the mind of the child, an exact number such as 85 per cent; the latter represents a step interval including several percentage points —A = 90 to 100 per cent.

There are several methods that you can use to indicate level of achievement of your pupils. You may reveal the degree of achievement in relation to that of the other members of the class; you may attempt to give an absolute measure of achievement; you may compare individual performance with norms of available standardized achievement tests in a subject. What most pupils are interested in is, "Where do I stand in my class?" Each child wants to know something about his achievement in relation to that of other members of his class, or of other classes in the school.

Importance of having standards understood by pupils. In your evaluation of pupil achievement you will make use of criteria in arriving at a mark. Pupils and parents need to know the standards that are used by you. You should utilize every available evaluating source, such as individual reports, daily recitations, weekly tests, notebook work, special projects, and final examinations. Not only should the pupils know that these are the criteria used by you, but it is of further value to them to know something about the relative weights assigned to each.

Factors Causing Variability in Marks

You must be on guard not to let child behavior influence your evaluation of achievement. Some teachers have a tendency to give higher marks to cooperative pupils than to troublemakers. A mark given to a child should represent your most accurate judgment of his learning progress and not be influenced by his attitudes or behavior. It should indicate your estimate of his accomplishment in the learning situation in relation to the achievement of all other pupils in your class. Evaluation of his other personal characteristics can be reported in other ways.

The fact that teachers do not agree upon nor use precisely the same standards in marking, accounts in part for the divergence among teachers' marks. Your set of values enters into marking more than you realize. A simple example can illustrate this point. Suppose you assign a grade to the following example on the scale from 0 to 10. What score did you assign to it? Do you give him credit for

$$\begin{array}{r} 786 \\ +249 \\ \hline 1025 \end{array} \qquad \text{Grade}\_\_\_\_\_$$

knowing the principle of addition even though his answer is incorrect? We have given this type of example to college juniors and seniors and to graduate students. It is never possible to get agreement on what the score or grade should be. The scores usually range from 0 to 9. Each student wants to explain his reason for his rating. What he means is that he has his standard that guides his evaluation. The purpose of this example is to enable you to understand that grades are based on your own mental standards and are far from being absolute.

Earlier in the chapter we reported that the marks of specialists on specific papers varied widely. Some teachers believe that minor errors should carry heavy penalties and are known as teachers who give low marks; other teachers are willing to overlook certain minor mistakes and accordingly assign higher marks. The latter become known as easy markers. Ironically, these standards vary from school to school and from teacher to teacher.

SUGGESTIONS FOR DISTRIBUTION OF MARKS

In an unselected group of learners there will be found a distribution of marks that follows closely that of a normal curve of distribution. (See Figure 3, p. 73.) Even in a class of pupils already equated on some ability basis or level of achievement, the scores earned by them tend to range from a low to a high with the larger number of scores falling near the middle of the distribution. In others words, when the achievement of a group of pupils is measured, you are likely to find a wide distribution of scores with which to deal. You then are confronted with the problem of using these scores in assigning marks.

Classes that are organized according to learning achievement and ability to perform constitute an excellent teaching-learning situation. When the learners have experiences that are somewhat comparable, your burden as a teacher is eased from one point of view. However, for the purpose of assigning marks, it is easier for you when you have an unselected group of learners. Here you have no difficulty in knowing what grades to give to the few at the low end and the few at the high end of the scale. When you have a class of gifted children you find a shorter range of scores, and you are less certain about the marks to assign the pupils.

Marks should reflect all of the evaluations that have been made by you during the course of the training period. There are various schemes of percentage distributions that you might use. You may have a school policy on this. If so, be sure to follow it. We present here several distribution schemes that represent the percentage of pupils who might be assigned respective marks.

TABLE 8

TYPES OF DISTRIBUTION SCHEMES FOR REPORTING MARKS

Letter Grade	Percentage Range	Percentage of Pupils in Each Range			
A	90–100	10	7	5	10
B	80–89	20	24	25	25
C	70–79	40	38	40	55
D	65–69	20	24	25	10
F	Below 65	10	7	5	0

If they are available, you might study the distribution of marks already given by different teachers. Much can be gleaned from these data. Also, you might be provided with the marks given by your college instructors in one or more of the subjects you are taking. You are likely to find that college instrutors vary in their marking procedures and standards in the same way as do teachers in the lower schools.

Even though the students who attend college are highly selected, the marks representing their achievement in any subject area vary with instructors and are distributed from low to high in any one class. In Table 9, we present representative marks given in three courses, including child development, adolescent development, and educational psychology.

TABLE 9

DISTRIBUTION OF MARKS IN THREE COLLEGE COURSES

Course	Marks				
	A	B	C	D	F
	Number of Students				
X	30	180	80	25	9
Y	35	103	64	24	6
Z	61	332	162	52	9

THE USE OF VISUAL GRADING

As a student teacher you are filled with enthusiasm. You want to be fair in your appraisal of pupil achievement and want to correct some of the grading abuses that you have observed. You want to put meaning into the marks that you assign. You proceed to construct an acceptable test and administer it to prevent cheating or any other abuse. You score the papers accurately and conscientiously. Once you have the raw scores, you are confronted with the problem of distributing them according to school policy. K. L. Russell [1] provides us with four criteria of a meaningful grading system. He says:

FOUR CRITERIA OF A MEANINGFUL GRADING SYSTEM

1. The grade for achievement in a given subject should be based on a comprehensive and extensive measurement program. There should be many measurements; they should be scattered over an extended period of time; and they should represent a number of different testing procedures.

2. The grade must be a symbol of comparison between student status and known and fair standards. The parent and the student want to know what the standard is. A standard in the mind of the teacher is not enough. The teacher must be able to describe these standards to both parents and students. Parent education is an absolute necessity.

Fairness needs no justification, but fairness does not just happen. The grade level and maturation of the student must be considered in establishing a fair standard. Fair standards are derived from a combination of perform-

[1] K. L. Russell, *Visual Grading* (Huntsville, Tex.: Educational Filmstrips, 1959). Reprinted by permission.

ance of students in the local school with a definition of competence by experts in the subject or field in question.

Percentage standards of and in themselves are of little or no value. A score of 80 per cent on a test has no meaning until we know something about other scores made by other students assigned the same subject matter and who took the same test. Without knowing the scoring practices of the individual teacher, we know little or nothing about the real meaning of percentage grades. A percentage score of 80 may represent the best achievement in the class or it may represent the worst. One teacher gives tests of a difficulty level designed to be a challenge to bright students with the result that 80 may be an above-average score. Thus we find that a percentage standard is not a standard at all since it can vary from day to day, from teacher to teacher, and from year to year.

3. Grades and reports should be realistic. Much has been written about frustrating the student with too much emphasis upon grades. Grading in such a way as to prevent frustration is impossible. "Over-grading" is certainly a disservice to the student because he will tend to over-rate his ability and be frustrated when he tries his skill in a non-school atmosphere. To under-rate the good student with low grades in order to prod him to more accomplishment may frustrate him and keep him from achieving as high as he should. Believe it or not, most of the progress of the world has been made by individuals who were frustrated in some way or another and set out to do something about it.

Some schools grade upon effort. Slow students are given good grades because they "try hard." Excellent students receive good grades for superior achievement. Without knowing whether the grade is for effort or for achievement, we know nothing about the effort or the achievement of the student. To average an *A* for effort and *F* for achievement, and report a *C* as the grade may indicate little about either effort or achievement.

There are good reasons for grading on effort, and where this is done there should be two grades—one for achievement and one for effort. The poor student is encouraged by his good grade for effort, yet recognizes his poor accomplishments. The good student may be reprimanded with a poor grade for effort and still be told that his achievement is of high quality.

4. The grade symbols must be understandable to students and parents. The meaning of grades should be clear and constant from year to year and from teacher to teacher.

Dr. Russell carefully explains the meaning of "Letter Grades" and defines what achievement is expected for each category:

LETTER GRADES

Letter grades provide a method of classifying achievement into meaningful groups. Experience suggests that teachers can place student achievement into approximately five groups. Finer divisions than this are impractical.

No two school systems define letter grades exactly the same way. The important thing is that schools clearly specify to all concerned what their letter grades mean. One such description is given here as an example.

The letter *A* is reserved for *very superior* achievement. It means that the student is prepared for high-quality advanced work in the field of study and usually represents a small number exhibiting outstanding accomplishments.

The letter *B* is representative of *highly satisfactory* achievement. It indicates that the student is prepared for above-average quality advanced work. The group receiving this grade is usually larger than the *A* group but much smaller than the *C* group.

The letter *C* represents *competent, satisfactory, average* achievement. It should mean that the student is prepared for advanced work. The *C* group is usually larger than the *A* and *B* groups combined.

The letter *D* signifies *poor* achievement. It represents work which is marginal for advanced work in the field of study. The group is similar in size to the *B* group.

The letters *E* and *F* are reserved for *very poor* achievement. The group is usually similar in size to the *A* group.

It is utterly futile to argue what per cent should be assigned the various grades. The proportions will vary from class to class, from semester to semester, and from community to community. However, over a two-year period or after 250 grades have been assigned, the distribution should be about 25–35 per cent *A*'s and *B*'s, 35–50 per cent *C*'s, and 25–35 per cent *D*'s and *F*'s. To be more exact than this is misleading. To stray too far from these figures, however, denies the definitions stated above. A teacher who persists in giving more than 50 per cent *A*'s and *B*'s or *D*'s and *F*'s has changed the definitions of the grades to fit his own purpose and thus his grades are meaningless to the rest of the school and the community. There may be exceptions to this where homogeneous grouping is attempted.

Many schools now use the mark of *E* for reporting very poor achievement. The *E* should be used when it seems advisable to "pass" or "promote" most children each year because of social, psychological, or economic reasons. This allows the teacher to report low achievement without the implications of failure and non-promotion. The *F* should be used when it seems advisable to "fail" or "retain" approximately 5 to 10 per cent of the students each year.

Five to 10 per cent of the students will generally fall in the very low group. No amount of juggling or adjusting of test scores can change this fact. If the school wishes to be realistic and report this fact to the parents, the school, and the community, it should adopt a system which makes it possible without implying failure and non-promotion. Parents will accept accurate reports of achievement. They will not accept arbitrary failure and non-promotion for their children. If the school is prepared for 5 to 10 per cent of its students to "fail" and is prepared to adhere to its decision, in spite of parental pressures, then it should use the *F*. If the school is unwilling for 5 to 10 per cent of its students to be in the process of repeating courses and grades, then it should use the *E*.

Advantages of Visual Grading

The advantages of visual grading as given by Russell are presented here:

The plotting of scores on cross-section paper for visual interpretation is one method of making grades more meaningful. It is a well proven fact that when a large number of unselected cases of any natural phenomenon are measured and plotted that a bell-shaped curve results. This fact has been the basis for improving grading practices for many years, but in practice the plans have proven inadequate. Most authorities who propose the "curve" as a background for grading forget that classroom teachers do not have the time to apply complicated statistical interpretations to student achievement. Moreover, the scores in any one class provide too small a sample to follow the statistics of the curve in daily practice. As a result the "curve" is extremely unpopular as a foundation for grading.

Visual grading adapts the phenomenon of normal distribution to small groups. This is done through visual interpretation rather than through a statistical one. Experience has shown that the visual interpretation of small groups of scores results in grade distributions which meet the criteria for meaningful grades. The following advantages can be attributed to visual grading:

1. Visual Grading makes it easy to include all types of evidence. Large groups and complicated statistical interpretations are unnecessary. It is not limited to any given number of measurements, to a period of time, or to any particular testing procedure.

2. Visual Grading provides a uniform basis of comparison regardless of the differences in scoring practices. The standard is verified by student achievement in any given area of learning. The system is fair to all students, while at the same time helping to provide a challenge to the bright students at all grade levels.

3. Visual Grading helps to keep grades constant from teacher to teacher and from year to year. Meaningless percentages are not used. Rigid "curve" grading is avoided. Achievement is classified into meaningful groups, not into artificial patterns dictated by blind percentages.

4. Visual Grades are realistic. There is no need to water-down the content of examinations. There is no need to be lax in evaluation procedures.

5. Visual Grading can be easily explained to students and parents in many ways. For convenience in explaining Visual Grading, a series of three film-strips has been prepared for use with teachers, students, and parents.[2]

6. Visual Grading is less time-consuming than many other methods. No complicated mathematical computations are involved. No averaging or percentage calculations are necessary.

[2] Kenneth L. Russell, *Grading Student Achievement,* Three Color Filmstrips (Huntsville, Tex.: Educational Filmstrips).

Charts That Illustrate Visual Grading

We now present four charts from Russell's *Visual Grading* that illustrate some of the ways that visual grading is used:

You are now ready for your first experience in the visual interpretation of test scores. Fairness seems to dictate that the same grade be assigned to similar scores.

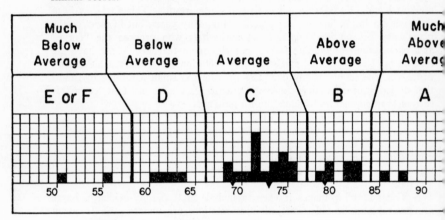

Fig. 7.—Assigning the grade.

The following is suggested as a beginning approach to the problem of visual grading with homogeneous groups. Experience is very limited in this area and the author will appreciate receiving distributions of scores from teachers who have been assigned homogeneous groups.

Assume a group of students selected from the upper 33 per cent of the student body. *A* and *B* students.

If the school requires the reporting of a percentage grade, in addition to a letter grade, the following procedure is suggested:

1. Chart the scores and grade according to the concept of visual grading.

2. Assign the lowest grade in each letter group the lowest percentage specified by the school for this particular grade. Adjust the other scores accordingly.

This adjusted percentage will now agree with the definition of the grade. This adjustment appears more desirable than to say that a score of 70 **is** average when in reality it may be above or below average.

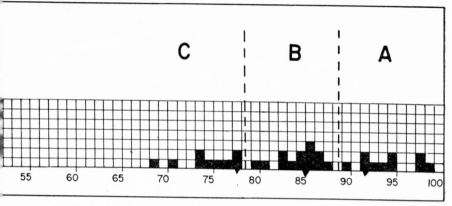

Fig. 8.—Grading homogeneous groups.

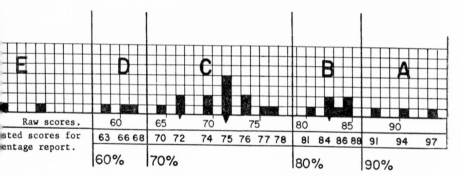

Fig. 9.—Adjusting to percentage scores.

REPORTING TO PARENTS

The pupil's report card, of which we presented samples in Chapter 4, represents an important medium for reporting pupil progress to parents. It is one of the most important documents that the child receives during his school life; it is important both to him and to his parents. On the report card is presented the story of the pupil's achievement according to the standards of the teacher in each learning area. The child deserves to have the marks on the card represent fairly his degree of achievement in learning progress and his personal qualities that are evaluated on it.

In many school systems informal reporting procedures are used to report progress for children in the kindergarten and first grade. These may take the form of parent-teacher conferences, of filling in general progress reports, or of general comments on progress, or all three. In Lansing, Michigan, the reporting procedures include both the conference and the informal report and, when requested, a letter grade.

As an aid to the teacher in his preparation for a parent-teacher conference the school system issues a *Parent-Teacher Conference Guide* to enable the teacher to confer successfully with parents. The teacher is expected to file a summary report on each conference held with parents. We present some of the suggestions here.

AN OUTLINE FOR PARENT–TEACHER CONFERENCE [3]

BASIC OUTLINE FOR PARENT-TEACHER CONFERENCES

A. Preliminary Planning for the Conferences.
B. Greeting the Parents and Establishing Rapport.
C. Orientation to Discussion.
D. The Main Part of the Conference.
E. Summary.
F. Closing and Parting.

DETAILED OUTLINE FOR PARENT-TEACHER CONFERENCES

A. Preliminary Planning for the Conference

1. An invitation should be sent to the parents. (The scheduling is planned by each individual school.)
2. Each conference should have a purpose. All areas of child growth and achievement can not always be discussed at one conference. Select the most important ones for the time.
3. A Teacher Preparation Form should be made for each child before the conference with the purpose of the conference in mind.
4. Some of the child's work should be ready for the parents to see.
5. A display of books to be used by the class during the year will be of interest to the parents.
6. The physical aspects of the room are very important.
    a. The parent is more at ease if the conference is held at a location other than the teacher's desk.

[3] Courtesy of Forrest G. Averill, Superintendent of Lansing Public Schools, Lansing, Michigan.

b. Comfortable adult sized chairs should be provided around a high table or in a group.

c. Two or three adult sized chairs should be placed in the hall near the teacher's door for parents who arrive early for their conference.

d. The room should be neat and attractive. A vase of flowers or a plant will give warmth to the conference.

B. *Greeting the Parents and Establishing Rapport*

1. Rise to greet the parents as they enter the room.
2. A friendly smile helps to put the parents at ease.
3. More time is needed with some parents than with others to establish rapport.

C. *Orientation to the Discussion*

1. The teacher and parents should know the purpose of the conference.
2. The teacher should assume responsibility for seeing that the purpose is clear to each parent.
3. The teacher must have definite information in mind about the child's accomplishments and his needs. The teacher must be ready with suggestions for the child's improvement.

D. *The Main Part of the Conference*

1. The conference is not a one way affair. The parents should be given an opportunity to talk. If the conference turns out to be just a time for telling the parents, a written report would be satisfactory.
2. Parents must be made to feel important in this conference. Don't be afraid to ask the parents for help.
3. Talk with the parents about the fine things their child is doing as well as his problems. Problems must be discussed but they should be presented kindly.
4. Try to convey to the parents the importance of the child as an individual and your realization of the importance of their role in his life.
5. Do not quote an I. Q. score. If the parent asks about tests, describe the child as average, slow maturing, or above average. Remember that a child's score will vary with different tests and on different days.

E. *Summary*

1. Always summarize the conference, remembering that the child is the focal point of the conference.

   2. Leave parents with the idea that they have contributed to a better understanding of their child and his needs.

   3. Invite the parents to visit the child's class to see his progress.

F. Closing and Parting

   1. Rise as the parents leave.

   2. Be friendly and make the parents feel glad they took the time to come.

SUGGESTED TOPICS FOR PLANNING THE CONFERENCE

Academic Adjustment and Work Habits

1. How does the pupil's progress in school learnings compare with his ability?
2. What are the characteristics of his ability to learn: for example—
   a. Is he a fast or slow learner?
   b. Is he eager to learn or does he have to be urged unduly?
   c. Is his retention reasonable as to time and amount of what is learned?
   d. Does he show initiative and self-direction in his learnings?
3. In what school learning, if any, does he excel or have marked difficulty?
4. In what situations and in what ways does he show intellectual curiosity?
5. What evidence does he show of ability to reason?
6. In what situations does he show imagination and creative ability?
7. What kinds of experience interest him and challenge him to purposeful activity?
   a. Are his special interests of an intellectual, physical, manual, or artistic character?
   b. Is he especially active along lines of planning, directing, and evaluating experiences?
   c. Is his activity directed predominately toward group undertakings, individual projects, or a balance of the two?
8. How able is he to listen to gain understanding necessary for intelligent participation and cooperation?
9. How responsible is he in working out his own learning problems?
10. What evidence does he show of growth in ability to evaluate his own work and that of the group?
11. In what respects does he show progress or lack of progress since his last reports?

SOCIAL ADJUSTMENT

1. Does the pupil have a friendly atttiude toward others?
2. Does he voluntarily participate in group activities?

3. Does he usually choose to work and play alone?
4. Does he always seek companionship?
5. Does he like to be the center of attention?
6. Does he avoid situations which draw attention to himself?
7. Does he often participate in group activities without seeking a major role?
8. Does he assume leadership on occasions?
9. Does he accept responsibilities in his relationships to others?
10. Can he be depended upon to carry through the responsibilities he accepts?
11. Is he genuinely considerate of others?
12. In group situations does he assert his rights, but at the same time respect the rights of others?
13. Does he respect the property of others?
14. Is he accepted by his peers?
15. Is he liked by his peers?
16. Is he at ease in social situations; neither overly timid nor overly aggressive?
17. Is he extremely competitive?
18. What is the pattern of his reaction to adults, dependent or resistant or well adjusted?
19. What is his attitude toward constituted law and authority on the social order?
20. Does his personal appearance operate as a factor in his acceptance by the group?

PERSONAL ADJUSTMENT

1. Is the pupil ordinarily contented, satisfied, independent; or is he discontented, disgruntled, complaining, faultfinding, worried, overly dependent?
2. Is he usually calm, composed, level-headed, well balanced, poised; or is he tense, high-strung, irritable, excitable, over-active, or apathetic, stolid, sluggish?
3. Does he tend to be happy, fun-loving, cheerful, sad, depressed, sullen?
4. Is his behavior consistent; or does it fluctuate between gaiety and depression, calmness and tension, self-control and loss of self-control?
5. Is he normal in persistence and able to work effectively; or is he easily distracted and quick to give up?
6. Is he able to apply himself actively and to the point; or is he a day dreamer, forgetful and indecisive?
7. Is he flexible, yielding and fair in adjusting to new situations; or is he fearful, inflexible, rigid, resisting, unreasonable?
8. Is he extremely neat, meticulous, devoted to detail, irritated and confused by disorder; or is he messy, sloppy, careless, disorganized?
9. Is he calmly self-confident, accepting his assets and liabilities without boast or apology; or does he tend to under-estimate his abilities and to be satisfied with goals too low for himself, to bully and brag as a cover for his insecurity, to be unduly sensitive and evasive?

10. Is he quick to anger? What sorts of situations arouse anger? Is his anger of long duration? Is there evidence of attempt at self-control on irritating situations or is there complete giving away to anger?
11. Does he have fears of a particular character? When and how does he show them? Can he manage to overcome them or does he give way to them?
12. From whom do his strongest pressures seem to come; from his parents, teachers, other pupils of his group, his brothers and sisters?
13. Does he appear to have sufficient rest and food; or is he tired and inattentive?
14. Does he appear to have good eyesight and hearing; or does he have trouble?
15. Has he established good bathroom habits?

The following are detailed suggestions for teacher-parent conferences. They should be most helpful to an inexperienced teacher.[4]

Go to the door to greet your guest, introduce yourself if you are strangers, and try to make the parent comfortable and at ease.

Walk about the classroom commenting on some activity under way, materials, the view, perhaps some irrelevant item. Don't plunge into the conference. Express appreciation for the opportunity of having the parents come to work with you. Assure them that you really need them and that your working together is a privilege.

Begin—and end—the conference with a positive comment about the child.

Try not to take notes during the conference. Jot them down immediately afterward. If you can't remember all the points covered, jot them down as unobtrusively as possible.

Hear criticism fully and get suggestions. Avoid arguments and, when it is desirable to change a point of view, do it diplomatically.

Try to put yourself in the place of the parent and try to imagine what effect your remarks will have. Be truthful, but remember that you are talking to a parent about his most precious possession, his child. Combine truth with tact.

Don't let your desk be a barricade between you. Use two or three chairs grouped together. The individual conference is a partnership, so don't let the presence of a desk "break up" the partnership feeling.

Don't get bogged down in generalities. "Johnny is doing all right . . . there are no problems . . . nice to have met you." This is nice for parents to hear but most of them would just as soon get it in a note or letter.

It is usually possible to evaluate a pupil's progress without being critical. Instead of "John is constantly annoying the other pupils," you might say "John seems unhappy in his relations with others." But be certain to be articulate about what you are trying to explain.

[4] *Conference Time for Teachers & Parents,* National School Public Relations Association in cooperation with Department of Classroom Teachers (Washington, D.C : National Education Assoc., 1961), pp. 23–25. Reprinted by permission.

When you offer suggestions to the parent, it's often good to offer alternative ones so that the parents may make the decision as to which to use. Most parents don't really want advice. They want support. But if they can be led to making their own decisions, the advice will more likely be accepted.

Find out how the parent is thinking and feeling about his child. This is important, because you can better understand Suzie's behavior if you know her mother's and father's attitudes.

If a parent tells you why he thinks his child is acting a certain way, accept it and lead the conversation on to other possible causes. He may be acting that way for a number of reasons.

If a parent suggests a plan of action, accept it if at all possible, but leave no doubt as to the proper roles of the teacher and parents as far as conducting the business of the classroom is concerned.

Avoid any tinge of an argument.

Keep your eyes open for possible signs of emotions: expressions, gestures, changes in voice. Sit so the light falls on both your face and the parents' faces so each of you can sense the emotional tone.

If you think it's necessary, assure the parent that your profession requires you to keep all information about pupils and parents confidential.

Don't take it for granted that parents want your help. Many of them will come for the first time only because they feel they should. If you give them the impression that you think they need help, your attitude may be taken for criticism. Let their suggestions come out in the course of the discussion.

If you have no suggestions for improving a bad trait, don't bring it up.

Don't send the parent away loaded down with countless suggestions. Concentrate on one or two things on which you can work together to help the child. Similarly, don't confuse the parent by trying to show every piece of work their youngster has done in the past months. What you don't show in the conference, the parents can look over at home.

Don't press inquiries if the parent is obviously reluctant. As one parent remarked: "I don't mind telling almost anything, but I don't like to be asked!"

You may get an unflattering earful about "that" former teacher who taught Eddie. Here you will want to be sure your attitude reflects only good of that teacher, and of other teachers and schools, too.

Similarly, don't let comments about other children enter the conversation. Don't compare brothers and sisters.

Don't suggest home activities that are really the responsibility of the school.

When you must say "no," take a long time to say it, and say it softly.

Don't ask prying questions about extremely personal matters.

Be on your guard for your own facial expressions. A wince or slight frown at a parent's comment may embarrass him. Especially avoid surprise or disapproval.

It is a mistake for you to try to tackle serious psychological troubles of children. Refer them to the consulting psychologist.

Don't show the parents only the poorest or best work. Show the whole range. If possible, show how the work has improved or changed.

Don't use educational "double talk." Words like "immature," "aggressive," "maladjusted," and "retarded" may have different meanings for the parent.

Provide paper and pencil for parents to use in taking notes if they want to.

You don't want to let the talk dribble off into inconsequentials past the point where nothing is accomplished. As a signal that the conference is over, you might suggest another meeting soon, or say: "I see Mr. and Mrs. Gordon are waiting for their conference."

Don't give parents the impression they have "had it" when this session is through. Make clear you welcome the chance to confer with them at any time: "We made a good beginning today, but we do need more time to talk together. Shall we make another appointment?" It may be possible to conduct some follow-up conferences by telephone, to conserve time.

The conference which you began with encouraging news should end on a note of optimism: "I'm so glad, Mrs. Taylor, that you suggested helping Karen to make the multiplication cards for use at home. I'm sure they will help her with her arithmetic."

Summarize major areas discussed.

Agree upon action needed.

Clarify next steps.

Extend an invitation to visit school any time.

See the parents to the door—allow yourself a 10-minute interlude, if possible—and welcome the next ones in with a smile, even if the last conference was a problem.

Keep the following checklist as a guide to help you conduct conferences with parents.

CHECKLIST FOR A GOOD CONFERENCE [5]

1. Make careful preparation.
2. Insure privacy.
3. Have an informal setting.
4. Set a time limit.
5. Establish rapport.
6. Begin on a positive note.
7. Encourage the parents to talk.
8. Listen attentively.
9. Develop an attitude of mutual co-operation.
10. Delay making numerous definite suggestions yourself.
11. Encourage suggestions from the parent.
12. Use parents' practical suggestions as a springboard for action.
13. Summarize points covered.
14. Make plans together for future progress.

[5] *Ibid.*, p. 27.

15. End on a note of continuing co-operation.
16. Make notes after parents leave.
17. Be informed about school purposes, methods, and achievements.

Parents' cooperation is more easily attained in school projects when they understand what is going on and how they can assist in encouraging their children to participate actively in their school-work.

QUESTIONS AND TOPICS FOR DISCUSSION

1. Explain what is meant by, "Evaluation is the final step in the educative process."
2. What intelligence test or tests are administered to the pupils in your school?
3. Compare the results of intelligence tests administered to the children in your class with their achievement ratings. To what extent do they agree? What specific differences do you find? How do you explain these differences?
4. If you have taken a personality test, report on your attitude toward it and your reaction to individual items.
5. With your cooperating teacher's approval, experiment with having your pupils prepare some daily quiz questions. What difficulties do the children encounter?
6. Which type of short-form questions do you prefer? Why?
7. Why should questions in a test become progressively more difficult?
8. What are the implications of item 10 of the principles of test construction?
9. What are some of the difficulties involved in assigning marks?
10. Which of the types of distribution schemes in Table 6 seems to you to be the most equitable? What factors can influence your opinion?
11. What have you learned about grades from reading Russell's comments? In what ways has he helped you in assigning marks?
12. How might your method of weighting different learning activities vary from the one presented in the chapter?
13. What are the advantages of teacher-parent conferences concerning children's learning progress? List needed cautions to be observed.

16

TEACHER PLACEMENT AND ORIENTATION

During your student-teaching experiences (probably earlier), you gave attention to the problem of securing your first position as a regularly assigned teacher. You will want to devote sufficient time and thought to this task so that you finally select and are accepted by a school in which you can achieve personal and professional satisfaction, and, through participation in the activities of which you are stimulated, grow in your chosen career. Too many teachers-to-be who make this decision hastily discover that, for one or more reasons, they are unhappy in their work. They may even come to believe that they are unsuited for teaching.

SEEKING EMPLOYMENT AS A TEACHER

Before you start to seek your first position, you need to ask yourself certain important questions concerning your teaching interests. For example: Do you want to teach in your home community or are you willing to accept a position in another community or even state? Do you prefer teaching in a large or a small school community? To what extent will size of salary affect your decision? How important to you are opportunities for professional growth and advancement?

Your answers to questions such as those given in the foregoing will determine in part the kind of school or school system in which you will attempt to secure employment. Fortunately for you, the population on the elementary school level is increasing. Hence teacher demand is greater than teacher supply. Yet, since the number of young people preparing to teach on this level also is increasing, you will have stiff competition. You may need to compromise somewhat in regard to what you consider to be an ideal teaching situation. Too, you must make certain that you meet the certification requirements of the state and locality in which you seek a position to teach.

Certification Requirements for Teaching

Each state has established certain requirements that must be met by an applicant for a teaching position in the elementary school before he can be given consideration for appointment in that state. Various states are increasing the minimum years of preparation for teacher eligibility. At present, all states except one require the baccalaureate degree for eligibility to teach. Although all states require the completion of courses in professional education and student teaching there are differences among them in the number of semester hours required.

In order to determine your accrediting status, it would be wise for you, before you apply for a position, to consult the latest edition of the National Education Association *Manual on Certification Requirements for School Personnel in the United States,* which publishes a revised edition about every two years. A college placement officer also may be able to help you check your eligibility in various states. In some states, the schools will employ you provisionally, giving you a period of grace in which to fulfill a specific requirement.

Approaches to Teacher Placement

There are various avenues of approach to securing a teaching position. You may have a friend or relative in a school in which you might be interested in teaching. If there were an appropriate vacancy in that school, the person could speak in your behalf and perhaps arrange an interview for you with a member of the administration. You might decide on geographical areas that would be convenient for you and visit locations in order to discover possible vacancies. These informal approaches may yield uncertain results, however. More formal approaches to seeking a position usually are to be preferred.

Value of a college placement bureau. Most colleges and universities maintain a placement bureau for the use of their students and graduates. Many schools and school systems report their faculty needs to certain selected institutions of higher learning that are engaged in teacher education. These vacancies are kept on file in the placement offices of the colleges, and attempts are made to fit graduates to available positions. Your first approach to finding a position might be to register with your college bureau. You will find that the director or one of his assistants will be more than willing to discuss with you any opportunities for placement that may be available. The bureau also will help you organize your credentials. Some elementary schools send recruiting officers to various colleges to review the credentials of possible teacher applicants and to meet them for interviewing purposes.

Other teacher placement services. There are commercial teachers' agencies to which you can apply. Although college placement officers usually do not charge a fee, commercial agencies exact a fee for placement of about 5 per cent of the first year's salary. Most of these agencies conduct a reputable business, but you should consult someone who knows about these agencies before you sign up with one. In some states there also are state-sponsoring placement services or services offered by state teachers' associations. These usually charge a small fee.

Other ways of locating a possible position are (1) to send letters of inquiry to selected schools to discover whether there are any vacancies in your field of interest, and (2) to apply by letter to schools in which you have heard that there are available positions. The *Education Director,* published by the U.S. Office of Education, can be used to find the names and addresses of all school superintendents.

Some of the larger school systems (New York City, for example) select their teachers by way of licensing examinations. Any qualified citizen of the United States is eligible to enter one of these examinations that are held at stated intervals. If you pass the various parts of the test (including a physical examination and a speech test) your name is placed, in rank position, on an eligible list from which appointments are made. One difficulty of this procedure is that many months may elapse between the taking of the examination and the date of the appointment.

Data to be included in an application. Any materials that are needed in applying for a position must be accurate and carefully prepared. You need to be sure that your credentials are properly stated. Someone in your college placement bureau can assist you in their preparation. File a set of credentials with the bureau for present or future use. Be sure that what you file is kept up to date.

Your college probably has a form for the listing of credentials. Fill in all items. These usually include identifying data, the position for which you are qualified, your personal qualifications, your training, and any experience you have had with young people, including your student teaching. Give specific dates and places. You usually are required also to include the names of at least three persons who can serve as references. Avoid using the names of close friends or relatives. The names could include those of (1) a college instructor, (2) your cooperating teacher in a school, and (3) your clergyman or other community leader. You should name individuals who will give a fair and impersonal evaluation of your personal qualities, your skill in working with children, your scholarship, and the like.

Most schools require a transcript of your college record of scholarship. This is furnished by the college upon request. The first transcript is sent without charge. You may be asked to pay a small fee for others. Also included with the credentials should be a small photograph of yourself (about 3×5 inches). Snapshots are not desirable. When you sit for the photograph, wear conservative business clothes, and be sure that your head and shoulders are in view. Avoid a "posed" expression.

The letter of application. A letter of application should be clear, brief, and to the point. This is a business letter and should follow the proper format. Type the letter, unless a school administrator prefers that you write in longhand. If so, make certain that you write legibly and in black or blue-black ink. Take care that your signature can be read easily. Be specific. State the position for which you are applying, and your training and experience. Either enclose a brief statement of your qualifications or refer the reader to the placement agency from which your credentials may be obtained. Specify when you will be available for appointment and indicate your desire to be called for an interview. End your letter by expressing appreciation of whatever consideration you may receive. Also, enclose a large self-addressed, stamped envelope for any forms that may need to be sent you.

The letter of application is an important document. Administrators often are shocked by the carelessly written and poorly organized letters of application they receive from college-educated young men and women. An attractively and properly prepared letter is a point in favor of your candidacy. After you have written your letter, proof-read it, noting any errors of form, spelling, grammatical structure, typing, and the like. If possible, submit it to a college instructor for criticism. Rewrite when any errors are found.

Many school systems require the completion by the candidate of a regular application form that requires the submitting of pertinent data. The application blank of the Westport Public Schools, West-port, Connecticut, for example, includes the following area items:

Teaching Position for Which You Are Applying
1. Personal Data
2. Employment Data
3. Military Service
4. Educational Preparation—Undergraduate Level
5. Educational Training—Graduate Level
6. Educational Credits
7. Teaching Experience
8. Student Teaching Experience—If New to Teaching
9. Other Work Experience
10. Other Professional Experience
11. References
12. Name and address of the Placement Office where your credentials are on file
13. Write a brief statement of your reasons for wanting to teach in Westport and your satisfactions in teaching thus far.
14. What do you consider your strongest and weakest characteristics as a teacher?
15. What reading have you done in the past six months?
    a. General Magazines
    b. Professional Magazines
    c. Books
16. List the professional, civic, and social organizations in which you hold membership.

Your interview with school administrators. School officials usually want to meet a candidate before deciding on his eligibility for a vacancy. This can be accomplished in one of two ways. The candidate is invited to the school on a particular day and at a specified time convenient to the interviewer and interviewee; a recruiting officer of the school may interview possible candidates at the college. In either situation, your displayed attitude during the interview is extremely important.

Your first interview probably will be a trying experience. Especially will this be true if the position for which you are being interviewed is one in which you are very much interested. You may tend to be "nervous." You may break out in a cold sweat and seem to be losing control of your voice. You may be inclined to fidget or to sit in a rigid position. You may be impelled either to overplay or underplay your qualifications for the position.

You need to become mentally set for the interview before you arrive. It is imperative that you be prompt, courteous, and honest. Before the interview, try to learn something about what might be expected of you. Avoid telling the superintendent how to run his school. Be willing to assess your own ability to meet the needs of the position. Reveal your interest in children and your interest in teaching as a profession. Somehow reveal the fact that you can be relied upon to discharge your obligations as a teacher when they are due and in the way they should be done. Convince the superintendent that you will reflect credit on the faculty and the school by your presence in the community.

Remember that the interviewer probably has had considerable experience in interviewing candidates for their first job and is able to recognize the symptoms of your inner perturbation. Hence he will make allowances for it. He is likely to prefer a modest young person to one who appears to be brash and overconfident. Listen attentively and answer questions simply and truthfully. Indicate by your manner that you appreciate the opportunity to be interviewed and that you hope that your qualifications are satisfactory. Although it is helpful to ask questions for clarification of the needs of the position, avoid any seeming attempt to interview the official.

Your final decision. The chances are good that you will receive at least several offers of positions. Deciding on the one to accept may constitute a problem. You do not want to be hasty. The first offer you receive may meet all of your expectations concerning teaching conditions, attitude of the administrator and other faculty members, salary schedule, kind of community, and living conditions. You probably will accept this position and look no further. It may be, however, that you have a question about one or more aspects of the vacancy. It is best then to wait for other offers. Yet, this procedure may give rise to difficulties of placement.

You cannot expect a school to hold a vacancy open to you indefinitely. You may need to meet a deadline for acceptance. Also, later offers may be less desirable than the one about which you are hesitating. Some schools do not object to your accepting the assignment tentatively, provided that you give your final decision within a reasonable period of time. It is unethical to accept several offers of employment and then to withdraw applications with no regard for the inconvenience caused to an employing school. Consult with the director of your college placement bureau concerning the ethics in dealing with employment practices.

Your teaching agreement. A teaching contract is a formal legal agreement between the employing school system and the teacher being employed. The form and interpretation of such contracts differ somewhat with states. Before you sign a contract you should read it through carefully. Make certain that you understand its provisions and are willing to abide by them. The contract includes specific information concerning length of tenure as specified in the contract, as well as the terms under which the agreement can be terminated by either party.

A teaching contract is binding on both the board of education and the teacher. Just cause must be shown by either for breaking the contract. If you are performing conscientiously and effectively, you need have little fear of being released from the contract. Likewise, you are expected to live up to it, except in the case of an emergency.[1]

Beginning teachers do not always appreciate the seriousness of contractual agreements. For example, a graduating senior of an institution for teacher preparation made application for a teaching position in several school systems in his state. During May, he signed a contract with the superintendent of school A. In early summer, he received what seemed to him to be a more favorable offer from school B. Thereupon he signed a contract with that school but neglected to notify school A of his changed plans until the end of August. When this matter was called to the attention of the head state authority, this young person's teaching certificate was sus-

[1] *Code of Ethics for the Education Profession* (Washington, D.C.: National Education Assoc., 1963), Principle IV, pp. 427–30.

pended for a period of six months, starting in September of the following year. This meant that, although the teacher was permitted to teach in school B for one year, he then was denied accepting a position in a public school in that state for the following September.

STARTING YOUR FIRST TEACHING POSITION

After you have made your final decision concerning the school in which you will teach and have signed the contract, you need to prepare yourself for entrance into your new field of responsibilities. Whether you have completed your plans before or after college graduation, various matters need to be attended to before you begin your actual teaching.

One of your first considerations is where you will live. If you are to teach in your hometown or close to it, this presents no problem. You probably will live at home and travel to and from school. If your new school is so far removed from your home that travel would be difficult or impossible, you need to find a temporary home for yourself. The school officials usually have a list of appropriate homes for their teachers. Obtain a list of such vacancies and investigate the possibilities in light of your interests.

Some characteristics of available quarters can be judged on inspection; others need to be lived with to be evaluated. For example, distance from the school; size, furnishings, and general appearance of the room; size of family, number of other roomers and boarders, and cost can be determined by means of a visit to the home, accompanied by tactful questioning. Such matters as kinds of meals, heating facilities, and extent of personal freedom and privacy can be discussed in advance, but no conclusions can be arrived at concerning them until you have lived with them. It probably is wise to make tentative arrangements that can be changed later if necessary.

You also should attempt to acquaint yourself with the community. Visit the town to discover its available facilities, such as libraries, religious organizations, community centers, educational and recreational facilities, and the like. Some schools send their prospective new teachers maps and other interesting material about the community. Try to become as well acquainted with the community as is possible before you become a member of it.

Another area of preparation, of course, is the assembling of teaching-learning materials that will be helpful to you on the job. Here again the school can be of assistance to you by giving you, ahead of your arrival for duty, whatever in the way of curriculum materials, courses of study, and lists of available aids that you will need. You also can visit the school, preferably before you sign the contract, to discover something about the school's policies, types of pupils, teaching schedules, available teaching-learning equipment, and similar matters. The better prepared you are to start your teaching, the greater will be your chances of successful accomplishment.

PROGRAMS OF TEACHER ORIENTATION

Modern school administrators are becoming increasingly aware of the value to all concerned of helping beginning teachers in a school system adjust with a minimum of tension to their new responsibilities. Most schools sponsor orientation or induction programs at the start of the school year and continue to offer assistance to new teachers throughout their first year in the school. Where this is possible, an experienced teacher of the school, usually on the same grade, is assigned to help the latter in the meeting of his various school-and-class, management-and-teaching obligations.

As interpreted by most school officials, the term *new teachers* can refer either to beginning teachers or to more experienced teachers who have transferred from other school communities. Although orientation or induction procedures are conducted for both groups, beginning teachers receive whatever additional sympathetic help that may be needed.

Assistance in adjustment is rendered either through the issuance of teacher handbooks and other information materials, or through the conducting of workshops or meetings before the regular school year begins, or both. We shall present briefly some examples of orientation procedures that have been selected from school systems in various sections of the country.

Handbooks and Brochures for Teachers

Written materials dealing with information of value to the teacher tend to be attractively organized and arranged. They vary in length in terms of their specific purpose. For example, the Omaha Public Schools have prepared a well-illustrated ten-page brochure entitled *You'll Like Teaching in Omaha*. It contains brief comments on the environment, possibilities of professional growth, orientation, opportunities for advancement, salary and benefits, professional associations, and living conditions. The purpose is to attract qualified teachers to Omaha.

Various types of such publications are illustrated by the orientation booklet of Syracuse, N.Y. *Welcome to Syracuse,* Rochester's *Now That You Are with Us,* and the two booklets of San Diego, California—*San Diego City Schools Elementary Program* and *New Teachers' Handbook*. Such handbooks include detailed information concerning policies, credentials, regulations, schedules, tenure, special services, and other types of data with which teachers in the particular school system should be acquainted.

Teachers' handbooks are generally intended for use by all the teachers of the school. Some schools include materials for new teachers in the same booklet; others prepare a separate pamphlet, as is the case with the San Diego schools. In fact, this school system goes a step further by presenting to new teachers an extremely attractive booklet entitled *San Diego Today,* which contains snapshots of some of their teachers at work with young people at various grade levels or in special subject areas. The St. Paul, Minnesota, Schools publish *A Handbook for Teachers* and a brochure *Welcome Aboard,* which includes information that is of special interest to the new teacher. You might be interested in reading the foreword of the brochure.

Welcome to the staff of the Saint Paul Public Schools!

You are now a member of a most congenial, skillful, and helpful staff. May I express the hope that you will find genuine enjoyment in your new work in Saint Paul and that out of the ensuing school year will come much of lasting benefit to you as a result of your personal and professional associations.

The role of a teacher in our present-day society is not an easy one, and the first year of teaching, or the first year in any new school situation, is always beset with special problems. It is within our intentions, throughout this rather difficult period of adjustment, to render you every possible assistance. Your principal, the directors and supervisors, and your fellow teachers are ready to help you. Do not hesitate to call on them. Your contributions and your successes will be the source of much satisfaction to us, in the same way that these successes will contribute to your own feelings of personal satisfaction and well-being.

Good Luck!

Forrest E. Conner

Superintendent of Schools [2]

Schools and school systems throughout the country are accustomed to list in writing certain definite materials concerning your professional relationships. The City School District of Syracuse, New York, for example, issues administrative bulletins that deal with teachers' orientation information. The current bulletin includes the following items:

Absence from your classroom

Absence (excused), request for

Certification

Change of name, etc.

Discipline, classroom

Helping teachers

Hospitalization, medical benefits

Leave of absence

Policies and regulations

Probational reports

Probational status

Professional record, personnel file

Retirement

Salary adjustments

Sick leave

Social Security

Termination of employment, notice of

Time schedule, daily

Transferral

Similar materials prepared by the Tenafly, New Jersey, public schools include brochures *Tenafly Invites You* and *Let's Get Acquainted,* and a salary guide dealing with matters such as salary range, salary increase, credit for previous experience, recognition for professional improvement, sick leave, pension and retirement, insurance, and sabbatical leave.

[2] Forrest E. Conner, *USS St. Paul Public Schools; Welcome Aboard* . . . (St. Paul, Minn.: Board of Education, 1962), foreword. (Mr. Conner is now Executive Secretary of the AASA.)

You also may be interested in reading answers to probationary teachers' questions as presented by the San Diego school officials. They deal with matters that concern you, regardless of the school system in which you have accepted an appointment. You need to discover what the policies of your school are in these respects:

FOR PROBATIONARY TEACHERS

ANSWERS TO YOUR QUESTIONS ABOUT YOU AND YOUR JOB [3]

ED. NOTE: Each year, our growing number of probationary teachers ask questions concerning matters which affect them directly as certificated employees of our district. The following questions and answers, prepared by the Personnel Department, are set forth in a sincere desire to improve understanding and communication on tenure, leaves, retirement, service evaluations, third-year physical examinations, and similar matters.

Ratings or Service Evaluations

Q. *How often am I to be evaluated as a probationary teacher?*

A. Each probationary teacher is rated by his principal twice during the year. These ratings are due in the Personnel Department not later than Nov. 15 and Feb. 15. The principal will discuss both ratings with the teacher and the teacher will sign the forms as an indication that he has seen them.

Tenure

Q. *What is the legal basis for tenure in California?*

A. *Education Code Section 13304:* "Every employee of a school district of any type or class having an average daily attendance of 250 or more, except a joint union or union high school district maintaining eight or more schools lying not less than six miles apart, who, after having been employed by the district for three complete consecutive school years in a position or positions requiring certification qualifications, is reelected for the next succeeding school year to a position requiring certification qualifications shall, at the commencement of the succeeding school year be classified as and become a permanent employee of the district."
Education Code Section 13328: "A probationary employee who, in any one school year, has served for at least 75 per cent of the number of days the regular schools of the district in which he is employed are maintained shall be deemed to have served a complete school year. In case of evening schools, 75 per cent of the number of days the evening schools of the district are in session shall be deemed a complete school year."

[3] From *San Diego City Schools: Elementary Program* (San Diego, Calif.: Personnel Department, 1963), pp. 36–37. Reprinted by permission.

Education Code Section 13331: "Service by a person under a provisional credential shall not be included in computing the service required as a prerequisite to attainment of, or eligibility to, classification as a permanent employee of a school district."

Q. *If I am absent for illness does my absence count toward the 75 per cent of the regularly scheduled teaching days in the school year which I must teach in order to have it count for tenure and a salary increment?*

A. No. According to legal opinions received by the Personnel Department, absence because of illness does not constitute service under the meaning of the Education Code section. Anyone absent more than 25 per cent of the school year for illness or other noncreditable reasons loses credit for that year toward tenure and must be considered "first-year probationary" again the following year. No salary increment is received for that year.

Q. *What are the standards for permanency?*

A. New teachers in the San Diego Unified School District are selected on the premise that they will achieve sufficiently high standards of service to become permanent. Prior to permanency, however, probationary teachers must demonstrate high professional competence and good physical and mental health.

Q. *How is the pre-permanency health exam handled?*

A. In the spring, health questionnaires are obtained from second-year probationary teachers and their principals. These are screened by the school physician, and those teachers who have no apparent health problems are exempted from the pre-permanency health examination. Appointments are scheduled with the Medical Board the following fall for those teachers not exempted. The expense for the routine exam is borne by the district; however, if any special report or medical care is necessary, the teacher obtains such from his personal physician at his own expense.

Leaves of Absence

Q. *Are probationary teachers eligible for leaves?*

A. Leaves of absence are granted only to permanent teachers with the one exception of leaves for compulsory military service.

Q. *May a teacher who is recommended for permanency after three years but who has not served the fourth year be granted a leave?*

A. Teachers who are recommended for permanency and who accept a contract for the fourth year of service are considered, for all practical purposes, as permanent employees. Therefore, such a person would be entitled to all the rights and privileges of a permanent employee, including leaves. However, because of the teacher shortage, all leave requests will be critically reviewed.

Q. *What job protection do permanent teachers have if their request for leave is not granted and they wish to resign?*

A. Under Education Code Section 13402, any certificated employee who is permanent and who resigns may apply for reemployment; and *if he is reemployed within 39 months* from the last date of *paid* service with the district, he is reinstated as a permanent employee with all the usual rights and privileges.

Sick Leave

Q. *What sick leave privileges do I have as a probationary employee?*

A. Full-time, 10-month, probationary employees during their first year are immediately eligible for 10 days of full-time sick leave at full pay. In addition, they are eligible for 100 days sick leave at half pay. Second-year probationary employees who have not used any sick leave during the first year are eligible for 20 days of full-time sick leave at full pay and 90 days at half pay. Full-time sick leave for which the employee is compensated by full salary is accumulative indefinitely under California Law. The sick leave policy appears on page 113 of the district *Rules and Regulations* available in the principal's office.

Absence on Personal Business

Q. *May I be absent to attend to personal business?*

A. Yes, if the business is of an urgent nature. The request should be submitted to the Personnel Department at least 3 days in advance on the "Personal Business Absence" form. Such absence entails loss of salary.

Administrative Examination

Q. *How do I achieve eligibility to be considered for administrative appointment?*

A. Administrative appointments are made from candidates who have qualified on the administrative examination. This exam is given once a year, usually near Christmas vacation, and the date is announced in the *Superintendent's Bulletin.*

Q. *What are the general requirements for taking the exam?*

A. Candidates must be permanent teachers or third-year probationary teachers who are being recommended for tenure, must hold a Master's Degree and the proper administration credential.

Transfer Requests

Q. *May I request a transfer from one school to another or from one level to another?*

A. Yes, any employee may fill out an Assignment Preference Request indicating his desire for a change in assignment. The deadline is Dec. 18 for changes desired the following September. In general, however, employees are expected to stay with a particular assignment for a full school year.

Retirement

Q. *Do probationary employees participate in the retirement program?*

A. Yes, all certificated employees must participate in the State Teachers Retirement System. Deductions for the employees' contributions to the program are made automatically by the Accounting Department.

Q. *If I resign, may I get back my retirement contribution?*

A. Yes, any employee resigning from the district may apply immediately for refund of the retirement contributions, plus interest, which the employee has made.

Q. *May I receive credit for teaching experience outside the State of California for retirement purposes?*

A. No. Under present legislation, there is no provision whereby an employee may obtain credit for teaching service outside the State of California.

Death Benefits

Q. *In the event of the death of an employee, are there any benefits to the estate or the beneficiary?*

A. Yes. There are four types of death benefits immediately available to the beneficiary of a deceased employee: (1) A refund of all contributions plus interest. (2) A lump sum death benefit of 1/12 of a year's salary for each year of service to a maximum of six years or half salary. (These benefits are paid to any beneficiary named by the employee.) (3) A survivor benefit of $90 for each dependent survivor to a maximum of $250 a month. These benefits are remitted to the immediate family of the deceased. Consult the Retirement Section for more details. (4) If the employee has reached age 55, the widow or orphan children of an employee may elect a retirement allowance of half the retirement allowance to which he would have been entitled had he retired at the moment of death. This benefit is paid in lieu of benefits (1) and (2) listed above.

Q. *In the event of a prolonged illness prior to the death of an employee, are sick-leave benefits available to the beneficiaries?*

A. Yes. Sick-leave benefits due an employee for days absent because of illness are available if claims for such benefits are made by the authorized executors.

Health Insurance

Q. *What provisions are made for participation of employees in health and accident insurance plans?*

A. Payroll deductions to cover the premiums for the Washington National Insurance Company income protection plan may be arranged. In addition, all employees who qualify are covered without cost by the Pacific Mutual Life Insurance Company's major health and accident group policy. Qualified employees may arrange for a salary deduction to cover dependents under this plan. Complete details of the coverage offered may be found in the handbook issued by the Pacific Mutual Life Insurance Company.

Even before you become attached to a particular school you can benefit from acquaintance with the policies and regulations that are common, to differing degrees, in most schools and school systems. Note the various areas of information that usually are regarded as being significant to the beginning teacher. Include them among the points to which you will give attention as you consider the pros and cons of service in any schools that may offer you a position. Perhaps your college placement office has copies of the handbooks of particular schools that you may consult to alert yourself to teaching conditions in them.

Orientation Practices

A common school practice, in addition to distributing pamphlets and brochures, is to bring teachers together for a day or more before the beginning of the regular school year in order to afford them an opportunity to prepare for the year's work. This preschool session usually includes general information meetings and special panel discussions of the teachers of respective levels. New teachers attend such meetings and, in addition, are briefed in other ways concerning their status and responsibilities. To acquaint you with what you can expect to have happen at such orientation sessions, we are presenting a few programs conducted in specific schools or school systems.

DULUTH, MINNESOTA. ORIENTATION PROGRAM FOR
NEW TEACHERS [4]

THIS IS YOUR JOB

You're a member of the biggest and one of the most important professions in the country—the *teaching* profession.

[4] L. V. Rasmussen, *Orientation for New Teachers* (Duluth, Minn., Board of Education, 1964), pp. 4–7. Reprinted by permission.

Be proud to be a teacher; be loyal to your profession.

As a teacher, certain attitudes, duties, activities and responsibilities are expected of you.

Basic

When you agree to teach, you obligate yourself to support the entire school program, K-12.

You have the responsibility of carrying out general policies of the board of education.

School is like any business, in that employees are expected to work in a manner satisfactory to the employers.

A chain of authority exists, so take your suggestions and criticisms to your principal first. It isn't ethical to breeze your complaints to others.

The Duluth taxpayers have a big investment in the schools; they have a right to know what they're getting for their money; and you have the knowledge and the responsibility to give this information.

Specific Responsibilities

Present your teacher's certificate, and transcripts of credits to the superintendent's office, on or before the orientation meeting.

Every Monday morning, in your school, read the newsletter from the board of education.

Have your lesson plans carefully prepared in advance. "Pre-planning prevents panic and propagates poise."

Leave your personal problems at home; but bring your sense of humor to school.

Use correct English—and spelling *always.*

Ask for help and advice from experienced teachers.

The common school is the greatest discovery made by man.

Relations with Pupils

Develop creative abilities without neglecting basic skills.

Treat students with courtesy and in a fair and impartial manner.

In promoting a pupil, consider both achievement and what is best for the individual.

It's a fundamental fact that the learning process is based upon law and order in the classroom. You're responsible for discipline in your class—take to the principal only cases you can't handle. (Never send a pupil to the principal alone; accompany him.)

In the matter of discipline, require a standard of behavior consistent to the age of the pupil; try to develop in him self-control, not fear of authority —to arouse self-respect, not humiliation or pain.

Relations with Parents

Take every opportunity to become acquainted with parents of your pupils. Talk freely to parents who inquire about their sons and daughters. Appreciate their interest. If you have to state an unpleasant fact, precede it with a sincere compliment about the pupil.

Join and participate in the PTA.

Meet even discourtesy with courtesy.

Relations with the Community

Learn about the community.

Get the history by reading *This Is Duluth,* published by the board of education.

Read the newspapers to keep up with current affairs.

Participate in community activities.

Have some friends who aren't school teachers—broaden your view.

Vote in elections.

Buy in Duluth; the merchants help pay your salary.

Publicity

Help to interpret the schools.

Develop a nose for school news.

You will experience heartbreaks as well as triumphs, but if you work conscientiously, you'll find your place and begin to feel the intangible rewards of teaching. You'll get a warm glow inside you as you watch youngsters grow up to take an important place in the world, knowing that you have had a part in their success.

WE'LL HELP YOU WITH YOUR PROBLEMS

In a new school, you may want a bit of assistance in your work. You can get it.

Principals, directors of elementary and secondary education, *helping teachers* in the elementary schools, and *supervisors* in certain subject matter fields will help you. You can make appointments for a conference or ask them to visit your building.

The audio-visual department, with an office in the Franklin school building, offers services in films and recordings correlated with your work.

The A. M. Chisholm Museum, a department of the board of education, has exhibits from all over the world and from most ages in history. You may take your class to the Museum or requisition, through the loan service, materials to use in your classroom.

A guidance department, with the director's office in the Administration Building, will give assistance with problems of pupils in elementary schools. Guidance counselors are available in junior and senior high schools.

Ask not what the school will do for you, but what you can do for the school.

If a child is too mentally slow for your class, you can get help from *the special education department;* if he is too intellectually gifted, from *the special services department.* Through the special education department, there are: classes for children with defective hearing, eyesight, or speech; Kate Barnes classes for children needing orthopedic care; and home instruction for children who are physically weak. There is also a reading clinic to help elementary school children who have reading disabilities. You make referrals to these classes through your principal.

The medical department is staffed with a school medical director, a director of nurses and school nurses to help you with health problems of your pupils. If you notice any problems in mental or physical health of a pupil, consult your principal.

INDIANAPOLIS, INDIANA. HELPFUL HINTS TO NEW TEACHERS.[5]

BEFORE THE FIRST DAY OF SCHOOL GET ACQUAINTED WITH YOUR SCHOOL

locate
  Principal's office
  Your room
  Nurse's room
  Custodian's room
  Children's rest rooms
  Auditorium and gymnasium
  Supply room
  Visual aids
  Bulletin board for notices

learn the meaning of all bells
  Dismissal
  Fire drill
  Air raid drill

You will also want to determine where to take your children during fire and air raid drills.

[5] George F. Ostheimer, *Handbook for Beginning Teachers* (Indianapolis, Ind.: The Board of School Commissioners), 1963, pp. 4–6. Reprinted by permission.

Prepare Your Home Room

You and your pupils spend much of your day in your room. You will want to make it attractive for them and for yourself. You might consider:
Growing plants and flowers
Colorful and intriguing books
Magazines
Pictures
Exhibits
You will also want to get your desk in order. In these activities, be creative and feel free to use your own ideas.

Perform Necessary Clerical Work

Write or print on the board
  1. Your name
  2. Room number
  3. Grade level
  4. Supplies to be furnished by pupils
  5. Book rental fee
Order supplies for your room through your principal
Sign nativity cards
Get cumulative record cards and folders for your grade
Get medical emergency record cards
Prepare a temporary registration sheet for children reporting the first day.
Check the inventory of text books and equipment in your room. Keep this record
Make seating chart form

CHECKLIST FOR YOUR FIRST DAY

While Pupils Are at School

—Collect report cards of children *new* to the building. Keep these until later.
—Get names of all pupils.
—List children new to school and city and check to see that each has enrolled in principal's office. If not, send to office.
—Check cumulative record cards * (pink and white) and inquire about children not present. Put information on cards with pencil.
—Pass out nativity cards * to all pupils new to the school. Explain the necessity for parents to answer every question.

* Definition on following page.

—Pass out medical emergency record cards.*
—Explain arrival time and tardy time.
—Discuss importance of not leaving home too soon or loitering along the way.
—Collect rental fee of those who bring it and record your receipt of it together with the child's name. Do not enter in the rental receipt book * until school registers have been officially opened.
—Prepare information to give your principal on the number of children reporting to you according to grades and the number you have learned who will report later.
—Complete seating chart.

After Pupils' Dismissal

—Check with your principal for any changes necessary in pupil enrollment, seating and supplies.
—Check your program for each day.
—Check your pupils' program for each day.
—Write pupils' program on the board (intermediate grades).
—Make out building cumulative record cards (white) for pupils new to your building. Enter only the child's name. Later add information obtained from nativity card: birth date, parents' names, address and telephone number.
—Make out "Request for Cumulative Records" * for pupils transferring from other city schools. This request card can be obtained from your principal.
—Check supplies necessary for following day's work such as pens, pencils, papers, textbooks and textbook lists for all pupils.
—Place number of boys, girls and total who belong to your homeroom on black board.

	B	G	T
4A	8	7	15
4B	9	9	18
	17	16	33

—Prepare a list of children for the nurse.
—Secure ink bottle and fill ink wells (upper grades).

YOUR DEFINITIONS

Cumulative records and folders—These are the records which follow each Indianapolis Public Schools pupil from the first through the twelfth grade. They include information on health, personal traits, tests, family, adjustment activities and academic record. They should be kept accurately up to date.

Enrollment and nativity card—Contains family information such as age, parents, siblings, birth, sex, race, remarks by parents. It must be signed by parents. It may be referred to as the enrollment card, but generally is called the nativity card.

Medical emergency card—Properly filled out, it can be used in locating the parents of a sick or injured pupil and the three doctors and three hospitals his parents want him to be taken to in case he needs emergency attention.

Monthly report—A record of attendance, accessions, and losses that is required of every school, is compiled from each teacher's register. It is extremely important because the distribution of funds from the state is based upon these reports.

Pupil accident report—Should be filled out by home room teacher if a pupil has suffered any accident necessitating medical attention or a half-day's absence or more. Your principal also has forms to be used for such purposes as pupil trips and pupils' leaving the building.

Register—The official attendance and promotion record of our schools. Information should be entered promptly, accurately and in accordance with directions on the front page.

Rental receipt book—Contains rental receipts in original and duplicate form. Original form is given to pupils who pay for the use of textbooks and supplies. Receipts are not given to indigents.

Request for cumulative record (Elementary Schools Only)—A white form obtained from the principal used to secure cumulative records of a pupil transferring to your room from another Indianapolis public school. Four weeks should be allowed before request is made.

School referral to social service department—A request to have a social worker investigate any of the following problems of any child: attendance, behavior, parental neglect, educational, or conomic. It is submitted at the discretion of your principal and you.

Seating chart—A diagram of the seating arrangement, giving name and seating position of each pupil. Even though you know the names and seats of your children, this chart is needed in case a substitute teacher comes to your room.

ROCHESTER, NEW YORK. CLASSROOM PROCEDURES [6]

ELEMENTARY SCHOOLS

Absence Cards

Most schools use a daily absence card for reporting absence to the office. When a child is absent, record an "A" in the appropriate space. If the reason for the absence is known, record the date of absence and the reason on the reverse side of the card.

[6] Robert L. Springer, *Now That You Are With Us* (Rochester, N.Y.: City School District, 1962–63), pp. 19–21. Reprinted by permission.

In most schools, the cards of absentees are sent to the office by classroom messenger or are picked up by the office messenger. Inquire about the method used in your school.

Admitting Pupils After Absence

When a pupil returns to school after a period of absence, he must have a written note from his parent or guardian. This note should be kept by the teacher for one year. If a pupil fails to bring a note from home after an absence, consult the principal.

Assemblies

A large variety of educational and recreational experiences is offered to students through assemblies. The teacher will be notified regarding the time and seating procedure for programs in the school.

Banking

Pupils in the Rochester schools may make weekly deposits in the Rochester Savings Bank. An easy system has been devised for the handling of this routine. Consult the school clerk regarding the present procedure and the banking day for your school. The banking chairman or office in your school will be able to supply each teacher with all necessary materials.

Book Rental

A letter to the parents stating the rental fee for each grade will be furnished by the school office. The teacher is expected to send these letters to the parents at the beginning of each term and to collect the rental as early in the term as possible.

A rental fee for the use of books is collected from each child at the beginning of each term, unless special home conditions exempt the family. In some schools, the rental for the entire year is collected at the beginning of the school year. The principal will furnish each teacher with a list of children who are exempted from the payment of rental.

The teacher should give the pupil an official receipt when any payment, partial or whole, is made. Receipts are available in the official Cash Receipt Book which each teacher is given.

All book rental money collected should be turned in to the school office immediately. This money should be taken to the office in an envelope marked "Book Rental" securely fastened and marked with teacher's name, grade, date, and amount. The teacher should receive from the school clerk a receipt for all money turned in.

Discipline

We believe that pupils should have considerable freedom of action, but we think of this freedom as an earned privilege that follows demonstrated ability to use it wisely. We expect a teacher to control his pupils at all times.

We believe that the control of a group through the development of self-control on the part of its members is the highest type. Rigid, formal discipline, autocratically imposed, should not satisfy a teacher. Freedom to the point of license has no place in the school. Between these two extremes, there is a middle ground that can usually be held by good teachers.

Pupils in the Rochester schools are expected to conduct themselves at all times in keeping with their responsibilities to others in the classroom. No purposeful classroom activity can be carried on if effective control and suitable behavior are not present.

In general, the best way to maintain class discipline is to anticipate and remove possible conditions which may lead to the necessity for discipline. A good program and good discipline usually go hand in hand. When, however, occasions arise, the teachers are expected to deal firmly with the situation. Do not be afraid to ask for help. It is better to work out a solution together than let the situation get completely out of hand.

Excused Absence

No pupil is to be excused from school during school hours except by permission of the principal.

Faculty Meetings

Faculty meetings are held in each school to deal with administrative and instructional needs.

Questions pertaining to school policy or administration are covered in general faculty meetings.

Instructional meetings deal solely with areas of curriculum. These meetings may be broken down into small groups according to departments, grade levels, or special interest areas.

A tentative schedule for faculty meetings will be available in the principal's office. Wednesday after school is reserved for building meetings.

Homework

A written statement of policy about homework is on file in the school office. Teachers are urged to read it, discuss it with their principal, and use it as a guide.

Lights

Lights should be shut off when room is not being used. Always shut off lights and lock the door when leaving your room at noon and again at the close of school. Notify the custodian regarding lights that need repair or replacement.

Milk

During the greater part of the school year, children are given an opportunity to purchase milk for the mid-morning. The collection of milk money is made once a week on a designated day to cover the following week. The rates to be charged are established through a bulletin issued by the Milk for Schools Committee. All money collected for milk should be turned in to the school office before the close of school.

In each school a number of children who need milk service but are unable to afford it are given free milk. The principal of the school will furnish each teacher with names of the children who are to be given milk without cost. Care should be taken to avoid publicizing the names on this list.

Money

All money collected by teachers should be turned in to the school office as soon as possible after collection. Always put it in an envelope securely fastened and properly marked with name, purpose, and amount. Under no circumstances is money to be left in the teacher's desk, either locked or unlocked, during day or overnight. Each school is provided with a safe for the keeping of funds collected. The school system cannot be responsible for any money lost through a violation of this regulation.

When a teacher collects money from pupils for book rental or for any supplies, a receipt should be issued to the pupil. The office in turn will issue a receipt to the teacher when the money is turned in at the office.

Plans

Check with your principal as to the requirements concerning daily, weekly and monthly plans and time schedules. There is no substitute for careful daily planning and evaluation.

Repairs

Consult the school clerk as to the proper method used in requesting the repair of City School District property.

Substitute Teacher Folder

Each teacher is provided with a folder for use by a substitute teacher. Such a folder will include such items as:

Daily Time Schedule
Weekly or Monthly Plan of Work
Milk Lists
Reading Group Lists
Pupil Committees
Special Group Lists—orchestra, choir, religious instruction

The above items will be filled out by the teacher. This folder is to be kept up to date for it is the basis for an on-going program in absence of the regular teacher. Nothing is more discouraging than coming into a room where there is no evidence of planning. The folder may be checked periodically by the principal. It is suggested that the folder be clearly marked "Substitute Teacher Folder" and be kept in top middle desk drawer for easy access.

Ventilation

A teacher should make sure that the ventilation in her room is adequate for the size of the class. If the room is uncomfortable, do not attempt to adjust the thermostat. Notify the custodian and ask him to do so.

General Housekeeping

Teachers are expected to maintain reasonable standards of housekeeping in their rooms. In general, the custodial staff is responsible for the following chores at the end of the school day:

Sweeping floors
Replacing furniture in the position it was found
Locking windows as required

The teacher is responsible at the close of the school day for:

Positioning furniture
Closing windows
Drawing upper shades
Turning off lights
Locking the classroom door

Responsibility for cleaning chalkboards and erasers varies from school to school. Consult your principal.

SPRINGFIELD, MASSACHUSETTS. ORIENTATION CONFERENCE
HELD FOR NEW TEACHERS.[7]

Thursday Afternoon 1:30

1:30   Grade Meetings in Second Classroom (see above schedule)

Friday Morning 9:00

9:00   Building Meetings with New Teachers
        To relate the background information obtained at the general orien-
        tation meetings to the individual school program and environment.
        To acquaint the new teacher with:
          1. School Community
                Kinds—residential, business, or industrial
                Types of families
          2. School Building
                Classrooms
                Special Rooms
                  Assembly—Gym
                  Cafeteria
                  Helping Teacher's Room
                  Library
                  Medical Rooms
                  Music Room
                  Storage Rooms
                    Books
                    Equipment
                    Supplies
                  Teacher's Room
                  Toilet Facilities
                Playground Areas
          3. Resources
                Records
                  Cumulative Folders
                    Progress Reports
                    Parent-Teacher Conference Reports
                    Test Results
                    Health Records
                    Special Information
                  Office Record Cards—Cross File Cards
                  State Register—City Enrollment Sheets

[7] T. Joseph McCook, *Conference for Teachers New to Springfield. Building
Meetings with New Teachers* (Springfield, Mass.), pp. 3–5, mimeographed. Reprinted by permission.

Supervisors, Co-ordinators, Special Teachers
Supplementary Teaching Aids
4. Building Policies
Banking
Discipline
Dismissals—early, regular
Fire Drills
Toileting
Milk Orders
Insurance
Weekly Reader
Field Trips
Concerts
Junior Red Cross
March of Dimes
5. Responsibilities Other Than Classroom Teaching
Supervision
Playground
Why?—To assure safe, wholesome play
When?—According to needs of individual building
Noon Hours—Varies according to building needs
Stress on importance of well-constructed lunch period
Remuneration
Bus   —Varies according to building needs
Safety of children
Feeling of security especially with younger children
Beginning and ending of day in orderly manner
Classroom Responsibilities
8:30–8:45 A.M. —Informal discussion groups
Centers of interest
Committee responsibilities (children)
Close of session—Evaluation
Next day's needs
Teacher's plans in order
Time Schedule—1 copy in desk
by day or week   1 copy in office
Committee Responsibilities
Audio-visual Co-ordinator
Corridor Bulletins
Library Bulletins
Equipment, Books, etc.
Parent-Teacher Conferences
Appointments
Reports

> Professional Meetings
>   Staff
>   In-service
>   Parent-Teacher Association
> Professional Organization Representatives
>   Teacher's Club
>   Schoolmaster's Club
>   Springfield Education Association
>   United Fund Drive
>   Association for Childhood Education
>   Junior Red Cross
>   American Education Week Plans
>   Advisory Cabinet

The discussion of the group of children assigned to the new teacher is purposely separated from the rest of the building meeting procedure because of the fact that this should be done individually with each new teacher. Time permitting, this may be either Friday morning, August 30, or Tuesday morning, September 3.

> 6. Group of children assigned to new teacher
>   Range of abilities
>   Personality differences
>   Physical defects
>   Home environment
>   Other pertinent information

Building Meetings for all teachers will be held Tuesday morning, September 3, at 10:00 A.M.

Regular classes start Wednesday, September 4.

Teachers are expected to be in buildings at least a half an hour before and after school.

The first week, there are half sessions for children; teachers remain all day.

NEW JERSEY. ORIENTATION PROGRAM FOR NEW TEACHERS

According to a circular issued in 1963, resulting from a study of New Jersey's public schools, the following practices were reported as constituting *Teacher Orientation Programs:* [8]

Part I : "New Teacher" Orientation Programs

One hundred seventy-six school districts reported special "new teacher" orientation programs. A large majority of these meetings (86 percent) were held prior to the official opening of school in September.

[8] *Teacher Orientation Programs for the 1962–63 School Year* (Circular No. 87) (Trenton: New Jersey Education Assoc.). Reprinted by permission.

However, at least fifteen school districts indicated that briefing sessions were also held after school began for these new personnel. Such sessions usually were after-school meetings, sometimes held in addition to preschool meetings and sometimes as a substitute for the special training sessions held in the summer. Examples: One district held six mandatory Monday afternoon meetings for new teachers. New teachers in one district met with various service people from 8:00 to 8:30 A.M. each morning for one and one-half weeks to discuss services and problems. One district set aside time before school opening in the fall as well as seven afternoons for subjects important to new teachers. One district allotted one to five days in the spring and one day in September for these sessions.

Even though one district in six did not specify length of orientation session, it was evident that one- and two-day sessions were most frequent. One-day meetings were held in at least 64 school districts and two-day meetings in 46 districts. Administrators in districts which did not specify length of meeting time commented that these meetings were held at the convenience of administrator and teacher, individually set, held at time of employment, held sometime during the summer, etc.

General Observations on "New Teacher" Orientation Programs

Local groups such as board of education, teacher associations, P.T.A. council, service clubs, and chamber of commerce often participate in "new teacher" meetings. They sponsor luncheons, dinners, and other social functions.

Many programs combine business with pleasure. They include one or more social functions such as breakfast, luncheon, social hour, reception, or dinner. One program featured luncheon in a local plant, guided bus tour, and reception and buffet supper at a local hotel. Other types of social gatherings mentioned were picnics (board, chamber of commerce, or teacher-association sponsored) and boat ride.

Many programs include tours of the community. At least 33 school districts included this activity on the agenda. Such tours are sometimes sponsored by local chambers of commerce and local teacher associations.

The major emphasis in "new teacher" orientation programs is effective adaptation to school environment and educational offerings within the district. To achieve this purpose, most programs include discussions of school philosophy, policies, curriculum, report cards, personnel policies, testing programs, and professional organizations. New teachers are alerted to available equipment, educational services, and special projects in operation. Programs often include departmental metings (high school), separate building meetings with principals, classroom demonstrations, workshops, etc.

Outside consultants such as State Department personnel, representatives from teachers colleges and universities, and other leading speakers are often used in more formalized programs.

Some districts use the person-to-person approach in their new teacher programs. The "buddy" system in which each new teacher is assigned to an experienced one for help and guidance is one technique used. One district holds individual meetings between the new teacher and principal and between the new teacher and the old teacher.

In a special effort to help new teachers, some districts prepare packets of information for this group. One district specified advance summer mailing of professional information.

Some districts invite teacher association representatives to speak on teacher welfare (retirement, legal rights, etc.)

Other ideas incorporated into new teacher orientation programs include the following:

—County helping teachers are sometimes used to help in setting up these programs, especially in rural counties.

—In one district, new faculty members and department chairmen worked during the summer in preparing courses of study, visual materials, library assignments, and audio-visual aids.

—Several districts stress public relations. One district spends considerable time on "quality" of teaching and salesmanship of education.

—One district devotes three days of its briefing session for teachers with provisional certificates, less time for new teachers with limited certificates, and one day for teachers with experience.

—After one month of service, one district invites new teachers to a dinner to evaluate their work and receive suggestions on improving the orientation program.

Detroit, Michigan Public Schools

Approximately nine hundred new teachers are employed annually in the Detroit Public Schools. Hence much of their orientation is done by the administration of the individual schools. Each fall, however, receptions are held in each of the nine districts, at which time the beginning teachers meet the Superintendent, the Board Members, and other administrative staff people. In addition to these meetings, the supervisors hold regular meetings at the Division of Staff Orientation for the Improvement of Instruction for the various subject areas.

At the end of each school year, a questionnaire is completed by each first year teacher. This is returned to the office of the Division of Staff Orientation, unsigned by name of school or individual. This questionnaire is presented here. More is said about it later.

The responses obtained to items on the questionnaire are summarized. The findings in the form of a report are then submitted to principals and supervisors. The main purpose of the study is to examine various aspects of the orientation program, its scope, its strengths, and its weaknesses, to aid in planning activities in the future.

DEPARTMENT OF STAFF ORIENTATION. ATTENTION—
FIRST YEAR TEACHERS. DETROIT PUBLIC SCHOOLS [9]

Dear Teacher:
You are just completing your first semester or year of teaching in Detroit. We are glad to have you with us and would like to profit from your experiences. The Department of Staff Orientation needs your help in planning specific aspects of the program for new colleagues who will join the Detroit teaching staff next year.

Will you please give your reactions to the following items? Your answers will guide us in knowing how to help other teachers. *You need not sign your name.*

Please return the completed form via the school pick-up to Room 738, Schools Center Building, 5057 Woodward *on or before June 17, 1965.*

Florence Kuhn

Assistant Superintendent

DIRECTIONS: Please check or fill in the blanks in accordance with your experience. Use the margins and the back of the last sheet for additional comments.

A. Is this your first or second semester as a   1. First   _____
    Probationary I teacher in Detroit?   2. Second   _____   (1)

B. What previous teaching experience have you had?
    1. As contract teacher in Detroit   _____
    2. As contract teacher elsewhere   _____
    3. As substitute teacher in Detroit   _____   (2)
    4. As substitute teacher elsewhere   _____
    5. None except as student teacher   _____

C. At what school level are you doing most of your teaching?
    1. Elementary   _____
    2. Junior High   _____   (3)
    3. Senior High   _____

[9] *Courtesy of Detroit Public Schools.*

D. Are you teaching in one of your fields of   1. Yes _____
    specialization?   2. No _____   (4)

E. Is there an official department head in your   1. Yes _____
    school for the subject which you are teach-   2. No _____   (5)
    ing?

F. Were you given your school assignment early   1. Yes _____
    enough to enable you to visit the school be-   2. No _____   (6)
    fore your first day on duty?

G. Did you have a conference with your princi-   1. Yes _____
    pal before you started teaching in his school? 2. No _____   (7)

H. Were you on duty the first day of your first   1. Yes _____
    semester?   2. No _____   (8)

I. Where did you do your student supervised
    teaching, last contact?
                1. School to which I am now assigned   _____
                2. Some other Detroit public school   _____   (9)
                3. A school other than a Detroit public school _____

J. Did you do substitute teaching in the school   1. Yes   _____   (10)
    to which you were assigned?   2. No   _____

K. Did you receive help from your school's   1. Yes   _____
    handbook of school policies and procedures?   2. No   _____   (11)
                                                    3. None
                                                       avail-
                                                       able   _____

L. How much help were the following hand-
    books to you?

				Did Not	
	Much	*Some*	*Little*	*Receive*	
THE HUMAN TOUCH	1. _____	2. _____	3. _____	4. _____	(12)
IT TAKES TEAMWORK	1. _____	2. _____	3. _____	4. _____	(13)
TEACHER'S BULLETIN NO. 3	1. _____	2. _____	3. _____	4. _____	(14)

M. Who, among the following, observed your
    teaching long enough or often enough to make
    an evaluation of your teaching?

District Administrator_____	(15)	Assistant Principal	_____	(18)
Supervisor _____	(16)	Department Head	_____	(19)
Principal _____	(17)	Other (specify)	_____	(20)

N. From which *one* among the following did you
   receive most help on your professional problems? *Check only one.*

District Administrator	1._____	Department Head	5. _____
Supervisor	2._____	Counselor	6. _____ (21)
Principal	3._____	Teacher	7. _____
Assistant Principal	4._____	Other (specify)	8. _____

O. Did you visit classes in your building to ob-   1. Yes   _____ (22)
   serve the teaching of others?   2. No   _____

P. Did you visit other schools for half a day or   1. Yes   _____ (23)
   more to observe teaching?   2. No   _____

Q. How helpful were the following to you?

	Much Help	Little Help	None Attended	
Supervisors' meetings	1. _____	2. _____	3. _____	(24)
Summer or Saturday workshops	1. _____	2. _____	3. _____	(25)
Demonstration lessons	1. _____	2. _____	3. _____	(26)
Department meetings in the school	1. _____	2. _____	3. _____	(27)
School's teachers' meetings	1. _____	2. _____	3. _____	(28)
Committee meetings	1. _____	2. _____	3. _____	(29)
Building orientation meetings	1. _____	2. _____	3. _____	(30)

R. Which *five* of the following sources of help or
   service do you think are *most* important to
   a teacher new to Detroit? *Check only five.*

Assistant principal	_____ (31)		Principal	_____ (39)
Counselor	_____ (32)		School secretary	_____ (40)
Demonstration lessons	_____ (33)		Supervisor	_____ (41)
Department head	_____ (34)		Teacher-sponsor	_____ (42)
District administrator	_____ (35)		Teacher's handbook	_____ (43)
District reception	_____ (36)		Teachers' meetings	_____ (44)
Observation of other			Other (specify)	_____ (45)
classes	_____ (37)		_____	
Other teachers	_____ (38)			

S. What do you feel was the reaction of the
   teaching staff toward you as a new colleague
   of theirs?

   Most of them were friendly and made me   1. _____
   feel welcome.
   Some of them were friendly and made me   2. _____
   feel welcome.
   Only a few of them were friendly and   3. _____ (46)
   made me feel welcome.

They seemed to be too busy to pay atten-   4. _____
tion to me.
They made me feel uninvited and left out.   5. _____

T. Would you, in general, recommend the Detroit   1. Yes   _____
system to a friend or acquaintance as a good   2. No   _____   (47)
place to work so that you would encourage   3. Doubtful _____
him to file an application for a position?

U. What is your reason for your answer to question "T"? (Your answer to this question will
be most helpful.)

(48)

V. What further comments or suggestions do you wish to make? (Use the
back of this sheet if you need more space.)

(49)

Please return this form to Room 738, Schools Center Building, 5057 Woodward, via the school pick-up. Thank you for your help.

Comment. The various examples of orientation programs cited
give you some idea of what you probably will experience on your
entrance to your first teaching job. Regardless of what a school does
to help its new teachers adjust to working conditions, real benefits
accrue to the individual teacher in terms of his own attitude toward
the program and his own efforts to profit from the assistance offered.

QUESTIONS AND TOPICS FOR DISCUSSION

1. In which states are you eligible for certification?
2. If you already have your teaching placement, how did you receive your
   position? If not, what are you doing about it?
3. Write a letter of application for a position and ask one of your college
   instructors to criticize it.
4. Compare the application blank of the Westport public schools with
   some that you have received. In what ways are they alike and different?
5. What has been your experience with interviews? What changes, if any,
   do you need to make in your attitude toward them?
6. If you have accepted a position, on what factors was your decision
   based?
7. Why do the regulations concerning teaching contracts need to be strict?

8. What are you doing to become acquainted with the community in which you expect or hope to teach?
9. What have you learned about teacher status from reading the answers of the San Diego Schools to teachers' questions?
10. Which of the orientation programs described in this chapter do you think would be the most helpful? Give reasons for your opinion.

17

YOUR PROFESSIONAL GROWTH

Your teacher-education program has prepared you for entrance into your chosen profession. Your student teaching experiences will enable you to put into practice the various aspects of theory that you learned in your college classrooms. You have been appointed to a school in which you hope to apply the principles of good teaching that you conscientiously have attempted to master. Through the orientation program offered to new teachers by your school, its administrators, and other faculty members have assured you of their sympathetic understanding of and friendly cooperation with a beginning teacher. They have alerted you to the many details of school organization and management that you need to know.

Now you are started on your career as a teacher and are more or less on your own. Your co-workers probably will continue to aid you in meeting effectively all of your many teacher responsibilities. Yet, what actually takes place in your classroom and the extent to which your pupils cooperate with you as you attempt to guide their learning activities depend in good part on your (1) knowledge of proper classroom procedures, (2) understanding of children, and (3) ability to plan, organize, and present effectively the learning materials you are attempting to teach.

You probably are starting your teaching activities with much enthusiasm and a strong desire to be a successful teacher. It is likely, however, that at first you will have some misgivings concerning your ability to handle the situation. These early fears usually are overcome as you gain confidence through continued experience. Your question could be "What kind of teacher will I be five, ten, or fifteen years in the future?" The answer to this question can be contained in another question, "What can I do to foster my professional growth?" It is with the matter of professional development that the remainder of this chapter is concerned.

YOUR FIRST YEAR OF TEACHING

Your first year of teaching can serve as a kind of proving ground. You will need to become acclimated to new living and working conditions. You will be attempting to develop friendly and cooperative relationships with your pupils, the school faculty, and members of the community. With the assistance of the school administrators and your fellow teachers, you gradually will improve your teaching techniques and procedures. You will acquire an increasing understanding of your responsibilities and rights as a teacher. From the beginning of your teaching activities in a school you can so plan for meeting your new responsibilities that you make a good start. The following suggestions for new teachers distributed by the Kansas City schools may have value for you.

SUGGESTIONS TO TEACHERS [1]

Introduction

Here are some suggestions that we hope may prove helpful on the first days in the classroom. Many of them are the same points that we discuss in our meetings with teachers new to the Kansas City School System. These suggestions are mimeographed so that you may have more time to look over them and make use of them. Some of them may seem small and rather unimportant but they are the things that go into building the kind of habits we hope to establish. If we begin at once with definite plans we help to eliminate situations that lead to disorder and confusion.

Getting Ready

1. Visit your school. Get room ready for arrival of children. Get needed materials such as chalk, erasers, pencils, books, and paper. Plan the best spots for reading groups, library, painting, etc., keeping in mind lighting, accessibility, and safety. Locate and plan best routes to restrooms and play spaces. Familiarize yourself with school rules.
2. Get list of pupils. Make name card for each child. Make seating chart for use as soon as possible.
3. Plan a schedule of activities for each hour of the day with approximate times. Plan more than you expect to do. Write out the plan. Place it

[1] *Suggestions to Teachers* (Kansas City: Department of Elementary Education, Kansas City, Missouri Public Schools, 1963). Reprinted by permission.

before you. Think it through in advance. Evaluate it at the close of the day.

4. Have easily accessible all materials needed for activities planned.
5. Plan for distribution of supplies and materials. Remember children like to help do this.
6. Make a complete list of supplies for each child to take home.

All Through the Year

1. Plan to be in your room early enough so that all work and materials are ready for children when school begins.
2. Greet the children when they arrive in the morning and take time to tell them goodbye at the close of school. This creates a feeling of friendliness. Observe the same courtesies you hope to teach the children.
3. Be consistent at all times. When you ask for the attention of the class, wait until you have it before giving any directions.
4. Speak in a calm and unhurried manner. The tone of your voice is most important. It needs to carry assurance in order to gain attention and respect.
5. Set up standards for good work and behavior *with* the children. Be sure everyone understands them and check to see that they are being followed. Stress only a few at one time.
6. Call the attention of the class to the ones who are doing the right thing. It is better to build on the *positive*, as: "I like the way Mary is getting to work." Speak privately to the ones who are not following directions and who need correcting. The best way to get children to do the right thing instead of the wrong is to make the right thing easier to do.
7. In matters of discipline act with confidence and restraint. Overlook petty infractions the first day or two, but disturbing conduct must be dealt with immediately. Do not hesitate to consult the principal or an experienced teacher on any and all perplexing problems rather than permit a situation to get out of hand.
8. Be familiar with school regulations. See that they are observed from the start.
9. Have your work well-planned for each day and needed materials ready. This gives you a sense of security even though these plans may be changed some as you work and plan with the children.

Plan enough work to take care of all the children. Arrange independent work material so that when one part is finished the children understand what to do next. This takes care of the faster workers.

Each day under the date on the board it is well to keep Plans for Today. Read and explain each one carefully. Take time for needed questions. Then be sure everyone begins to work promptly.

Have something definite each morning for children to do immediately when they get to their places. Be sure it is work they can do without asking questions. This gives you time for morning duties such as attendance and collections. Plan to get samples of children's work as a guide to planning.

10. Get all reports in promptly and accurately.
11. Teach children their responsibility in the proper care of all materials such as books, *boxes,* crayons, paints, pencils, and play equipment. Check to see that children always have needed supplies.
12. Collect and label all art materials with the exception of crayons. Store so they can be passed out easily.

It is better to collect tablets in first and second grades and distribute paper as needed, otherwise children waste it.

Show children how to arrange and keep materials in their desks or tables in an orderly manner. Do not let children keep workbooks or writing books in their desks.

13. Have a definite time for sharpening pencils. It can be at the beginning of each morning or at the close of the day. Have a child call one row or a table at a time while the others are busy. Each child should have two or more pencils. Keep a box of extras at your desk to be loaned in emergencies.
14. Set up definite standards for all written work on each paper as:
   1. a heading   2. a margin   3. letters double spaced   4. capital letters
   and punctuation.
   (See *Teaching English in the Elementary School,* Curriculum Bulletin 125, Kansas City, Missouri Public Schools, 1961.)
15. Keep writing in all Primary Grades two spaces high *all year.*
16. Change room helpers each week. Keep record on Helper's Chart.
17. Plan definite games for play periods and noon. Set up the games before leaving the room. Evaluate the games when returning to the room. List games as children learn to play them. It quiets children after a play period if you establish the habit of relaxing with heads on desks or tables and eyes closed for a few minutes.

The First Day

Look your freshest, prettiest, happiest.
Wear something becoming to you and that gives you a lift.
Arrive early enough to be ready.

1. Some children come early. Greet each child, but ask him to play outside. Otherwise he will get restless.
2. Get essential information from parents. Thank them graciously for coming. Let them leave before class. Ask them to come back soon to visit. If they do not leave don't feel compelled to talk to them. At this time your work is with the children.
3. Plan to be in a position where you can observe children enter; near the door where you can catch the eyes of those who come in boisterously. Let them choose their own seats at first.

4. As the bell rings or promptly at the starting time if no bell rings move to the front of the room. Always wait for their attention before beginning to talk.
5. Maintain friendly, calm, relaxed attitude. Show by your manner you expect orderliness and courtesy.
6. Talk in a pleasing not loud voice, so those in the rear can hear you.
7. Ask a child to lead in flag salute and in singing one verse of a song they know.
8. Check names to see who is missing and the number of children you have. Children can often tell why some are not there.
9. Have a get acquainted time. Tell them who you are. Write your name on the board. Tell a little of what you have done during the summer. Have children stand and introduce themselves mentioning summer activities. Pronounce names correctly. Jot down names on seating chart at this time.
10. Follow your planned activities. (See Suggested Activities) *Plan more than you think you'll have time for.* Write out your plans.
11. Discuss list of needed supplies for children to take home. Check to see that all supplies are in by a definite time.
12. Take your children to the rest room about mid-morning. See that they go quietly in line.
13. Set up a game for a twenty minute play period before you go with children to the playground. Let them choose a game they know. Show them another game before play period is over.
14. Have a five minute quiet rest period with heads on desk or table after playtime.
15. Make directions clear and be sure the children understand.
16. Save time to *evaluate your day's activities with the children* before leaving. Let children tell what they have done. End the day as it started all together, with a smile and a plan for what tomorrow will bring.

Developing Friendly Relationships with Pupils

Much that was said about your interrelationships as a student teacher applies to your experiences as a beginning teacher. However, these relationships are on a more permanent basis and you must chart your own course. You do not have a college supervisor and a cooperating teacher available to ease the way for you.

Most children admire young teachers. They seem to feel that a beginning teacher will understand them and their problems. They also may catch some of his enthusiasm for his teaching. You usually can afford to be friendly with them and let them know that you are interested in their activities. At the same time, you should maintain an attitude of dignity and objectivity as befits your position.

A few of the less well-controlled pupils may attempt to "test" you. They may submit poorly prepared home assignments, talk out of turn in class, act the clown, and in other ways try, as they express it, "to get your goat." Difficult as this may seem, you need to keep calm in situations such as these, indicating by your attitude that you want to be fair in your treatment of them but that you will tolerate no nonsense.

Beginning teachers sometimes are hesitant about referring to the authorities a pupil whose behavior in class is troublesome. They believe that doing so is a sign of personal inability to maintain proper discipline. You would not, of course, report minor infractions of school or classroom rules or regulations. These lie within your domain of authority. If a child by his display of uncooperative behavior persists in interfering with the work of the class, you will need to use measures that will correct his behavior.

If your efforts at control are ineffectual, consult his file and teachers who are acquainted with the pupil. If you still are unable to reach him, consult his guidance counselor or another school official. When this last approach is used sparingly, the administration will respect your recognition of the limits of your power to treat recalcitrant children. In some elementary schools, there is an attempt to avoid assigning a newly appointed teacher any pupil who is known to be difficult in classroom situations.

Relationships with Faculty

Experienced teachers differ in their attitude toward a newcomer. For the most part, remembering their own neophyte experiences, they are sympathetic toward him and his problems. They are quick to recognize his needs and give him whatever assistance they can. Teachers on the same grade can offer him the use of their instructional materials, help him in lesson planning, and introduce him to other faculty members. He is invited to join a lunchroom group and encouraged to participate in small- and large-group social events.

You are likely to find in the school a few teachers who seemingly resent you. If the pupils appear to like you, some teachers will be jealous of your popularity, perhaps claiming that you are trying to undermine school discipline. To the extent that you utilize more modern methods than they do, they may accuse you of adding "fads and frills" to the program. These persons make you or any other beginning teacher the target of their criticism.

In your dealings with your co-workers you must face up to the fact that they are evaluating your potential worth as a teacher. They are willing to make allowances for any minor lacks in your ability to function efficiently because of your inexperience. They are extremely sensitive, however, to your displayed attitudes toward them, school policies, and your various school duties. There are various forms of behavior that you should avoid. Some of these are the following:

1. Even though you believe that the teaching approaches taught you at college are more effective than those commonly employed in the school, do not say so. Quietly introduce as many newer techniques as you can with administrative approval and without disrupting school-accepted procedures. You may find that some teachers gradually will come to follow your lead.

2. Do not complain about the kind or number of routine duties to which you are assigned in comparison with other members of the faculty. The more experienced teachers probably are carrying other responsibilities that you are not yet prepared to assume. Be willing to take your share of responsibilities for good school management.

3. Avoid participating in unfavorable criticism of administrative officers or other faculty members. As members of a faculty, teachers sometimes possess what may seem to be a peculiar kind of loyalty. They feel that it is their privilege to question the rightness of what is done by members of their group, but take umbrage at attempts of a comparative outsider to be critical.

4. Refrain from any display of superiority among your fellows. Be modest. Do not boast about your college, your family, or your hometown. Let the members of the group discover for themselves that you are a fine person with an excellent background. You may find yourself talking too much about yourself without meaning to make invidious comparisons. One young teacher was accustomed to recount, with pride, stories about the accomplishments of family members. She was much chagrined one day when a fellow teacher responded to such a story with this old saying, "He who boasts of his illustrious ancestors is like the potato; the best part of him is underground."

Relationships with the Community

Your relationships with the community should follow a pattern similar to that which is desirable for school relationships. Be courteous and friendly with parents, enlisting their aid in helping their children fulfill their potentialities. Attend parent-teacher meetings and show by your attitude that you are interested in the welfare of children and their families. Accept invitations to participate in community-sponsored activities insofar as doing so does not interfere with the meeting of school responsibilities. Avoid listening to or taking part in gossip concerning members of the teaching staff, pupils, or community leaders. If you are living in the home of one of the school's pupils, be careful to refrain from discussing anything about the school with family members. You know that an innocuous remark can be much exaggerated.

At one time, school communities tended to exercise considerable control over the behavior of the members of the school staff. Community leaders attempted to decide what a teacher should or should not do in personal matters such as religious affiliation, recreational activities, dating, time to arrive home at night, marital status, and the like. These community attitudes have undergone considerable modification, especially in the larger urban areas. Some small communities, however, still prescribe certain restrictions that the teacher is expected to respect. It would be advisable for you, therefore, to ascertain, before you accept a teaching position, what the community's attitude is toward a teacher's private life. By so doing you can avoid the experiencing of considerable frustration while you are on the job.

Desirability of Teaching in Your Home Community

A question often raised is whether a teaching candidate should accept a position in a school that he attended as a student or in the neighborhood in which he was reared. Whether or not this should be done depends on the kind of person he is and his reputation and that of his family in the community.

To some people, a child never grows up. If you accept a position in a school that you attended, you may find that some of your former teachers may embarrass you by describing to others in detail some of your childish feats of accomplishment or other less desirable activities. They may treat you as though they still hold a position in regard to yourself of *in loco parentis.* They may overwhelm you with attention or feel called upon to criticize your every activity. Neighborhood friends and acquaintances may give evidence of a similar attitude toward you.

In spite of these apparent disadvantages of teaching in your home community, there are many advantages. You know the school and the community. You do not need to become acquainted with it and perhaps commit social blunders while you are doing so. A feeling of belonging is quickly and easily established. Because you grew up in the neighborhood, you are likely to understand the children whom you are teaching. Consequently, you probably are better able to motivate their learning activities and to share their interests. Your former teachers and neighborhood friends are proud of your achievements. They are ready to accept you and to do what they can to help you earn success in your chosen profession. Teaching in your home school and community can be a rewarding experience.

Improving Your Teaching Procedures

No matter how much success you achieve as a student teacher, you will find that assuming full responsibility for the learning progress of your pupils gives rise to problems of planning, organizing, and presenting learning materials that you did not encounter in your earlier experience. You will need to prepare lesson plans that will meet the needs of these children. You also must adjust your utilization of teaching aids to the materials and equipment available in the school. You will need to adapt your teaching approaches to school approved courses of study, class organization, and teaching procedures, as well as to the learning needs and abilities of the pupil population.

If you participate in a well-organized preschool program of teacher orientation, you receive many worthwhile suggestions concerning the school's teaching policies. At the beginning, however, you are likely to find the going to be rough. You may try some of your "pet" procedures only to find that they do not produce desired results. You will realize that you need both to improve your teaching techniques and to receive the assistance of more experienced individuals. Two of the more commonly used procedures to help beginning teachers are (1) intelligent and sympathetic supervision and (2) observation of the teaching of master teachers.

Value of Constructive Supervision

It is a common plaint among teachers that they fear and dislike supervisory observation. This teacher attitude probably is the result of experience with the kind of supervision that was too prevalent in the past—destructive rather than constructive (emphasis on what is wrong with the lesson rather than recognition of its commendable aspects). As a beginning teacher, you should welcome supervision as the primary means of helping you develop professional competence and improved satisfaction in your work.

In most elementary schools at present, the purpose of supervisory observation is to bolster your morale rather than to tear it down. During your first year of teaching, you can profit much from this experience. At first, administrative personnel probably will visit your class for short periods of time in order to discover your teaching attitudes and needs. Later, at your invitation, one of them will visit you for longer periods, observing complete lessons. Such a visit should be preceded by a conference in which you talk over your plans for the lesson, indicating to your supervisor what you hope to accomplish. You receive an evaluation of the lesson as you later discuss it with him.

Your reactions to supervision exercise a potent influence on the extent to which it can assist you in improving your teaching techniques. Your attitude should be positive rather than negative. Insofar as the supervision is friendly and constructive and you give evidence that you are eager to learn, good rapport can be established between you and your principal as supervisor.

Value of Observing a Master Teacher

Your observation of the presentation of a lesson by an experienced teacher in your grade is a valuable experience. You know that your observation of your cooperating teacher enlarged your concept of the teaching process. Now that you have begun to recognize some of your faults, you are ready to apply to your own work some of the approaches used by the master teacher.

You can give evidence of your desire to improve by requesting that opportunities be arranged for you to observe other teachers at work. When permission to do so is granted, enter into the experience with an open mind. Look for those elements in the lesson that are an improvement over what you have been doing. A short conference with the observed teacher has value. In it you can express your appreciation for the help he has given you and stress the points of the lesson that were especially worthwhile. In addition, of course, throughout the year you should constantly evaluate your own performance and strive to make whatever changes in techniques that seem to be advisable.

LEARNING ABOUT YOUR RESPONSIBILITIES AND RIGHTS

During your preteaching educational experiences you probably became somewhat acquainted with your responsibilities and rights as a teacher. Now, as a regular teacher, you are becoming concerned in a practical way with ethical standards in teaching and a teacher's legal status. You should discover early in your teaching career what is expected of you as a member of the profession and in what ways your legal rights are protected.

Ethical Standards

In common with other professional and business groups, members of the teaching profession are limited in their activities by certain generally accepted dicta to which they should adhere. The most widely known set of ethical standards for teachers is *The Code of Ethics of the Education Profession* that was constructed by the *NEA Committee on Professional Ethics* and adopted by the *NEA Representative Assembly,* Detroit, Michigan, July 1963.

THE CODE OF ETHICS OF THE EDUCATION PROFESSION [2]

Preamble

We, professional educators of the United States of America, affirm our belief in the worth and dignity of man. We recognize the supreme importance of the pursuit of truth, the encouragement of scholarship, and the promotion of democratic citizenship. We regard as essential to these goals the protection of freedom to learn and to teach and the guarantee of equal educational opportunity for all. We affirm and accept our responsibility to practice our profession according to the highest ethical standards.

We acknowledge the magnitude of the profession we have chosen, and engage ourselves, individually and collectively, to judge our colleagues and to be judged by them in accordance with the applicable provisions of this Code.

Principle I

Commitment to the Student

We measure success by the progress of each student toward achievement of his maximum potential. We therefore work to stimulate the spirit of inquiry, the acquisition of knowledge and understanding, and the thoughtful formulation of worthy goals. We recognize the importance of cooperative relationships with other community institutions, especially the home.

In fulfilling our obligations to the student, we—

1. Deal justly and considerately with each student.
2. Encourage the student to study varying points of view and respect his right to form his own judgment.
3. Withhold confidential information about a student or his home unless we deem that its release serves professional purposes, benefits the student, or is required by law.
4. Make discreet use of available information about the student.
5. Conduct conferences with or concerning students in an appropriate place and manner.
6. Refrain from commenting unprofessionally about a student or his home.
7. Avoid exploiting our professional relationship with any student.
8. Tutor only in accordance with officially approved policies.
9. Inform appropriate individuals and agencies of the student's educational needs and assist in providing an understanding of his educational experiences.
10. Seek constantly to improve learning facilities and opportunities.

[2] The Committee on Professional Ethics, National Education Assoc.

Principle II

Commitment to the Community

We believe that patriotism in its highest form requires dedication to the principles of our democratic heritage. We share with all other citizens the responsibility for the development of sound public policy. As educators, we are particularly accountable for participating in the development of educational programs and policies and for interpreting them to the public.

In fulfilling our obligations to the community, we—

1. Share the responsibility for improving the educational opportunities for all.
2. Recognize that each educational institution may have a person authorized to interpret its official policies.
3. Acknowledge the right and responsibility of the public to participate in the formulation of educational policy.
4. Evaluate through appropriate professional procedures conditions within a district or institution of learning, make known serious deficiencies, and take any action deemed necessary and proper.
5. Use educational facilities for intended purposes consistent with applicable policy, law, and regulation.
6. Assume full political and citizenship responsibilities, but refrain from exploiting the institutional privileges of our professional positions to promote political candidates or partisan activities.
7. Protect the educational program against undesirable infringement.

Principle III

Commitment to the Profession

We believe that the quality of the services of the education profession directly influences the future of the nation and its citizens. We therefore exert every effort to raise educational standards, to improve our service, to promote a climate in which the exercise of professional judgment is encouraged, and to achieve conditions which attract persons worthy of the trust to careers in education. Aware of the value of united effort, we contribute actively to the support, planning, and programs of our professional organizations.

In fulfilling our obligations to the profession, we—

1. Recognize that a profession must accept responsibility for the conduct of its members and understand that our own conduct may be regarded as representative.
2. Participate and conduct ourselves in a responsible manner in the development and implementation of policies affecting education.

3. Cooperate in the selective recruitment of prospective teachers and in the orientation of student teachers, interns, and those colleagues new to their positions.
4. Accord just and equitable treatment to all members of the profession in the exercise of their professional rights and responsibilities, and support them when unjustly accused or mistreated.
5. Refrain from assigning professional duties to non-professional personnel when such assignment is not in the best interest of the student.
6. Provide, upon request, a statement of specific reason for administrative recommendations that lead to the denial of increments, significant changes in employment, or termination of employment.
7. Refrain from exerting undue influence based on the authority of our positions in the determination of professional decisions by colleagues.
8. Keep the trust under which confidential information is exchanged.
9. Make appropriate use of time granted for professional purposes.
10. Interpret and use the writings of others and the findings of educational research with intellectual honesty.
11. Maintain our integrity when dissenting by basing our public criticism of education on valid assumptions as established by careful evaluation of facts or hypotheses.
12. Represent honestly our professional qualifications and identify ourselves only with reputable educational institutions.
13. Respond accurately to requests for evaluations of colleagues seeking professional positions.
14. Provide applicants seeking information about a position with an honest description of the assignment, the conditions of work, and related matters.

Principle IV

Commitment to Professional Employment Practices

We regard the employment agreement as a solemn pledge to be executed both in spirit and in fact in a manner consistent with the highest ideals of professional service. Sound professional personnel relationships with governing boards are built upon personal integrity, dignity, and mutual respect.

In fulfilling our obligations to professional employment practices, we—

1. Apply for or offer a position on the basis of professional and legal qualifications.
2. Apply for a specific position only when it is known to be vacant and refrain from such practices as underbidding or commenting adversely about other candidates.
3. Fill no vacancy except where the terms, conditions, policies, and practices permit the exercise of our professional judgment and skill, and where a climate conducive to professional service exists.
4. Adhere to the conditions of a contract or to the terms of an appointment until either has been terminated legally or by mutual consent.

5. Give prompt notice of any change in availability of service, in status of applications, or in change in position.
6. Conduct professional business through the recognized educational and professional channels.
7. Accept no gratuities or gifts of significance that might influence our judgment in the exercise of our professional duties.
8. Engage in no outside employment that will impair the effectiveness of our professional service and permit no commercial exploitation of our professional position.

Read the code thoughtfully. Note that its provisions deal with a teacher's responsibility to his pupils, the community, the profession, and professional employment practices. Each of these areas of commitment includes practices that should be known to and followed by all members of the teaching profession, since the principles apply to all persons engaged in the professional aspects of education.

Legal Aspects

As a teacher, you have certain rights and responsibilities that are granted or implied by law. The legal status of a teacher may be decided in light of federal and state constitutional provisions, statutory enactments, and judicial decisions.

Various aspects of a teacher's professional relationships have legal implications. We already have referred to their application to employment and contractual practices and their possible effect on a teacher's private life. Other areas of possible legal controversy include the political activity of a teacher, academic freedom, and collective bargaining. The law also has something to say about proper disciplinary approaches and pupil sustained injuries. You should acquaint yourself with the legal provisions that apply to teachers, especially those of the state in which you are teaching.

Teachers sometimes tend to resent what they consider to be too strict legal restrictions on their professional rights. They fail to recognize the fact that the law also protects their rights as citizens and teachers. The teacher needs to carry out the directives of his superiors even when he disagrees with the policies involved.

A generally law-abiding citizen and a conscientious member of the teaching profession is unlikely to become embroiled with the law because of his own participation in illegal activities. Hence any legal problems that arise and in which he becomes involved are likely to be initiated as the result of undesirable or outmoded statutory enactments or the incorrect interpretation of the law by school officials. It is advisable that you refrain from challenging a particular law as it is upheld by your superiors as long as it is on the statute books. If you believe that it is unjust or no longer mandatory, join with other school people in efforts to have it removed or changed to meet existing conditions more adequately.

EVALUATION OF YOUR PROFESSIONAL PROGRESS

During your first year of teaching, you should attempt periodically to appraise your effectiveness in and attitude toward teaching. The end of that year is a good time for you to evaluate your progress as a teacher in the particular school in which you have been functioning. Some school officials help you in your self-evaluation by making available for your use questionnaires similar to the one prepared by the Detroit school system and presented in the preceding chapter.

By the end of your first year in the field, you probably will question the effect on you of your year's experiences. Do you still believe that your selection of teaching as a career was a wise decision? What satisfactions have accrued to you in your work? Recently, the United States Office of Education published its report of a survey of beginning teachers.[3] Among the many areas of beginning teaching surveyed was one that concerned teachers' satisfactions with various aspects of their positions. The items included in this part of the questionnaire are listed here: [4]

Your Satisfaction with Various Aspects of Your Position: Please write the code number which best expresses your feeling about each item in the space to the left of each item. Use the following code:

4 - Very satisfactory
3 - Fairly satisfactory
2 - Fairly unsatisfactory
1 - Very unsatisfactory

—— Adequacy of your school building
—— Adequacy of supplies and equipment furnished to you by the school
—— Your present salary

[3] Ward S. Mason, *op cit.*
[4] *Ibid.*, p. 195.

—— Maximum salaries for classroom teachers in your school system

—— Time needed to reach the peak salary in your school system for teachers with full qualifications for their positions

—— Provisions for sick leave

—— Provisions for retirement

—— Your salary compared to that of other occupations in your area open to people with your level of education

—— Your teaching load

—— Your non-teaching responsibilities

—— Total time you spend on school duties, including both teaching and non-teaching responsibilities required or definitely expected of you

—— Helpfulness of the supervision you receive

—— Fairness with which duties are distributed in your school

—— Your relations with your superiors

—— Your relations with fellow teachers

—— Your relations with students

—— Your relations with parents

—— Pupil attentiveness and discipline

—— The amount of interest shown by your students

—— General community attitude toward teaching as an occupation

—— Your position as a whole (except salary)

—— Your position as a whole (including salary)

The resulting data, representing responses from about 7,000 beginning teachers, is presented in Table 10.[5]

The report includes these comments concerning the rank order of the satisfactions:

Given a generally high level of satisfaction, we may still ask which aspects of teaching are most satisfactory and which are least satisfactory. A glance through the ordering of items quickly indicates some clear-cut patterns in this regard. The items with the top four ranks all have to do with the teacher's social relationships—with fellow teachers, superiors, students, and parents. There is a nearly unanimous feeling that all these relationships are satisfactory, and in each case a majority of teachers say "very satisfactory." This finding would seem to indicate that the attention often given to orienting the new teacher to his job and integrating him in the organization and community tends, on the whole, to be successful.

At the other end of the rank order is a clustering of four items all having to do with salary, and a fifth item in which the influence of salary is undoubtedly very large. Here is strong evidence to the effect that beginning teachers find their salaries the least satisfactory aspect of teaching. They say this about three separate aspects of salary: the salary currently received, the maximum salary, and the time needed to reach the maximum salary.[6]

[5] *Ibid.,* p. 80.
[6] *Ibid.,* pp. 79–80.

TABLE 10

SATISFACTION OF BEGINNING TEACHERS WITH SELECTED ASPECTS OF THEIR JOB, WITH ITEMS RANKED IN TERMS OF MEAN SATISFACTION EXPRESSED, BY TEACHING LEVEL AND SEX: 1956–57

Satisfaction Item [1]	Item Scores		All Beginning Teachers — Percentage by Degree of Satisfaction					Percentage Saying Very or Fairly Satisfactory, by Teaching Level and Sex			
	Rank	Mean [2]	Total [3]	Very Satisfactory (Wt.=4)	Fairly Satisfactory (Wt.=3)	Fairly Unsatisfactory (Wt.=2)	Very Unsatisfactory (Wt.=1)	Elementary Men	Elementary Women	Secondary Men	Secondary Women
	2	3	4	5	6	7	8	9	10	11	12
Your relations with fellow teachers	1	3.77	100	79	20	1		98	98	99	99
Your relations with your superiors	2.5	3.65	100	70	26	3	1 [4]	98	97	95	95
Your relations with students	2.5	3.65	100	67	31	1		98	100	97	98
Your relations with parents	4	3.57	100	61	35	3	1 [4]		98	95	95
Fairness with which duties are distributed in your school	5	3.41	100	55	35	7	3	93	93	85	83
Your position as a whole (except salary)	6	3.40	100	48	46	5	1	93	96	91	91
Provisions for sick leave	7	3.20	100	43	42	9	7	84	84	83	85
Provisions for retirement	8	3.19	100	36	51	9	4	84	91	80	90
Amount of interest shown by your students	9	3.14	100	29	58	10	3	88	94	78	82
Your nonteaching responsibilities	10.5	3.12	100	35	47	13	5	82	84	79	80
General community attitude toward teaching as an occupation	10.5	3.12	100	34	48	13	5	79	90	69	83
Pupil attentiveness and discipline	12	3.08	100	26	59	11	4	88	90	81	78
Helpfulness of supervision you receive	13	3.04	100	38	37	15	9	77	77	81	72
Your teaching load	14	2.99	100	30	47	15	8	75	81	71	77
Adequacy of supplies and equipment	15	2.98	100	28	49	16	7	78	82	71	73
Adequacy of your school building	16.5	2.96	100	31	44	14	10	74	80	68	73
Total time you spend on school duties	16.5	2.96	100	25	53	17	6	78	81	73	74
Your position as a whole (including salary)	18	2.83	100	17	55	21	6	59	83	57	76
Your present salary	19	2.63	100	12	52	22	13	46	75	50	69
Time needed to reach peak salary	20	2.62	100	13	49	23	14	56	71	49	62
Maximum salaries	21	2.61	100	14	47	25	14	54	70		61
Your salary compared to that of other occupations in your area open to people with your level of education	22	2.36	100	13	34	28	24	28	62	27	52

1 The wording of some of the items is abbreviated; for complete wording see item 53 of the questionnaire in app. D.
2 The mean is based on the weights as indicated in cols. 5 through 8.
3 Because of rounding, detail does not necessarily add to total.
4 Less than ½ of 1 per cent.

A study of Table 10 and accompanying comments may be fruitful. Where would you rank yourself in the satisfaction items? In regard to attitudes expressed toward salary and salary schedules, keep in mind that much has been done since the study has been completed. Hence greater satisfaction toward adequate salary schedules can be expected to prevail among beginning teachers as time goes along than was the situation at the time of the study.

CONTINUING YOUR PROFESSIONAL DEVELOPMENT

Let us assume that you have made a good beginning as a teacher. Your first year of teaching has been rewarding and satisfying. For the most part, your pupils are responding well to your guidance of their learning. You have developed good rapport with the school's administrative staff and your fellow teachers. You have found a place for yourself in the school's community. Where do you go from here?

You cannot rest on your laurels, believing that continued success will be yours if you do no more than maintain the status quo. New educational demands will be made upon you. Changes constantly are taking place in teaching-learning approaches as a result of experimentation. Research brings to light new data with which you need to be acquainted if you are to continue to perform adequately in the classroom. Public interest is increasing in providing effective teaching and teaching facilities for children. You dare not stand still amid all of the many factors of change that are characteristic of progress.

Perhaps there is no more pathetic individual than the teacher who began his professional career with enthusiasm and relative success and then became so bogged down by the mass of detail inherent in his work that he found no time or energy for self-improvement. You probably have encountered teachers who have become routinized to the point that they seem unaware of the changes that have taken place in education. They attempt to meet their teaching responsibilities according to a pattern that they found effective ten, fifteen, or more years ago. You can avoid getting into a rut by taking advantage of all the opportunities that now are available to you.

General Approaches to Teacher Growth

As an active member of your school's faculty, you will continue to engage in various activities that can strengthen your teaching skills. You will be expected to participate in faculty meetings and educational conferences. Your classroom work will continue to be supervised. You may be invited to participate in the development of curricular materials and the planning of teaching approaches.

At the same time, you can utilize other growth media on a more or less voluntary basis. Regardless of the program of self-improvement that you select, it is essential that you continue to engage in periodic self-evaluations to determine, as best you can, your outstanding strengths and your particular weaknesses.

Membership in Professional Organizations

Many and varied educational organizations have been established on the local, state, and national levels. These professional groups are intended to serve both general and specific needs of school people. Membership in these organizations is voluntary, but their value usually is so great that you cannot afford to refrain from joining those that meet your interests and that can benefit you professionally. These associations have periodic meetings, some of which you could attend with profit to yourself. Most of the professional groups publish periodicals for their members. These publications can keep you informed concerning what is happening in the field of education, both generally and specifically.

As a beginning teacher, you would be wise to affiliate with the local teachers' association. Here you will have an opportunity to cooperate with your colleagues in attacking and attempting to solve educational problems that have local and immediate significance. Also worthy of consideration is affiliation with statewide professional organizations that bring together teachers from all parts of the state and from various fields of professional activity. The state organization usually is primarily concerned with the important aspects of teacher welfare, such as the legal status of teachers in matters dealing with teachers' salaries, tenure, and retirement, although other professional areas are not neglected.

Certain teacher federations also are active in promoting teacher welfare. Some of these are associated with the labor group and are especially active in large cities.

The National Education Association (NEA), with a membership of about one million, exercises a potent influence on American education. It has 33 departments, serving all educational levels and professional ranks. Its monthly publication, the *NEA Journal,* keeps association members informed concerning all aspects of educational development. The *Research Bulletin* reports studies and investigations conducted by its research division. The bulletin contains many articles dealing with teacher welfare and the improvement of teaching and teaching conditions. The association sponsors a general meeting every summer. Also, the various special departments and divisions publish bulletins and yearbooks, and conduct annual meetings.

Value of Continued Study

Not only is preteaching education increasing in extent and depth, but considerable emphasis is being placed by school people on a teacher's need to participate in one or another form of in-service education. When you are graduated from college and start to teach, you probably will feel that for a year or so you will want to devote your time and energy to your teaching job. This usually is a good decision, but you should not delay study activities to the point that you find it difficult to resume the student role.

Some school systems require teachers to take appropriate courses in order to be eligible for their annual salary increments. In school systems where there is a three-year probationary period, a teacher may be excused from engaging in in-service education until he is preparing to enter his fourth year of teaching. In addition, some large school systems provide nonfee in-service courses for their teachers. These courses usually are staffed by administrators, supervisors, and experienced teachers of the system. New York City sponsors over six hundred such courses.

Many colleges and universities offer graduate courses, either on campus or at off-campus centers, to meet teachers' educational needs. If you are teaching in a community that contains an institution of higher learning or one of its off-campus centers, opportunities will be provided for you to study after school hours and/or on Saturdays. Many teachers devote some of their summers to study, perhaps also taking a leave from their school for a term or a year in order to complete the requirements for a higher degree.

One purpose for continued study is to complete advanced study in one's teaching field or to keep up-to-date concerning changes in educational policies, curriculum development, and instructional methods. Another purpose is to prepare oneself for entrance into a field of specialization, such as administration, supervision, counseling, and the like. Whatever your purpose is, plan ahead for your educational progress, and stay with it. Be careful, however, that you do not become so involved in your study activities that your teaching responsibilities are neglected.

In-service education is an important area of professional growth. Your growth as a teacher depends in good part on the effect of continued education on your attitudes toward your work. The expanding body of knowledge and the increasing complexities of teaching literally require continuous study to keep abreast of the new developments in the teaching-learning situation.[7]

Other Media of Professional and Personal Growth

Some school systems and institutions of higher learning, and educational organizations foster the formation of summer workshops. Groups of teachers having similar educational interests gather together (usually from two to six weeks) under the auspices of the sponsoring agency. Here they consider their common problems and attempt to work out tentative solutions to them. Recommendations arrived at during a workshop session are then applied, insofar as this is possible, to the next year's teaching activities and evaluated in light of results. The workshop approach is an excellent means of encouraging creative activities among school people.

Another way in which you can keep up-to-date, of course, is to follow a planned program of professional reading. Both public and school libraries are giving increased attention to the need for supplying good reading materials in the various areas of general world affairs and in education. Also available are many professional

[7] For an excellent discussion of "Continuous Growth for the Teacher," consult *Educational Leadership* (November, 1962).

periodicals. As a beginning teacher, you should develop the habit of becoming acquainted with current educational literature.

It may seem to you as you reflect on the foregoing that we have stressed unduly the various aspects of professional growth to the neglect of your development as an individual. That is not our intent. You cannot grow professionally—in the best connotation of the term—unless you also are constantly developing your personal interests and activities.

Many avenues of personal growth are open to you. As a teacher you have relatively long summer vacations. Some of that time can well be spent in travel. Do not confine your reading to professional literature. Become interested in the arts, perhaps developing a hobby. Take time out for recreational activities. Select some of your friends from among people who are engaged in occupational fields other than your own. Devote a reasonable amount of time and energy to participation in community affairs. Engaging in wholesome out-of-school activities can take you back into the classroom with renewed vigor and enthusiasm for your professional responsibilities.

QUESTIONS AND TOPICS FOR DISCUSSION

1. Why should you begin now to consider ways in which you can grow personally and professionally?
2. To what extent and in what ways do you think that your present experiences with children will help you as a beginning teacher?
3. What should be your attitude toward a teacher who seems to resent you?
4. What is your attitude toward teaching in your home school or home community? Be explicit.
5. Which of your experiences as a student teacher do you think will help you most as a regular teacher?
6. As a student teacher, what has been your attitude toward supervision? Give reasons for it.
7. Differentiate between an ethical standard and a legal enactment.
8. If you already have contracted for a teaching position, how well satisfied are you with the salary you expect to receive? If you have not accepted a position, what salary is your goal?
9. Name professional organizations that you could join as a student teacher. As a regular teacher. In what ways could you benefit from membership in them?
10. Name the books, in addition to those in education, that you have read during the past year. How have you benefited from reading them?
11. What are your favorite recreational activities? How can participation in them encourage personal and/or professional growth?

READING LIST

ADAMS, H. P., and DICKEY, F. G. *Basic Principles of Student Teaching*. New York: American Book Co., 1951.

ARMSTRONG, W. E., and STINNETT, T. M. *A Manual on Certification Requirements for School Personnel in the United States*. Washington, D.C.: National Commission on Teacher Education and Professional Standards, National Education Association, 1964.

BARR, A. S., *et al. Teacher Effectiveness*. Madison, Wis.: Dembar Educational Research Services, Inc., 1963.

BARUCH, D. *New Ways in Discipline*. New York: McGraw-Hill Book Co., Inc., 1949.

BILLARD, V., and STRAND, R. *Parent-Teacher Conferences*. New York: McGraw-Hill Book Co., Inc., 1963.

BOUGH, G. O., and SCHWARTZ, J. *Elementary School Science and How To Teach It* (3rd ed.). New York: Holt, Rinehart & Winston, Inc., 1964.

BROWN, E. J., and PHELPS, A. T. *Managing the Classroom* (2nd ed.). New York: Ronald Press Co., 1961.

BROWN, T. J., and BANISH, F. *Student Teaching in an Elementary School*. New York: Harper & Row, Pub., Inc., 1962.

BURR, J. B., HARDING, L. W., and JACOBS, L. B. *Student Teaching in the Elementary School* (2nd ed.). New York: Appleton-Century-Crofts, Inc., 1958.

BURTON, W. H. *The Guiding of Learning Activities* (3rd ed.). New York: Appleton-Century-Crofts, Inc., 1962.

BUSH, R. N. *The Teacher-Pupil Relationship*. Englewood Cliffs, N.J.: Prentice-Hall, Inc., 1954.

BYERS, L., and IRISH, E. *Success in Student Teaching*. Boston: D. C. Heath and Co., 1961.

CLEMENTS, M., FIELDER, W. R., and TABACHNICK, R. R. *Teaching Social Studies in the Elementary School*. Indianapolis: Bobbs-Merrill Co., Inc., 1965.

CONRAD, G. *The Process of Art Education in the Elementary School*. Englewood Cliffs, N.J.: Prentice-Hall, Inc., 1964.

CORLE, C. G. *Teaching Mathematics in the Elementary School*. New York: Ronald Press Co., 1964.

CROW, L. D., and CROW, A. *Readings in Guidance*. New York: David McKay Co., Inc., 1962.

———. *Educating the Academically Able: A Book of Readings.* New York: David McKay Co., Inc., 1963.

———. *How to Study.* New York: Collier Books, Inc., 1963.

———. *Mental Hygiene for Teachers: A Book of Readings.* New York: Macmillan Co., 1963.

———. *Human Development and Learning* (rev. ed.). New York: American Book Co., 1964.

———. *Workbook for the Student Teacher in the Elementary School.* New York: David McKay Co., 1965.

CROW, L. D., CROW, A., and MURRAY, W. *Teaching in the Elementary School: Readings in Principles and Methods.* New York: David McKay Co., Inc., 1961.

CURTIS, D. K., and ANDREWS, L. O. *Guiding Your Student Teacher.* Englewood Cliffs, N.J.: Prentice-Hall, Inc., 1954.

CUTTS, N. E., and MOSELEY, N. *Better Home Discipline.* New York: Appleton-Century-Crofts, Inc., 1952.

DALE, E. *Audio-Visual Methods in Teaching* (rev. ed.). New York: Holt, Rinehart & Winston, Inc., 1954.

DEVOR, J. W. *The Experience of Student Teaching.* New York: Macmillan Co., 1964.

DUROST, W. N., and PRESCOTT, G. A. *Essentials of Measurement for Teachers.* New York: Harcourt, Brace & World, Inc., 1962.

FRENCH, J. L. *Educating the Gifted: A Book of Readings* (2nd ed.). New York: Holt, Rinehart & Winston, Inc., 1964.

GARRETT, H. E. *Testing for Teachers.* New York: American Book Co., 1959.

GERBERICH, J. R., GREENE, H. A., and JORGENSEN, A. N. *Measurement and Evaluation in the Modern School.* New York: David McKay Co., Inc., 1962.

GREEN, J. A. *Teacher-Made Tests.* New York: Harper & Row, Pub., Inc., 1963.

HARRIS, A. J. *Effective Teaching of Reading.* New York: David McKay Co., Inc., 1962.

HASKEW, L. D., and McLENDON, J. C. *This Is Teaching* (rev. ed.). Chicago: Scott, Foresman & Co., 1962.

HUSBANDS, K. L. *Teaching Elementary School Subjects.* New York: Ronald Press Co., 1961.

HYMES, J. *A Child Development Point of View.* Englewood Cliffs, N.J.: Prentice-Hall, Inc., 1955.

INGRAM, C. P. *Education of the Slow-Learning Child* (3rd ed.). New York: Ronald Press Co., 1960.

KAMBLY, P. E., and SUTTLE, J. E. *Teaching Elementary School Science.* New York: Ronald Press Co., 1963.

KINDER, J. S. *Audio-Visual Materials and Techniques* (2nd ed.). New York: American Book Co., 1959.

KIRK, S. A. *Educating Exceptional Children.* Boston: Houghton Mifflin Co., 1962.

KLAUSMEIER, H. J., and DRESDEN, K. *Teaching in the Elementary School.* New York: Harper & Row, Pub., Inc., 1962.

KRUG, O., and BECK, H. L. *A Guide to Better Discipline.* Chicago: Science Research Associates, Inc., 1954.

LAMBERT, P. (ed.). *The Teacher and the Machine.* Madison, Wis.: Dembar Educational Research Services, Inc., 1964.

LINDSEY, M., and GRUHN, W. T. *Student Teaching in the Elementary School.* New York: Ronald Press Co., 1957.

McKIM, M. G., HANSEN, G. W., and CARTER, W. L. *Learning to Teach in the Elementary School.* New York: Macmillan Co., 1959.

MASON, W. S. *The Beginning Teacher: Status and Career Orientation.* Washington, D.C.: U.S. Department of Health, Education and Welfare, 1961.

MEEKER, A. M. *Teachers at Work in the Elementary School.* Indianapolis: Bobbs-Merrill Co., Inc., 1963.

MILNER, E. J. *You and Your Student Teacher.* New York: Teachers College, Columbia University, Bureau of Publications, 1954, reprinted, 1962.

MORRISON, I. E., and PERRY, I. F. *Kindergarten-Primary Education: Teaching Procedures.* New York: Ronald Press Co., 1961.

MURRAY, T. R. *Judging Student Progress* (2nd ed.). New York: David McKay Co., Inc., 1960.

PETERSEN, D. G. *The Elementary School Teacher.* New York: Appleton-Century-Crofts, Inc., 1964.

PETERSEN, D. G., and HAYDEN, V. D. *Teaching and Learning in the Elementary School.* New York: Appleton-Century-Crofts, Inc., 1961.

REDL, F. *Understanding Children's Behavior.* New York: Teachers College, Columbia University, Bureau of Publications, 1960.

RICKEY, R. W. *Planning for Teaching* (3rd ed.). New York: McGraw-Hill Book Co., Inc., 1963.

ROGERS, D. *Mental Hygiene in Elementary Education.* Boston: Houghton Mifflin Co., 1957.

RUSSELL, K. L. *Visual Grading.* Huntsville, Texas: Educational Filmstrips, 1959.

SHEVIAKOV, G. V., and REDL, F. *Discipline for Today's Children and Youth* (rev. ed.). Washington, D.C.: Association for Supervision and Curriculum Development, National Education Assoc., 1956.

SMITH, M. F. *Teaching the Slow-Learning Child.* New York: Harper & Row, Pub., Inc., 1954.

SMITH, N. B. *Reading Instruction for Today's Children.* Englewood Cliffs, N.J.: Prentice-Hall, Inc., 1963.

STRATEMEYER, F. B., and LINDSEY, M. *Working with Student Teachers.* New York: Teachers College, Columbia University, Bureau of Publications, 1958.

Teaching Career Fact Book. Washington, D.C.: National Education Assoc., 1963.

The Supervising Teacher. Thirty-eighth Yearbook. Cedar Falls: Association for Student Teaching, Iowa State Teachers College, 1959.

THOMAS, R. M. *Judging Student Progress* (2nd ed.). New York: David McKay Co., Inc., 1960.

VAN DALEN, D. B., and BRITTELL, R. W. *Looking Ahead to Teaching.* Boston: Allyn & Bacon, Inc., 1959.

WHITE, V. *Studying the Individual Pupil.* New York: Harper & Row, Pub., Inc., 1958.

WIGGINS, S. P. *The Student Teacher in Action.* Boston: Allyn & Bacon, Inc., 1957.

WINGO, G. M., and SCHORLING, R. *Elementary School Student Teaching* (3rd ed.). New York: McGraw-Hill Book Co., Inc., 1961.

Yearbooks of the Association for Student Teaching. Cedar Falls, Iowa.

APPENDIX

The 16 mm. films listed here can be used to supplement the material in the text as indicated, chapter by chapter. The running time is given for each film. We recommended that the instructor preview each film before showing. The names and addresses of the producers and publishers are included at the end of the list of films.

Audio-Visual Aids to Learning (United World Films, 11 minutes). Shows how audio-visual aids can be used in class. Chapter 11.

Chalkboard Utilization (McGraw-Hill, 15 minutes). Presents ways in the classroom chalkboard can be used more effectively in teaching. Chapter 11.

Curriculum Based on Child Development (McGraw-Hill, 12 minutes). Shows how the methods employed by an elementary school teacher are adapted to meet the curriculum needs of her fourth-grade pupils. Chapters 3, 6.

Developing Self-reliance (Coronet, 11 minutes). Shows the importance of self-reliance in successful endeavor. Chapters 13, 14.

Discovering Individual Differences (McGraw-Hill, 25 minutes). The teacher learns about each pupil and adapts his teaching to the needs of each. Chapters 4, 10.

Dry Mount Your Teaching Pictures (McGraw-Hill, 10 minutes). Shows a teacher how to mount pictures for classroom use. Chapter 11.

Each Child Is Different (McGraw-Hill, 17 minutes). Explains the importance of knowing the different backgrounds of the children, as well as their individual abilities and needs, in order to adjust the teaching program to meet these needs. Chapters 4, 9, 10.

Effective Learning in the Elementary School (McGraw-Hill, 20 min-

443

utes). A fifth-grade teacher tells some of her own experiences in making learning more effective. Chapters 6, 7, 9.

Family Circles (McGraw-Hill, 31 minutes). Presents several cases of children, showing how their home life affects their school life. Chapters 3, 13.

Feltboard in Teaching (Wayne University, 9 minutes). Presents various ways of using feltboard in teaching. Chapter 11.

From Sociable Six to Noisy Nine (McGraw-Hill, 22 minutes). Illustrates the behavior that may normally be expected in children from six to nine. Chapter 3.

Frustrating Fours and Fascinating Fives (McGraw-Hill, 22 minutes). Shows a modern nursery school in operation; takes up problems of discipline, and shows what may be expected of and explained to a child at four and five. Chapters 3, 13.

Guiding the Growth of Children (McGraw-Hill, 18 minutes). Shows that one of the most important parts of a teacher's job is to guide the growth of the pupil as an individual. Chapters 3, 6, 14.

He Acts His Age (McGraw-Hill, 13 minutes). Explains that a child's emotional development normally keeps pace with his physical growth. Chapter 3.

How to Make and Use a Diorama (McGraw-Hill, 20 minutes). Demonstrates the construction of the diorama framework and the preparation of its realistic miniature scenes. Chapter 11.

How to Use a Classroom Film (McGraw-Hill, 18 minutes). Introduces the basic principles leading to the most effective presentation and utilization of a classroom film. Chapter 11.

I Want to Go to School (McGraw-Hill, 32 minutes). Shows how the teacher stimulates pupils' interest by using different objects for the purpose of demonstration. Chapters 7, 8.

Planning for Personal and Professional Growth (McGraw-Hill, 18 minutes). Presents some of the problems faced by teachers in professional growth. Chapter 17.

Preparation of Teachers (United World Films, 20 minutes). Presents the need to stress personality traits in teachers. Chapters 2, 16.

Principles of the Art and Science of Teaching (Iowa State University, 55 minutes). Concerning the assignment, this film presents the setting up of objectives, selecting content and activities, and adapting procedures. Chapters 7, 8.

Problem Children (Penn State University, 20 minutes). Presents
the ways in which home and school experiences affect the personality of two children. Chapter 13.

Promoting Pupil Adjustment (McGraw-Hill, 20 minutes). Shows
how the classroom teacher promotes social and emotional adjustment. Chapters 4, 14.

Speech: Group Discussion (Young American Films, 10 minutes).
Shows how a group can be organized for group discussion. Chapter 9.

Teacher and Pupils Planning and Working Together (McGraw-Hill,
19 minutes). A teacher and pupils work together to develop plans
for the day's work. Chapter 8.

Teaching (Mahnke, 11 minutes). Presents the qualifications and
characteristics of teachers in this country. Chapter 2.

The Problem of Method (McGraw-Hill): Part I, *Defining the
Problem and Gathering Information* (18 minutes); Part II, *Using
Information to Solve the Problem* (16 minutes). Chapter 7.

The Teacher as Observer and Guide (Teachers College, 20 minutes).
Suggests ways in which the teacher can help pupils with their
learning and adjustment problems. Chapter 3.

Three R's Plus (McGraw-Hill, 27 minutes). Presents a graphic
overall view of the teaching program—the curriculum, materials,
and techniques—in the elementary school. Chapters 7, 8, 9.

We Plan Together (Teachers College, 20 minutes). Presents ideas
for teacher-pupil planning. Chapters 7, 8.

What Greater Gift (National Education Association, 28 minutes).
Shows the teacher as a professional person, as well as something
about the nature of teaching. Chapter 2, 17.

Producers and Suppliers of Films

Coronet	Coronet Instructional Films, 65 E. South Water St., Chicago, Ill. 60601
Indiana University	Indiana University, Bloomington, Ind.
Iowa State University	State University of Iowa, Bureau of Visual Instruction, Iowa City, Iowa
Mahnke	Carl F. Mahnke Productions, 215 E. 3 St., Des Moines, Iowa
McGraw-Hill	McGraw-Hill Book Co., Text-Film Department, 330 West 42 St., New York, New York 10036
National Education Association	National Education Association, Press and Radio Section, 1201 Sixteenth St., N.W., Washington, D.C. 20036
Penn State University	Pennsylvania State University, State College, Pa.
Teachers College	Teachers College, Bureau of Publications, Columbia University, 525 West 120 St., New York, New York 10027
United World Films	United World Films, 1445 Park Ave., New York, New York 10029
University of Michigan	University of Michigan, Ann Arbor, Mich.
Wayne University	Wayne University, Audio-Visual Materials Bureau, Detroit, Mich.
Young American Films	Young American Films, Inc., 18 East 41 St., New York, New York 10017

INDEX

Index